EMBODYING

STUDIES IN THE BODY PEDAGOGICS OF SOUTHERN WHITENESS

JOSHUA I. NEWMAN

EMBODYING DIXIE

STUDIES IN THE BODY PEDAGOGICS OF SOUTHERN WHITENESS

JOSHUA I. NEWMAN

Common Ground

First published in Australia in 2010
by Common Ground Publishing Pty Ltd
at Sport and Society
a series imprint of The University Press

The National Library of Australia Cataloguing-in-Publication data:

Embodying Dixie: Studies in the Body Pedagogics of Southern Whiteness
Joshua I. Newman

Bibliography.

978 1 86335 723 4 (pbk.)
978 1 86335 724 1 (pdf)

1. University of Mississippi.
2. Racism in higher education--Mississippi.
3. Sports and race relations--Mississippi.
4. Educational sociology--Mississippi.
5. Universities and colleges--Sociological aspects.

378.9762

The cover image is reprinted with permission from Special Collections, University of Mississippi.

Table of Contents

Acknowledgments

This book was written over the course of five years, starting when I was a PhD candidate in the Physical Cultural Studies program at the University of Maryland and ending here in New Zealand. I spent large parts of the intervening period in the US South; teaching, researching, learning, and living. Along the way, I met a lot of good people in the Mid-South, many of whom inform the best parts of this study and to whom I owe a great deal of gratitude. Specifically, I need to acknowledge the contributions of the following people (and numerous others I am no doubt forgetting):

First, I want to commend Kathryn Otte from Common Ground for her expert and efficient stewardship in seeing this book through to completion. The book's best rhetorical twists owe to her subtle guidance, while any errors, both large and small, are mine. I would also like to acknowledge the assistance I received from the kind folks at the University of Mississippi. Further, I would like to thank the editors of the *Journal of Sport and Sociology Issues*, *Sociology of Sport Journal*, and the *International Review for Qualitative Research* for allowing me to reprint parts of previously published or forthcoming articles in this book (particularly Chapters 7, 8, and the Epilogue).

Second, I would like to thank all my friends and co-conspirators at the University of Maryland for their inspiration, mentorship, and critical imaginations. This project has greatly benefitted from the prescient insights offered by Bryan Bracey, Jessica Chin, Michael Friedman, Woo-Young Lee, Sheri Parks, Jennifer Sterling, Jamie Schultz, and Deborah Young. I would also like to acknowledge the invaluable supervision and support I received from Richard Irwin, John Amis, Robert Pitter, Michael Huffman, Ralph Wilcox, and Stan Walls during my time at the University of Memphis.

Third, while the book's weaknesses are reflective of my own shortcomings as a scholar/writer, its strengths echo the conscientious insights offered to me by my colleagues at Towson University and the University of Otago. While at Towson, I was fortunate to work with genuinely wonderful people such as Lisa Swanson, Jessica Braunstein, David Zang, Jennifer Ballengee, and Matthew Durington. And during my short time at Otago, I have had the privilege of engaging in stimulating, collegial, and punctilious dialogue with Mark Falcous, Steve Jackson, Doug Booth, Mike Sam, Allen Hill, Luiz Uehara, Sally Shaw, Tania Cassidy, Lisette Burrows, Jon Shemmell, Chris Button, Elaine Rose, Ken Hodge, Sandy Mandic, Ojeya Cruz-Banks, Melanie Bussey, Alex Kolb, Chris Sullivan, and Hamish Gould. I would also be remiss not to also mention the support I've received from compatriots across the broader academy, including: Jennifer Metz, Darcy Plymire, Michelle Donnelly, Janelle Joseph, Ben Carrington, Shirley Steinberg, and the late inspirational critical pedagogue, Joe Kincheloe.

Fourth, I want to thank all my friends in the States and abroad who, while being smart enough to avoid academia, have nonetheless contributed to this piece of scholarship in ways that extend far beyond its limited rhetorical or interpretive scope. Special thanks to John Hyden for being so selfless, sincere, and dependable; to Brian Loeffler for being the funniest and most genuine person I know; to Brian Cook for showing me how to mature; to Russ McSwain for always giving more than you take; to Cory Fisher, Steve Mosher, Steve Wilburn, and Eric Beukema for standing beside me (and tolerating my politics) in spite of your better judgment; to Jeff Perlman, Wilson Stone, and David Ruch for your reliable humanity.

Finally, I want to specifically acknowledge those folks who, through their individual and collective contributions to my own human journey, have added to my life in ways I'll never be able to repay: Fiona McLachlan for her unbending criticality and commitment to social justice; Michael Silk for always demanding the best of me; Geoff Kohe for his inspirational effervescence; Michael Giardina for sharing his genius and kinship; Adam Beissel for all that he is and will become (I proudly sigh); Andrew Grainger for being the kindest person I have ever known; Carolyn Albright for always, *always* being my friend; Ryan King-White for his unyielding comradeship through it all; and David Andrews for, well, *everything*.

This book is dedicated to my family; to Frank and Dolores Handy for all their love and support along the way; to my brother Seth, who by every important measure is a far better human being than I ever could be; to my Mom, for her sacrifice and incredible strength; and to my Dad for teaching me not to pre-judge people or to take anything at face value. Finally, this book is dedicated to Anne for being perfect in *every way*; and to Rhys, who everyday brings such incredible joy into my life.

Introduction

Of Confederacies and Corporealities

Few institutions have been identified so closely with the Old South legacy, good and bad, as Ole Miss – (Lederman, 1993)

If you want to study racial relations in the South, look at the University of Mississippi – (Nossiter, 1997)

DATELINE: Oxford, Mississippi, USA, October 1, 1962, or later

"GO HOME YOU FUCKING NIGGER, YOU DON'T BELONG HERE!"
"GET BACK TO THE SLAVE QUARTERS!"
"GO TO HELL, YOU COON!"
"STUPID FUCKING SPEAR-CHUCKING MONKEY!"
"HOTTY TODDY, GOSH A'MIGHTY . . ."

Nearly half a century has passed since James Meredith gained admission into the University of Mississippi (more affectionately known as 'Ole Miss');[1] a half-century since a young black man risked his life to penetrate what

---

1. On September 30, 1962, the college town of Oxford, Mississippi, erupted in violence following the U.S. government's interventions to allow James Meredith, an African American, to register at the all-white University of Mississippi. The federal government insisted that the state of Mississippi honor the rights of all its citizens, regardless of race, and allow admittance to Meredith. Mississippi Governor Ross Barnett's refusal to admit Meredith led to a confrontation between state and federal authorities, and resulted in a violent siege on the campus led by segregationists, which resulted in the death of two people and injuries to dozens more.

many Civil Rights activists referred to as the 'fortress' of educative white solidarity; a half-century since Meredith was assailed by a lynch mob of young white men hurling projectiles and equally vicious racist epithets (such as those above) onto his 'interloping' body; a half-century since President John F. Kennedy summoned Federal troops to march against their fellow citizens in order to end racial segregation at that institution of higher learning; a half-century that has washed away the blood that soiled the campus that riot-scarred autumn night. Looking back to see how far the University and the South more generally have come—and listening as the malicious discords of race reverberate through the ages—we cannot help but be reminded of that most famous passage from Oxford's Noble laureate son William Faulkner: "the past is never dead. It's not even past."

Historians point to the 'James Meredith crisis'—described by then Mississippi Governor Ross Barnett to be "the moment of [the South's] greatest crisis since the War Between the States"—as one of the most significant flashpoints of the US Civil Rights Movement, particularly in its usurpation of practices of racism in the post-plantation South. Nearly eight years after the *Brown versus Board of Education* decision, five years after Little Rock Central High School was forcefully integrated, and situated between the Freedom Rides of 1961 and the 1963 March on Washington, Meredith's 'infiltration' of one of the South's most revered all-white cultural institutions—considered to be the 'deep South's citadel' of racial separatism; the institution where the "height of plantation upper-class segregationist Mississippi culture" (James Meredith, Marshall, & Doar, 2002, p. 2) coalesced around symbols and practices of the solid [white] South—is marked by many as the decisive rupture in white Mississippi's solidaritous resistance to the Civil Rights Movement (K. T. Andrews, 2004; R. H. Barrett, 1965; Dittmer, 1995; Silver, 1984).[2]

Set against a backdrop of new racisms embedded in the post-Reconstruction South, this ephemeral convergence of segregationist attitudes and integrationist bodies located Meredith and the institution as diametrically-opposed symbols of the pervasive racial polarity existing in the Deep South,[3] with Meredith occupying the role of crusader and the University

---

2. For instance, the National Civil Rights Museum in Memphis, Tennessee has for many years featured an extensive exhibit on Meredith's enrollment efforts and the integration of Ole Miss.

3. Throughout this manuscript, my uses of the terms "Deep South," "Dixieland", and "Dixie South" are meant to signify not only the Mississippi Delta region of the United States, but perhaps more importantly the romanticized, if not imaginary cultural and political economic formations of the region. Whereas the "Delta" is more often used to refer to the geographic and economic region from Memphis, TN to Vicksburg, MS, the term "Dixie" evokes the more livid and robust imaginings of a broader 'Southern Ethic' of parochial tradition. "Dixieland" is best known for its evocation in the song "Dixie," which was the battle song of the Confederate troops during the Civil War. My use of the term "Deep South", then, is in reference to the cultural and geographic locus of these Dixieland imaginings—born of the places and peoples of the plantation South, Mississippi, Georgia, Alabama, and Louisiana.

standing at the symbolic fulcrum of separatist ideology. Bestirring the fundamentalist and traditionalist ideologies that galvanized many Southern states to secede from the Union in January of 1861, segregationist whites from a century later rallied around the notion that integration of the University of Mississippi effectively 'disenfranchised the state and its rights to operate in sovereignty and separation.' As then Mississippi Governor Ross Barnett proclaimed on September 13, 1962:

> The day of expediency is past. We must either submit to the unlawful dictates of the federal government or stand up like men and tell them no. The day of reckoning has been delayed as long as possible. It is now upon us. This is the day, and this is the hour. Knowing you as I do, there is no doubt in my mind what the overwhelming majority of loyal Mississippians will do. They will never submit to the moral degradation, to the shame and the ruin which have faced all others who have lacked the courage to defend their beliefs. (quoted in R. H. Barrett, 1965, p. 64)

Echoing the century-long legacy of formal and informal *Black Laws* that often allowed for black Mississippians only fractional democratic vocation (e.g. three-fifths voting laws), Barnett's contentions that the outspoken *majority* of Mississippians principally supported segregation at Ole Miss, and that Federal intervention threatened the 'Mississippi way of life,' authorized the directive, or what former US President George W. Bush might refer to as the "mandate," to act upon the groundswell of white support for the University's segregationist imperative.[4] On campus, the University's student newspaper, *The Mississippian*, published a poll in late January, 1956, reporting that 74 percent of the students on campus favored segregation; and of the 19 percent supporting integration, a sizeable majority were 'non-Southerners' ("Ole Miss students favor segregation," 1956). A similar poll conducted by the conservative, state-sponsored Citizens Council three years later concluded that 98 percent of white residents in Jackson, McComb, and Greenwood (three of Mississippi's most populous cities) favored segregation in all of Mississippi's colleges and universities (Silver, 1966).

For many of these adherents to the traditionalistic logics of a divisive plantation cultural economy, the prospects of Meredith's enrollment at the state's flagship university endangered the pedagogical symmetry they had been able to construct prior to, and reconstruct following, the failings of the 'Confederate Cause' their ancestors had formulated in the lead-up to the US Civil War. For stalwarts of separatism such as Barnett, the social and material consequences of integration jeopardized the function of Ole Miss as an institutional cog of a broader repressive state-sponsored apparatus: which was to create separate spaces—and thus separate opportunities—for young Mississippians. The prospect of integrating the Oxford cam-

---

4. A more thorough explication of the origins and meanings of the cognominal 'Ole Miss' will be offered in Chapter Eight. Here, let us suppose that perhaps the politics of the moniker are linguistically allied to the Old South vernacularisms of racial hierarchy and gendered expressivity.

pus signaled the epochal rupture in the continuities of a strategically-constructed social and spatial institution designed and mobilized to publically-celebrate and pedagogically-reinforce plantation privilege and white exceptionalism. From its inception, the University of Mississippi had been an important edifice for the proliferation and advancement of a state-sponsored parochial white orthodoxy—*the* preeminent pedagogical enterprise in what then University of Mississippi professor James Silver (1966) famously referred to as Mississippi's 'closed society.' The admission of black students was perceived by many within Mississippi's white power elite as a "mongrelizing" (Silver, 1966, p. 126) campaign against the social Darwinist plinth of Anglo-Saxonism moulded at the state's flagship educational institution.

Following a turbulent three-year enrollment, and upon completing his degree, James Meredith (1966) irreverently celebrated the ostensibly revolutionary effect of his desegregationist crusade by extolling, "Today . . . I am a graduate of the University of Mississippi. For this I am proud of my country" (p. 1). For social reformists and civil rights activists of the early 1960s, this important victory signified a decisive symbolic and material turning point in Southern social and cultural relations—and was heralded as *the beginning of the end* of the racism[s] of Mississippi's, as well as the Deep South's, past. In a somewhat concessionary retraction following the forced integration of the University of Mississippi, Governor Ross Barnett's professed that black and white Mississippians now "enjoy[ed] a wonderful and peaceful relationship" (qtd. in Silver, 1966, p. 23). The Governor's sentiment was echoed by then Senator James O. Eastland in his assertion that by the mid-1960s, "There [was] no longer discrimination in the South" (qtd. in Silver, 1966, p. 23).

In spite of these and other 'post-racist' declarations, it would be misguided to assume that the *politics of race* in the Deep South, and more specifically the *racist politics* of Ole Miss, ended in the fall of 1962. The University of Mississippi has since the days of Meredith been witness to a proliferation of pyrrhic and physical confrontations around issues of race. A cursory survey of post-Meredith race relations at Ole Miss renders a bevy of tumultuous encounters, each of which illuminates the diachronic interplay between the segregation-era identity politics and the primordial social practices and relics of the post-Civil Rights campus body. In 1988, for example, Ole Miss made national headlines when the new building that was set to house the first black fraternity on the Ole Miss campus was burned to the ground by arsonists (Dabney, 1988). Only one year later, members from one of the University's many all-white fraternities branded "KKK" and "I hate niggers" on the chests of two students, drove them to nearby Rust College (an historically black college), and abandoned their epithet-emblazoned white bodies on the Rust campus (S. Mason & Yarbrough, 1989).

In 2001, another racially-charged incident at the Garland-Hedleston-Mayes dormitory again brought Ole Miss into the national popular when students were found displacing and altering Black History Month flyers—incorporating antagonistic racial slurs into the modified brochures

(Thomas, 2000). Also in 2001, two members of the Alpha Tau Omega fraternity were expelled from the organization following their role in creating a racially-charged, mordant photograph taken on the night of fraternity-sponsored Halloween party. The photograph depicted a fraternity member, outfitted as a police officer, holding a gun to the head of another member dressed in blackface. The member in blackface was wearing a straw hat while kneeling on the ground as if picking cotton (Finley & Yoste, 2001). In 2002, two unidentified students were accused by the University of scribbling racist graffiti on the dorm room doors of two black students in the Kincannon residence hall. Among the hateful soubriquets: "Fucking Nigger" and "Fucking Ho Nigger." The culprits also left a tree with a noose and hanging stick figure in the dormitory and vulgar imprints of genitalia drawn in blue window chalk along walls on three floors of the dorm (Kanengiser, 2002).[5]

Of course, these forms of overt racism are by no means exclusive to Ole Miss. For such examples are certainly suggestive of the broader specters of racist and segregationist logics—spawned during slavery and maintained by Jim Crow laws[6]—which continue to haunt this and many other social and academic institutions throughout the US South. Imbricated by the historical pervasiveness of racist 'Old South' ideologies, these examples are representative of the outward manifestation of social hierarchies that become coded in parochial discourses of racialized objectification (of the black "Other") and subjectification (of the privileged white norm)—each collapsing upon the politics of identity within the Mississippi Delta region. As Silver (1966) poignantly proscribed, "Mississippi invariably represents the South, and the South is always regarded as a solid unit" (p. 29). Likewise, history suggests that such machinations of Southern [white] solidarity have become both meaningful and powerful, and at the same time fractured and unstable; an *order of things* bound to both supremacist ideologies of the past and institutional orthodoxies of the present (Brattain, 2001; Hoelscher, 2003; hooks, 1992; McPherson, 2003).

---

5. It was later concluded by the Ole Miss campus police that the inscriptions had been perpetrated by three black students who lived in the dorms as part of a 'hoax.' As a result, there was a journalistic assault from the Right against these "accused sickos" who employed "crude and twisted acts of Tawana Brawleyism" to reignite charges of racism against the University's white students (Malkin, 2002). In a preposterous recount of the incident, columnist Michelle Malkin identified the problem as such: "how the young beneficiaries of the civil rights movement are squandering and desecrating its legacy of equal respect and justice for all" (Malkin, 2002).

6. These new logics of an old racist order were further ordained through a number of inter-state segregation laws—or what are more often referred to as Jim Crow Laws. The Laws—the etymology of which can be traced back to the popular antebellum blackface minstrel *Jump Jim Crow*—legitimated the segregation of public schools, public buildings and parks, public transportation, and the segregation of restrooms and restaurants along racial lines. For an excellent rejoinder to the Jim Crow Era, see Stetson Kennedy's (1959/1992) *Jim Crow Guide*.

Most problematically, however, the material history of the US South illustrates continuities and patterns whereby much of the young white population has been "educated to believe in [its] superiority" (Silver, 1966, p. 151). Historically in Mississippi, an institutional constellation of civic and service clubs, educational institutions, churches, business and labor organizations, sport and leisure formations, and political and judicial groupings have comprised an interconnected universe underpinned by white supremacist, social despotic, and cultural pathologic dictums. However, in this book I follow others in arguing that perhaps the most distinctive, and significant, methods for promulgating Mississippi's symbolic technologies of racism among its elite class can be found in the pedagogies, discourses, and physical practices of the state's educational system. More specifically, I focus this study on the pedagogical architecture of Ole Miss: an institution which from its conception was designed to "transmit culture—customs, values, history, and habits—'across the generations'" (Cohodas, 1997, p. 14).

I am not alone in fixing a critical eye on the Oxford campus. Numerous social commentators and critical historians have interpreted and documented such explicit racism which diachronically transverses the University of Mississippi's troubled political, cultural, and economic [trans]formations throughout interwoven epochs (R. H. Barrett, 1965; Cabaniss, 1971; Cohodas, 1997; W. Doyle, 2001; Hendrickson, 2003; J. Meredith, 1966; D. G. Sansing, 1990, 1999; Silver, 1966, 1984). Perhaps more than any other Southern social space, the campus of Ole Miss (and practices therein) has long been the archetypal 'ideological state apparatus' (Althusser, 1971) for perpetuating the material and symbolic power of Dixieland's 'normative center.' From the outset, Ole Miss was created to mask the social inequities of Mississippi's past and present, while simultaneously functioning to reproduce the 'preeminence' of Southern white hegemony. "Its traditional mission," wrote Adam Nossiter (1997), "has less to do with imparting Shakespeare than with passing on the culture of white Mississippi" (p. 1).

In the tradition of modernist social history and modern conceptualizations of racial difference (Hall, 1985, 1986b, 1992c), these journalists, anthropologists, and historians have typically rewritten or rearticulated the 'social facts,' practices, and processes of explicit racism in and around Ole

Miss, Mississippi, and the Dixie South.[7] But there is something more complex, more divisive at work in Oxford: a social configuration which has gone virtually unnoticed by journalistic and scholarly luminaries, and which, while operating on the everyday experiences of people from this region, occupies a clandestine, and perhaps *normal*, quality within these analyses. For at the intersection of a living, vibrantly romanticized heritage culture and Old South nostalgia on the campus and the physical and material discords of polarized/racialized human beings operating therein, post-Meredith Ole Miss looks a lot like the university of white plantation gentry from generations past. While times have changed, the function of the institution—to transmit the cultures and power relations of the past onto the future—has largely remained the same.

These analyses do share the common basis for interpretation: that of the racialized body. In their attempts to understand the sociological element of embodied relations at social institutions such as Ole Miss, cultural analysts have often overlooked the relevance of the creations of discourse and discursive formations; of what Deleuze and Guattari (1983a) describes as an elusive, discursively constituted 'body without organs.' Here I follow

---

7.The social relationships of the South, generally, and Ole Miss particularly, have traditionally been framed and conceptualized around logics of what Lincoln and Guba (2000) would refer to as 'modernist' or 'positivist' epistemological positions. In other words, through narratives and conventions borne of a white male dominated social scientism, analyses bound to conventions of modern sociology have typically engaged the Southern agent as standing outside the structure of power, rather than as a subject position operating within the schisms of subjectification and identification (Frow & Morris, 2000). Such theories are made and remade to reinforce modern idioms of power because they remain within the strategic norms of modern, positivistic, scientific hegemony (Denzin, 1994). As Grossberg (1996) asserts, "the modern transforms all relations of identity into relations of difference . . . the modern constitutes not identity out of difference but difference out of identity" (p. 93). However, a promising striation has recently emerged within cultural studies research on the *discourses* of identity—a logical bent which aims to disrupt traditional ways of theorizing race, gender, sexuality, and ethnicity (cf. Woodward, 1997). While in the modern social sciences identity was typically conceptualized around conventions of a binary logic (black/white, masculine/feminine, heterosexual/homosexual, male/female, etc.), this new strand of critical engagement, which originated out of recent internal debates in, and external challenges to, critical cultural studies, instead problematizes the broader discursive and ideological regimes which categorize human agents around such outdated schemas (Hall, 1992b, 1992e, 1995, 1996a). As Lawrence Grossberg (1996) postulates, post-modern cultural critics and researchers must abandon the hermeneutic posture of modern social science, and instead reflexively problematize issues of identity around contextually-specific formations of discourse, identification, and subjectivity. Paraphrasing Grossberg (1997b), and following Stuart Hall (1983; 1985; 1996b), any critical engagement of the identity politics of the South would be well-served to elicit a poststructuralist interpretive position grafted out of a synthesis of Derridian (1974; 1977; 1982) post-Sausurrian semiotics, and Foucauldian (1977; 1982a; 1982b; 2001) discursive politics—whereby local identity is constructed within formations and interconnections of *discourse*. Here I interpret the ways in which gesticulations of meaningful signification act upon the everyday experiences of the individual (Grossberg, 1986a; Grossberg & Slack, 1985).

the thinking of various French poststructural theorists in examining how ra-
cialized-, classed-, and gendered human beings came "to be interpreted as
knowing subjects, and at the same time objects of their own knowledge"
(Dreyfus & Rabinow, 1983, p. xix). As such, I draw upon the work of Michel
Foucault, Jean Baudrillard, Roland Barthes, Michel de Certeau, Jacques
Derrida, Henri Lefebvre, and Guy Debord (very few of whom, if any, would
identify themselves as 'poststructuralists', per se) to interpret the relations
of power, knowledge, bodies, space, spectacle, pedagogy, and spectacle in
the construction and contestation of a synchronically- and diachronically-
constituted set of identity politics. In particular, I make use of Foucault's
historically-grounded theories of subjectivity—and that which will be adopted in this analysis—in studying the construction of discourse, the essence
of ideology (truth), and the formation of power within social spaces such
as the one under inspection here. For Foucault, formations of discourse,
through language, image, narrative structure, mediated message, etc., actively organize human activity (Smart, 1983).[8] Whereas traditional sociological paradigms have often embraced the quest for social facts, causal relationships, and universal truths, this striation of poststructuralist thinking has called for new interpretations of the social world—interpretations
that seek not to test hypotheses or apply theory to the empirical world,
but rather that seek to understand how human agency is constitutive of,
and constricted by, formations of discursively-organized power (Seidman,
1998).[9] In this way, to exist in the world, and in various social contexts, is to
at once be subjected to various structural forces and to create individual experience and identity through the systems of representation existent thereof.

To understand and disrupt these modern axioms of representation, I will
shift the focus away from the conspicuous confrontations and contradictions of pluralistic identities, and instead brazen out the 'structural phases'
(J. Baudrillard, 1983a) which operate in, and reproduce through, pronounced
portents of commonality and 'difference.' Lawrence Grossberg (1996) argues that scholars must escape the conventions of oppression, both the 'colonial model' of "the oppressed and the oppressor" and the 'transgression

---

8.The power of discourse is evident in social fixtures such as sexual taboos, technologies of science, the justice system, and education. In each of these discursive fields
(as well as many others), power is imbedded in the language and implementation of
discipline.

9.In this project, I will attempt to update the corporeal manifestations of these 'back-
wards' relations. Drawing from theoretical works on the social and cultural complexities of late modernity (or postmodernity), namely those of: alienation, reification, and ideology (as theorized by Situationist thinkers such as Guy Debord and
Henri Lefebvre); social class (namely Pierre Bourdieu and Georg Lukács); whiteness
(Henry Giroux, Ruth Frankenberg, and bell hooks); critical pedagogy (Joe Kincheloe, Paulo Freire, Shirley Steinberg, and Stanley Aronowitz); representation and semiotics (Jacque Derrida and Jean Baudrillard); and the discursively mobilized political body (Michel Foucault), this project is one part historical analysis, one part critical interpretation of the present.

model' of "oppression and resistance" (p. 88). Rather than think in terms of binaries of oppression or forces of oppression versus forces of resistance, he proposes that we rearticulate the question of identity into a "question of constructing historical agency" (Grossberg, 1996, p. 88). If scholar-researchers reproduce a popular pedagogy entrenched in a discourse of binaries, whereby white is privileged over black and masculinity over femininity, rather than negotiating the pluralities of the postmodern subject position, then those social researchers fail to disrupt the logics which often privilege one side of a binary logic (Frankenberg, 1997; H. A. Giroux, 1997b; J.L. Kincheloe & Steinberg, 1998). Furthermore, if dominant and marginalized *subject positions* are products of modern power relations (and modern discourses therein), as well as producers of the discursive systems and structures which distribute power through subjectification (and thus objectification), then we must instead problematize the institutions and institutionalization processes through which such hegemonic systems are activated (Beatriz & Patterson, 1998; H. A. Giroux, 1998; J. L. Kincheloe, Steinberg, Rodriguez, & Chennault, 1998; Rains, 1998; Ware & Back, 2001).

Thus, my aim within this study is to complicate these unspoken, clandestine, normative discursive formations, practices, and systems of power-knowledge at Ole Miss. I do so not to offer a generalizable indictment on past or present students, academic and professional staff members, administrators, or members of the Oxford community; I have no plans or ambitions here to typecast University constituents as seething racists (or vile misogynists and class elitists) or subordinated dupes. Further, my purpose in this book is not to document overt practices of racial (and to a lesser extent patriarchal and class-based) 'oppression' at Ole Miss, as that has been done elsewhere. Rather, I want to engage the ways in which discursively-constituted pedagogical practices (and praxis), and pedagogical practice as discourse, continually bring to life the iniquitous *cultural physicalities* of the Old South. In overly simple terms, in the coming pages I will endeavor to write a history of what Shilling (2007) might refer to as a distinctive formation of Southern 'body pedagogics'; or "the central pedagogic *means* through which a culture seeks to transmit its main corporeal techniques, skills and dispositions, the embodied *experiences* associated with acquiring of failing to acquire these attributes, and the actual embodied *changes* resulting from this process" (p. 13, author's emphasis). My aim here is to de-institutionalize the contextually- and parochially-raced body, the classed body, and the gendered body; and interpret how those bodies have been read, performed, and institutionalized in ways that concatenate the generations to power relations forged in plantation times.

The institution does not exist outside the social relationships in which it constitutes and is constituted by, but rather it is an active formation in the 'signifying system' (R. Williams, 1981) of imaginary conservative, Anglo-centric identity politics. Thus, I will further venture to explore how the body, what Stuart Hall (1996)—borrowing from the conceptual rhizomes of Jacques Derrida (1976, 1982)—describes as that 'most transcendental of signifiers,' is both *a product of* the broader social, economic, and political structures of the Dixie South and *produces* the power relations therein. As Maurice Merleau-Ponty (1945/2002) reminds us, it is through the body, and in relation to 'Other[ed]' bodies, that we come to understand our cultural world (and our place therein):

> The body is our general medium for having a world. Sometimes it is restricted to the actions necessary for the conservation of life, and accordingly it posits around us a biological world; at other times, elaborating upon these primary actions and moving from their literal to a figurative meaning, it manifests through them a core of new significance: this is true of motor habits such as dancing. Sometimes, finally, the meaning aimed at cannot be achieved by the body's natural means; it must then build itself an instrument, and it projects thereby around itself a cultural world (p. 146)

The *flesh cultures* of Ole Miss are at once political and powerful because they are made of 'knowing bodies'—discursively constituted bodies that evoke not only corporeal aesthetics, but knowledge-power relations imbedded in the hierarchical logics of the Old South. They ignite the politics of what Peter McLaren (1988) describes as 'enfleshment'; or, the "dialectical relationship between the material organization of interiority and the cultural forms and modes of material production we inhabit subjectively" (p. 61). This enfleshment, as McLaren continues, "occurs not just at the level of the materiality of the flesh, but through both the corporeal embodiment of symbols and metaphors into the flesh and 'fleshing out' of ideas at the level of cultural forms and social structures. That is, the body *both incorporates ideas and generates them.*" (p. 61, author's emphasis).

For it was the body—both the isolated body (shackled under the sweltering mid-day sun to the cotton field, fearfully pacing across the backcountry dirt road at dusk, or lording over the land [and thus the bodies of others]) and the collective configurations of embodied whiteness, patriarchy, and gentility—upon which systems of power, misogyny, lynch mob-terrorism, and slavery were exchanged and diffused across the ages and the land. Through embodied praxis, "knowledge is embodied as the effects of processes of inscription. These processes, and the embodied knowledge they install, are shown to be central to acculturation and socialization, and to the production and reproduction of social order" (Lattimer, 2009, p. 3).

As but a few critics have begun to contemplate, to understand the power relations of the modern US South, we must wrestle with how the *visible nature* of these identity politics has served as "a conceptual space for desperately clinging to the social relations of an imagined past" (C. R. King & Springwood, 2001, p. 154)—to understand how the body is a conduit through which power can be inscribed, performed, read, and thusly mobilized as cultural currency. In this way, the body is oriented, objectified, subjected, and brought into the realm of ideas through flesh; to quote Maurice Merleau-Ponty (1968), it is a fold "coiling over the visible upon the visible" (p, 138). Hence, my objective is two-fold: 1) to read the body as it has been discursively constituted at the University over time, in hopes of prying loose those cultural codes by which some bodies are privileged over others; and

2) deconstruct the pedagogical mechanisms by which these codes are systematically inscribed, knocking down the walls and barriers which are allowed to float freely throughout the campus by way of the symbolic, the performed, and the ingratiated.

On the Politics of Interrogating Dixie

I suppose then, that I should make a confession about this project's political intent. It was never fashioned in the tradition of modern scientific objectivity, neutrality, or value-free epistemology; quite the opposite, actually. Prior to beginning the project, I, like anyone else who has spent time in the Deep South, had become all-too-familiar with the politics of race and racism that are to this day omnipresent both in Mississippi, my home state of Tennessee (where I became well-versed in the symbolic and practiced codes of Southern whiteness), and most other parts of the region. Hence, while in an auto-biographical sense I did not seek out the South—but rather the South chose me—empirically and epistemologically I could think of no other place to explore how the racisms and race-based identity hierarchies of the past are learned, performed, brought to life through the body cultures of the present. Nor did I seek out Mississippi or Ole Miss to demonize its various constituents; but rather to extrapolate from the *crucible of the Old South* a better understanding of how knowledge and power can be inscribed in the body pedagogic—and the pedagogic body. It is my hope that interpretations that follow might lead us toward a better Ole Miss, a better Mississippi, and a better South; whereby the individual acting therein can be more critically aware of how her or his body is subjected to the weight of history, of power, and of oppression.

Indeed, by revealing the socially-constructed body cultures of the Dixie South across various historical contexts, I hope to foster critical consciousness among both those individuals whose social, cultural, and economic status is inextricably linked to past cultures of alienation and exploitation and those individuals whose lives continue to be challenged as a result. In this way, I follow the Brazilian pedagogue Paulo Freire (1970/2006)—whose pedagogical method was a *mélange* of counter-oppressive politics and emancipatory education; of classroom instruction and everyday encounters—in cultivating a form of popular education intended to share in the communal practice of raising individual consciousness ('conscientization') of the political and oppressive regimes acting against the human condition. For Freire, critical consciousness, or *conscientização*, comes about when individuals develop an epistemological awareness of the ways dialogic, political, and economic structures act upon their everyday lives. That awareness is nurtured through constant dialogue with, and consideration of, the oppressive elements of one's life; and actively imagining and working to make real alternative, egalitarian social formations. It is my hope that through education, both the individuals within a society and the society itself are best able to achieve autonomy and emancipation from those anti-humane forces that restrict freedom.

In the spirit of the Stuart Hall's New Left and their efforts to better understand how Thatcherism had captured the working class British imaginary, this multifaceted study evolved into a politically-driven project directed toward such an interventionist public pedagogy (Greenwood & Levin, 2000). The philosophy which undergirds the work of Hall's British Cultural Studies, and guides my empirical and epistemological endeavor here, is this: by way of critically theorizing and thoroughly empiricizing, scholar/researchers can discover the dominant and marginal formations of society, and reformulate a politics of existence which subvert those marginalizing forces. As Lawrence Grossberg (2001) posits, "I think cultural studies is about the integration of rigorous theory, empirical research and political commitment" (p. 144). Framed around the notion of 'social justice,' such a politically-driven cultural studies is borne of the urge, if not the impetus, to implode the iniquitous social relations which are allowed to remain pervasive throughout society. This type of interventionist polity is reflected in Henry Giroux's (2007; 2000, 2001) notion of a 'performative pedagogy.' Giroux (2001) argues:

> As a performative act, cultural studies involves using theory as a resource to think and act, learning how to situate texts within historical and institutional contexts, and creating conditions for collective struggles over resources and power . . . such a gesture not only affirms the social function of oppositional cultural work (especially within the university) but offers opportunities to mobilize instances of collective outrage, if not collective action. (p. 11)

Ours is a cultural studies "fundamentally concerned with understanding, with a view to transforming, people's lived realities" (Howell, Andrews, & Jackson, 2002, p. 154)—"always at some level marked . . . by a discourse of social involvement" (Frow & Morris, 2000, p. 327).[10]

Whereas social scientists of the modernist tradition are often in the business of generalizing, categorizing, and (to some extent) commodifying ideologies, discourse, and practices, following Pierre Bourdieu (1998b), critical cultural scholars tend to distance themselves from a traditionalist sociology throttled by *"escapism of Wertfreiheit"* (p. 16)—which is essentially the

---

10. Acknowledging that cultural phenomena "can be interpreted in any number of equally valid ways because there is no one correct interpretation" (Flaherty, 2002, p. 481), researchers in the cultural studies vein disregard static, formulaic, and objective positivism of modern social science.

notion of being free from value.[11] As Frow and Morris (2000) suggest, cultural studies more specifically has "been less concerned with debating the pros and cons of essentialism as a philosophical stance than with examining the political conflicts at stake, in concrete contexts and for particular groups of people" (p. 318). This is a cultural studies that, first and foremost, emanates from the political Left; and as such our shared endeavor is fixed on demonstrating how within certain contexts "cultural objects negatively affect the lives of specific people" (Denzin, 2002, p. 486).

A prevailing critique of the vanishing activist Left in the academy is the "crisis in representation" (Marcus & Fischer, 1986, p. 7) imbedded in the nature of critical analysis of discourse. As a result of the increased relevance of poststructuralism and the 'cultural turn,' a great deal of cultural studies research interprets and formulates responses to discourse and discursive formations. As Denzin (2002) queries: "How is it possible to effect change in the world, if society is only and always a text?" (p. 483). The debates around public intervention, reciprocity, and activist research create a bit of a conundrum: when interpreting discourse, and particularly in the practice of Derridian deconstructionism, scholar/researchers are saddled by the challenge of separating language, text, rhetoric, physicality, and other forms of signification from the human action which they dialectally produce.

While these circuits of representation offer insight into the ideological regimes acting upon human experience, researchers often fail to articulate the connections between discourse, ideology, and the lived experience. These various postulations emanating from the cultural studies milieu have increasingly failed to engage a progressive, political-activist charge in the tradition of the New Left.[12] At this point there are two competing courses of thought: the first is that no substantive social change can take place from poststructuralist deconstructionism, as discourse is abstract and amorphous and thus disconnected from human experience and the potentialities of soc-

---

11.I thus follow Hall, Grossberg, and their contemporaries in rejecting Max Weber's 'value free sociology' (see Lewis, 1975), instead fashioning a philosophical bent that those who have the chance to devote themselves to the study of the social world "cannot stay neutral, indifferent, and away from the struggles whose stakes are the future of the world" (Mesny, 2002, p. 63). As Norman Denzin (2002) submits, "there is no possibility of theory- or value-free knowledge" (p. 484), rather, in doing social research we immerse ourselves in the social world, and as social beings, cannot divorce ourselves as researchers from the activities we are analyzing. Contrary to the Durkheimian/Weberian traditions of modern sociology, the interventions of postmodernism and poststructuralism have reintroduced the authorial politics into the intellectual text.

12.Giroux (2004) has argued that in recent years, the public sphere is increasingly marked by "a poverty of critical public discourse, thus making it more difficult for young people and adults to appropriate a critical language outside of the market that would allow them to translate private problems into public concerns or to relate public issues to private considerations" (p. 207).

ial justice. However, a second trajectory[13] suggests that not only is discourse relevant, but an understanding of the complex and oppressive discursive formations which shape, and are shaped by, human activity is imperative for any type of contemporary sociological analysis. Interpretive analysis of qualitative power relations seeks to understand and critically undermine "how power and ideology operate through and across systems of discourse, cultural commodities, and cultural texts" (Denzin, 2002, p. 484). The study of discourse is the first and last step in a poststructuralist analysis of the social world. By deconstructing the taken-for-granted nature of power relations encoded in practices of signification, representation, and mediation, researchers can show "members of the underclass how to find their own cultural homes within . . . shifting oppressive structures" (Denzin, 2002, p. 487).

Released from the bindings of foundational and positivistic social science, many contemporary cultural studies researchers of the academy and beyond are now exploring the limits and social effects of performance-based ethnographic research and interventionist texts (Denzin, 2000). The challenge for these researchers is to create a reflexive dialogue between researcher as political informant and the prevailing modalities of public discourse (Grossberg, 1997). In other words, progressive scholar/researchers "need a language of critique and possibility, one that connects diverse struggles, uses theory as a resource, and defines politics as not merely critical but also as an intervention into public life" (Giroux, 2004, p. 208). To 'discover the marginal text,' and perhaps more importantly, to identify the normative discursive formations which create marginality, is surely the first step toward disrupting existing regimes of power in society. To get somewhere 'better,' we must understand the social construction of discourse, and the politics written into that discourse.

Although my study is an interrogation of enfleshed and bodily discourse, and the processes by which discursive formations are produced, I have no intent to write myself out of this text. Throughout this research project, mine was, and continues to be, *a body of the South*; encoded in the corporeal language and deportment of that which I interpret here. Having spent the past five years exhaustively dialoging with the body cultures of the Dixie South, it would be misleading to suggest that I am writing this from the outside. On the contrary. I attended tailgate parties before Ole Miss football games, drank a few toddies, meandered about political rallies, spent hundreds of hours on campus speaking with students, administrators, and staff members, exhumed millions of pages of antiquated text from the University Archives and various newspaper's microfiche vaults, dined at cafes in the Square, spent many a warm spring afternoon lounging on the Grove's plush fescue, and so on.

Thus, I am of the opinion that a rigorous investigation of the body cultures and pedagogies of the Dixie South cannot—and make no mistake, I

13.This trajectory is more fully described in Appendix I, whereby I delve further into the political nature of discourse and the attempts to breach the discursive/practical divide (see discussions on articulation, context-building, and discourse).

am signaling a departure here from most of the work done under the banners of cultural studies, physical cultural studies, and body sociology—rely solely on 'textual analysis,' discourse analysis, semiology, or other disengaged methodological teleologies. This is indeed a study of discourse, but I do not assume that discourse is encoded, decoded, contested, negotiated, and made meaningful in ways that can be understood by only 'reading' them from the sofa. For, as Kathy Davis (2007) reminds us, "the body is more than a surface, a cultural 'text', or a site for the endless deconstruction of Cartesian dualisms. Bodies are anatomical, physiological, experiential, and culturally shaped entities" (p. 61). To do so would assume a common scheme of decoding complex corporealities that simply does not exist. For the bodies I encountered were dynamic, operating within the formations of race, gender, class, ability, and regionality—but never, *never* in ways that were predictable, categorical, or *guaranteed*.

More importantly, rather than suggest that all who attend Ole Miss are 'racist whites' or 'complicit blacks,' I want to elucidate the ways in which persistent identity politics shape human action within the Ole Miss space, and then undermine the *taken-for-grantedness* of oppressive physical cultures. In more explicit terms, this project is an attempt to *peculiarize* the power dynamics of identity in the Dixie South as expressed through the social praxis and physical discourses of the University of Mississippi; how, through schooling, "the physical bodies of students [and non-students alike] are patterned to fit our social and economic structures" (Shapiro, 1999, p. 24). Writing as a part of this society, rather than some 'enlightened' outsider, I did this to better understand the complexities of embodied Southern culture. And yet, it is this embodied South, and imaginaries of a 'Southern ethic,' which I aim to scrutinize, disrupt, and implode throughout these pages.

So who is this research for, and why do it? Paraphrasing James Silver, author of 1966's controversial *Mississippi: The Closed Society*, a scathing doctrine of white supremacy in the deep South, it is my intention that the reader—and I am mainly concerned with the reader from the US South—will look upon this manuscript with an open mind and will consider the implications proposed within not as an attack on their way of life, but as *entrée* into a discussion about the iniquities of the present-day South, the nation, and beyond. For it was the 'son of the South,' Senator William Fulbright from Arkansas, who reminds us:

> To criticize one's country is to do it a service and pay it a compliment. It is a service because it may spur the country to do better than it is doing, it is a compliment because it evidences a belief that a country can do better than it is doing. Criticism, in short, is an act of patriotism, a higher form of patriotism, I believe than the familiar rituals of national adulation. (quoted in Sage, 1990, p. 12)

This book is for those who have chuckled off with flippancy another's evocation of wicked epithets such as 'nigger.' This is for those who do not wave Confederate flags at Ole Miss football games, but yell 'Hotty Toddy' with the same vigor as those segregationists who fought to keep James Meredith out of Ole Miss. This is for those who are aware of the clandestine practices of racism in the Deep South documented in this manuscript, and fully sentient to the wealth of racist practices which evade these pages, and choose to let them be. This is for 'NASCAR dads,' Southern Belles, and 'Rebel Rousers' everywhere who stand by, and allow for, the persistence of the powerful center. Finally, this is for the Indiana University student, the North Dakota sports fan, and the Eli Mannings of the world, who, in reading this, might see their own, local, oppressive whiteness in their daily lives and recognize how the divisive politics of race continue to plague progress in this US and beyond. In sum, my aim is to 'make visible,' to polemicize, the material and discursive manifestations of white supremacy at Ole Miss.

Dialectics of Knowing Whiteness

As Ruth Frankenberg (1993; 1994; 1997) suggests, to understand these forms of power—and particularly the dialectics of embodied power—we must start by turning our attention to the *center*: to the everyday, taciturn regimes of representational power which effectively [re]produce dominant subject positions through the construction of prevailing social discourses. For Frankenberg, as well as a sizeable contingent of social researchers (Allison, 1998; M.W. Apple, 1997; W. C. Ayers, 1997; Bonnett, 1996, 2000; Delgado & Stefancic, 1997; Dyer, 1997; Feagin & Vera, 1995; Fisher Fishkin, 1995; Frankenberg, 1997; H. A. Giroux, 1997a, 1997c; Hall, 1995; hooks, 1997; Ignatiev, 2003; J.L. Kincheloe & Steinberg, 1998; Mahoney, 1997; Malin, 2003; McIntosh, 1990; Peck, 2000; D.R. Roediger, 1997; D. R. Roediger, 2002; Semali, 1998; Sleeter, 1993, 1996; Stowe, 1996; Ware & Back, 2001; Wray & Newitz, 1997; Young, 1990), such an enterprise begins at the core of representational power: the adjudication of monolithic, uninterrupted whiteness. The earliest such petition for the critical study of whiteness as social construction can be located in W. E. B. Du Bois' *Black Reconstruction*. As Hartman (2004) suggests, Du Bois' (1903/1996) luminary text:

> ... elevated the concept of 'whiteness' as an analytical problem in determinations of class and stratification. He theorized that even white workers enjoyed a 'public and psychological wage', regardless of their position in the social hierarchy, [one] that was derived from their whiteness and reinvested in it. White privilege validated, and was validated by, racism (pp. 23-24).

Du Bois' (1903/1996) appeal for critical examination of the structures and processes of whiteness, however, went largely ignored until the early 1990s.

Unfortunately, rather than a neo-Du Boisian assault on the specters of white privilege, the initial strand of a public pedagogy on whiteness was (for the most part), and continues to be, a self-victimized and self-centered trope emerging from the political Right in response to the changing nature of 'multiculturalism' and post-modern social relationships brought on by affirmative action, 'political correctness,' and other recourses of class-based and race-based Civil Rights Movements in late-Twentieth Century America (Gabriel, 1998; H. A. Giroux, 1997c; Wellman, 1997). In Western 'intellectual' dialogue, a broad range of responses to issues of whiteness materialized—including pseudo-academic works such as Richard J. Herrnstein and Charles Murray's (1994) *The Bell Curve* and Dinesh D'Souza's (1995) *The End of Racism*—each of which offered quasi-substantiated claims of white disenfranchisement through the propagation of racial difference.

This loose adaptation of 'whiteness' was effectively a conservative reaction to political and cultural threats to white male hegemony: a clinging to the vestiges of the previously unchallenged (material and symbolic) spaces of privilege reserved for white males (Hartigan, 1997a, 1997b; McIntosh, 1990; McIntyre, 1997; Stowe, 1996). This trajectory of white disenfranchisement extended beyond the academy, into popular cinema such as the feature films *Falling Down* and *Lone Star* (K. W. Kusz, 2001; Somerson, 2004) and radio and television narratives such as *The Rush Limbaugh Show, The O'Reilly Factor, Sean Hannity,* and *Imus in the Morning.* Ultimately, 'whiteness,' or 'being white,' became the recalcitrant posture for white, middle-class "resistance to taxation, to the expansion of state-furnished rights of all sorts, and to integration" (Winant, 1992, p. 166). Thus, most early discussions of whiteness centered on the reclamation project of the 'angry white male,' whereby opposition to 'new racism' or 'reverse racism' was "coded in the language of 'welfare reform, neighborhood schools, toughness on crime and illegitimate births'" (H. A. Giroux, 1997c, p. 377). Whiteness was articulated within the popular sphere as an alternative discourse for whites assailed by the changing dynamics of immigrant labor, leftist multiculturalism, and a professed 'reverse' racism in the job market (Omi & Winant, 1993).

In contrast to this trend of cumbersome reactionary conceptualizations to the 'problem' of whiteness, a concurrent—and ontologically-opposed—wave of theorizing the prevailing discourses of identity emerged in the early 1990s. This trajectory took a more critical approach to the *problems* and *consequences* of dominant subject position[alitie]s. The forerunning texts which located whiteness as something more than white backlash to 'bleeding heart' liberalism were Toni Morrison's (1992) *Playing in the Dark* and bell hooks' (1992) *Black Looks.* 'Whiteness' in this strand of theory thus came to be conjuncturally defined as "a practice, a social space, a subjectivity, a spectacle, an erasure, an epistemology, a strategy, a historical formation, a technology, and a tactic . . . it is unified through privilege and the power to name, represent, and create opportunity and deny access" (King & Springwood, 2001, p. 160). Echoing Du Bois (1903/1996), this new tack of theorizing recognized that whiteness as a social process exists to reinforce dominant ideologies of race, but is not desideratum of all those who identify themselves as white.[14] In fact, the most compelling thread of whiteness research frames whiteness as a process best understood as historically constructed

---

14.Morrison and hooks, as well as George Lipsitz (1998) after them, argued that it is erroneous to conflate the oppressive forces of whiteness with the social activities of all white people. Put more simply, and borrowing from Marx: whereas certainly some white [masculine] subjects perpetuate these ideologies, not all necessarily do so under conditions of their choosing (Giroux, 1994).

yet *internally differentiated* and *externally contested* (T. Allen, 1994; Bonnett, 2000; Delgado & Stefancic, 1997; Feagin & Vera, 1995; J. Z. Wilson, 2002).

To use the Martiniquan philosopher Frantz Fanon's (1986) terminology, this theorizing of whiteness sees white privilege and racially-constructed power as "epidermal," not biologically fixed but rather a product of social relations and diachronic materialism. In this way, whiteness is both challenged from within and contestable from the outside; *not all whitenesses are the same.* In fact, there is an infinite cultural lexicon of complementing and competing whitenesses operating within any historically or culturally specific context (Mahoney, 1997). Whiteness can be both a source of privilege and underprivilege; of both hegemonic and marginalized positionalities.[15] However, in US 'American' culture, whiteness has often evaded critical examination in part due to the rampant fetishism of the racialized and ethnicized 'Other' by modern sociologists (hooks, 1997, 2000a). Consequently, most theorizing on race tends to reify cultural variance, carving up ethnicity into measurable, visible ethnological qualities (and quantities)—except in the case of whiteness. The clandestine nature of whiteness within the academy has led to a non-reflexive understanding of the structures and discourses which create ideological power for the 'invisible center' (Sandoval, 1997).

In the US South, varying formations of whiteness have shaped social relations since long before Jim Crow, featuring, but not limited to: discourses of white supremacy, 'white trash,' and the occupant suburban white middle class. The critical eye of identity scholarship and whiteness only recently turned its attention to the South (Aanerud, 1997; Alexander, 2004; Applebome, 1997; Brattain, 2001; Delgado & Stefancic, 1997; Ferber, 1998a; Fisher Fishkin, 1995; R. Frankenberg, 1994; Frankenberg, 1997; Hale, 1998; Hartigan, 1997a; M. Hill, 1997; J.L. Kincheloe & Steinberg, 1998; J. L. Kincheloe, et al., 1998; Lipsitz, 1998; Mahoney, 1997; Newitz & Wray, 1997; Rodriguez, 1998; Stowe, 1996; Ware & Back, 2001). Ruth Frankenberg (2001) rightly postulates that "whiteness as a site of privilege is not absolute but rather cross-cut by a range of other axes of relative advantage or subordination" (p. 76). In the South, whiteness often intersects with patriarchy, heteronormativity, and late capitalist class politics in a conjunctural panoply of social power. As the scrupulous gaze of the critical scholarship has fixed its sights southward, it has been met by a social and cultural order still echoing social divisions and hierarchies of the Jim Crow era—yet a society confronted with unfamiliar remonstrations to the homogeneity of post-plantation white hegemony. Particularly in spaces of white privilege such as Ole Miss, the cultural trends of postmodern identity-fracturing have in recent years resulted in an unsettling of the dominant location of the upper-class, white, male subject position (H. A. Giroux, 1997a; Hall & Jameson, 1990; Jameson, 2001; Lury, 1996; Mukerji & Schudson, 1991). Borrowing from W.

---

15. For example, the privileged subject position brought upon by whiteness might not have the same resonance for Southern working class whites, often referred to in the popular sphere as "white trash" (Wray & Newitz, 1997).

J. Cash (1941/1991), the reign of the white supremacist 'helluvafella,'[16] which has been at the core of Dixieland social praxis since the genocide of the native peoples of the region during the early part of the 18th Century, has come under attack. The increased inspection of whiteness in civic and vernacular discourses, and the privileges imbedded within experiences therein, has in many ways challenged the fundamental social ordering of 'helluvafella' dominance over those on the margins (Brattain, 2001).

Paralleling broader trends in whiteness research, early theorizing on Southern whiteness assumed that to 'be white' in the South meant entitlement to the fruits of racist hierarchies which abound throughout American society. However, as bell hooks (2000b) rightly points out, in recent years the research has turned toward a more complex reading of whiteness, and its diverse and complex manifestations and experiences therein. Whereas the early research flirted with the conflation of Southern 'whiteness' and 'new racism,' more recent work has begun to problematize the complexities of the "oppressive, invisible center" (H. A. Giroux, 1997c, p. 376). In other words, while there is an undeniable history of sexism, racism, and social class exclusion which has operated on, and continues to operate within, the everyday experience of all Dixieland Southerners (Brattain, 2001)—one which has, and will continue to be, well documented, there is a noticeable gap in research dedicated to the critical examination of the contextually-specific responses and reclamations of the 'invisible center.'

The task of illuminating the complexities of Dixie South whiteness, and thus challenging the normative nature of social relations emanating from the core of the Old South's power structure, is closely linked to the interrelated outcomes of postmodern fracturing of Southern identities and the symbolic diffuse of power brought about by contested paradigms of difference. The old logics of race and gender in the Dixie South have been met by convergent tensions brought forth by softer forms of social conservatism (which elucidate the region's social inequities) and the new realities of a terrestrial post-industrial economic order (which further isolate the region's revenue streams). In these messy postmodern times, such a signified instability threatens to undermine the longstanding hegemonic location of Dixieland whiteness within the pantheon of representational politics.

As such, articulations of Southern whiteness, and particularly whiteness in the contemporaneous Dixie South context, operate outside conventions of most critical studies of whiteness. Whiteness research often starts its analysis from an unspoken, clandestine center of power. And while the centrality of a Southern knowledge-power dynamic is pervasively located within a white center, the *conspicuous* response of (and from) the empowered white center has been the promotion of a more noticeably pronounced, *vis-*

---

16. In his famous 1941 manuscript, *The Mind of the South*, W. J. Cash (1941/1991) describes such a southern white masculine subject as "helluvafella": the proverbial 'good ole' boy' grounded in language and practices of southern tradition.

ible center.[17] Unlike Eric Lott's (2001) reworking of Arthur Schlesinger's (1997) notion of the 'vital center,' in which the author imagines a subversive, yet all-encompassing center of power, or Giroux's (1997a) 'invisible' whiteness, I want to explore the possibilities of whiteness as conspicuous performance—whereby an overt *theater of white power*[18] is brought to life in and through the embodied practices of Dixie South identity at Ole Miss.[19] For any culture, as Thomas Csordas (1990) makes clear, is a culture indivisible from embodiment: "The body is not an object to be studied in relation to culture, but it is to be considered as the subject of culture, or in other words as the existential ground of culture" (p. 5).[20]

This book, then, is in some ways a response to Frankenberg's (1997) call to understand contemporary whiteness by focusing on corporeal knowledge-power and the diachronic making of those body pedagogics.[21]

---

17. The notion of a 'visible' quality to whiteness, or more accurately the physical propagation of centralized identity politics around whiteness, is briefly introduced in Derald Wing Sue's (2004) paper on 'ethnocentric monoculturalism.'

18. Much like the 1936 Olympic Games constituted a theater of power for expressing Aryan supremacy, solidarity, and political ideology, this theater acts to reinforce the normative nature of preferred whiteness in the Dixie South context while simultaneously authorizing the practices of the oppressive center.

19. The complex axes of the identity politics and Southern whiteness are suggestive of the pluralistic nature of representation and identification in advanced postmodernity, where ultra-conservative traditionalism is expressed through a body politic and cultural economy dominated by *New South imagery* with an *Old South feel*. This is not to suggest that Dixie South whiteness is just another selection in the cornucopia of identities, but rather that over time the centralizing mechanisms and processes imbedded into local culture have created a gravitational pull, always bringing power back to the normative white epicenter of social power. As such, this study is a journey into the center of identity politics within the Dixie South, a core drilling project which aims to understand how whiteness becomes normalized and centralized, and how it is inevitably and imminently perceptible through active expressions, practices, and discourses within social institutions such as Ole Miss.

20. Research on whiteness and what Protevi (2001) refers to as the body's 'political physics' is relatively embryonic in its development. The earliest theorizing to emphasize the political nature of the body in relation to whiteness, primarily informed by the post-positivist social sciences, was produced by Alexander (2004), Delgado and Stefancic (Delgado & Stefancic, 1997), Bonnett (1998; 2000), Dyer (1997), Feagin and Vera (1995), Gabriel (1998), Long (2000; Long & Hylton, 2002), Mahoney (1997), Solomos and Back (1996), and Wellman (1997). And while this list is not comprehensive, it is no doubt suggestive in terms of the recent influx of this trajectory of research. However, essentially every previous contribution to the growing corpus of work on whiteness and physical culture (or body culture) offers broad sweeping analysis of the discourses of whiteness.

21. In using the terms "corporeal" and "corporeality," I am aiming to elicit double meaning. In the first instance, my use of the term is to refer to things related to the body. Concurrently, the term suggests a relational quality between the body and a broader social and cultural body politic. An interesting third reading could be the notion of a physicality governed by the logics of late capitalism, whereby [corpor-]ation infiltrates all aspects of human life.

In this way, *Embodying Dixie* is both a history and ethnography of embodied whiteness; and the intricate structures and process which shape racialized discourse in the US South. In the first instance, racial discourse and the politics of whiteness intersect at the body. While whiteness as a cultural formation extends beyond embodiment, both license to, and construction of, identity politics are in the most banal sense 'occularcentric' (McLaren, 1999)—individual skin color, gait, posture, and physicality (Marcoulatos, 2001). As such, this is fundamentally a study of contemporary 'physical culture' (D. L. Andrews, 2006; D.L. Andrews, 2008; David L. Andrews & Giardina, 2008; Hargreaves & Vertinsky, 2007; A. G. a. F. Ingham, 1997; Vertinsky & Hargreaves, 2007)[22]; an exploration of the body, perhaps more than any other site of signification, as the "condensation of subjectivities in the individual" (Hall, 1996, p. 11). Peter McLaren (1999) perhaps puts it best when articulating relations of the body to broader social and political formations:

> No matter how distant, removed, and powerless human beings feel in relations to the complexity of contemporary social and economic life, they carry the mega- and microstructures of social life in the machinery of their flesh, in the pistons of their guts, and in the steely wires of their tendons. (p. ix)

In the Dixie South, the body often [re]presents a vessel for, as well as an expression of, the mega- and microstructures of white supremacy. Foucault (1977a) refers to the promotion of the self through the politics of the body as an 'aesthetics of existence'—a strategic layering and performance of identity politics over the body. Elizabeth Grosz (1994) argues that such a body schema "unifies and coordinates postural, tactile, kinaestehtic, and visual sensations so that these are experienced as the sensations of the subject coordinated into a single space" (p. 83). Corporeal discourse not only objectifies the carrier of bodily signifiers, but also subjectifies the informant through the process of signification, which "itself is a regulative and regulated formation" (Hall, 1996, p. 11) which acts upon the political body. In other words, the formation of bodily discourse, and the discursive formations of the political body, moulds the body as text through normative regulation—which often reinforces social power relations and creates what Foucault (1977a, 1988a, 1988b) often refers to as 'docile bodies.' And thus, the theater of the body (and embodiment) becomes both a site for governance as well as a site for reproduction (or contestation) of the prevailing social order.

This theater of cultural embodiment has many acts and many actors. In the South, country western music, stridently segregated religious congregations (i.e. burning churches and radical cloth-bearers), sporting traditions such as NASCAR and college football, the Ku Klux Klan, Confederate flags, and the hyper-racist Nationalist Movement have all been associated

---

22. In recent years, there has been an upsurge in research devoted specifically to expressions of the political discourses of the body in relation to both the popular and the local (Cole, 2000; Harvey, 1986; Harvey & Sparkes, 1991; Maguire, 1993; Vasterling, 2003).

such a longitudinal [re]centering routine. These discursive formations of local identity have contributed to an imaginary 'Southern ethic' within the public sphere[23] (and corollary hierarchies with regard to gender and social class). In the Dixie South context, and particularly through the social practices of its more visible institutions, the performativity of racialized representation offers a return to a cultural politics of the power of the ubiquitous, 'normative center' (D. R. Roediger, 2002).[24] Therefore, I offer the following interpretations on Dixieland with intentions of augmenting the existing literature by developing a radically contextual analysis of Dixie South whiteness and expressions of the *visible center*. This analysis is part historical account, part cultural analysis, of the ways in which social power is espoused and expressed in and through discourses of bodily praxis, the mediated body, and the body in space at institutional locus of visible Dixie South whiteness.

Embodying Dixie

Embodying Dixie is essentially an analysis of the disciplined and spectacularized body within various historical contexts, and how physical culture at today's Ole Miss interacts with racialized (and to a lesser extent gendered- and social classed-) hierarchies of the Old South. Rather than offer a sociological analysis of the present that assumes relations of historical continuity and discontinuity, or conversely to take up a reconstructionist historian's labor in seeking to 'set the record straight' about body politics of the past, this book creates a dialogue between the past and present. Following Michel Foucault, *Embodying Dixie* is an amalgamation of both a 'genealogy' of diachronically-constituted power relations (a social history of discourse) and an 'archeology' of the what Don Johnson (1983) refers to as "body knowledges" unique to, and pervasive within, this context (an excavation of formations of discourse). It offers a cultural forensic of the construction, contestation, and performance of Dixie South body pedagogics across both time and space. Perhaps most importantly, throughout the book I en-

---

23. Throughout this manuscript, I will refer to 'blackness,' 'Southern blackness,' and 'blackness at Ole Miss' in a number of different ways. Often I slip in and out of using these terms to describe cultural experiences and discourse of black identity in a homogenous way. This is in no way attempt to suggest that all blacknesses and black experiences are similar, or that black identities are uniform, but rather I use the terms in this way to describe the prevailing attitudes about black 'Otherness' as discursively constituted in relation to dominant white identities/whiteness. Further, it is not my intention to overly-victimize blackness, but rather to locate the oppositional discourses of blackness which antithetically locate and relocate whiteness.

24. While "critical studies of whiteness" (Roediger, 2002, p. 15) are becoming increasingly relevant within the academic community, and Southern whiteness has been a growing part of that sociology, there is a liminal amount of research which critically considers how the body, as a discursive terrain, reproduces power structures of localized Southern white hegemony.

deavor to articulate the two; to interpret how the historically-constructed race-based body pedagogics explicated in the first half of this manuscript (Chapters One, Two, Three, and Four) come to life and are made meaningful in the present day body cultures of the Dixie South. Thus, the first part of what follows is a genealogical forensic of cultural physicalities of hegemonic whiteness at the University of Mississippi. Following Nietzschian and Foucauldian modalities of genealogical analysis, these chapters represent my efforts to contextualize and historicize the transitory politics of the body within various moments of the Ole Miss and Dixieland body politic.[25]

The first chapter primarily focuses on the disciplining of white bodies during the antebellum period at the University of Mississippi—and specifically how the body was both an instrument and object of white supremacist performative politics in a slave-based cultural economy. It traces how the faculty of the University, in conjunction with its Board of Trustees and the state government, enacted a series of measures meant to discipline and watch over Mississippi's young white men to better impose upon, and subject these students to, regimes of contextually-important power-knowledge formations. It explores how, through 'correct training' at the University, these white bodies were conditioned to capitalize upon and expand the cultural and economic empire of Mississippi's white elite. Such training entailed strict governance of the student body (*double entendre* intended), primarily through the implementation of a "Deportment Grades." This chapter ends by investigating the public and private discourses of institutional regimentation of Mississippi's young white elite prior to the Civil War—an episode which formulated the basis for the functionality of the University for years to follow.

---

25. At Ole Miss, there are numerous ways in which Dixie South whiteness is theatrically articulated, and a variety of formations of Dixie South whiteness which mask the iniquity-bearing cultural economy of the region. As James Silver (1966) suggested, "Mississippi has long been a hyper-orthodox social order in which the individual has no option except to be loyal to the will of the white majority" (p. 154). Historically, the inequities and incongruence of cultural interactivity in the plantation South can be traced back to the Mississippi Delta, which was arguably "the most racially restrictive and oppressive [region] during the entire segregation period" (Hoelscher, 2003, p. 659). With regard to the discourses of race, no other region holds such a turbulent and incendiary place within the nation's historical imagination. The memorialized, yet segregated Dixie South perpetuates "a dialectic that unites 'race' and 'place' through their mutual construction" (Hoelscher, 2003, p. 659), whereby binaries of white/black and privilege/poverty are inextricably linked to one another. To such an end, the region has long been castigated as America's 'crucible of race' (Williamson, 1984), a portrait of inequality and the ill-fated logics of the antebellum and Reconstruction US South. Not only has the history of these complex interactions affected race relations of the region, but also held broader implications for US society. As Hoelscher (2003) suggests, "a primary root of modern American race relations can be found in the southern past" (p. 657). The complex and oftentimes perplexing interactions of the Delta region are even more problematic when considering the pervasiveness with which some of these conventions remain in a region often referred to as "the South exaggerated" (Silver, 1966, p. 154).

The second chapter offers a critical examination of the [re]construction of Dixieland whiteness at the University during the Reconstruction Era. More specifically, following feminist-poststructuralist theorists this chapter looks into how identity and corporeality were constrained by, and in dialogue with, collective longings for social order of the Old South (Grosz, 1994). If the formative (antebellum) years of the University were spent operationalizing and defining the function of Mississippi's white elite within the region's interwoven political and cultural economies, the Reconstruction Era Oxford campus played the role of reappraising and reconciling the hegemonic position of whiteness in the New South and beyond. The institution became a nuclear vessel for re-inscribing the politics that brought about secession into the cultural and social fabric of the region. This chapter explores how history, and particularly the discursive histories of what came to be known as the Confederate secessionists' 'Lost Cause,' were mediated and manipulated to better promulgate the imaginings and power relations that so many Dixie Southerners had in years prior died trying to 'defend.' And in turn, the articulations, memorializations, and performativities of that 'Cause' linked the Ole Miss body pedagogic to a broader consensus for the politics which that 'Cause' represented.

In Chapter Three, I examine the ways in which whiteness as body pedagogic was at once institutionalized, embodied, and rarely contested in what came to be known as the 'New South.' As Grace Elizabeth Hale (1998) posits, "If whites no longer owned African American bodies, they had new, more flexible means of maintaining differential power" (p. 23)—and access to the University of Mississippi was one such establishment. In spite of the *Emancipation Proclamation*, from the end of the Civil War until 1962, the University of Mississippi remained an all-white establishment. While black Mississippians were not allowed to attend Ole Miss, the absence of black bodies in and around campus defined the era of uncontested postbellum Dixieland whiteness at Ole Miss. I argue that the institutionalized bodies of this 'New South' order were subjected to the trifurcated conscription of sporting excellence, religious sanctimony, and scholastic dogmatism that further spectacularized local imaginings of Dixie South whiteness.

The fourth chapter outlines the process of integration and its effects on race relations at Ole Miss from the start of the Civil Rights Era onward. It details the convergence of political and scientific thinking that foregrounded the bodily politics of the institution during the era of desegregation—highlighted by Southern Democrats break from the Democratic Party over the issue of desegregation in the early 1950s and the prevailing scientific racisms that came to be a significant part of the instructional mechanics at the University around the same time. The chapter then recounts James Meredith's entry into the University in 1962, and the passages of episodic unrest that followed. While the *entrée* of black bodies into a theretofore solidaritous white educative space interrupted white reign at Ole Miss—whereby black students periodically (and often spectacularly) confronted the white hegemony of the institution—by bringing *bodies of dif-*

ference in close proximal contact, integration also produced spatial disjunc-
ture and discursive formations of a *louder* racist praxis (see Deleuze, 1994).
The presence of black bodies on the Ole Miss campus created new [re]con-
figurations and overt expressions of whiteness (i.e. the removal of the Confederate battle flag from the on-campus football stadium led to an influx of
flags out side the stadium), yet concurrently failed to eradicate the iniquitous social relations within the University's imagined and physical spaces.

The second half of this manuscript offers a collection of interrelated
studies that investigate the discursive practices that produce what Peter
McLaren (1988) refers to as 'body/subjects' as sites of modern power at the
University of Mississippi. Individually, each chapter seeks to explore how
the body, to follow McLaren (1988), becomes "a terrain in which meaning is
inscribed, constructed, and reconstituted." As such, the "body is conceived
as the interface of the individual and society, as a site of embodied or 'enfleshed' subjectivity which also reflects the ideological sedimentations of
the social structure inscribed into it" (pp. 57-58). Collectively, these chapters
make up an archeological project set on "mining the epistemic domain of
discourse amounts to a critique of thought; i.e., what amounts to analysis
of the conditions of the existence of our thought" (Mahon, 1992, p. 6).
This form of archeological dig is "concerned with objects . . . articles left
from the past, silent moments" (Ritzer, 1997, p. 38). As Foucault (1976)
rightly surmises, archeology in this sense is a matter of tracing the "relations
between statements, between groups of statements and events of a quite
different kind (technical, economic, social, political)" (p. 29). As such, following Foucault, I aim to excavate discursive formations from human activity, in order to better understand the 'unities' and 'fissures' of discourse and
the power relations therein. Whereas the first half is more focused on definitive passages in the social construction of Dixie South whiteness within
the imagined and material spaces of Ole Miss, the second half of the book
(Chapters Five, Six, Seven, and Eight) anthropologically interrogates more
contemporaneous systems and practices of representation and signification
within the institution. As a composite work, the chapters that follow constitute an exploration in the dynamics of power and the manifestations of
Dixie South whiteness *made visible* through articulations and gesticulations
of the 'body/subject.' The book will focus on both the origins and development of power-knowledge regimes and the language (spoken, written, and
most importantly, embodied), or the unity of discourse, which perpetuates
the objectification and subjectification of campus agents.

The fifth chapter strips back the celebrity skin of some of the institution's most lionized embodiments of Dixie South whiteness. It decon-
structs the public pedagogies of Dixie South whiteness as proliferated
through the narratives and imagery of sporting prowess, local ingenuity,
and freckled white skin. More specifically, this chapter explores the discursive legacy of fabled coach John Vaught; and then Archie Manning's
celebrity in the Civil Rights Era, his transcendental legacy (both imaginary
and blood—in the form of Eli Manning), and the re-articulations of supremacist visions of the white sporting South eclipsed the moment of in-

tegration, and thus re-centered the Ole Miss sporting popular around a hyper-white orientation. The chapter then interrogates the racial politics of 'Gentle' Ben Williams, the first black football player at Ole Miss; as well as Chuckie Mullins, a player who died following an injury suffered on the field, became popular figures in the symbolic system of black reticence. Gentle Ben emerged as the archetypical post-Civil Rights 'docile' black interloper-turned-insider, while Mullins' celebrity a return to the deservingly iconized black servant/laborer. In many ways, this has led to a homogenization of difference for the purpose of a more perfect binary—vociferous blackness as oppositional text to the Ole Miss normalized, sterile black body. And in place of that oppositional blackness, post-Meredith blackness has become more corroborator of, rather than acrimonious to, the preferred white-nesses of Ole Miss's past.

The sixth chapter of this manuscript focuses on the built environment of the Ole Miss campus—a polysemic spatiality founded upon the classic Greek architectural influence seen in many plantation-style Delta South homes and buildings. From the administration buildings and fraternity houses to the strategic campus-wide use of shrubbery and florally infused color schemes, the ocular experience of the Ole Miss campus is unique in its commitment to a socially and historically distinctive post-plantation aesthetic. In their design and manufacture, each building strategically incorporates various elements of style, texture, and color to correspond with and compliment an existing structural aesthetic. As such, it can be argued that this economy of the built environment constitutes a 'signifying system' (Williams, 1981) coded in the prevailing logics of race relations within the region. Such a signifying system, since the days of slavery, has long granted affirmation and licensure to a code of racist praxis and social inequality. And while the University has made great strides in allowing equal opportunity for admittance of black students, one could argue that the spatialities of the Ole Miss built environment to this day serve as symbolic and material edifices for restricted access and reconstituted indoctrination. One critic has gone so far as to suggest that "for many whites in the state, the University of Mississippi isn't so much a school as a kind of secular temple" (Nossiter, 1997). If the implicit nature of a racialized 'kinaesthetic' is not evident, the control of space and organization therein has historically functioned to maintain exclusivity. The thoughts, bodies, and conduct of agents operating in the Ole Miss space are organized in a calculated theater of disciplinarity, power, and hyper-normativity. For white students, the ideological and physical spaces of Ole Miss reinforce the normative structures of power imbedded in their whiteness: "Ole Miss is an intangible experience rather than just a place. It is the beauty of the Grove, the sound of 'Dixie,' and the charm of Oxford itself" (Evans, 2004, p. 2). Quite contrarily, those operating in the margins of Mississippi Delta society have historically been less comfortable in the almost phantasmagoric manifestation of the pervasively racist "liberal conscious" (Cohodas, 1997) of the region.

Of course, space alone is not the sole determinant of the pervasive discursivity of Dixie South whiteness. The practices therein, and the governance of those practice, become a discursive space upon which bodies are regulated, regaled, regurgitated in fashion of a preferred state of whiteness. In particular, the spectacular dynamics of the 'body/subject' in territorialized spaces such as the "Grove," an on-campus courtyard which is famous for pre- and post-game fetes, reinforce the power-knowledge dynamic of the body, space, practice as discourse, and thus ideology. As such, the spectacle of the Grove or the ritualistic carnivalesque of the Confederacy (more later) offer *entrée* into the empirical phenomenon of post-plantation Delta South sporting identity.

Chapter Seven examines the significance of the Confederate flag in the local sport cultures of Ole Miss. Perhaps if we are to adopt Baudrillard's (1983) position of postmodern sign as simulacrum, whereby the decoded signifier is two degrees separated from the referent authentic version, then we can optimistically reduce these symbols to introspective caricatures, divorced from the inequalities pervasive throughout the 'real' world. However, if we concurrently examine the social practices historically performed under the guise of Confederate symbols, we find a more troubling correspondence between sign and praxis. Informed by (1) a critical historiography and (2) an exhaustive four-year ethnography, this chapter mediates on the intersection of an exclusionary history and contemporary signifying acts of Dixie South Whiteness articulated through the sporting local. I also offer interpretations from a 'micro-ethnography' of the memorial services for the Confederate dead held on the Ole Miss campus in spring of 2005. In the end, this chapter is meant to offer a better understanding of the complex social relationships between the body and the built environment, and how such relationality might reinforce or subvert the social hierarchization which is pervasive throughout other forms of Delta South culture.

In the eighth chapter, I deconstruct the signifiers and signification of the Ole Miss symbolic popular, in order to reconstruct the possibilities of obfuscation encoded therein. In recent years, the discourses relating to the practices and expressions of Ole Miss identity have come under intense public scrutiny, primarily because of the habitual fetishization of Old South imagery, such as the waving of the Confederate flag during home games, and the continued use of ethnically-coded signifiers such as school's sporting mascot, Colonel Reb[26] (Sindelar, 2003). To such end, a virulent debate has emerged between traditionalists and progressives as to the 'appropriateness' of Old South imagery at Ole Miss sporting events. The semiotic traditions of Ole Miss formulate a 'taxinomia' (Foucault, 1994, p. 71), or a lexicon of representation, for promoting an emphasized bodily deportment within university spaces. As such, this chapter contributes to an already vibrant discussion on the politics of race and ethnicity as mobilized through the semiotic embodiments of sporting mascots. This chapter more specifically explores how the University of Mississippi's ("Ole Miss") sporting mascot,

---

26. Colonel Reb's image is akin to a white plantation owner in antebellum American South. I will discuss the origins of the signifier in greater depth in Chapter Five.

Colonel Rebel, constitutes an important discursive space through which (a) the corporatized academic institution accumulates sign-valued capital and (b) the power/knowledge relationships formed under a localized spectator/ fan subjectivity—constructed out of a parochial, conservative, "Old South" Whiteness—become incontrovertibly bound to the symbolic territories of a localized sporting neo-Confederacy.

In Chapter Nine I examine how the spectacular dynamics of the body in territorialized spaces such as the "Grove," an on-campus courtyard which is famous for pre- and post-game fetes, reinforce the power-knowledge dynamic of the body, space, practice as discourse, and thus ideology. As such, the spectacle of the Grove offers *entrée* into the empirical formation(s) of post-plantation Dixie South sporting identity. Has the Ole Miss spectator experience moved beyond the signifiers of the plantation South, or do the supporters cling to the vestiges of an era of southern white privilege? Or, is it that activities in the Grove and other spaces of sporting consumption at Ole Miss comprise a new spectacle of southern white privilege, whereby the social interactions of the white upper class are performed in such a way as to reinforce the status orientation of contemporary social relations within the Mississippi Delta region? To better understand the social practices in and around the Grove, I conducted a four-year ethnography of the activities before, during, and following each Ole Miss home football game and other Ole Miss sporting events. In total, this chapter is meant to offer a better understanding of the complex social relationships between the body and the spectacle, and how such relationality might reinforce or subvert the social hierarchization which is pervasive throughout other forms of Dixie South culture.

The coda brings together the various elements of this book to offer new insights into the problematic nature of whiteness and the political nature of the 'body/subject' in the contemporary Dixie South context and beyond. Through analysis of the different ways in which whiteness is encoded and decoded through discourses of the political body, particularly through the political and cultural, I explicate how the increased *relevance of the South* and the interpellating forces of conservative institutions such as Ole Miss are further suggestive of a possible *rise of the visible white center*, where penetration of an embodied politic now canvases the cultural, the economic, and the social formations of broader Western society.[27] More importantly, I conclude by offering a brief commentary of how the problems of race, body, and culture discussed throughout the study are in no way unique to Ole Miss, the US South, or North America more generally, but rather are pedagogically symptomatic of a more globally-extensive 'recovery movement,' to borrow from Joe Kincheloe, that now reveals itself across various sociopolitical locals.

The epilogue offers a reflexive [re]discovery of my own whiteness, my own Southern-ness, and my own masculinity through ethnographic engagement with the body cultures of the 'new New South'; reporting on the juxtaposition of my new [Leftist critical scholar] self onto the spaces and social relations once inhabited by my old [working class, parochial, 'Southern'] self. While the epilogue is primarily a retrospective on my return to Southern sporting fields in Mississippi, it is also a critical inspection of the performative politics of engaged cultural studies research on the body. For mine is a political project, bent on contextualizing, and thus problematizing, the seemingly banal nature of Southern cultural physicalities. The more time I spent in these spaces, 'observing' the physical cultures from which I sprung, the better I was able to trace a series of ostensibly inescapable patterns of oppression: 1) the cultures of racism, sexism, and patriarchy are still highly active within these local pedagogies and spectacles; 2) my white skin, Southern drawl, 'hillbilly' vernacular, and masculine deportment allowed access to the most exclusive/divisive of these social spaces (whereas others might have been denied); 3) to prolong engagement with various groups, I was forced to 'perform' my 'old' Southern self (laughing at racist jokes, admiring Confederate-flag emblazoned garb, etc.); and 4) in an effort to create change (through critical interrogation of the sporting empirical), I was most often 'read' as a [re]productive agent of these regressive cultural politics. To this end, I argue that any politically-'progressive' outcomes from this type of

---

27. I would be remiss if I failed to acknowledge here the limited scope of this study. This analysis of whiteness and corporeality at Ole Miss is over-determined by issues of racialized identity and the discursive fabric of oppression and empowerment. As such, I develop only part of the full equation of the visible center, failing to fully confront the problematic configurations of gendered, sexualized, and classed inequities of one of the Dixie South's last bastions of privilege. It is not my intention to dismiss or trivialize the importance and severity of these formations, but to begin illuminating the visible center here through the racial problematic in hopes of expanding the sociology of embodied Southern inequality. For this study begins to fill the fissures opened up by the generational reign of Dixie South whiteness and body pedagogics of power and privilege, but leaves many other cracks to be sorted. There is no doubt a need to critically engage at least the following aspects of power at Ole Miss: the lived experience of the racialized 'Other;' the creation and reproduction of Southern gentility through the social interworkings of the institution; the articulations of a hypermasculine governance over the feminine subject; and the heteronormative constrictions on sexuality and sexual relations for campus bodies. In this project, I hope to begin the broader venture of rearticulating the ways of representation and identification which reinforce the social power encoded therein.

qualitative research must be weighed against the symbolic violence created therein.

Part I

Genealogy of the Southern Body Pedagogic

The Making of Dixie South Whiteness

The University of Mississippi was conceived amidst the throws of ubiquitous intellectual expansion throughout the American South. Following the establishment of a major public university in Georgia in 1785[1] and in Tennessee and North Carolina ten years later, the decades following the American Revolution saw a proliferation of state-funded institutions of higher learning throughout the South. Through significant (in relative terms) subsidies from respective state governments (and after the war in the form of land grants), these institutions and their neighboring successors in South Carolina (1801), Virginia (1819), Alabama (1831), Florida (1853), and Louisiana (1860) typically hired a small faculty of men (and only men in each case) well-versed in the classics, political economy, and rhetoric to shepherd late adolescent boys (again, only boys) through the philosophies, mechanics, and logics of the emerging plantation-classed society.

This explosion of state-based institutions was reflective of two important, interrelated features of the antebellum American South cultural economy: educating the future generations of genteel Southern patriarchs in the techniques of capital accumulation within the region's burgeoning agricultural economy; and promulgating the cultural logics by which that economy was legitimized, and by which race-based power relations thereof were normalized. To understand the socio-political formation(s) of University of Mississippi, and specifically of the cultural institution 'Ole

---

1. While the University of Georgia was first chartered in 1785, it did not begin enrolling students until 1801—a point of contention amongst historians seeking to anoint the institution the 'oldest public university in the US.'

Miss,' it is within these diachronic cross-hairs that we might best begin to sketch our genealogical analysis.

Cultural Economics of the Cotton Gin

In admittedly simple—albeit critical—terms, the political economy of the antebellum US South can be triangulated within three points of Cartesian-cotton [in]dependence (economic dependence on slave labor and the autonomy to exploit other humans without intervention): the diasporic black body as economic instrument; the Euro-centric narcissism of the rugged white individual; and the rationalizing state polity which marshaled the two through the fabric of everyday life (Yates, 1999). This triumvirate of oppression was oriented around, and toward, a *manifest destiny* of the auto-cratic white South, and laid the foundational principles of the 'Confederate cause' (or what came to be known as the 'Lost Cause').

That destined course was catalyzed by a series of continuities—ranging from American independence to innovations in shipping and distribution of goods, to re-entrenched mercantilist economic policies, to the genocide of the native peoples of the region. However, perhaps no singular techno-logical shift outweighed Eli Whitney's advent of the cotton gin in shaping the political and cultural economies of the Cotton South (Yafa, 2005). The introduction of a machine that could exponentially out-produce a human laborer not only induced a radical transformation toward mass production (and thus mass consumption), but also led to a spike in the demand for the region's foremost cash crop. And in places like Mississippi—with its sur-plus of arable land, proliferated slavery-based systems of accumulation, and cotton-friendly climate—cotton became the boon crop of the early-indus-trial economy. To such an end, the total cotton production for the region went from 180,000 pounds in 1793 to 93 million tons by 1810 (North, 1966). Gavin Wright (1978), drawing upon the theories of Malthus and Ricardo, argues that the principles of the pre-industrial cotton-slave economy of the American South can perhaps best be described through this heuristic:

> If land is available to all comers, and if cultivation may be practiced at any scale without major loss of efficiency, then there will be no way for an entrepreneur to achieve a large absolute profit except with unfree labor. Under a free labor system, wages would rise and exhaust all land rents. (p. 11)

The plantation economy of 18th and 19th Century US South, and the subse-quent over-reliance on indentured servitude, created a social and econom-ic hierarchy which recycled the gesticulations of corporal surveillance, poli-cing through violence, and racialized self-importance for the greater good of many of Mississippi's white elite—all of which deprived black laborers of human equality, sovereignty, or spirit (O'Rourke, 2004). Despite the fact that white settlers only began their takeover of the Mississippi Delta from the indigenous Chickasaw and Choctaw peoples a few decades earlier (Bil-lington & Ridge, 2001), the adjudicated population redistributions of the Mississippi Delta region suggested these white immigrants brought with them an over-reliance on slave labor. For example, by 1850 the average family in Washington County (which borders the Mississippi River, to the southeast of Oxford and Lafayette County) held nearly 82 slaves in servitude. Across the Mississippi Delta more generally, black inhabitants outnumbered whites by a ratio of five to one (Cobb, 1992).

On the whole, the [agri]cultural landscape of the 19th Century Mississippi plantation could thus be described as an economic and social amalgam moulded out of the antediluvian Linnaeus-inspired binaries of the *disciplined black body* and the *disciplining white cerebrum*. For the presentist Structuralist, the delineations of white-power/black-subordinate can be seen as revelations of trans-Atlantic colonial mercantilism (W. Johnson, 1999). This line of interpretation has—and rightfully so—been extensively drawn out elsewhere (Franklin & Moss, 2000; Genovese, 2003; H. S. Gutman, 1977; Stampp, 1989; Starobin, 1970), with these scholars typically tracing patterns of migration, exploitation, and racism from the metropole through to west Africa, and on to the fields of a formative outpost. These histories often shed new light on the inhumane ends power elites would go to in order to protract commercial and somatic dominion over those bodies from which their power was extracted.

With due deference to those analyses, here I want to focus on how such an unequal and disproportionate power structure created a *subjective* dualism whereby the [black] body became a discursive site mobilized for the regeneration of race-based inequalities and the [white] mind was that mechanism around which power was organized. Following Michel Foucault, my use of the word 'subject' comes with double meaning: both "subject to someone else by control and dependence, and tied to his [sic] own identity by a conscience or self-knowledge. Both meanings suggest a form of power which subjugates and makes subject to" (Foucault, 1982b, p. 212). Most conceptualizations of these antebellum South power relations suggest that the dominant white 'subject' exercised physical power over the black laborer, and thereby the cerebral white bourgeoisie retained a positionality of authority over the black body. However, this form of power was brought about by more than just repression of the black body, as such a notion of repression "is quite inadequate for capturing what is precisely the productive aspect of power" (Foucault, 1984b, p. 60). Rather, the socio-economic power of slave owners in antebellum Mississippi was equally bound to their ability to shape discursive knowledge and leverage of representational politics. For the freedoms of whiteness inculcated the flows of human capital—but as Paulo Freire (1970/2006) reminds us, the oppressor's sway is inexorably linked to both bodily and social control.

Perhaps a more perfunctory equation can describe the Cotton South political economy: the processes of dehumanization allowed for profitability and power. In the first instance, black bodies of the Cotton South were beaten, maimed, raped, abused, and tortured under the oppressive regimes of the antebellum Southern slave economy (Bontemps, 2001). In this way, the 'body/subject' became spectacle: 'productive' both in being a site of disciplinarity for agricultural yields (and thusly reproducing related economic power relations) and in constructing 'codes' of bodily conduct along the lines of black worker-subordinate and white profiteer-authoritarian. By the 1840s, Mississippi was home to the most expansive plantations on the continent, and subsequently produced higher cotton and tobacco yields than any other state in America (Hawk, 1943). This, of course, resulted in a disproportionate abundance of economic wealth for white plantation owners across Mississippi, and especially in the Delta region. The ironic incongruence of plantation wealth was ultimately bound to the hazards and hierarchies of the body. The rewards of this plantation-era whiteness were so alluring that early white settlers were willing to endure great financial and physical risks to procure profit from the rich sediments and racial hierarchies abounding throughout the Yazoo-Mississippi alluvial flood plains (Cobb, 1992).

Subsequently, to ensure profitability, or return on their socio-economic investments, white 'gentlemen-planters' implemented a number of physically-oppressive 'disciplinary technologies' onto the labouring slave body. Rephrasing Foucault (1977a, p. 198), slave masters of the Mississippi Delta often relied on common practices of corporal punishment such as whipping, beating, detaining, and hanging in order to forge a 'docile body' that may be 'subjected, used, transformed and improved' (Silver, 1966). These practices of constructing and refining productive bodies "through drills and training to the body [and] through standardization of actions over time" (Rabinow, 1984, p. 17) were common throughout antebellum Mississippi. Marcel Mauss (1934/1973) noted some time ago that in this way the body is at once subjected to "modes of training, imitation and especially those fundamental fashions" and simultaneously to "the modes of life, the *modes*, the *tomus*, the 'matter', the 'manners', the 'way'" (p. 78).

To be effective, however, such disciplinary technologies had to be both imagined (through the threat of violence against the black body) and operationalized within a spatiality of confinement. Thus, the control of space was an equally important ingredient in the regulation and discipline of the labouring black body. As Paul Rabinow (1984) suggests, "discipline proceeds from an organization of individuals in space, and it requires a specific enclosure of space" (p. 17), and the preservation of that space, and the conduct therein, was essential to reproducing cerebral/corporal dichotomy of the plantation economy. A system of inspections and detainments secured such an incarcerating spatiality, one that shaped social life in the plantation South for decades thereafter (O'Rourke, 2004; M. M. Smith, 1998; Starobin, 1970). In this and other oppressive cultural economies, such active praxis of disciplinarity creates:

> subjected and practiced bodies, 'docile' bodies. Discipline increases the forces of the body (in economic terms of utility) and diminishes these same forces (in political terms of obedience). In short, it dissociates power from the body; on the one hand, it turns it into an 'aptitude', a 'capacity', which it seeks to increase; on the other hand, it reverses the course of the energy, the power that might result from it, and turns it into a relation of strict subjection. If economic exploitation separates the force and the product of labor, let us say that

36

disciplinary coercion establishes in the body the constricting link between an increased aptitude and an increased domination. (Foucault, 1977, p. 138)

Consequently, the 'subjectified' body, by way of cotton yields and corporeal yielding in the context of the antebellum Mississippi plantation, was productive both in terms of the production of commodities and the [re]production of a race-based power dynamic.

Control over the black body on the punitive plantation fields became systematized not only through spatialized antebellum praxis, but also through the normative pedagogies of surveillance, disciplinarity, and subjectification active within a number of the regions foremost social institutions: the gospel of racial hierarchies espoused by members of the church; the rhetoric of inferiority postulated by members of the 'scientific' community; the oppressive administration of power emanating from racist police state; and the indoctrinating oppressive normativity learned in the academy (Black, 1997). In the antebellum South, social institutions functioned to align common polity, common law, and common capital along the trifurcation of a slave-based plantation economy, Protestant ethos, and agricultural interdependence (Lee & Passell, 1979). In so doing, these settler-pioneers sought to establish a new order of Southern gentility—with the patriarchs of commerce, faith, and governance wielding both considerable status and sway over the emerging political economy of the plantation South.

An Institutional Cornerstone

Just as the spectacle of the tortured black body was both productive of, and produced by, these regimes of governance and govenmentaility, so too were the spectacular[ized] pedagogies of white power and antebellum whiteness cultivated within the institutions upon which those logics congealed. And from the first meetings of the organized state government of Mississippi, its leadership sought to create a flagship academic institution that would not only educate Mississippi's youth, but perhaps more importantly, promulgate the 'social traditions' and 'Southern ethic' that gave license to this emerging gentility of the plantation economy. Fearing that young white men from Mississippi might seek higher education in neighboring states,[2] the impetus for the creation of the University of Mississippi is perhaps best captured in the famous 1839 edict by then Governor Alexander G. McNutt, who implored: "Those opposed to us in principle can not safely be entrusted with the education of our sons and daughters" (quoted in D. G. Sansing, 1999, p. 13).

---

2. A sentiment echoed in the Governor's decree: "Send your sons to other states and you estrange them from their native land [and thus] our institutions are endangered" (quoted in D. G. Sansing, 1990, p. 36).

With the 'principles' of isolationism and unionism[3] as early-1830s ideological backdrop, Mississippi's leadership set out to identify a site for the flagship public institution of higher education in the state (D. G. Sansing, 1990). In the decade that followed, forty-eight disparate locales throughout the state—from Mississippi City in the southernmost part of the state to Pontotoc County in the northeast—vied for the economic and political power invested in the local government's newest and most coveted institution. On January 21, 1841, the selection was finally awarded to the northern community of Oxford, based on, among other things, the "general character of the people" (Sansing, 1999, p. 21)—but this decision was not simply a scholastic or linguistic coincidence but perhaps rather an example of early industrial 'place wars.' The township's founders promoted the area as the perfect place for such an educational body—featuring rolling hills, vast greenery, and a moderate climate (by Mississippi standards)—and in an attempt to turn the eye of state parliamentarians northeasterly, purposively named the town after the celebrated British academy (Cabaniss, 1971).[4]

On January 24, 1844, Governor Albert Gallatin Brown signed the University's charter, and shortly thereafter the cornerstone was laid at the site of the University of Mississippi's first building, the Lyceum ("Points of interest at the University of Mississippi," 1984). Largely subsidized by revenues from a bourgeoning Cotton economy, Mississippi's flagship university opened its doors on November 6, 1848. Bound by a conviction of preparation for the future, but perhaps more so to unwavering ideologies affixed to the past's present, the inaugural class of eighty young men—all but one from the state of Mississippi—took their places at the desks of the Lyceum for the first time (Cabaniss, 1971).

In many ways, the University of Mississippi was no different than other state-sponsored institutions of higher learning in the US during the middle part of the 19th Century. The University's initial curriculum was aligned with the prevailing academic disciplines of the era, organized around thematics such as: logic (Whatley's Logic); rhetoric (Campbell's Philosophy of Rhetoric); moral philosophy (Stewart's); and political economy (Mill's) (J. N. Waddell, 1848). On the surface, the University of Mississippi professed an institutional *façade* which promoted principles of egalitarianism, Christianity, and classless meritocracy—seemingly committed not to training the next generation of gentlemen planters, but to a broader spectrum of South-

---

3. Southern 'unionism' refers to the notion of a regional collectivity, or intrastate union, not the interstate union of an imagined American community.

4. The central business and social area of Oxford was subsequently developed with designs of bringing the state's preeminent university to that specific elevated space. This area would later come to be known as the 'Square,' which is now the business and cultural center of Oxford, featuring retail spaces and the town's central government and judicial buildings. However, the state legislature eventually settled on a site just to the west of College Hill, in a wooded area near a proposed throughway for the north-south Mississippi Central Rail line (Sansing, 1999).

ern white solidarity.[5]

Moreover, as Professor Emeritus of the University of Mississippi David Sansing (1999) later suggested, the University's pedagogical modules were often modeled after vocations of bourgeois intelligentsia:

> Mississippi's practical-minded planters wanted more information about soil chemistry and the science of agriculture. As they looked to the state university for this information, they encountered a faculty that was opposed to 'grafting' experimental science onto the classical curriculum. Such courses, the traditionalists argued, were incompatible with the role of the university, which was to provide a liberal education, build character, and produce Christian gentlemen. (p. 67)

More critically, we might argue that the regimes of 'character building' extolled through the practices of the institution were mobilized to bring whiteness—and particularly a contextually-specific manifestation of Dixie South whiteness—to the *center* of Mississippi Delta cultural politics. Although white Mississippians from varied social class backgrounds were admitted to the University, they were uniformly trained in the techniques of plantation status and operations of racialized white privilege. These 'body techniques,' to rephrase Nick Crossley (2007), became embedded in the cultural contexts where they had a symbolic significance, were normatively regulated, and thusly *rationalized* (p. 86). Hence, the University became a leviathan of institutional whiteness, through which the exclusively-white student population was systematically subjected to both alchemies of plantation privilege and practices of on-campus lordship over black servants. In this way, the university was from the outset dialectically and symbiotically adjudicated around a Cotton South cultural economy, the all-white status of the University, and the malicious treatment of black campus slaves; and in sum demarcated the hierarchical identity politics operating on both black and white bodies of the institution.

Dehumanizing 'College Negroes'

> *"whiteness has been and is still often experienced as terror by people of color, they can easily reach back to the autobiographies of slaves for examples"* – (D. R. Roediger, 2002, p. 23)

In spite of its all-white student population, the University of Mississippi, like most other schools in the antebellum South, was not without a formidable presence of black individuals. In the earliest years the number of black individuals on the campus in Oxford was equal to, if not greater than, the number of whites (D. G. Sansing, 1990). All the campus laborers were

---

5. While those students with lower economic capital were granted admission into the University, and were not responsible for remuneration of tuition, books, or fees, they were not allowed to live in the on-campus dormitories. In the recorded minutes from the first faculty meeting in the school's history, the University's stewards proclaimed: At the University of Mississippi, "there will be not difference in the treatment of different classes of students" (J. N. Waddell, 1848).

black, as were the slaves of the academic staff; and each student was expected to bring his own black servant onto campus upon enrolment[6] (Cohodas, 1997). As in any other slave-based economy, these individuals were treated as commodity-objects (Black, 1997), property of either the school or the masters of its halls.

In the antebellum years of the University of Mississippi, the reign of plantation hegemony on the campus produced articulations of cyclical representations of the black body as subordinated servant-machine (see Mercer, 1994). The faculty minutes of September 16, 1856 unambiguously outline the mechanistic duties of the college servants:

> . . . it was Resolved, That it shall be duty of the servants employed in the dormitories to sweep the rooms and entries daily, adjust the bedding, carry fuel, make fires, bring water daily, from the 1st October till the first April, and twice a day the rest of the college year. (W. G. Richardson, 1856)[7]

This regimentation, of course, was not uncommon in other spaces of antebellum Mississippi. And by most accounts, the working life of the campus servant at the University of Mississippi was no less dehumanizing than that of a slave on any given nearby plantation (yet no less deplorable).

However, the slave labor scheme devised within institutional purview tells only part of the story of early Ole Miss race relations. Beyond the institutionally-devised routines of exploitation and indentured servitude, the all-white student body frequently and persistently tortured and assaulted campus slaves. While it was against university policy to assault servants, doctrine in practice usually meant acquiescence to white interests (even at the expense of economic and human capital). Despite no reported incidents of provocation, university records show that in the early years students were regularly reprimanded by University President Frederick Barnard (whose title was later renamed 'Chancellor') or other members of the faculty for the maltreatment of campus servants—but regardless of the viciousness of the offense, were rarely met with severe consequence. The faculty minutes from May 7, 1860, offer insight as to the types of offense and tolerance with which such aggression was given:

> The Proctor reported Mr Gage of the Senior class as having severely beaten one of the college negroes, and as having acknowledged the act: Whereupon the Chancellor was instructed, unanimously, to converse with Mr Gage upon the subject and to refer the case to the Executive committee unless he (Gage) showed a proper spirit in relation to the occurrence in the interview with the Chancellor. (Harrison, 1860a)

---

6. I use the masculine pronoun when referring to the antebellum student body at the University of Mississippi because the institution did not allow women enrollees until 1882.

7. When referencing minutes from the faculty meetings at the University of Mississippi, I will not make use of page numbers. When recording the minutes, faculty members kept a series of journals and logs, each of which has since been replaced in the University Archives by typewritten transcriptions of those records. As such, the page numbers of the manuscripts in the Archives do not correspond with the actual pages of written text from the recorded minutes.

This judgment, and the punishment rendered thereafter, was far less harsh than that given for other 'indiscretions.' For example, 'suspension' was the penalty given to two students who had damaged the walls of their sleeping quarters in the Lyceum only a few months earlier (Harrison, 1860a).

In the late antebellum years, student aggression against black laborers on campus had become an importunate problem. However, the plantation logic was not based on the objection toward inflicting pain to another human, but rather as inhumane relations whereby abuse of servants was a means to further suture the bonds of disciplinarity between institutional hierarchs and their striplings. According to most reports and university records, cruelty toward campus servants was interpreted as a way to antagonize the faculty rather than as a confrontation between two individuals—to conduct malice against the property of the institution. In the summer of 1860, university administrators encouraged students to organize a "Vigilance Committee" for patrolling and punishing inklings of perceived 'Negro insurrection' (Harrison, 1860c). At once a masterstroke of govenmentality and surveillance, as well as panopticism over the potentially deviant campus slave, they indicted a number of students on various instances of abuse: from branding black servants on the face (Harrison, 1860d), to whipping campus slaves (Harrison, 1860c), to repeated acts of sexual assault and battery.

Brutality against "College Negroes" became so rampant in late 1860 and early 1861 that the faculty institutionalized a demerit scheme specifically designed to curb the malevolence. The first case against a student was held during the faculty meeting on January 14, 1861:

> Mr Melton was called before the Faculty and examined relative to a charge which had been preferred against him and be which he was accused of having beaten one of the college negroes, in violation of a regulation recently passed by the Faculty and announced by the Chancellor at the Chapel. He plead guilty, but so far succeeded in justifying the act, that, under the circumstances, he was no farther punished than by the imposition of 25 demerit marks and be required to sign a paper promising never again to attempt to chastise one of the College Negroes. (Harrison, 1861a)

In the years leading up to the Civil War, and as a form of rebellion against what some in the community and on campus considered a 'questionable position' on the slave issue by some members of the faculty,[8] the inhumane treatment of campus slaves reached a climax. Random acts of violence against 'Campus Negroes'—and particularly against those servants 'owned' faculty members deemed to be sympathetic to idioms of racial equality—became patterns of body terrorism. While it would be wrong to suggest that slaves at the University of Mississippi were categorically stripped of any political or social agency—as indeed there were some instances of resistance

---

8. These challenges were primarily directly the Chancellor, who was repeatedly confronted about his position on the slavery issue. At the end of his appointment, which was brought about in part because of 'questionable character' with regard to this issue, Chancellor Barnard moved north and became an outspoken proponent of racial equality.

to these schemes of torture and malice—the spectacular formations of bodily discipline and persecution across the racial binary often over-determined any possible equality within that context. The assaulted black body was
rearticulated as an embodiment of plantation racial control (on display at
work), a site for contesting campus policy and Union sympathies to eliminate those controls, and as a spectacle of the prevailing anti-abolitionist cultural politics of the region (Genovese, 2003).

The flesh politics of campus slaves were not unlike those of their subjugated plantation-laboring peers, the stakes of which were masterfully captured in the following passage from Toni Morrison's (1987) *Beloved*:

> In this here place, we flesh; flesh that weeps, laughs; flesh that dances on bare
> feet in grass. Love it. Love it hard. Yonder they do not love your flesh. They
> despise it. They don't love your eyes; they'd just as soon pick them out. No
> more do they love the skin on your back. Yonder they flay it! And O my people
> they do not love your hands. Those they only use, tie, bind, chop off and leave
> empty. Love your hands! Love them . . . and no, they ain't in love with your
> mouth. Yonder, out there, they will see it broken and break it again. What
> you say out of it they will not heed. What you scream from it they do not hear.
> What you put into it to nourish your body they will snatch away and give you
> leavins instead. No they don't love your mouth. . . . And O my people, out yon-
> der, hear me, they do not love your neck unnoosed and straight. (pp. 88-89)

Writing about a fictional context all too similar to the plantation-like confines of the Ole Miss campus, Morrison paints a vivid picture of the racialized, dehumanized bodies of servitude from which race-based power was exercised. The regimes of terror imposed onto the black[ened] slave body produced dichotomous body pedagogics in which slave subjectification—and
body-specific systems of torture—both granted the human qualities of subjectivity to some and denied humanity to the subjugated 'Other.'

Conversely, the unrestrained *mindful white body* (to borrow from Shilling,
2003, p. 67)—capable of unjustified and unfettered violence against the
'Campus Negro'—was all-the-more empowered by this antithetical state of
dominion. In the wake of an impending 'War between the States,' abuse to
campus black bodies was a tangible measure of both power and solidarity for
white Mississippi students.[9] The dehumanizing project of corporal castigation within the campus boundaries was reflective of broader Southern ideological and cultural formations, as the looming threat of a gradual recession
of the dichotomous power dynamic of black/white, slave/master resulted in
an increased backlash against black bodied servants in the years leading up
to secession (Stampp, 1989).

In the context of an era of persistent episodes of brutality against black
laborers on campus, perhaps no instance of slave abuse illuminates the de-

---

9.As some conservative commentators have suggested (cf. Smith, 1998), the power-
knowledge Civil War tensions initially arose between oppositional white positionalities, namely in the form of states rights versus Federal law. In Mississippi, the issue
of slavery was viewed not as a contest between white profiteers and black indentured
proletariats, but rather the exercise of statist white power over local white individualism and bigotry.

humanizing convictions and supremacist ideologies of the institution and its bearers better than the incidents of mid-May, 1859, and the related polemics that dominated campus life in the year that followed. On May 23, 1959, a student, S. B. Humphreys was brought before the faculty on the following charges:

1. "Visiting the dwelling of the President in his absence and while it was occupied by defenceless (sic) female servants, with shameful designs upon one of the said servants."

2. "Committing a violent assault and battery upon the servant aforesaid, and inflicting severe personal injury, whereby the said servant was for days incapacitated for labor, and of which the marks are still after the lapse of many days, plainly visible." (Harrison, 1859a)

The proposed punishment, if found guilty, would have been suspended from the University (which at the time was still not the most severe of punishments afforded the faculty). Despite no corroborating evidence to support his case, and testimony of his guilt from a number of sources (including those 'female servants' noted in the indictment), Humphreys was found *not guilty* by a vote of five to three. Even more disturbing was the resolution which passed immediately followed the decision: "the Faculty are morally convinced of Mr Humphrey's guilt, yet they do not consider the evidence adducted to substantiate the charge, as sufficient, legally, to convict him" (Harrison, 1859a). A recorded statement by the minority voters from the faculty minutes of February 2, 1860 further illuminates the partialities of the case: namely that the defendant failed to produce an alibi, and one fellow student in particular, who was trespassing on the Chancellor's premises during the same time on the attack, failed to respond to whether Humphreys was in his company (Harrison, 1860a).

The majority responded with a callous tone and staggering rationale, developed in two themes. With regard to the first, Professor Carter of the majority wrote:

> . . . when Prof. Richard[son] impeached & discredited Jane's (the victim) statements, Dr. Barnard contended for their credibility & admissibility, — putting, in the course of the discussion, this question to Prof. Richardson – 'Prof. Richardson, if your servant Harry were to tell you he had seen a certain student take your horse or saddle from your stable, would you not believe him?' The Prof. replied, 'No! I would not, if it came in good conflict with that student's denial' . . . In view of our social & political economics, I consider Jane's statement, as testimony, altogether in admissible. (Harrison, 1860a)

Perhaps this statement could be interpreted as the situating of the black slave (already colonized under the generic Anglo-centric 'Jane') below the white University students on the Ole Miss racial hierarchy. Such was common practice and pathology throughout the Old South (Black, 1997; Mercer, 1994), and certainly reinforces that which has already been fleshed out with regard to issues to servitude and humanity under these conditions. However, a second set of grounds by which the majority had found reason to dismiss the charges against Humphreys as articulated in Professor Carter's long edict offer a second tangent of dominant awareness:

> Prof. Boynton stated before the Faculty, that he knew the accused was guilty—When asked if he made this affirmation from personal observation he said he did not. When requested by Prof. Whitehorne & myself, to give his authority, he refused to do so. When farther (sic) asked by Prof. Richardson whether his informant was a white person or a negro, he declined to tell. From the positive character of his first assertion, I supposed, he was personally aware of the guilt of the accused; but when he refused to answer the question propounded by Prof. Richardson, I was constrained to be believe his informant was a negro & I consequently rejected the testimony. (Harrison, 1860a, author's emphasis)

Thus, the power imbedded in Professor Boynton's bodily discourse (his whiteness) was not only defused, but usurped by the *assumption* that his testimony *might* bear the observational inflections of a dark-bodied servant. Moreover, this *one-drop paradigm of truth* signals the turgid anti-humanity at work within the institution, but also the parallax of knowledge and truth filtered through crystalline of white authority.

The 'Humphreys incident' also elucidates the sway of the dehumanizing racist logic which dialectically influenced conduct and ideology at the University of Mississippi—whereby ideologues freely propagated a polarity of opposites: whiteness as the embodiment of cerebral sagacity, human subjectivity, and congenital superiority; and blackness as the embodiment of commodity physicality, subhuman objectivity, and misbegotten inferiority. After an accumulation of 'indiscretions,' Chancellor Barnard eventually dismissed Humphrey's from the University of Mississippi. That ultimate dismissal, however, would fuel a protracted "whispering campaign" (D. G. Sansing, 1999, p. 97) against the Chancellor by those faculty members voting in the majority for years to come.

Student Bodies and Oxford Orthodoxy

The tolerance and hypocrisies of the 'Humphreys case' are further illustrative of the two-part function of the University of Mississippi during the pre-Civil War Era: which was both to discipline objectified black bodies operating within that space (as in the plantation space)—linking the plantation economy to the edicts of the institution—and also to produce the bodies of young white males and manufacture the next generation of plantation gentry and racist despotism. Through proper instruction in conduct and logic, and the aegis of what Foucault (1984a) refers to as a 'new economy of power,' the University operated as a channel for advancing the tenor of segregation and the synchronization of physical and economic control over Mississippi slaves. As such, the University as institutional space allowed for disseminating the "procedures which allowed the effects of power to circulate in a manner at once continuous, uninterrupted, adapted, and 'individualized' throughout the entire social body" (Foucault, 1984b, p. 61).

And it was the body, both a malleable, corporeal discursive canvas, and an objectified instrument of economic and social hierarchy, which was central to the project of developing this 'new economy of power.' Such was the purpose of the University of Mississippi—a school building; a social and pedagogical institution; what in Derridian terms we might refer to as a 'logocentric' apparatus (Derrida, 1977)—that *made flesh the logics of a slave-based political economy*. For Foucault, Western educational institutions such as the University of Mississippi have historically operated as an extension of the disciplinary function of the prevailing political economy, meant to:

> Train vigorous bodies, the imperative of health; obtain competent officers, the imperative of qualification; create obedient soldiers, the imperative for politics; prevent debauchery and homosexuality, the imperative for morality. A fourfold reason for establishing sealed compartments between individuals, but also apertures for continuous surveillance. (Foucault, 1977a, p. 172)

In this way, antebellum Ole Miss has many parallels: whereby, much like the universities of Mussolini's Italy or Hitler's Germany, the academy was transformed into a place of training for, and for fetish of, the young, able-bodied, white, masculine body. In turn, the subjected body becomes a signifier of morality, of solidarity, and of adherence to the protocols of power. Chris Shilling (2003) writes that in this regard, bodies "are highly malleable phenomena which can be invested with various and changing forms of power" (p. 69). The malleable body becomes an extension of dominant social formations which in inhabits. As Rolland Munro (1996) suggests, "we are always in extension. Indeed, extension is all that we are ever 'in'" (p. 264, author's emphasis).

During the antebellum years of the University of Mississippi, the primary disciplinary technology used by the faculty in organizing and institutionalizing the 'conduct of conduct' (see Bratich, Packer, & McCarthy, 2003) was the institutional practice of governing students based on bodily "Deportment." On April 1, 1851, the faculty members adopted a code of conduct, whereby white students received a "Deportment Grade" based on the following measures: presence/absence/tardiness at recitation; presence/absence/tardiness at study room; presence/absence/tardiness at prayer; boisterous conduct—whereby students were to "obstain (sic) from indulgence in ardent spirits"; and disorderly conduct – fighting (J. N. Waddell, 1851). As a measure of internal governance, students were asked to 'pledge their honor' not to violate any of the rules of the University. The accumulation of deportment "marks"—later termed "demerits"—against the student resulted in probation, suspension, or expulsion. Each student was given a "Green Card" (Harrison, 1860b), which effectively outlined the parameters for such conduct and tracked the accumulation of 'marks' throughout the academic year.

In this way, the body was a site of accountancy; an auditable node of corporeality through which the systems of govenmentality could be instilled, monitored, and adjudicated as those in power saw necessary. In the years following its introduction, the 'Green Card' system graduated into a more comprehensive, if not omnipresent, system of bodily governance. As I aim

45

to make clear in the following three subsections, the modalities of deportmental governance evolved into three striations of corporeal subjectification over the course of the antebellum era: 1) the disciplining of the body in relation to its location within space and time; 2) the correct corporo-moral training of the [student] body; 3) and the exercise of Michel Foucault has often referred to as discursive formations of 'bio-power.'

The Disciplines of Spatio-Temporal Whiteness

In the first semester of the 1850 academic year, faculty members at the University of Mississippi were confronted with importunate incidents of students leaving the campus grounds at night to go 'carousing' in the town of Oxford. To escape the vigilant gaze of the faculty, students regularly disguised themselves in blackface and set forth on an emancipatory one-mile voyage into Oxford (Waddell, 1850). The blackface escapism of the white Ole Miss students offers an interesting juxtaposition of burden and privilege, whereby evading their whiteness meant escaping the disciplinary arm of the University. In one sense, we can read this incident as white apposition to, or co-optation of, contextually-specific readings of embodied black deviance. In that context, however, we might also see how embodied blackness was a socially-conditioned space of enfleshment through which whiteness (perceived as both burden and privilege) could be simultaneously usurped and reinvigorated. Just as legions of Mississippi's black slaves were channeling underground railroads to escape the plantation prison and life of indentured servitude forced upon them therein, Foucault, borrowing from the work of Jeremy Bentham (see Bentham, 1995), refers to such organization of surveillance as panopticism,[10] whereby the surveyor is physically positioned in a manner in which the vigilance of surveillance, rather than surveillance itself, governs human activity.

Such a model, both metaphorically and literally, mirrors the philosophical orientation of the faculty at the University of Mississippi during the ante-

---

10. In Bentham's prison panopticon, the guard is situated in the center of a circular structure, and the prisoners are located in individual cells that are completely exposed on the side facing the center. The prisoners are unable to see into the guard tower, but after the consistent rendering of corporal punishment to offending (and non-offending) inmates, they begin to assume that the eye of the watchman is fixed in their direction. Thus the surveyed is governed not by the gaze of the watchman, but by the possibility of such a gaze (Foucault, 1977a). This, of course, leads to the self-governance of behavior amongst the prisoners; whereby the assumption of surveillance holds its own power, and disciplines and regulates physical conduct within the setting. The notion of a panopticon, according to Foucault (1977), offers "a generalizable model of technologies of functioning; a way of defining power relations in terms of the everyday life of men [sic] . . . it is in fact a figure of political technology that may and must be detached from any specific use" (p. 205).

bellum era. While the circular orientation of the Lyceum[11] and its neighboring buildings on the Mississippi campus failed to have the central, watchtower-like edifice,[12] the specters of control were even more pervasive and subversive, more clandestine than Bentham's panopticon. The expansive sterilizing ether of the University panopticon created a particularly vivid instance of how "political technologies of the body function" (Rabinow, 1984, p. 18), and how corporeality was to be regulated within that context. As the following examples illustrate, the exercise of power onto the [student] body was at the core of the labors of the University faculty during the antebellum years, to such an end that they relentlessly evoked new standards of behavior and incarcerations in the training of their subjects within the campus space.

The first measure taken by the faculty under the new system of Deportment Grading was to regulate the spaces the student body inhabited, and to mobilize a more enveloping relational panopticism between student corporeality and built environment. In the faculty minutes from the September 27, 1852 meeting, it was noted:

> That it will be the duty of a member of the faculty once every week to visit every room in each Dormitory building as well as the public building of the University and note all damages done to the rooms and entries and report such damages to the Faculty at their weekly meeting on Monday evening. (J. N. Waddell, 1852)

This disciplining of the body in and through space utilized the power availed through the philosophical impetus of care for the university property—the same [fleeting] philosophy which had indicted numerous students on counts of servant battery. Such investigative expeditions were unannounced, and thus had a more significant effect on the conduct of students in their quarters than the preservation of campus property. It created an ether of temporal governance and inevitability; much like the organization of space allowed for disciplinarity through both action and inaction, schemes of temporal surveillance such as this enliven an ever-present possibility of time-deviant deportmental regulation.

The potential of these visits served as a means of governance, whereby student behavior was burdened and regulated by *the inevitability of possibility*. According to faculty minutes from the months that followed, this and other new measures to control the conduct of the student population were not

---

11.At that time the Lyceum was the largest building on campus. Today the Lyceum is the central administration building, and the architectural hallmark of the University of Mississippi. It's central location, along with its cultural and symbolic relevance have resulted in the profile of the Lyceum becoming the academic mark of the University.

12.Ironically, the contemporary layout of the campus bares the same orientation, with six buildings organized in a circular fashion. However, today's campus does feature a central edifice: a three-story tall flagpole upon which the American and state flags fly—the latter emblazoned with the Southern Cross of the Confederacy—perhaps suggestive of a panopticism of the Confederate imaginary.

well-received. So much so that by May of 1853, the University faced the problem of abandonment, as students were relocating their residences to the town of Oxford—away from the watchful eye of the faculty (J. N. Waddell, 1853a). An excerpt from the faculty minutes from May 23, 1853 illustrates the faculty's solution to the problem of campus desertion:

> Resolved unanimously that all students now lodging in town be ordered back to the Dormitories, as it is in direct violation of the laws, that students should sleep out of the University buildings, unless under circumstances specified, until the Dormitories are filled. (J. N. Waddell, 1853a, author's emphasis)

Both in the management of where the students lived, and the conduct of the 'body/subject' therein, the faculty controlled most aspects of student activity. Students were arranged in the classrooms in alphabetical order, and on days when class was not in session (e.g. Saturdays), as the March 7, 1854 faculty minutes suggested, were subjected to other forms of corrective training: "every student in the University shall be compelled to attend the one (Phi Sigma Society) or the other (Hermean) Society or remain in his room until 12, m. on Saturdays" (J. N. Waddell, 1854a). In many ways, these strategies for regulating the body within the University space were aimed at creating what Foucault (1977) refers to as a "political anatomy" (p. 138)—whereby the body was disciplined for political purposes whilst subjected to prevailing power-knowledge norms by way of correct[ive] training.

Such a political anatomy at the University of Mississippi was a product of the intersection of regulated space and time discipline. For example, in the early years of the University, the conduct of students was metered by rigidly constructed activities within the day. The hours of recitation and study began immediately following morning prayers and breakfast, at nine o'clock, and continued on through the day until five o'clock (with an adjournment for lunch). At early candlelight the college bell rang and each student was "required to repair to his room and occupy himself diligently in his studies until 9 o'clock" (Sansing, 1999, p. 62). During the hours of study, it was compulsory that every student remain in his room and "attend to his business without noise, or performance of any musical instrument; no excuse for absence from his room, except on absolute necessity, during those hours [would] be accepted" (J. N. Waddell, 1854b). The political anatomy of the University of Mississippi, was thus in the first instance, built upon the surveillance of the body in relation to space, and subjected to approved training for a preferred white-bodied institutionalized corporeality.

Dixieland [Deport]mentalities

At the intersections of eugenics pedagogy, spatial control, and plantation panopticism, both black and white bodies on the Ole Miss campus featured in the reproduction of the social and economic logics of the plantation South. However, just as logic and disciplinarity were central to the pedagogical formations of the antebellum institution, so too was the faith in God's plan for the peoples of the South: both black and white. If the University of Mississippi were to properly train its constituents for the perpetuation of a hierarchical race- and gender-based iniquitous society, then the white-bodied student population would have to endure disciplinary technologies of a different kind. Echoing the prescribed 'Protestant ethic' (Weber, 1958/2002) of the region's cultural and economic context, campus leaders sought to curb any use of the body for pleasure. The correct training of the Mississippi student involved the rigid three-part equation of enlightened mind, sanctified spirit, and asceticized body—and there was neither need nor want of deviance outside the norm. Those white bodies operating outside the norms, or showing signs of departure from idealized Southern manliness, were disciplined into a desirable docility.

On February 1, 1853, it was unanimously resolved at the faculty meeting "that hereafter this Law be so interpreted as to forbid all association of any student with an expelled or suspended student or other person of notoriously bad character at any time, in Oxford, or its vicinity" (J. N. Waddell, 1853a, author's emphasis). This process of normalization, what Foucault refers to as the "means of correct training" (Foucault, 1977, p. 170), entailed three interrelated instruments: hierarchical observation, normalizing judgments, and the examination. The faculty gaze and the implementation of regulations meant to contain and control student bodies allowed for the prison-like hierarchical observation of student conduct. The authority over white masculine conduct proffered by the antebellum faculty of the University focused on the regulation of activities such as dancing, gambling, dress, and playing vernacular sports such as fencing and boxing. For example, on September 26, 1853, it was unanimously resolved by the faculty that:

> . . . no student shall be allowed to attend dancing-school, during the Session without written permission from his Parent or Guardian first deposited with the Recording Secretary and not even then, during study-hours, under the penalty of suspension. And it was further unanimously Resolved, That no student shall be allowed to attend any public Ball or public dancing Party, or Party given be a dancing Master, during the Session, (always excepting the Annual Commencement Ball) under penalty of thirty demerits first offence, suspension 2d. (J. N. Waddell, 1853c, author's emphasis)

While disciplining white bodies at the University of Mississippi first meant implementing a system of punishment (Deportment Grades) as a means of reinforcing norms and the concurrent power structure, the faculty of the University later developed what is considered to be "a forerunner of the modern grading system" (Sansing, 1999, p. 83): a thorough and complex scheme of marking conduct, academic performance, and attendance. Within this later system, parents were notified at 'convenient intervals' as to the standing of their sons. Such academic regulations "extended far beyond student discipline and admissions . . .They went to the core of college governance" (Sansing, 1999, p. 83). In many instances, the faculty 'advised' students to uphold a preferred posture and deportment, only to 'require such action' upon the 'advice' not being heeded. Proper dress was a focal point for the such sheathed discourse; for example on May 16, 1854, "It was resolved that Mr. Hall be reprimanded for general low standing, & for his eccentricities in dress" (J. N. Waddell, 1853b) and on October 10, 1859, "At Prof. Whitehorne's suggestion students are from this time *forbidden to appear at the college exercises in dressing gowns*" (Harrison, 1859b, author's emphasis).

Perhaps Foucault's notion of 'governmentality' best illustrates the penetrating nature of power, discourse, and surveillance in this instance. Like disciplinarity, governmentality refers to the "arts and rationalities of governing, where the conduct of conduct is the key activity" (Bratich, et al., 2003, p. 4). However, governmentality is further descriptive in how the conduct of conduct takes place at innumerable sites and thus how the strength of powerful institutions is dependent upon "the proper disposition of humans and things" (Bratich et al., 2003, p. 4). In other words, governmentality refers to the promulgation of power over individuals, but also how such power schemas are adopted by, mobilized, and reinforced through the ideologies and practices of those individuals. For example, On December 5, 1853, the faculty reported of an incident where:

> Messrs. Ashe E. Thompson, & Calhoun, who were found guilty of being in town after 9 P.M. at a Confectionary, were each sentenced to have 15 demerit marks imposed upon them, to be reprimanded, and warned that if they should be found guilty of any similar offence hereafter, they should be sent off. (J. N. Waddell, 1853d)

The language-ing of the proclamation is suggestive of the examination/punishment dynamic that was essential to the governance of the University subject—whereby the possibility of further examination, and of the potentialities of punishment, weighed on the everyday conduct of the students. Punishments such as the 30 demerits given to "Messrs G. Thompson and Christian Sile . . . for playing cards" (Eakin, 1856) were commonplace, as were any and all efforts to stray beyond the University's code of conduct.

It was Chancellor's Barnard's philosophy that student conduct should be regulated by student conscience rather than litany-ridden preambles—ruled by "a hand of iron in a glove of velvet" (Sansing, 1999, p. 80). On January 23, 1860 the faculty assembled to discuss an unauthorized visitor to the campus:

> Dr Barnard reported the presence of a 'boxing and fencing Master' upon the College grounds contrary to the 'law' and to its special request, and asked the Faculty how to proceed in the premises. He was instructed to notify the students of the existence of the law prohibitory of such exercises in any room belonging to the College authorities, and requested to 'speak' with the Fencing master personally. (Harrison, 1860a)

The notion that the 'boxing and fencing Master' might be invited to a college campus of the US South in the years prior to the Civil War will certainly come as no surprise to most historians. However, for the administrators of the University, the 'master's' un-commissioned appearance presented a threat to the power-knowledge dynamic of the institution's hierarchy. For if the students were acting autonomously and without fear of recourse, and training their bodies in ways that might enhance the collective's potential to create physical violence, the entire system of correct training at the University of Mississippi might fall.

Therapeutic Whiteness

From 1853 to 1859, the interwoven discourses of health and sickness framed much of the disciplinary techniques between faculty and students at the University of Mississippi. Student health became an important formation of power relations between the two groups, as the faculty regimented the 'care for the self' as an auxiliary installment of control and surveillance. Foucault refers to such power accrued by the defining of principles and conditions of corporeality as 'bio-power,' which has historically "brought life and its mechanisms into the realm of explicit calculations and made knowledge-power an agent of the transformation of human life" (Foucault, 1978, p. 143). For Foucault, bio-power is manifest through 'nosography,' or the "unquestionable foundation for the description of diseases" (Foucault, 1975, p. 129) and definitions of the proper care for the self. During the antebellum years of the University, in the context of heightened fears throughout the country concerning the spread of terminal disease (Grob, 2002), the faculty relied on the matriculated scientism of clinical nosography and medical 'gaze' to constrain and police the student body. Although an inexact science (as misdiagnosis parlayed into at least two student deaths in the late 1850s), and often misguided in rationale, the 'free gaze' of medicine, averting the esotericism of social scruples, thus acted as the organizing power-knowledge standard of human activity at the University. The 'disciplinary power,' as Foucault suggests, of bio-power is in the internalization of clinical governance. Like the subjugation of black bodied slaves, the exercise of disciplinary bio-power was intended to foster a chimera of governmentality, whereby distributional paranoia policed each student internally, producing a subjected body for the correct training offered by the institution (the state) (see Dreyfus & Rabinow, 1983).

An example of the contestation of disciplinarity is evinced in an 1853 exchange, when a committee of students signed a petition which "Resolved that under the present circumstances" (a rumor of small-pox near Oxford), "it is expedient immediately to withdraw [from the University]" (J. N. Waddell, 1853b). The faculty responded by resolving that no such leave would be granted, and further, "that there would be greater probability of safety in remaining here, than in leaving" (J. N. Waddell, 1853c). Thus, the student subjects were detained by the intersection of 'bio-power' and spatial governance in a sterile heterotopia[13] — defined by the logics of policing

---

13. A notion often used in Foucault's work to refer to a space in which contradictory elements are juxtaposed. In other words, here I am referring to the corruptive nature of racialized bio-power and the governance of the body in the antebellum spaces of Ole Miss.

the body in space, and through the regulation of physical spatialities.[14]

In the continuing spirit of panopticism, and as a means of diffuse governmentality, the faculty established a policy in 1857 whereby students claiming absence based on sickness were required to 'declare upon their honor' that they were indeed sick, and report their whereabouts during the illness and how said illness was being treated. To ward off further disease, and "for the encouragement of healthful bodily exercise" (Sansing, 1999, p. 81), Chancellor Barnard persuaded the Board of Trustees in November of 1857 to finance the construction of a gymnasium—one of very few institutions in antebellum America to afford such a facility. Influenced by the broader shift of muscular Christianity[15] in US society, the gymnasium allowed for the advancement of a pedagogy of physicality—and a valorization of sterility and muscularity within the discourses of masculinity. However, the material outcomes of these ideologies fell short, for soon after the opening of the gymnasium—during the fall semester of 1858—the University suspended all exercises as a result of the 'temporary' evacuation of "nearly the entire student body" (Harrison, 1858) due to concerns over a number of illnesses on the campus.

Earlier in the semester, typhoid pneumonia had afflicted 'some' university students. One student died from acute hepatitis in mid-semester, and numerous other cases of typhoid fever had been reported throughout the course of the semester. By semester's end, only twenty students remained on campus, prompting the faculty to discontinue activities until the start of the new year (Harrison, 1858). Citing their firm belief that no "local influence pernicious to health" existed on campus, and that "no causes predisposing to disease exist[ed at the University] . . . and that none such ha[d] at any time existed . . . which ha[d] not been equally prevalent at the same time, over the whole adjacent country," the faculty required the return of the students to campus no later than January 3, 1859 (Harrison, 1858). The faculty's 'clinical gaze,' that is, the mythical qualities of expertise mobilized by the faculty to retain and detain students, much like those of in the field of medicine, was illustrative of the powerful nature of scientifically-defined discourses of expertise. In this instance, this ability to exercise power by gazing and antiseptic disciplinarity was a result of the vast internalization of observations by the University's constituents.

---

14. Much later, in 1872, the threat of small pox in the town of Oxford compelled the faculty to order students to avoid the town, and remain quarantined on the campus where the Chancellor would endeavor to provide for the vaccination of all students.

15. Muscular Christianity can be defined as a Christian commitment to health and manliness. Its origins can be traced to the New Testament, which sanctions manly exertion (Mark 11:15) and physical health (1 Cor. 6:19-20) (Ladd & Mathisen, 1999).

In the Gloaming of Antebellum Dixie

The effectiveness of disciplinary technologies and bio-power governance waned as the Civil War approached. The power-knowledge dynamic imbedded in pedagogical narratives and systems of 'care' for the student body lost traction as the educational practices and body-governmental auspices of the university waned amidst rising anxieties of a coming Civil War. The 'Cause' thus became the principal concern amongst most University constituents, and in turn the pedagogical authority that had held sway over the campus in its formative years was usurped by broader passions for an emergent Confederate nationalism. Ironically, the institution—which more than any other carried forward the idioms and technologies of a slave-based cultural economy—was now unraveling due to its adherents' steadfastness in preserving those practices and ideologies that brought them together.

The first mention of militarism on campus was in the faculty minutes from October 24, 1859, when Professor Boynton "communicated a request from the Students requesting permission to organize a military company" (Harrison, 1859c). From that meeting forward, student ownership and use of firearms parlayed into chronic anxiety of campus administrators. First the faculty attempted to regulate the use of firearms, through a December 4, 1859 decree that consented to the use of 'fowling pieces,' but only for "sport purposes . . .[and] only on Saturday, providing said fowling pieces are deposited, at all other times" (Harrison, 1859d). The continued use of guns and other weapons on campus eventually led the faculty to adopt an unbending compact. On March 11, 1861, the faculty resolved to ban the use and ownership of firearms, and every student in the University was required to sign the following pledge:

> I, the undersigned, do hereby declare and pledge my word of honor, that I have not now, nor will I have, so long as I am connected with the University of Mississippi, in my possession or under my control any firearms or other deadly weapon of any description, under any circumstances whatever, without the express permission of the Chancellor or Faculty. (Harrison, 1861b)

However, as the North/South conflict neared, the campus became saturated with firearms, along with the recalcitrant sentiments which had brought many of the guns into their owners' possession. A University infantry had been forming for many months, and with the encouragement and direction of the state government, had seized much of the authority of the faculty (Cabaniss, 1971). By meeting in secret, electing officers, and surreptitiously traveling to Jackson to meet on matters of the upcoming secession, the new militia of the Oxford campus had formed their own society; their own power structure; their own social hierarchy.

Popular sentiment in Mississippi favored secession in the months leading up to the disunion of the states (Stampp, 1992). Both in the popular discourse (such as the state's newspapers) and in local sentiment, Mississippi was "the storm center of secession" (Sansing, 1999, p. 101). On January 9, 1861, Mississippi became the second state to secede from the Union (following South Carolina). While the reason(s) for secession have been the subject of great scrutiny and debate amongst historians ever since (i.e. States Rights versus slavery) (Tulloch, 1999), the declaration offered by separatist Mississippians of the eve of the war should leave no question as to their purpose:

> Our position is thoroughly identified with the institution of slavery—the greatest material interest of the world. . . . (The Union) advocates Negro equality, socially and politically, and promotes insurrection and incendiarism in our midst. (Declaration of the Delegates to the Mississippi Secession Convention, 1861)

In the first of "many bonds that would be forged between the Oxford campus and the Confederate cause" (Cohodas, 1997, p. 8), the articles of secession adopted by the Mississippi state government were drafted by L. Q. C. Lamar—a prominent Mississippian and mathematics professor at the University. The students, who were once critical of the Board of Trustees for censoring anti-slavery texts, were burning the University's only two abolitionist manuscripts on the campus green in the winter of 1861. By May 2, 1861, it was reported in the faculty minutes that only five students remained on the Oxford campus following the departure of the student Confederate infantry, the "University Greys," (Harrison, 1861d). Two weeks later, the faculty members held an informal meeting at which time it was determined to suspend University activities due to the ensuing Civil War. Burton N. Harrison, the Faculty Secretary at the time, concluded his notes from the meeting with three ominous lines:

WAR!

WAR!

WAR!

The coming war would bring change to the University: both in the function the institution would play in postbellum Dixie South society and the impetuses of Southern gentility which the University served. However, the early years of the University of Mississippi—especially those before the outcomes of the Civil War and the Emancipation Proclamation muddied the clearly demarcated racial hierarchy of the Dixie South—the foundation was laid for ideological and physical boundaries within which white subjects were disciplined in the order of racial hierarchy, class-based privilege, and plantation exclusivity. Following feminist theorist Judith Butler (1990; 1997), we might argue that through various forms of governance, surveillance, and biopolitics, the student subject was captive to a new pedagogy of performative politics; whereby the educated body was subjected to broader structures of a contextually-specific power-knowledge. In this way, the body was an ongoing project of reform toward performativity, inculcated by the "power of discourse to produce the phenomena that it regulates and constrains" (J. Butler, 2000, p. 108). Simply put, the university was a place to [re]educate white boys to embody—as performative vessels of white power and plantation wealth—of the conditions of production which brought them together.

From the beginning, the university was created not with the primary purpose of teaching Mississippi's young people the precepts of post-Enlightenment society. Rather, as the 'Crisis between the States' deepened and intra-national agitation over the issue of slavery intensified, the university was more consequentially created as the "last bastion in the defense of the Southern Way of Life" (D. G. Sansing, 1999, p. 19). It became a vessel for "transmitting culture . . . across the generations" of Mississippi's white genteel class (Cohodas, 1997, p. 14). And in the context of mounting pressure from the North to abolish slavery in the 1820s and 1830s—a shift that threatened to compromise the economic and social aristocracy which brought many white settlers into the region—the state's political intermediaries installed the university as what the Marxist-Structuralist Louis Althusser (1971) would refer to as a key *ideological state apparatuses* that might further institutionalize both Southern sentiment and parochial praxis within the social fabric of the region (Cash, 1941/1991).

Leaders of the state of Mississippi were certainly not lonesome in this pursuit. However, as Nadine Cohodas (1997) suggests, no other state-funded educational institution was conceived with such an explicit *raison d'être* as the University of Mississippi for becoming "a training ground for white supremacy" (p. 2). Due to the interdependency with which the political economy of the state relied on the institution of slavery and the economic and social *epistemes* which legitimated servitude as profit, perhaps no school rivaled Mississippi in its programmatic propagation of race-based ideologies and oppressive, slave-based economies (see also Knottnerus, Monk, & Jones, 1999). In sum, the University of Mississippi was created "not to challenge the status quo but to preserve it" (Cohodas, 1997, p. 5).

For the state's ruling elite, the university, perhaps more than any other social organism, would both *reaffirm* and *crystallize* the repressive social relations in the Cotton South. Put simply, it was an institution created to advance and protract a cultural and political economy which favored the Southern white plantation aristocracy. In this 'new economy of power,' the learned whiteness of the institutional orthodoxy organized discourses of race and power around the prevailing visible center of whiteness, the centralized power structure and Dixie South body politics.

Bodies congregated to learn, but in the process were subjected to regimes of ideological, racial, and pedagogical hierarchization, alienation, and disciplinarity. These bodies were disciplined in a way that produced not only political action within the confines of the institution, and not only in the moment in which they were forged, but in a way that could be transmitted across the region, for years to come. Paraphrasing Jennifer Gore (2001), Ole Miss pedagogy's governmental influence, both within and beyond the schooling institution, is enormously powerful in the control of populations. The governance of bodies within this epifocal space, was made effusive not by its ability to mirror the society from which it sprung, by rather as a dialectic formation that was both constituted by, and as we will see in the coming chapters became constitutive of, race- and class-based power relations across the region and beyond.

Post-Confederate Mythscapes

In more ways than one, the US Civil War (c. 1861-1865) brought tumult to the doorsteps of the uninhabited[1] school property in Oxford, Mississippi. Only a few months after the University's student militia, the 'University Greys' departed for battle, Governor John J. Pettus directed state political and military leaders to establish a war-time sanatorium on the abandoned university grounds (D. G. Sansing, 1999). The campus's central location in northern Mississippi, near major battle sites in Shiloh, Fort Pillow, Corinth, and Vicksburg, and its relative proximity to a munitions storage depot in Holly Springs, Mississippi, made Oxford an ideal place for such an outpost. During the war, the Lyceum was converted into a military hospital, equipped with surgical tools and dressed with operating and infirmary rooms. Local plantationers provided eighty-five slaves to serve as orderlies, and dozens of Oxford women served as nurses for the makeshift hospital (D. G. Sansing, 1999). Although the campus space was reserved for harboring wounded Confederate soldiers, by the autumn of 1862 the Northern armies had forcefully taken control of the region and established a military camp upon the college grounds. In December of that year, Union Generals Ulys-

---

1. Only four students returned to the University of Mississippi in the fall of 1861, and thus the Board of Trustees decided to suspend the exercises of the University until the war concluded. The campus grounds and buildings were maintained by two faculty members who remained on campus throughout the war.

ses S. Grant and William Tecumseh Sherman[2] made their way into Oxford, and began making preparations for the oft-mythologized 'Vicksburg campaign'—arguably one of the seminal passages of the war, during which the Union gained control of the Mississippi River, and the naval and transport capacities therein (see Ballard, 2004).

Despite most local newspaper reports to the contrary, no damage was done to the campus buildings during the Union's occupation of Oxford,[3] and the institution was turned back over to the campus faculty in the condition it had been seized.[4] When the war concluded in 1865, that fall's enrollment at the University of Mississippi exceeded both the Board of Trustees' and the faculty's expectations. By November, 86 young men made their way onto the Oxford campus, almost double what had been projected by state and University policymakers. Most historians agree that nearly every member of the company that included the University Greys was killed in the Battle of Shiloh—and if any Greys did make it out of the war alive, none ever returned to the Oxford campus (Ginn, 2003). In light of the fact that thousands of college-age males in the state—including the Greys—were killed during the war, the University relaxed admissions requirements to allow for a broader constituency of student pupils. During the chancellorship of John N. Waddell immediately following the war years, for example, the Board of Trustees established a new policy that allowed the enrollment of students as young as the age of 13 in the 'Preparatory Program' (*Catalogue of the officers and students of the University of Mississippi*, 1866).[5]

---

2. These men were arguably two of the more celebrated Generals in the Union army. Each is considered my most Civil War historians to be an important leader in the Union's military advances into the South.

3. Sans an episode in which a few intoxicated Kansas Jayhawkers broke some shelving units and furniture in the observatory (Sansing, 1999).

4. Some historians have suggested that this was in large part due to the long-time friendship between General Sherman and Chancellor Barnard, to whom the General regularly corresponded with during his time in Oxford (Sansing, 1999).

5. In practice, this awkward arrangement created a learning atmosphere whereby these adolescents were often in the same classrooms as much older Civil War veterans. However, the heterogeneous post-war student population was less versed in the practices of the academy. Thus, in addition to the circumstances of initiating a callow student population to the codes and curriculum of the institution, the recurring problematic of the University of Mississippi became the continuing dilemma of student discipline. To such an end, "Student hazing, kangaroo courts, gambling, cheating, and disrespectful behavior toward the faculty were serious problems and were given wide currency in Mississippi newspapers" (Sansing, 1999, p. 146). Hence, the 'less refined,' younger pedigree of Mississippi's elite descended upon a university grounds not ravaged by war, but tethered by the symmetric conjuncture of adulation (for the 'Lost Cause') and designation (for reclaiming the South's lost splendor).

Deconstructing Reconstruction

Of course, while the business of the University of Mississippi resumed at the conclusion of the Civil War, it did so under very different circumstances and within a very different context than it had during its formative antebellum years. At the conclusion of the 'War Between the States,' the Federal government assumed greater jurisdiction over economic and social affairs in former Confederate states like Mississippi. This post-war period came to be known as the Reconstruction Era,[6] an era following the 'War Between the States' in which the United States government enacted a number of reforms meant to reconnect the polity and commerce of the South to the rest of the union. This 'reconstruction' began with Abraham Lincoln's Federal mid-war mandates such as the Emancipation Proclamation of January 1, 1863—which effectively declared the end of slavery—and carried on through the subsequent Constitutional amendments promising equal rights. These measures were followed by mechanisms to reinstall the hierarchs of the local-Federal judiciary and legislative systems put in place by Lincoln's successor, Tennessean Andrew Johnson (E. L. Ayers, 2007; Woodward, 1971). Following the highly contentious presidential election of 1876, Rutherford B. Hayes was awarded the presidency over Samuel J. Tildon on the condition that Hayes' predecessor and Civil War General Ulysses S. Grant would remove the remaining Federal troops overseeing reconstruction in South Carolina, Florida, and Louisiana.

In response to these and other Reconstruction Era Federal initiatives, Democratic leaders within former Confederate states formulated various countermeasures to resist Reconstruction; or better yet, to recreate the antebellum society that so many had died trying to preserve. The *Compromise of 1877* gave state leaders of the post-bellum South autonomy to begin a quite different reconstruction project of their own: that of reinstituting various socio-political schemes seeking to re[produce] the antebellum order of things. Southern state leaders instituted a series of 'grandfather laws' limiting the voting rights of freed slaves, Native Americans, and (to a much lesser extent) poor whites and 'union sympathizers' (Woodward, 1971). Perhaps most significantly, local and state governments enacted a number of laws which resuscitated the 'Black Codes" of antebellum times; laws that in effect stretched the intent of numerous post-war resolutions in order to return to a quasi-slave-based economic and social order. An oft-cited quote of Ellis Oberholtzer (1917), worth quoting at length, details the economic conditions of the newly-Emancipated South:

6.When capitalized, the term "Reconstruction" refers to the period immediately following the Civil War, and particularly the political, economic, and cultural rebuilding era of the American South (Foner, 2002). In this instance, my use of the term is meant to elicit the double meaning of the broader era of political reconstruction and the reformation of a political identity bound to the University of Mississippi, the region, and the Confederate imaginary more generally.

... persons of color contracting for service were to be known as 'servants,' and those with whom they contracted, as 'masters.' On farms the hours of labor would be from sunrise to sunset daily, except on Sunday. The negroes were to get out of bed at dawn. Time lost would be deducted from their wages, as would be the cost of food, nursing, etc., during absence from sickness. Absentees on Sunday must return to the plantation by sunset. House servants were to be at call at all hours of the day and night on all days of the week. They must be 'especially civil and polite to their masters, their masters' families and guests,' and they in return would receive 'gentle and kind treatment.' ... A vagrant law of some severity was enacted to keep the negroes from roaming the roads and living the lives of beggars and thieves. (pp. 128-129)

These new logics of an old racist order were further ordained through a number of inter-state segregation laws—or what are more often referred to as Jim Crow Laws. The Laws—the etymology of which can be traced back to the popular antebellum blackface minstrel *Jump Jim Crow*—legitimated the segregation of public schools, public buildings and parks, public transportation, and the segregation of restrooms and restaurants along racial lines. Further, starting with Mississippi in 1890, former Confederate states passed new amendments that effectively disfranchised most blacks (and tens of thousands of poor whites) through a combination of poll taxes, literacy and comprehension tests, and residency and record-keeping requirements. The Laws, at work long after the *Brown v. Board of Education* ruling, defined the separate social relations, opportunities, vocational and educational activities of the US South throughout the post-war century. And in the decades that followed the *Compromise of 1877*, Jim Crow Laws laid the foundation for a new tension between the North and South; between local authority and Federal democracy; between ideologies of autonomous reign and integrative equality. This tension—between Southern sovereignty to propagate antebellum race-relations versus the Federal government's various interventions to disrupt that sovereignty—would frame the political and cultural economies of the Deep South for the entirety of the 20th Century (Litwack, 1998).

Closing Ranks around 'New South' Whiteness

It was within this post-war political, economic, and cultural landscape that the project of *reconstructing* the University of Mississippi ensued. With a comprehensive faculty in place, and no repairs needed to the campus's physical structures, the task of Reconstruction at the University had more to do with [re]institutionalizing [white] Southern identity—restoring Mississippi's inequitable social configuration and valorizing the 'Lost Cause'—than any type of material restoration.[7] As Edmund Husserl (1973)

---

7. The notion of the 'Lost Cause' refers to the popular sentiment in the South following the Civil War. This notion was popularized in Southern literature and newspapers during the early to middle part of the Twentieth Century (Gallagher & Nolan, 2000).

reminds us, while bodily practices are fleeting, their meanings and modes do not necessarily disappear:

> This lived experience itself, and the objective moment constituted by it, may become 'forgotten'; but for all this it in no way disappears without a trace; it has merely become latent. With regard to what has become constituted in it, it is a *possession in the form of a habitus*, ready at any time to be awakened anew by an active agent (p. 122, author's emphasis)

Against the specters of union pressure and the ghosts of the region's war-elicited depopulation, state officials made it clear that University officials were to reestablish the University as a 'sanctuary' for 'awakening' these corporealities of white Southern orthodoxy. As such, the Faculty and Board of the University re-established many of the corporeo-moral programs that had been created during the antebellum years; particularly in subject areas such as 'elocution,' 'Deportment,' and 'Religion.' Despite losing the war, and the subsequent imposition of Federal mandates that would eventually eliminate the emaciated slave-based economic structure, university administrators obligingly moulded the pedagogical locus of the institution around the preservation of plantation-forged race- and class-based hierarchies.

As a vessel of the preferred statist body politic throughout the period during and immediately following Reconstruction, the educational activities at the University were formatively structured and actively organized around the traditionalist edicts of populist leaders such as Governors James K. Vardaman and Theodore G. Bilbo. One of the first measures James K. Vardaman initiated upon taking the office Governor was the appointment of his own selections to the University of Mississippi's Board of Trustees. The newly installed Board immediately took drastic measures to police and censor the academic freedoms of University faculty. Those pedagogues teaching outside the prescribed literacies of separatism and racial Darwinism were ostracized and often forced to resign their posts within the university. The tight controls of Vardaman's Board prompted former Chancellor Robert Fulton to resign from the University, exclaiming: "I could not serve with self respect even my own alma mater whom I love more than all others [under a board] swayed by the will of the master, Vardaman" (qtd. in Sansing, 1999, p. 180).

While he was not Vardaman's immediate successor, Governor Theodore G. Bilbo maintained, if not [re]invigorated, this constrictive relationship between the state and the University well into the Twentieth Century. At his inaugural address, Governor Bilbo announced the intention to "build a bigger and better University" (Sansing, 1999, p. 220) by taking a more active role in overseeing the activities of the institution. That 'active role' included the hiring, firing, and rehiring of a series of Chancellors, along with the infernal purge of pro-integration texts from the campus library (Cabaniss, 1971). Furthermore, in the years leading up to the Civil Rights Movement, Bilbo's favorite socio-political armature, the state-sponsored Citizen's Council, unrelentingly pressured faculty to enforced the Jim Crow segregation on the campus and encourage isolationist ideals within the curriculum (McMillen, 1971)—a collective effort to further thwart any 'scalawag liberal thinking' at the University (Sansing, 1990).

In concert with the Southern Nationalist Party (later renamed the Nationalist Movement)—which held a great deal of sway over Mississippi politics throughout the Twentieth Century—the Citizen's Council became a significant force in shaping the protracted racist ideologies and practices imbedded in Mississippi's political and cultural economies. In turn, the Council maintained an influential presence on the campus during the years leading up to and following desegregation (McMillen, 1971). The interposition of the state's social and political ruling elite interests in the university was both a symbolic response to its failures in 'War of Northern aggression' and an interjection which reconstituted the precepts and pretexts from which 'being white' was affixed to old discourses of entitlement articulated through the identity politics of the New South (Dailey, Gilmore, & Simon, 2000; Williamson, 1984). Through an upsurge of the sensationalized newsprint vernacular, solidarity in white civic and community-based organizations, and vehement church- and state-sponsored campaigns geared toward separatism, white and black Dixie Southerners found themselves immersed in a new lexicon of identity and new formations of subjectivity with an Old South feel (Winders, 2003).

Through an epochal post-bellum parade of white robes, political stumps, hellfires, brimstones, and corruptive public spectacles, the public pedagogies of New South whiteness were ceremoniously and pervasively articulated within the language of white supremacy during the era of Reconstruction. More importantly, the pheno-*typicality* of whiteness became the abstracted norm of social power; whereby spectacular displays of white bodies exercising white power enacted an embodied link between traditionalist ideologies of slavery and the memorialized spectral embodiments of the 'Lost Cause.' Again rephrasing Foucault (1976), to understand the power formations imbedded in this common vision of Dixie South whiteness we must deconstruct the discursive formations upon which these New South identities were forged—severing the racialized signifiers from the localized social practices therein.

In the years following the Civil War, at the University of Mississippi, much like in the rest of the Dixie South, whiteness as a process and as a discursive formation was constructed out of two interlocking planes: 1) competing spatialities "within the national formation of the South, delineated as white, versus the nation" and; 2) contested [pheno]typicalities (the normative cultures of the white body in the South) "within the regional dynamic of ex-Confederates versus ex-slaves" (Hale, 1998, p. 9). As such, the conjunctures and contestations of New South power formations fell upon both the visceral, volatile, and subjugated bodies at work within those Southern spaces. Those bodies were thusly framed in epistemes of phenotypically-layered racial autonomy whereby collective imaginings of Old South, 'Confederate' whiteness was often constructed as antithetical to the interloping unionism of the North (Faust, 1988).

Exhuming the Greys

On the post-war Ole Miss campus, the archetypal site for promoting the *Southern man as courageous defender* trope was captured in the celebration of the University-sponsored regiment which fought for the Confederacy during the Civil War—the 'University Greys.' The celebration of a distinctive Dixie South masculinity at Ole Miss during the era of Reconstruction was galvanized in the first instance following the Civil War; in the adoration reserved for the exploits of the University's regiment that fought for the 'Southern cause.' These 'soldiers of impulse' (M. M. Brown, 1940) heeded the call of the Confederate States in the earliest stages of the conflict, rushing in solidarity to the secessionist call-to-arms in defense of the 'Southern way of life.'

The first mention of the student group known as the 'University Greys' on the University of Mississippi campus came in early April of 1861, as the faculty minutes reported "various members of the 'University Greys' [were] in the habit of using their muskets for hunting and other purposes, in violation of the terms of agreement by which they were allowed to remove their muskets from the 'arsenal' to their rooms for better keeping" (Harrison, 1861c). These soldiers of the South joined the Confederate cause near the end of that spring semester, just as the early stages of the war were taking shape. With the 'winds of insurrection' at their backs—and to the axiom of *Ducit amore patria* (the love of my country leads me)—these mostly teenage boys were thrust into battle. That eagerness to come to the defense of the South became a popular fixture in the discursive celebration of the 'University Greys.' As one University historian proclaimed, "The regiment was animated by impulse—the impulse of valor" (Brown, 1940, p. xi). By most accounts, that valorous impulse brought about the untimely death of nearly every member of the regiment—the ultimate sacrifice of these sons of the Confederacy.

The spirited collective endeavor of the Greys from the first outburst of the military spectacle was posthumously glorified in the epic film *Gone with the Wind*. In the film's well-known 'Twelve Oaks scene,' the Greys and their Confederate compatriots prepare for what would eventually lead to their penetration of Union entrenchments atop Seminary Ridge (only to ultimately suffer massive causalities) (Brown, 1940). As another example, native Mississippian William Faulkner weaves the fate of two mythic 'University Greys' into his 1936 novel *Absalom! Absalom!*. Despite the mass slaughter of the Greys at Gettysburg, the homage-inations (or, the homogenous nature of celebrated Confederate whiteness) of their efforts to defend the Confederate South are inscribed into the campus spatial fabric via a memorial to soldiers on the Ole Miss campus—in imagery and inscriptions such as a large stained glass window in a classroom building which "reflects the reverence for tradition" and honors those "who with ardent valor and patriotic devotion to the Civil War sacrificed their lives in defense of principles inherited from their fathers and strengthened by the teachings of the Alma Mater" (Cohodas, 1997, p. 11).[8]

A second constant in the posthumous memorialization of the 'University Greys' was the attention given to the band of combatants' military garb. The legend of the Greys is propounded by reports that upon their arrival to the battle lines in Harpers Ferry, Virginia, the Inspector General of the Confederate Army noted that the 'University Greys' took "much pride in their appearance" (Sansing, 1999, p. 107), and that the Greys were known as the most 'handsomely dressed' unit in their battalion. One commander of the Confederate Army further admired the fashion sensibilities of the student regiment: "The University Greys were an unruly lot, but they were well dressed and good shots" (Sansing, 1999, p. 107).

These and other accounts of the 'nobility' of the outfit's outfits further contributed to the mythologization of the Greys. As time passed, the import and reverence of the 'respectful' adornments of the Greys materialized in Faulkner's post-Reconstruction South, which saw an ironic, if not awkward juxtaposition of the political body and politicized decorum; whereby the military recourses inflicted upon a ravaged South were turned asunder by the 'kinaesthetic' lifeline of an 'unvanquishable' bodily adornment of Dixie South whiteness (Meyer Jr., 1995). These imaginings of class-conscious Confederate *sureshots* thus embalmed the valor of the Confederacy through the ornamentation of a venerated, imagined code of dress. During the University's centennial celebration in 1948, the senior ROTC group, which was renamed the "University Greys" in 1942 as a tribute to "one of the most gallant fighting groups of the Confederate Army" (Furr, 1942, p. 1), procured Confederate uniforms and other accoutrements, including a replica of the colors (unit battle flag), and reenacted the enlistment of the University Greys. For many campus events during the year-long celebration, the ROTC unit donned its Confederate regalia, and, in "the mind's eye, the storied Greys who won imperishable glory at First Manassas and suffered 100 percent casualties at Gettysburg, reappeared on the campus they had abandoned for war in 1861" ("ROTC celebrates the Old South," 1948, p. 1).

This feted existentialism of the ephemerally-constituted bodily aesthetic culminated in the practice of students honoring the 'University Greys' by dressing 'in their Sunday best' for home football games during the middle part of the Twentieth Century. The ritual of spectacular titivation[9] to celebrate the Confederate courage and Old South masculinity of the 'University Greys' continues today, in the ethereal preponderance of a stylish eulogization. The institutionalized code of dress, much like the informal

---

8. In Chapter Six I present a more thorough examination of the relationship between space, ideology, and racialized discursive expressions of the body, in particular how the memorialization of the Confederacy acts to redistribute representational power—recentering whiteness through romantic visions of a Confederate collective.

9. This practice of 'dressing up' for home football games during each fall at Ole Miss as an act of homage to the Greys will be examined in greater depth in Chapter Nine of this manuscript.

code of conduct, is intently located in the preferred logics of masculine desire and class-based fashion taste (Lipovetsky, 1994). In this instance, the governance of fashion transcended, and continues to transcend, physical and imaged space, whereby the fashionable body becomes a site for the convergence of ideological forces, discursive formations, and corporeal collectivity. Moreover, borrowing from the Nietzschean notion of 'eternal return,' the fashion-fashioned homage to the Confederate dead can thusly always already be current and new, and yet resuscitative of the cultural politics to which they confer.

Walter Benjamin (1969), following Nietzsche, suggests that fashion in this way articulates itself as an act of imperialism over the 'body/subject' by always masking itself as something new, in spite of the return to diachronic forces of symbolic materialism.[10] By mobilizing the fashions of Confederate passions, the modern Ole Miss subject of the Reconstruction Era could be re-situated, and thus subjected, to the regimes of antebellum power and the logics of hierarchical society. In this instance, the post-Confederate stylization presented itself as "the unique self-construction of the newest in the medium of what has been" (Benjamin, 1999, p. 64). And the rearticulated fusion of Confederate fabric and the 'eternal return' of Old South public masculinity extended, and continues to extend, beyond fashion as *recherché*—what Benjamin (1999) described as the "always vain, often ridiculous, sometimes dangerous quest for a superior ideal beauty" (p. 66)—into the realms of 'kinaesthetic' governance and adornment as disciplinarity. The unreal bodies of the 'University Greys' thus operated on, and continue to discipline, the active subjects on the Ole Miss campus through the specters of an adulated imaginary of the ghosts of the 'University Greys' (this point is further discussed in Chapter 9).

[Re]Collections of a Fallen Body Politic

The 'University Greys' offered a story—and perhaps more importantly, an idealized corporeality—through which New South body politics could be framed, contested, and reified. In this way, mystique and mythology was transformed into performative praxis; with the University becoming a main artery in propagandizing the traditions and ideologies associated with the Southern cause and forging the linkages between ante- and postbellum formations of whiteness (D. Goldfield, 2002; D. R. Goldfield, 2003). At the University of Mississippi, like other Southern cultural institutions, the necessity to define the 'history' of the Civil War and its causes became the "first battle in the creation of modern southern whiteness" (Hale, 1998, p.

---

10. In other words, adornment operates in the dominion of modern, masculine power, whereby women and men are unable to escape from the aesthetic discourses of the past—and instead are subjected to a constant reinvigoration of ocular disciplinarity through the conventions and reinventions of the antithetical and synthetic tastes of fashion.

49). And in this regard, the Greys were victors. They were native Mississippians—students of the flagship cultural institution in fact—and their sacrifice became a locus upon which new identity politics of the Reconstruction Era were forged.

The Greys, however, were but one facet of a broader post-Confederate mythscape. At the University of Mississippi, re-articulating and re-membering the identity politics of the past was dialectically connected to reverent tropes of the 'Lost Cause' and the language of victimization (through forced intrastate unification) (W. Doyle, 2001). As an illustration of the historicized Old South public pedagogies brought to life on the post-bellum Ole Miss campus in the postbellum years, the state legislature invited the well-known Confederate sympathizer Reverend T. D. Witherspoon to speak at the 1867 spring commencement ceremony.[11] The Reverend spoke candidly about how the university, much like the church, would be a key conduit for 'passing on' the cultures and ideologies of the past through to Mississippi's future generations. In concluding the address, the Reverend implored the stewards of the University to "embalm in literature, and thus preserve in . . . memory [that] civilization which has been an ornament to the South" (qtd. in Sansing, 1999, p. 121).

A few months later, on June 19, 1867, Confederate protagonist Jefferson Davis was awarded an honorary degree of LL. D. by the University for his leadership of the armies of the Southern states during the Civil War (Shoup, 1867c). The image of Davis and his Confederate contemporaries—as iconic embodiments of a seminal Southern masculinity—was further *embalmed* into the University's geometric aesthetic through a number of monuments and statues erected in the years that followed (see Chapter 6). These and numerous other activities in the early postbellum years of the University constituted a recurring outline of adoration and reverence for the Confederacy, and further sutured the institution to the symbolic and ideological edicts of the 'Lost Cause.'

The active role of community-based organizations such as the United Confederate Veterans further advanced the *history-writing project* undertaken by adherents to the Confederacy who held sway over the University of Mississippi—travailing to combat what Southern conservatives perceived to be the "back-stabbing" tendencies of an "unthinking Northern populace" (A. S. Johnson, 1951, p. 2) in recording the history of the Old South. For instance, in the years during and following the Reconstruction Era, the Unit-

---

11. This was the first graduation ceremony for matriculating students who initially populated the University in the fall of 1865, the semester in which the school reopened following the war.

ed Daughters of the Confederacy (UDC)[12] annually sponsored numerous social activities on the university grounds. On March 22, 1912, the UDC invited the sole survivor of "Stonewall" Jackson's staff to address the students of the University, an individual who was hailed as "an excellent type of that class of Southern gentlemen who supplemented a liberal education with the stirring school of a great war" ("Dr. J. P. Smith makes address," 1912, p. 1).

To further signify the close ties between the Confederacy and Ole Miss, members of the UDC commissioned and erected a monument valorizing their fallen Confederate ancestors on the University of Mississippi campus from 1902 to 1904—and a replica was constructed a year later near the government buildings on the 'Square' in Oxford (Cox, 2003). Like their sibling counterparts, the Sons of Confederate Veterans (SCV), a direct heir of the United Confederate Veterans, was also a fixture on the Ole Miss campus during the era of Reconstruction. And similarly, the SCV played an active role in shaping public culture at the University of Mississippi in the postbellum years. Organized at Richmond, Virginia in 1896, the SCV sponsored historical and 'patriotic' events at numerous Southern universities during the era of Reconstruction (Foster, 1987; D. Goldfield, 2002). At the University of Mississippi, the SCV became a featured participant and organizer of most social events—and particularly those themed around the Confederate cause—throughout the remainder of the century.

In the passage between the post-Civil War rebirth and reunification of the ideological South (Reconstruction Era and the ephemeral configurations of the 'New South') and the re-emergence of pre-Civil Rights Era racial traditionalism and conservatism, the connection between universal praxis and idealized Old South chivalry became the galvanizing thread by which many Dixie South whites affixed their identities. In the first two decades of the Twentieth Century, the Old South statist vanguard was confronted by a 'New American' political conscious, one echoing the social and religious conservativism of the Confederacy but somewhat supplanted by 'radical' notions of American egalitarianism and collectivity (D. Goldfield, 2002). For example, after the United States entered the colossal massacre that was World War I on April 6, 1917, many Mississippi students withdrew from the University during that spring semester and enlisted into military service—thus answering 'the call of their country' to go to war ("Ole Miss men prepare for country's call," 1917).

As a result, Mississippi's white elite began to fear that local identity politics and the 'reign' of white privilege were beginning to fade in the

---

12. Perhaps the most involved of post-Confederate organizations on the Oxford campus, the United Daughters of the Confederacy was created as the outgrowth of many local memorial, monument, and Confederate home associations and auxiliaries to camps of United Confederate Veterans that were organized after the 'War Between the States' (Cox, 2003). The National Association of the Daughters of the Confederacy was organized in Nashville, Tennessee, mainly to preserve the heritage culture of the Confederacy and memorialize the 'Lost Cause' through the construction of monuments scattered throughout most Southern towns and cities.

early and middle Twentieth Century. The seductive antithesis of which, one that gained momentum through the late-Century 'Solid South,' was an American hyper-nationalism bound to the momentary interventions of war-time solidarity, McCarthyism, and rhetoric of an imagined 'Great Society.'[13] At the University, the insular, post-war cohesion of the 'New South' imagined community crystallized around the 'oppositional reading' (R. Williams, 1981) to an intensifying industrial-era *pax Americana* and the increased relevance of the diffuse ideological power of the American nation-state (Woodward, 1971). And the South's front line institutions such as Ole Miss[14] functioned as those spaces for resisting the symbolic and material impulses of such an imaginary American collective. For Mississippi's political leaders of the era, rearticulating the local—along with a buzz in the public discourse that the University faculty and students were shifting toward the political Left—was promulgated through a state-wide backlash discourse against the University as a space for free expression (Howard, 1917). To brazen out the interloping ideologies of post-war solidarity and nationalistic unification, the stewards of the University of Mississippi closed ranks around a common, yet implicit circuit of Southern power: the chronological authority invested in a shared whiteness.

As such, the cultural and political intermediaries of the Mississippi Delta began a longitudinal propagation of a discursive North (authoritarian)/ South (libertarian) dichotomy (see E. Williams, 1963) which by century's end would be etched into the conscience of Mississippi's citizenry and political franchises. The ironies of this pre-Civil Rights Movement, 'democratic' Dixie South were thusly revealed in the dyad within an expansively interconnected local economy thrust into the national consciousness for its necessity and its abhorrence—both an antagonism to unionism and a metonym of the broader national industrial formations into which it was integrated. Nonetheless, local Dixie South identity politics were centralized around a *liberal,* individualistic (almost anarchic), local whiteness. As one University lecturer proscribed in 1913, 'progress' for Mississippians meant a 'man against the mass' attitude, or a 'siege mentality' against the forces of unified US nationalism (Dixon, 1913). The Southern 'man'—and especially the Ole Miss 'man'—was thus in part moulded out of, and into, iconographies of power defined by a loyalty to the Southern cause in the face of homogenizing American unionism and industrialism.

---

13. The ephemeral challenges to this parochial hegemony are perhaps best illustrated in the context of turn-of-the-century Rooseveltian masculine America captured in the Whitman-esque tropes of rugged individualism, the and symbolic representations of 'common people.'

14. See Chapter Eight for a more comprehensive history of the origins and meanings of the hypocorism "Ole Miss." I will only use the nickname when referring to the university after 1901, when the nickname was adopted. Furthermore, my usage is likely intended to mean more than just the physical and political structure of the university, evoking the broader culture of inequity pervasive throughout the University.

The concentrated relationship between the introverted neo-Confederacy and representational discourses within the University of Mississippi reached an early (bested only by the pre-civil rights return to a segregationist ethic) *denouement* in the fall of 1927. Following a series of local newspaper animadversions on the University—most of which cited the spatial and (growing) ideological distance between the state's capital and its seminal institution of higher learning—mounting sentiment which favored the relocation of Ole Miss to Jackson festered within the public sphere ("Bilbo endorses removal of Ole Miss to capital," 1928). To counterbalance and refute the movement championed by legislators and Governor Theodore G. Bilbo, Chancellor Alfred Hume invoked the nostalgic circuits of Mississippi's popular conscience of the 'Lost Cause.' He wrote:

> The University of Mississippi is rich in memories and memorials and a noble history. If its children did not come to its defense, the very stones of the memorial arches and the Confederate monument would cry out. The memorial window in the old library erected in loving memory of the University Greys, the Confederate monument nearby,[15] and the Confederate soldiers' cemetery a little farther removed are as sacred as any ancient shrine, altar, or temple. Instead of moving the University away that it might be a little easier to reach, ought not the people of Mississippi look upon a visit here as a holy pilgrimage. (Hume, 1928, p. 1)

Hume's petition was a success in two regards: political leaders reversed their tack, endearing themselves to the romantic tropes of Ole Miss and its Oxford locale and a newly romanticized, and publicized, sense of Confederate *noblesse oblige* afforded the University and its caretakers (D. G. Sansing, 1990).

Through valorized Old South nomenclature and appeals to the collective imaginary of a 'new' Dixie South imagined community, the efficacy of Hume's plea is exhibitive of both the cohesive symmetry between the Confederacy (its ideologies and symbols) and the institution and the broader mission of the University to reinvent those articulations within discourses of postbellum Dixie South whiteness (Winders, 2003). Framed by the demarcation of [white] Southern distinctiveness from the imagery and narratives of American nationalistic homogeneity, postbellum Ole Miss—like other *ideological state apparatuses* of white privilege—emerged as the preeminent conservatory of a Confederate parochialism within the Deep South. From the musings of Jackson's journalists, to the parliamentarian proclamations of die-hard 'Sons of the South,' to the spectacular rituals of posthumous homage for 'the Cause,' the pact to keep Ole Miss in Oxford ignited a bevy of multi-modal discursive formations that lionized the university as the 'nuclear' state institution through which the Old South would 'live forever.'

---

15. The University faculty approved a measure for faculty members to pursue "the erection of a monument to the honored Alumni of this Institution who have fallen in the service of the state" in the late 1890s.

Rhetoric of this newly historicized Dixie South whiteness was popularized in the public sphere through various threads of the hyper-white power structure as described in campus publications and public spectacles. For example, in the years following the Civil War, students organized the publication of the University of Mississippi's first student newspaper, *The University Record*, which was distributed weekly. The publication openly stated its purpose was to keep students informed of coming events and to facilitate their 'remembrance of the past' (Cohodas, 1997). As an exemplar of the romanticized idioms of the postbellum campus [senti]mentality, a columnist from the *Record* reminded readers in the May 5, 1899, issue that several hundred Confederate soldiers who lost their lives at the Battle of Shiloh were buried on the University of Mississippi campus, and that "these heroes [of] Shiloh, belong to us of the University, and . . . it is our duty to cherish their memory" ("Confederate heroes," 1899, p. 1a). The incendiary politics of this publication, and the subsequent versions of the student newspaper—the *Mississippian* and later the *Daily Mississippian*—offered an [inter]textual phantasmagoria of editorials, commentaries, scientific postulations, and 'stories' which framed (and continue to frame) the centralized white subject as arbiter and preserver of Southern gentility and victim of 're-verse discrimination,' as well as other discursive formations which link the pleasures of a homogenous past to the [white] collective loathing for a pluralistic future.

Looking at these and other examples, we might follow Maurice Halbwachs in reading that the composite intersections of Confederate rememberings and histories cannot simply be understood through temporally-exclusive thinking.[16] In *Les Cadres Sociaux de la Mémoire*, Halbwachs writes "Depending on its circumstances and the point in time, society represents the past to itself in different ways: it modifies its conventions" (quoted in Ricoeur, 2004). As discursive formations within the social world, these public pedagogies are bound not only to the manipulation of time, but perhaps more so to the re-situation of space therein. Maurice Mandelbaum (2001) reminds us of a core precept of Marx's historical materialism, that history is not a series of sequentially-absolute moments, but rather a collection of passages dialectically and diachronically interwoven into the conceptions of time: "a relationship of part to whole, not a relationship of antecedent to consequent" (p. 56). Likewise, through his cleverly formulated 'Theses on the Philosophy of History,' Walter Benjamin (1969) offers an important interpretation of Marx's historical materialism which might help us here:

> The true picture of the past flits by. The past can be seized only as an image which flashes up at the instant when it can be recognized and is never seen again. 'The truth will not run away from us': in the historical outlook of historicism these words of Gottfried Keller mark the exact point where historical

---

16.Much like Foucault (1976, 1994a), Halbwach's thinking is instructive in framing the language(s) of history, rather than the singular historical event (or sequence of historical events), as the impetus from which politics and power relations are imbedded in historical renderings.

materialism cuts through historicism. For every image of the past that is not recognized by the present as one of its own concerns threatens to disappear irretrievably. (p. 255)

In metaphysical *and* ontological terms, and following Marx, both Mandelbaum and Benjamin would concur that these new memories of the old Confederacy do not simply evolve through linear patterns from antebellum to post-bellum times (and thus the future), but rather *histories* are mobilized by intermediaries of the present to protract, contest, or re-make the hegemonic readings of collective memories of the past.

Furthermore, as Pierre Nora (1989) suggests, history is often seen to hold a deathly quality; it comes to haunt our social lives through the processes of remembering.[17] As such, cultural memories of the imagined community are always already political in that they arouse and bring to life dominant positionalities. In the case of the pedagogical stylings of New South Ole Miss, the past was made political through its normative qualities—socially-constructed readings of the past mobilized to reify, and glorify, the racial banalities of 'the Cause.' Whereas history "represents and reflects the past," writes Louise Weissberg (1999), memory in this way is "'a perpetually actual phenomenon' that can capture the present eternally. It is absolute, while history is relative; it claims objects, images, and space for itself, while history insists on the passing of time" (p. 17). Through remembering (and forgetting) we selectively mobilize the past, linking historical events while separating others; privileging select individuals, events, and narratives and marginalizing or erasing others.

Paul Ricoeur (2004) argues that rememberings such as those active throughout the institutionalized pedagogies of the early-Century University coalesce through a "memory which mocks history: the past is then, according to François Furet, 'immemorialized' in order better to 'memorialize' the present" (p. 408). By 'mocking' history, the student of such a history engages in processes of collective remembering that best transforms the plasticity of the past into political currency of the present. Thus, I argue here and again in coming chapters that these machinations of a memorialized Confederacy produce a collective accord of *ersatz continuum*—in which the white, settler, plantation mystifications of the Confederate past are projected onto the history making projects of generations that followed. In such times, we are reminded that those "who *posses history*," as Guy Debord (1967/1994) suggests, "give it an orientation—a direction, and also a meaning" (p. 96). Hence, the architecture of the Confederate mythscape became an im-

---

17.Over the course of some forty texts on the subject, Pierre Nora develops the notion of 'national memory'—broadly conceived (in order) as: 'founding memory' (or the period of defining and affirming the existence of the sovereign state); state-memory (circulations of representations of the state); 'national-memory' (the re-centering of national memories around collective machinations of the nation); and 'citizen-memory' (the sense of 'belonging to' the nation is diffused through the internalizing processes of the atomized masses). In his theorizing of French national memory, Nora contemplates the state as a generational mythology upon which modernity's longings for 'place' are thrust unto the national imaginary.

portant mechanism for transecting the spaces of uncertain Reconstruction times. As Nora (1989) posits, the memorial site (*les lieux de mémoire*, or place of memory) is not only a site for the further temporal extraction, but also *replace* the collective along powerful socio-political and cultural trajectories.

In the case of the New South, the Janus face of the mythscaped Confederacy both reconstructed the politics of the slavery South onto the post-bellum era, and projected that past onto social and economic relations of the future. Beyond teleology, these discursive formations reinvigorated the diachronic-synchronic intercese of a post-Confederate cultural geography. In this way, space and time were reorganized in the meaningful interplay of ideological oppression and national building memorialization. As Debord (1967/1994) suggests, "to reflect upon history is to reflect upon power" (p. 98). The 'body/subject' is thusly situated within the *durée* of everyday life; whereby cultures of the body and embodiment align with history in powerful ways. Under such a historically-subjected present, Latimer (2009) writes, "the body is more or less busy trying to get 'in line' with narrative. So that when someone becomes 'out of place', even momentarily, the body registers its being out of line" (p. 13). In this way, through the honorary degrees, campus monuments, patriating praxis, and other Confederate-related reclamations of not just the social relations—but the power dimensions—of the Old South, history re-colonized the past to project power onto the present.

This point is made quite clear in the following example: Just as the embodied and performed politics of Dixie South whiteness at the University of Mississippi during the Reconstruction Era further spectacularized, and thus coalesced (by allowing the visible center to stand unfettered), the ever-permeating racist discourses which connected the Old [South] with the New [South], so too did public confidence in 'a second Reconstruction'—one which would reorganize the racial hierarchy of the South around the logics of desegregation—abound.[18] During, and especially following the World War II era, University of Mississippi students revitalized a series of Confederate-inspired rituals, such as 'Dixie Week,' on the Ole Miss campus. To such an end, on November 27, 1950, the inaugural Dixie Week was held on the Ole Miss campus, featuring: the erection of a fifty-foot-high statue of Colonel Reb in the heart of the campus space, a reading of the Ordinance of Secession, ritualistic consumption of mint juleps, orations praising the life's labors of Robert E. Lee, and beard-growing contests to honor the hardships faced by their soldier ancestors ("First Dixie Week celebration gets into full swing," 1950).

The highlight of the first Dixie Week was the conveying of ninety-eight year old 'General' James A. Moore, one of six surviving members of the Confederate Civil War veterans. He was escorted to the Ole Miss-Mississippi

---

18. I will offer a more in-depth discussion of the Civil Rights Movement and the dialectic of the institution and the Movement in Chapter 4.

State football game[19] in a parade featuring a horse-drawn carriage, and was saluted at halftime by an aircraft flyover in the shape of the Confederate flag. After the game, General Moore was the featured guest of the Confederate Ball, which featured twenty 'Ole Miss belles' escorted by Rebel students in Confederate uniforms (Pulitzer, 1950). The annual Dixie Week celebration thus became a campus staple: a tribute to the Confederacy and a discursive space where "the spirit of the Old South [could] live again" (Brigance, 1951, p. 7) through the crowning of 'Miss Dixieland' and the other rituals of the white, genteel Cotton South.

In 1954, six months after the *Brown versus Board of Education* decision, the students at Ole Miss organized the fifth annual 'Dixie Week,' this time approximated more by the racial imperatives of the Confederate cause than by reverie for 'the spirit of the Old South.' That year's Dixie Week featured reenactments of secession from the Union, a slave auction, and on-campus speeches from members of the Ku Klux Klan. *The Mississippian* recorded the chairman of 'Dixie Week' promising "enough activities to please the whims of every Southern Belle and Confederate Gentleman" on campus (Flautt, 1954a, p. 1). The first day of Dixie Week 1954 began with the ceremonial raising of the Southern Cross, accompanied by drum and bugle corps. This was followed by a reenactment of the "assassination of Lincoln in the grill [a popular gathering place near campus], secession from the Union, a parade at noon, endoctrination (sic) of Yankee students, a salute at twilight to the Confederate Dead, flag lowering, and an evening pep rally" ("Dixie Week events may be reported by *Chicago Tribune*," 1954, p. 1).

The second day of 'Dixie Week' featured appearances by members of the Ku Klux Klan, followed by the purchase of Confederate war bonds and a reenactment of induction into the Confederate army. The third day was highlighted by the week's featured activity—the slave auction—whereby campus leaders and cheerleaders (all of whom were white) were cheerfully sold into servitude to the highest bidder. The remainder of the week was filled with activities themed around antebellum plantation life, from a mule race to a formal dance and campus-wide dinner (Flautt, 1954b).

This hyper-racist iconoclastic fete of the "unreconstructed Rebel" (Burgin, 1954, p. 1) suggests the reverence of the Confederacy and its racist ideologies and the relevance of physicality in pursuing and institutionalizing a racist hegemonic Dixie South whiteness. White bodies occupied the spaces of privilege and power within the University spaces and the state's hierarchical political and social structure, and white supremacy was acted-out in the textual narratives and corporeal discourses of post-Reconstruction Era Ole Miss. Thus, Dixie South racist ideological orthodoxy was channeled through, and dialectically reinforced by, the physicalities of the preferred white student subject. The imperatives of an epochal racial hierarchy, situated in the post-war Reconstruction and its cultures of segregation, were

---

19. The rivalry between the two schools came to be known as the 'Egg Bowl' in 1927, in honor of the victor's trophy: a golden egg.

defined throughout by the menial gesticulations of the white center, and promulgated by the hegemonic transparency of identity politics imbedded therein.

Body-Pedagogy and Confederate Continuity

The Civil War certainly weakened the jurisprudence of a plantation whiteness that had been woven into the fabric of the antebellum Dixie South cultural economy (Faust, 1988). However, through the region's key cultural institutions (such as the university, civic groups, the church, etc.), many elites were able to *reconstruct the 'order of things'* in the Dixie South as it was before the war came. In so doing, the university closed its ranks, indeed its *raison d'être*, around resurrections of 'the Lost Cause'—a cause inextricably linked to the formations of power produced in and through the identities, ideologies, and practices of antebellum slavery. In his book *The Closed Society*—a text that to this day holds great controversy on the Ole Miss campus[20]—former university professor James Silver (1966) defined the characteristics of Reconstructionist insularity in this way:

> . . . the community sets up the orthodox view. Its people are constantly indoctrinated—not a difficult task, since they are inclined to accepted creed by circumstance. When there is no effective challenge to the code, a mild toleration of dissent is evident, provided the non-conformist is tactful and does not go far. But with a substantial challenge from the outside—to slavery in the 1850s and to segregation in the 1950's—the society tightly closes its ranks, becomes inflexible and stubborn, and lets no scruple, legal or ethical, stand in the way of the enforcement of orthodoxy. (p. 6)

Restoring the formations of Dixie South whiteness meant reestablishing both a *collective emotion* and *iniquitous social order* in the South, what Benedict Anderson (1991) might proffer the return of an oppressive Anglo-centric 'imagined community.'

The university had to reinvent itself—but through an all-too-familiar Old South *lingua franca*. Like all Americans seeking social order in the post-Civil War era, white Dixie Southerners receded back to culturally established 'geographic anchors,' both in the imagined spaces of nostalgic narrative and the physical spaces of "spectacular whiteness" (Hale, 1998, p. 9). The demiurgic creators of the University had fashioned the institution as a citadel that reflected their collective imaginings and privilegings of antebellum whiteness; of the power invested in the discursive solidarities of qualitative bodily deportment (white versus non-white) and perceptible social status

---

20. The state's powerful elite held much distain for the book, suggesting that it was a threat to their 'way of life' and ordered that private detective spy on Silver in order to build up a case for his dismissal. After an arduous search which rendered no wrongdoings, the state senate and the board of trustees asked for Silver's resignation. Having already taken a year's leave to serve as visiting professor at Notre Dame University, Silver took the advice of University officials and did not return to Ole Miss, instead opting for a full-time position at Notre Dame (Sansing, 1999).

(plantation royalty versus subhuman servility). As such, during the postbellum remainder of the Nineteenth Century and beyond, Mississippi's political stalwarts devoted substantial resources and attention toward reclaiming the specters of a satiated power-knowledge imbedded within their 'anchor' of higher education and the center of their Old South imaginations (Cabaniss, 1971). What emerged, to borrow from Bryan Turner (1992), was an historically-constituted substrate of the Old South 'somatic society'; a *closed* society in which the linkages between bodies of the past and bodies of the present organized the "principal field of political and cultural activity" (p. 162).

History came to life at the postbellum University not simply as a matter of historical accord. Nor were the 'uses of history' were confined to the realm of recollecting the region's cultural, economic, or political antecedents. Rather, the uses of Confederate history in the postbellum present became generative of old identities, and old power relations (Hall, 1992a)—projecting the past economic, political, and cultural formations onto the relations of everyday campus life. Tradition was [re]invented, to echo Hobsbawm and Ranger (1983), but those inventions were not only products of the context from which they emerge. These mythscapes, as Laclau and Mouffe (1985) would not let the student of these Old South pedagogies (public or classroom) forget, *produce* the current society whose past they recount.

We might then, in refining our own [critical] historical literacies of postbellum Ole Miss, come to some sort of tentative conceptual closure by asking, and partially answering, the following question: Can history, in Saussurian terms, be both *syntagmatic* (linear and sequential) and *associative* (having an undetermined order)? In engaging the histories that were brought to life around those students of the Reconstructed university, I might offer a cautionary 'yes.' For while the region's pre-war history was indeed brought back to life in post-war fragments—selective narratives of the Confederate cause, episodic Old South identity politics, and carefully organized schemes of governance—the new pedagogies and selected (raced, classed, and gendered) subjects upon which those pedagogies were cast ultimately forged an institutional legacy more closed aligned with Old South racism, class-hierarchy, and patriarchy than any 'new' Southern ontology. Through racialized, classed, and gendered discourses of identity, emergent post-war Dixie South whiteness was thus fused from, and cemented to, the remains of antebellum Confederate hegemonic whiteness and the recalcitrance of a *retaliatory center*. From the start of the Civil War through to the latter part of the following century, the arbiters of a dominant political identity "used the fragments to erect more binary orderings, imagined as natural and physically grounded" (Hale, 1998, p. 5).

In turn, Ole Miss became an instrument for creating "a common whiteness to solve the problems of the post-Civil War era and build their collectivity on not just a convention or a policy but on segregation as a culture" (Hale, 1998, p. xi). Symbolic, inclusivity of the New South thus gave way to

75

the realities of cultural exclusivity harnessed around Dixie South whiteness (E. L. Ayers, 1993)—and the University was fundamental in re-centering postbellum, normative, masculine white elitism. Both in the mediated and practiced discourses of the University, students became both the objects and subjects of a performative politics of race, antediluvian chivalry, Old South gentility, and normalized[ing] schemas of the visible center. By creating new pedagogical and social formations through which members of the student body were encouraged to become active agents of the knowledge-power dynamic of postbellum Dixie South whiteness, the collective configurations and holistic integration of conservative patriarchy, racist ideology, parochial discourses of representation, and the language of performative embodiment were diffused, if not concretized, on the Ole Miss campus.

Embodiments of the New South

In this chapter, I detail the endeavors of University and state intermediaries to *galvanize Dixie South whiteness* at the University of Mississippi in the post-bellum years. Just as the past came to life in romanticizing, legitimizing, and re-institutionalizing an Old South Confederate whiteness, so too did the technologies by which a New South whiteness was instructed, performed, and made powerful. Thus, I first want to turn to the centralizing practices in which the bodies of the masculine, white student subject were disciplined in the order of Hume, Bilbo, and other white supremacists of the Deep South and moulded in the image of their Fallen Confederate brethren such as the University Greys. Later in the chapter, I explore how Old South identity politics also acted upon those non-dominant subjectivities that had come to inhabit the University's physical and pedagogical spaces during the post-Reconstruction Era.

Learning Whiteness

As I have suggested, from the outset the malleable body as a representational discourse was the core resource for redefining and reconstructing the politics of whiteness within Dixieland Mississippi. The governance of the student body at Ole Miss became so intensive and concentrated during Reconstruction that by the turn-of-the-century, the Ole Miss campus was considered a "self-contained community with its own customs, mores, and value system" (Sansing, 1999, p. 165). The systems of surveillance and governance over atomized, yet complex modalities of whiteness had become so codified, and normalized, that by the end of the 19th Century the University issued a handbook to all entering freshmen which came to be known as the *M-Book*—a catalog of the abundant 'opportunities' in physical culture, religious activity, and social organization.[1]

As the following illustrations indicate, the objective of the post-war University of Mississippi was to churn out productive white bodies, bodies which would summon and duplicate the bygone racial discourses of Mississippi society and reclaim the vestiges of the 'Lost Cause.' The task of the University throughout the latter part of the Nineteenth Century and first half of the Twentieth Century was to juxtapose the Dixie South power-knowledge lexicon onto the white-bodied student populace, creating a uniformed Dixie South corporeal 'hexis'—a fusion of supremacist ideology and separatist deportmental discourse coded in the language of the local.

In his seminal texts *Outline of a Theory of Practice* and *The Logic of Practice*, the late Chair of Sociology at the Collège de France Pierre Bourdieu (1977, 1990) defines such a bodily 'hexis' as "political mythology realized, *em-bodied*, turned into a permanent disposition, a durable way of standing, speaking, walking, and thereby feeling or thinking" (p. 93; p. 69). For Bourdieu (1977; 1990b), the notion of 'hexis' was both the reification of an idealized deportment and the concurrent reconstitution of dominant ideologies through the exhibition of somatic capital. Bourdieu (1993) stressed that hexis was primarily exhibited through visible means, particularly in performances of a normalized corporeal stylishness: exclusivity through expressivity. At Ole Miss, as in the South more generally, the preferred institutional hexis disciplined onto the student subject was a three part amalgamation of the visible center: post-*Emancipation* segregation, post-plantation 'egalitarianism,' and post-gender integration objectification (Woodward, 1989).

At the University of Mississippi, the discernible, spectacular nature of whiteness was fostered through such a systematic indoctrination as expressed through the multi-layered 'making' of signified corporeal conduct and observable performativity. Chris Shilling (2003) explains such a paradox of embodiment this way: "the capacities and senses, experiences and management of bodies are not only central to the exercise of human agency and constraint, but also to the formation and maintenance of social systems" (p. 19). Unlike the uncontested whiteness of the antebellum South, or the "invisible," "reticent," or "silent" whitenesses of a more contemporaneous post-Civil Rights moment, in the years during and following the Reconstruction era, whiteness was overtly flaunted like a badge of Southern privilege. In this *spectacle of Dixie South whiteness*, the diffusion of representational power radiated outward from the visible center—shaping human activity through an imaged *langue* of thesis (white center) and antithesis ('Othered' pole). While the narratives of Old South white privilege remained omnipresent, more visible, polyvalent articulations of New South white entitlement began to emerge.

---

1. The M-Book is still distributed to campus freshman each fall.

Unlike rhetoric or narrative, race representation in the New South "could convey contradictions and evoke oppositions like white racial supremacy, white racial innocence, and white racial dependency more easily and persuasively than a carefully plotted story" (Hale, 1998, p. 8). As such, the spectacle of Dixie South whiteness not only became the discursive conduit by which power was exercised, but also the paradigm by which racialized subjects 'learned' their identities within what figurationalist sociologists might refer to as the 'tensions and co-operations' (Elias, 1982) of the reordered Dixie South. The social hierarchy of Mississippi's race relations had to be relearned in the New South, and the apparatuses of the Old South were mobilized by the state's power elite to resuscitate the remains of an old social asymmetry. Through strategic controls, the University's function was reformulated to arbitrate and indoctrinate 'preferred meanings' (Hall, 1980) of a 'civilized,' ocular New South whiteness.

Whiteness was thus encoded through the deportmental features of a signifying system constituted by an antiquated class-based, race-based, and gender-based social hierarchy. To do this, the Chancellors, faculty members, the Board of Trustees, and other cultural intermediaries embarked on a nearly century long campaign to reorient and indelibly imprint the student body with the meaningful discourses, languages, and semiotics of Old South traditionalism and gentility. If the 'Other' at Ole Miss during the Jim Crow/ Reconstruction Era was constituted by the imagined intrusion of black bodies, feminine objects, and scholastic working class vagabonds, the visible center was reconstructed and reinstalled in the University's white masculine student subject through technologies of an idyllic, discursive infusion of a sacrificial deportment (Gaston, 1989; Tindall, 1989).

By interjecting a hyper-normative, state-sponsored curricular programmatic of instruction at the University of Mississippi—concretized immediately following the Civil War—Dixieland politicians seized the cultural physicalities and ideological possibilities of the institution's student body. A tight relationship, or regime of control, was established between the state and the university—one which reinforced the University's function as an extension and armature of the state and its ability to construct social and identity politics. The rigid management over the University was exemplary of the degree to which the institution was acting a vessel of the state's political agenda.

By the order of the Governor, in the early 1930s Chancellor Joseph Neely Powers replaced Chancellor Hume for a short interval, only to be removed after two years for what the Board of Trustees and the state legislature felt were initiatives attempting to revolutionize or 'annihilate' the principles and 'foundations' of the University. In his efforts to transform the University into an establishment for advancing the state's economic and social 'progress', the Board's perception was that Chancellor Powers had abandoned the elitist strata[fication] upon which the University had been serving. Shortly after resuming office, however, Governor Bilbo removed Hume and appointed Alfred Butts to the Chancellorship in 1935—his appointment, and the dismissal of Hume, was part of the 'whirligig game of politics' operating on the institution, where Ole Miss was an extension of the state's political maneuvering (D. G. Sansing, 1999).

For instance, at the request of the state legislature and the Board of Trustees, the formulaic program of "Anglo-Saxon" was developed as a central part of the Ole Miss curriculum during the early Reconstruction Era (Cabaniss, 1971; Garland, 1874). Anglo-Saxon was an essential ingredient of a new curricular recipe which abandoned the antebellum classical holistic programmatic in favor of a more nuanced and multifaceted indoctrination of genteel Dixie South whiteness. Courses in Anglo-Saxon promoted and crystallized the Eurocentric behavioral norms and epistemological values of regional whiteness, effectively teaching Mississippi's young elite how to *be white*. Furthermore, the process of Anglo-Saxonization immersed Oxford students in the parole of a Dixieland hegemonic bourgeois 'signifying system' (R. Williams, 1981); the hyper-masculine and hyper-racist domain of privilege and power within a conservative, plantation political economy. The study of Anglo-Saxon included coursework in Indo-European language arts (English literature, English composition, etc.), performative politics (theatre, calisthenics, etiquette, etc.), and—despite repeated appeals from the students—Greek philosophy and Western European orthodoxy. These performative processes of signification were fossilized in the "*natural* methods of 'Elocution,'" or the correct training of gait, posture, and linguistics (Garland, 1872b).

Elocution became such an imperative ingredient of the University's indoctrination project that by the late 1880s, the faculty had added a comprehensive "elocution" program to the catalog. Through "Physical Training, Respiration, Vocal Culture, Articulation, Orthcepy, Gesture, and the Laws of Inflection and Emphasis" (*Catalogue of the officers and students of the University of Mississippi*, 1887, p. 44), the 'body/subject' as discursive space was transformed into a palpable text; regulated by the institution, and encoded with a meaningful language of privilege and supremacy. Further, these students learned how to read, or 'decode' (Hall, 1980), the corporeal text and ascribe meaning to the signifiers of spectacle whiteness. At the intersection of Bourdieu's notion of hexis and Foucault's conceptualizations of power-knowledge, the children of Mississippi's once economically prosperous aristocracy were thus imparted with the knowledge by which to mobilize social (or linguistic) capital, cultural capital, and bodily capital in place of their fleeting familial economic capital (Bourdieu, 1986b). White empowerment, in this instance, was accomplished by learning the customs and value system entrenched in the discursive formations of a pervasively Eurocentric Dixie South.

Such an Ole Miss 'indoctrination project' was both intensive and dogmatic, allowing virtually no leverage for expressions counter to the prevailing logics of Mississippi's antiquities and traditions. During the period of Reconstruction, deviations from a normative Anglo-Saxonism were not tolerated on the University of Mississippi campus. On May 23, 1867, the faculty addressed the problem of political and religious insolence by adopting the following law into the University's code of conduct: "Resolved: that no student shall be allowed to introduce any contemporaneous political of controversial religious matter in any speech or essay for public exhibition in this University – Adopted" (Shoup, 1867b). Rather than allowing students to explore alternative politics, the University required that students join one of the two literary societies: the Hermaean Society and Phi Sigma Society. The Hermaean Society was formed only five months after the campus opened, and was perhaps the most intimately allied social organization to the campus's indoctrination project during the early years. By 1934, the group had produced all but two of the University's Rhode's scholars, and was the longest standing student organization on campus. Further, the organization had played a significant role in pre- and post-war collegiality of the University: celebrating their anniversary with a number of orations, functions, and social events each year in the early spring ("Hermaean Society has long and proud history on university campus," 1934).

While the rival organization of the Hermaeans, Phi Sigma's purpose was identical to its older predecessor—to shape the attitudes,[2] politics, and oral conduct of the University student body. Under the close supervision of faculty 'sponsors,' both the Phi Sigma and the Hermaean Societies demonstrated their linguistic and deportmental politics through chosen recitations at each year's commencement ceremony. Despite waning relevance of these societies during the 1940s, the active diligence of University socialization was still instrumental in layering the tapestries of contested Old South identity politics, one which revolved around competing discursive striations of: reverence for, and hypermasculine celebration of, the Confederacy, the caricaturization and disarmament of the new strength of blackness (i.e. blackface minstrelsy), and rebuilding a harmonious plantation phantasmagoria which supposedly existed prior to 'Northern aggressions.' At the cost of a practical, philosophical, or critical educational environment, the University of Mississippi served as an extension of the fallen Confederate state rather than a beacon of intellectual prosperity. The closed university within a 'closed society,' the faltering quality of education throughout the Reconstruction Era can be traced back to the elitist mentality and isolationist trajectory of institutional affairs.

As a result of the tightened organizational constrictions the state had put on University administrators, a study commissioned Governor Henry A. Whitfield, and conducted by the University of Wisconsin in the late 1920s to examine Mississippi's educational system, concluded that the institution had neglected the economic and social needs of the state in favor of maintaining an imposing exclusivity. Directed by Michael O'Shea and of-

---

2. As an example of the types of 'attitudes' constructed under the guise of these organizations, during the 81st Anniversary Celebration of the Phi Sigma Society, guest speaker J. F. Hawkins proffered: "The thing that has last brought the negro problem into prominence is the rise of the so-called new negro . . . this new negro seems to be a sort of demigod with large stature, manly features, a wide knowledge, and a powerful intellect" ("Large crowd in attendance Friday morning," 1928b, p. 1).

ten referred to as the *O'Shea Report*, the findings suggested that in general Mississippi's institutions of higher learning were adhering to the "genteel tradition [that] was in vogue throughout our country fifty years prior," and that those institutions failed to "train the youth of the State to become efficient in the performance of tasks that most need to be accomplished in Mississippi at present" (M. O'Shea, 1925, p. 200). O'Shea cited that a common theme in the faculty and administration interviews conducted at the University of Mississippi was that courses were organized "to develop character in [Mississippi's] young people," rather than designing a curriculum which would "train young people to develop the agricultural, industrial, economic, and human resources of the state" (O'Shea, 1925, pp. 201-202).

O'Shea (1925) pointed to the vague objectives of Mississippi's higher educational institutions—"'building of character,' 'inculcation of good habits,' 'training for citizenship,' development of a religious life,' 'making of men and women,' and 'the cultivation of moral conduct'" (p. 200)—and the deviation from a more practical, industrial educational foray as the shortcoming of the higher education system. Unlike most other American colleges of the era, in O'Shea's estimation, Ole Miss failed to prepare its students to contribute to the unique challenges of the state's economic, cultural, and agricultural demands in favor of the programmatic orientation of social and cultural elitism. The shackles of indoctrination—or the "educational and psychological dogmas" (O'Shea, 1925, p. 201)—at Ole Miss became so overwhelming that at the same time the *O'Shea Report* was being published, University faculty members were taking measures to exorcize any books referring to communism or desegregation from the campus library. The campus' praetorian of whiteness, Chancellor Alfred Hume, was adamant in his hostility toward an oppositional voice on campus and his service to the controlling interests of Mississippi's white elite—"keeping Ole Miss tethered to Oxford and secure in the 'worthy traditions' he lauded" (Cohodas, 1997, p. 32). The University—which operated under the auspices of what an Ole Miss undergraduate referred to as an "absolute monarchy"—rather than working for the betterment of its students and the community, remained "a group of buildings, lorded over and absolutely controlled by men careless or else heedless of student welfare, intent only on pouring into a docile student body their ideas concerning education" (Lomax, 1927, p. 4).

The oppositional voice brought forth by the small segment of student detractors was met with the claim by Hume that "academic freedom" can sometimes be "academic nonsense" (qtd. in Sansing, 1999, p. 226). One of the detractors of Hume's leadership was *Mississippian* Editor W. A. Lomax, who was critical of the weighted texts residing in the campus library. He argued, "Outstanding among the deficiencies in the Library is the spirit of conformity, which rules and prevails. . . . If a book even hints at disturbing the established political, social or religious questions of the day, it is not on the University Library shelves" (Lomax, 1928, p. 4). The strength of the academy, Lomax scathed, was undermined inasmuch as:

the spirit of endeavoring to find out for one's self the essential truth of things should be given free range, not stifled [as is the case at] the University of Mississippi. . . . Original thinking on the part of the student simply can't be done. Kant, Haeckel, Hegel . . . In their stead we find some priceless gems such as 'How to get Pep' or such other soothing syrup philosophical treatises. (Lomax, 1928, p. 4)

As we will soon see the issue of academic freedom at Ole Miss abounded in the public sphere throughout the Twentieth Century. During the first semester of James Meredith's enrollment at Ole Miss, the Academic Council imposed censorship measures against the most radical and outspoken faculty members who favored desegregation for years to come ("Works both ways: Freedom discussed," 1962). The first step of the indoctrination project of Ole Miss following the Civil War was to contain, and constrict, the mentality of its young constituency. As James Silver (1966) would later suggest, "To perpetuate itself the closed society must keep a firm control over what goes into the minds of its young people" (p. 60).

The Sanctified Student Body

By the 1940s, the University "would have more than met its goal, infusing generations of young white Mississippians with an immutable pride in their heritage and a belief in a social order accepted as divinely ordained" (Cohodas, 1997, p. 5). The University of Mississippi's anticipated end product was thus an amalgamation of 'preferred' whiteness and consecrated "symbolic violence" against outliers of the Closed Society. The former was learned through rigorous study of 'Anglo-Saxon' and other forms of instructional whiteness, while the latter was created through the symbiotic inseparability of church and state channeled through the institution. The administration of campus activities took on a decidedly sanctimonious posture during the Reconstruction Era. For example, echoing the early disciplinary logics of antebellum student governance, and illustrating the desire for dutiful morality embodied by the idealized student subject, the faculty suspended an undergraduate from the University in 1867 with the following explanation:

> The Faculty of the University regret to find you so frequently absent from recitation, and to perceive other indications of a general indifference to your college duties. They also learn with astonishment and regret that you are exceedingly profane in your language. Such indifference to college duties, & such disregard of the common decencies of society and of the laws of Morality, the Faculty cannot tolerate. (Shoup, 1867a authors emphasis)

The indoctrination of New South whiteness saved little room for those operating outside the conventions of moral Christianity. The hyper-Christian orthodoxy shaped student conduct and discipline in this and numerous other instances throughout the postbellum chronological epoch. Such discourses of the 'Southern Ethic' were underwritten by a firm asceticism, and what Max Weber (1958/2002) referred to as the 'rationalization,' or methodicalness, of the body operating in space over time. The regimented body, doing God's work, was operationalized at the University of Mississippi around a *status naturae* (Weber, 1958/2002)—a sublimation of the body politic onto the political body as social text.

The preferred *status naturae* in Mississippi was ingrained in the representational systems and cultural encounters of the state's flagship educational "instrument" (*Catalogue of the officers and students of the University of Mississippi*, 1866, p. 39) with an academic militancy of an ideological police state. To arrest deviations from a consumptively pious institutionalized student body, the faculty instituted a number of "Liquor Laws" in 1872 to curb the purchase and ingestion of spirits by University students (Garland, 1872b). As the wave of Prohibition swept across the United States, city and county government leaders sought to expand their sovereignty over the campus by imposing this new "Liquor Law" upon the students (by way of faculty governance) (Garland, 1872a).[3] Such an edict was intended to control what went into the preferred, temporal bodies of the students at the University.

As another example of the asceticization of the Ole Miss student body, the antebellum practice of dormitory inspections—which, in the tradition of West Point, were conducted at any time during the day or night—was reinstated after an incident in 1881. During the course of that academic year, members of the faculty were "mortified" to find that a postmistress was found in a student's dormitory room, and that several students had "visited" her during her stay (Sansing, 1999, p. 147). The reinstitution of inspection reestablished a disciplinary gaze and the chains of governmentality which had shackled students of the University prior to the war. Furthermore, the return to a regimented panopticism, similar to that which operated on the student subject in the antebellum period, signaled a reprise to the conduct of student conduct and the sanctimonious examination of the body in relation to space.

The hyper-religiosity of the University of Mississippi was fostered, if not sermonized, by the campus leaders in the decades following the Civil War. For example, Chancellor Hume's opinion on the matter of religion at the University was this: "fundamentally and historically the University of Mississippi is essentially a Christian institution. . . . It goes without saying that anything tending toward atheistic teaching will never be tolerated by me" (quoted in Cohodas, 1997, p. 25). The spiritual austerity with which Hume directed the University prompted one journalist to brand Ole Miss "Hume's Presbyterian University" (quoted in Cohodas, 1997, p. 25). In an endeavor to solidify public opinion concerning the godliness of the University, the early part of the Twentieth Century saw the faculty produce and disseminate 5000 copies of a brochure promoting the sanctimonious nature of campus life, citing the rituals of weekly prayer meetings and a generally "strong religious element in the student body" and announcing the extinguishment of the intrusive propensities of gambling, drinking, "extravagance and dissipation of every kind" (Sansing, 1999, p. 133).

3.Lafayette County is still considered a 'dry county,' where the purchase and consumption of alcohol remains illegal, with but a few exceptions.

Despite receiving state and Federal operating funds, Ole Miss was transformed into a publicly-petitioned Protestant university, an armature of the religious state which it served. In 1923, the student editor of *The Mississippian* proclaimed that while other state universities had become "strongholds of atheism, deism, rationalism, infidelity, and various other sectarian ideas out of accord with the tenets of Christianity, . . . the University of Mississippi is and always has been essentially Christian" (Lyon, 1923, p. 2). The internalization of a conjunctural convergence of the influence of the moral majority, the power arrangements emanating out of and descending upon Dixie South whiteness, and a pseudo-philanthropic genteel traditionalism preserved the fabric of an imagined 'Southern ethic.' However, the contradictions residing within such an ill-fated ideology simultaneously reinforced existing social hierarchies, and stood in opposition to human equality and 'righteousness.'

One such contradiction was the rationale for racial segregation at Ole Miss, which was grounded in Christian dogma, specifically in three passages from the Bible (Silver, 1966):

Genesis 9:25 *"And he [Noah] said, Cursed be Canaan; a servant of servants shall be unto his brethren."*

Genesis 28:1 *"And Isaac called to Jacob, and blessed him, and charged him, and said unto him, Thou shalt not take the wife of the daughters of Canaan."*

Leviticus 19:19 *"Ye shall keep my statutes. Thou shalt not let thy cattle gender with a diverse kind: thou shalt not sow thy field with mingling seed: neither shall a garment mingled of linen and woolen come upon thee."*

The liberal interpretation and immoral materializations of these doctrines are suggestive of the overarching cultural economy of segregation and supremacy operating on the white bodied power elite in the Dixie South. Rather than deductively finding themselves in their religion, Mississippi traditionalists interlaced racist social politics into their spirituality, accumulating a self-constructed licensure to hate the ethnicized 'Other' on the grounds of fundamentalism (Barkun, 1994).

At the University of Mississippi, every year starting in 1932 the campus hosted a Religious Emphasis Week, attempting to infuse the close relationship between the student conduct and the religious doctrines of the South ("Program for Religious Emphasis Week," 1938). In the fall of 1955, the director of religious life, Will Campbell, invited Reverend Alvin Kershaw to Oxford to participate in the ceremonies and events of that year's Religious Emphasis celebration. Reverend Kershaw had recently won a large sum of prize money on a popular television program and committed a sizeable portion of his winnings to the National Association for the Advancement of Colored People (or NAACP). Reverend Kershaw's generosity was met with resistance from Mississippi's traditionalist faction, who pressured the Chancellor to cancel the engagement. Citing the possibility that Reverend Kershaw's presence might disrupt the educational process, Chancellor John D. Williams revoked the invitation—a decision which prompted the resignation of Sociology professor Morton King and the protests of several local and regional ministers who had planned to attend the festivities. However, Dr. Morton's protest was one of a negligible number of internal detractions from the hyper-racist religious indoctrination project at the University. The prevailing conservative faction that defined Reconstruction Era whiteness in the frame of Christian principles and righteous moral conduct, and as another layer of Dixie South whiteness, religious exclusivity was harnessed and its principles mobilized to further the indoctrination project.

God and Football

Through a carefully crafted academic program which required study in classical whiteness (Anglo-Saxon and Greek) and a calculated baptism to conservative hyper-religiosity, University of Mississippi intermediaries created a rigid program for initiating students into the identity politics of the New South. However, perhaps more than any other social construct during the Reconstruction Era and beyond, the complex discursive formation of physical culture at the University of Mississippi produced the material and symbolic culmination of Dixie South whiteness and the political function of the University. As early as 1867, the faculty of the University had considered institutionalizing a course in 'physical culture' and appointing an instructor in calisthenics (Shoup, 1867b). From 1893 to 1906, the year of Chancellor Robert Fulton's resignation, the University developed a complete program of physical culture, in which students could receive credit for courses in physical education: including gymnastics, cycling, swimming, boxing, and wrestling. Corporeal emphasis in Ole Miss space became so concentrated that by the 1920s students in the physical culture program performed regular public demonstrations for the community, alumni, and fellow students. These demonstrations included: "pyramid building, medicine ball games, and several special drills from classes in the boys department," and the girl's classes performed general calisthenics with the accompaniment of music ("Physical Ed classes plan demonstration," 1927, pp. 1, 4). In the context of the matured American muscular Christianity movement, these activities resonated, and indeed embodied, the logics of the mind/spirit/body asceticism pervasive throughout the University and the community. As Foucault (1988a) reminds us, the origin of *gymnasia* is "training in a real situation, even if its been artificially induced. There is a long tradition behind this: sexual abstinence, physical privation, and other rituals of purification" (p. 37). As a social discourse, the body became a site for the exercise of power through correct training and preferred posture, and for further indoctrination into the ideologies of the New South. The preferred Ole Miss hexis emerged out of the intersecting discourses of a "clean muscular Christian" physicality ("The Y.M.C.A stands for clean muscular Christian manhood," 1912, p. 4) and a regimented disciplinarity of an 'kinaesthetic,' productive bodily deportment (Ladd & Mathisen, 1999).

After the Civil War, adaptations of masculine gait at the University were expressed through social organizations such as the Young Men's Christian Association and intra-campus and intercollegiate sport. Sport and well-ness evolved into important sites of disciplinarity, and expressions of spec-tacular Dixie South whiteness. For undergraduate men at the University of Mississippi, the Y.M.C.A. was promoted as an outlet for those who desired "to make the college a better place in which to live; to make it a strong-hold for righteousness; to train themselves and others for efficient services; to increase the religious faith of the students, and to direct that faith in-to the channels of higher living and noble thinking." ("The Y.M.C.A stands for clean muscular Christian manhood," 1912, p. 4). The Y.M.C.A. became the largest and most popular student organization on campus during the early part of the Twentieth Century. And while a Young Women's Chris-tian Association was eventually established on campus, its role and impact on campus activities was negligible in comparison to its masculine counter-part. This inconsistency was in part due to the hypermasculine nature of the Ole Miss power structure, but also to the masculine hegemony of sport and physical culture in America. While men occupied positions in the public spheres of political, governmental, business, and sporting environs, women were confined to roles within the 'domestic sphere'[4] — and the role of moral guardians rather than agentive sporting participants.

No social institution was more instrumental and significant in develop-ing the preferred deportment of the genteel, masculine student body than intercollegiate sport. The first semblance of an intercollegiate university team arrived when students organized a baseball club in 1876 and called themselves "The Red and Blue"—a group that eventually toured the re-gion and played most of its games against private and semi-professional teams (Khayat, 2003). Some two decades later, the University of Mississippi played its first intercollegiate football game on November 11, 1893, at the University Park on campus against Southwestern Baptist University of Jackson, Tennessee (Sorrels & Cavagnaro, 1976). The end-of-century expan-sion of intercollegiate sports also included the creation of new teams in tennis, women's basketball, track and field, and cross country. The sport-ing boom of the Reconstruction Era was part of a concerted effort by the University administration to embrace the development of a desirable and proper student physicality and foster a more cohesive social capital amongst the student population. In his annual report on June 12, 1893, Chancellor Fulton declared to the Board of Trustees that the university faculty was en-dorsing intercollegiate athletics, and specifically football for the regulatory benefits the sport would bring to the campus (Sansing, 1990). Many institu-

---

4.The notion of separate spheres "embodied the vision of a social order based on a po-larity of roles and personalities rooted in presumed biological and sexual differen-ces between the sexes. Men were rational, instrumental, independent, competitive, and aggressive; women were emotional, maternal, domestic, and dependent. Eng-land's nineteenth-century emerging bourgeoisie, idealized and popularized by the sentimental novel, advice books, and medical and religious writings, emphasized the concept of a society structured around supposedly "natural," God-ordained distinct male and female spheres" (Smith-Rosenberg, 2005).

tions, the Chancellor argued, had found that sport acted "as a safety valve to the exuberance of youthful spirits that would frequently find vent in some harmful way" (quoted in Sansing, 1999, p. 169).

And thus sporting performativity as an expression of disciplinarity became a central element of campus life, dominating the social actions and popular discourses on campus from the latter part of the Nineteenth Century onward. A survey of the editions of *The Mississippian* between 1911 (the newspaper's first year) and 1950 renders a gross over-saturation of sport coverage[5]—which is telling as to the importance of intra-campus and intercollegiate sport at Ole Miss during that epoch. Between the intramural dormitory, majors, religious, and literary squads (each had their own featured competitions in the various sports), and intercollegiate teams in men's varsity, junior varsity, and campus high school basketball, baseball, track, and football teams, and women's basketball, track, and volleyball teams, agonistic sport pursuits dominated the social lives and social texts of the University.[6]

But such a prevailing cultural import was not as organic in its development as it might at first appear. Those who failed to be interpellated into the culture of sporting physicality at Ole Miss, either by way of irreverence or indifference, were met with hostility by campus administrators. In a speech given to the students in the spring of 1918, Judge Kimbrough, a popular political leader in the Oxford area, implored every student to buy season tickets for all the University's intercollegiate athletic teams. He argued that students who failed to support the team financially "were either stingy or else they were against athletics at the University of Mississippi, for if a person [wasn't] for a thing, then he (sic) [was] against it" ("Judge Kimbrough speaks on athletics," 1918, p. 1). The indoctrination into a preferred physicality was effectively manifested through the physical (participant) and the ocular (spectator), and under the guise of the conservative political and religious appendages of the figurations of campus governance. As school spirit swelled under the disciplinary gaze of the University, administrators tempered the enthusiasm of the student body (for the student body) by reigning in the fervent collectivity of the Ole Miss imagined sporting community. In a speech to the students in 1915, Dr. Hendleston warned: "college spirit is truly a clan spirit and with whatever it is, it is largely a spirit of pride. But, because pride is both very useful and is very dangerous and is possible for it to go in the wrong as well as the right direction, it should be well guided" ("Dr. Hendleston talks on college spirit," 1915). Such an edict was illustrative of the administration's broader project of sterilizing student conduct, while simultaneously adjudicating positive emotional and psychological relationships between physical culture and the University.

---

5. During that span, sport content typically filled half of the six to eight pages of each edition of the school newspaper.

6. Sport dominated the front pages of *The Mississippian* during the early Twentieth Century, in part due to the dictum that half of the editorial staff of the newspaper be occupied by members of the Athletic Association.

A number of intercollegiate participant and spectator sports were popular at the University of Mississippi during the postbellum era. In the earliest years of the Twentieth Century, baseball captured the attention of students and campus intermediaries. As an example of the high profile the sport had attained at the University during the Reconstruction Era, administrators approved an undisclosed, yet reportedly significant monetary contract for former Brooklyn Dodger Casey "Dutch" Stengel to coach the University's baseball team for a stint in the mid-1910s. Using a method of strict physical training and protracted lectures on "inside baseball"—the mental approach to winning in the sport—to prepare the team (""Dutch" Stengel coaching baseball," 1914, p. 1), Stengel's teams rendered considerable success during his tenure. Following his resignation prior to the 1919 season, the reign of baseball as the preferred intercollegiate sport on the Ole Miss campus retracted to the popularity of another springtime sport: basketball. By the middle part of the 'Roaring '20s,' spectacles of intercollegiate basketball held sway over the sporting imaginations of the Ole Miss student public. As a writer for *The Mississippian* proclaimed in 1924, "Ole Miss stands as the premier basketball university of the South. Students are great devotees of the game" ("Ole Miss leads the South with interest in mid-winter sports," 1924, p. 1). In *The Mississippian*, substantial coverage was allocated for the exploits of the University's basketball team (which during that era were commonly referred to by the nickname 'The Flood'[7]). For a brief time in the decade the University added lacrosse to the pantheon of intercollegiate sports, in part for the associational prestige which administrators deemed the sport would bring by playing institutions ("Athletic heads go to meet; Ole Miss to play La Crosse," 1925). By the end of the era, however, the institution which promoted itself as 'a great Southern university' would have one singular sporting passion—intercollegiate football.

The sport's mass cultural appeal at the University was part of a larger contextual convergence of idealized rugged individualism and embodied, postbellum rituals of the new masculine white South. At Ole Miss, the "complimentary nature of white expressions of Southern pride and football is undeniable" (Borucki, 2003, p. 490), as the sport and its spectacular, masculine, dogged configurations became the lucid sporting expression of Dixie South whiteness. For Dixie Southerners, college football emerged during the Twentieth Century as the cultural form by which politics of race, locality, and tradition could be rekindled and the sense of pride for the South could be juxtaposed onto the sporting bodies representing their local universities.

---

7. Mississippi Flood was chosen as the team nickname, beating out 'Rebels' (2nd choice), 'Democrats' (3rd Choice), and 'Ole Marsters' (4th choice) ("'The Mississippi Flood' picked as name for athletes," 1929, p. 1). This play of the rhetorical-symbolic was but one example of the re-narrativized New South, whereby the conquest of the black subordinate and the resistances of the lost cause could be re-articulated through the linguistic dominion of the Dixie South's power elite, a point I will return to later.

As Andrew Doyle (1996) argued, football was the amalgamation of regional esteem, bourgeois persnickety, and symbolic modernization:

> Progressive Southerners adopted the fashionable sport of the Northeastern elite in the early 1890s as a cultural component of their program of modernization. The Machine Age sport of 'scientific football' provided a perfect vehicle for bringing bourgeois values to a region striving for inclusion into the American cultural and economic mainstream. Yet postbellum Southerners steeped in the mythology of the Lost Cause also imbued this Yankee game with the romantic trappings of the Cavalier myth and exalted their football heroes as modern incarnations of Confederate warriors. (p. 74)

The spectacle of college football interlaced with the spectacular nature of Reconstruction Dixie South whiteness created a palatable fusion of sporting and institutional prowess, one which has thrived throughout the succeeding generations.

From the first Reconstruction (following the Civil War) to the Second Reconstruction (during the Civil Rights Movement), intercollegiate football evolved into the centerpiece of muscular Christianity at the University of Mississippi—a cultural formation constructed upon the triangulation of Dixieland rugged masculinity, spectacular Dixie South gentility, and revisionist histories of the Confederacy. Borne of the ideologies of Rooseveltian rugged masculinity, from its inception football at Ole Miss was first and foremost a meaningful and symbolic formation which located the institution within the broader cultural economy of the postbellum Southern manhood. In this period of the modernizing and re-masculinizing South, we see the body re-emerge not just as the corpus of the pedagogically subjected self, but a socio-institutionalized project unto itself. The British sociologist Anthony Giddens (1991) writes extensively on what he terms 'the juggernaut of modernity', and offers this important interpretation on the politics of embodying the logics and cultural modalities of modernity:

> The body used to be one aspect of nature, governed in a fundamental way by processes only marginally subject to human intervention. The body was a 'given', the often inconvenient and inadequate seat of the self. With the increasing invasion of the body by abstract systems all this becomes altered. The body, like the self, becomes a site of interaction, appropriation and reappropriation, linking reflexively organized processes and systematically ordered expert knowledge . . . Once thought of as the locus of the soul . . . the body has become fully available to the 'worked upon' by the influences of high modernity. (p. 218)

Resonating the modernist ideological procession toward a hypermasculine perfect, the student editor of a special commencement issue of the *University Magazine* proclaimed: "today's colleges and universities" in large part due to on-campus and intercollegiate athletics, produce "strong and vigorous men" rather than "the weak and sickly bookworms of twenty years ago" (quoted in Sansing, 1999, p. 174).

Secondly, the marriage of college football and corporeal logics of Ole Miss created a discursive venue to transmit the cultural and elitist values of the University's genteel elite. Several years after the inaugural football game, the head football coach, Professor Alexander Lee Bondurant, recalled the colloquial merger of the Dixie South genteel social ellipses and the carnival-like exposition of Ole Miss football:

> The square presented a festal appearance, hung everywhere with crimson and blue bunting. . . . The afternoon was bright with just enough crispness in the air to inspire vigorous play, and the crowd of vehicles and pedestrians that surged up University street . . . showed that the community was prepared to enter with zest the excitement attendant upon a football game. (quoted in Sorrels & Cavagnaro, 1976, p. 16)

The footballing festival of 1893 and beyond illustrates the seemingly natural affinity the University community had for football, but perhaps more importantly is illustrative of the amiable [visce]realities of spectacle whiteness and the sporting spectacle. Finally, like most Southern schools, Ole Miss football grew into a site for celebrating Southern redemption following the 'Lost Cause' (Watterson, 2000). The football field, in some respects, became a space for reclaiming the lost glories of the Confederacy—a battlefield upon which the 'Lost Cause' could be won, if only symbolically (Borucki, 2003).[8]

In sum, sport culture, spearheaded by a pseudo-populist brand of football, became the organizing feature of social relations and somatic expression at Ole Miss during the postbellum era. College football in the South generally, and at Ole Miss particularly, became a metaphor for persisting animosities between the North and the South, with brimstoned head coaches instructing their troops to 'do or die for old Dixie' and sportswriters endeavoring to relocate the gridiron battles in the imaginary battlefields of Shiloh, Gettysburg, and Vicksburg.

New South, New Subjectivities

I have thus far argued that the symbolic continuities of the Old South haunted the cultural and identity politics of the University of Mississippi in the post-war years-draping an 'ideological blanket' over the pedagogical, spatial, and social arrangements thereof. Indeed, it would be hard to argue against the notion that 'traditional' agents of this and other Deep South social institutions were subjected to a panoply of conservative, parochial power-knowledge formations in the late-Nineteenth and early-Twentieth Centuries. However, individuals within the halls of the university did not exist within that space under conditions of their own choosing. For the old [South] epistemologies and pedagogies acting upon the dominant Ole Miss student subject (the young, white, hetero-masculine, inheritor of post-plantation status and wealth) bore a continuity of patterns of Old South privilege. And as I extrapolate in what follows, those new postbellum institutional subjects (former slaves, working class whites, and women) from the

---

8. The second part of this book will develop the meaningful and qualitative relationship between sport practices and social discourse at the University of Mississippi in much greater depth than space allows for here.

heterogeneous margins were more rigidly integrated into systems of subjectification, colonization, and subordination.

Emancipation or Re-articulation?

The most obvious challenge to white exclusivity at Ole Miss came through
the passing into law of the *Emancipation Proclamation* and the artificial 'lib-
eration' of black Southerners (Guelzo, 2004). Since the university's student
population remained exclusively white for a century after the Civil War
ended, however, those challenges came more in the form of disrupting, or
in many cases reproducing, the *status quo* of established Old South binary racial politics than in any radical transformation in the material and social relations on the Ole Miss campus. For in the antebellum South, the circuits
of slavery had "founded and fixed the meaning of blackness more than any
transparent and transhistorical meaning of black skin founded the category
of slavery" (Hale, 1998, p. 4). Before the war, black identities were largely
constructed by slaves and understood by white plantationeers within the
cultural hierarchy of organized slavery, and the knowledge-power dynamics
imbedded therein. As such, slavery constituted a dyad of superiority/inferi-
ority ensconced in both black and white Mississippi's racial imaginary in the
lead-up to, and period after, the Civil War (E. B. Brown, 2000).

However, after the war, that paradigm was undermined, if only on the
surface, by new conceptual formations of race and inter-relational politics
(Blight & Simpson, 1997). With the changes brought forth by the Proclamation, which destabilized the prevailing slave-based antebellum power-knowledge configuration, many white Southerners—and particularly those who
had accumulated plantation wealth—remained anxious about the emancipatory New South cultural economy that might shape social relations
therein. "For the first time," wrote Ralph Ellison in his classic sojourn *Invisible Man* (1952), Southern whites could not "walk, talk, sing, conceive of laws
or justice, think of sex, love, the family or freedom without responding to
the presence of Negroes." In other words, postbellum Dixie South whiteness was perhaps for the first time produced by, and productive of, the discourses and discords of racial *difference*; as whiteness was now conceived in
relation to the perceived cultural and physical variations between the tau-
tologically monolithic 'white race' and the eclectically abecedarian 'Negro
race' (Woodward, 1989).

Following a series of early Reconstruction Era ratifications to the state
constitution, it was evident that Mississippi's power elite had no intention
of allowing for political or social equality to the state's newly freed slaves
(Hale, 2000). Rather than a break from antebellum superiority/inferiority
logic to a postbellum egalitarian humanism, the post-war epoch of Mississippi race relations was reformulated through cultural segregation, and a
"culture of segregation" (Hale, 1998, p. 45). This culture of segregation appeared at the doorsteps of the University of Mississippi immediately following the Civil War. The undercurrent of apprehension toward the possible

admission of a black student into the University of Mississippi was captured in an 1870 open letter to then Chancellor John Waddell written by Judge Robert S. Hudson of Yazoo City, who inquired: "will the faculty as now composed, receive or reject an applicant for admission as a student on account of color?" (qtd. in Sansing, 1999, p. 123). Waddell and the faculty unanimously responded with the following points:

1. The Uny. Was (sic) organized for whites alone–
2. A change of policy can be effected only be an ordnance of the Board of Trustees
3. The Trustees have not effected a change—& as far as our information extends they have no such purpose.
4. If such a change of policy should be enacted, all the members of the Faculty present would resign. (Garland, 1870)

In late 1870, Chancellor Waddell followed the response to Robert Hudson with a declaration carried by most Mississippi newspapers, reassuring a unanimous and unequivocal segregationism of postbellum Ole Miss: "should a black apply for admission, we shall without hesitation reject him . . . [this university] was founded originally and has been conducted exclusively, in all its past history, for the education of the white race" (J. Waddell, 1891, pp. 465-466). Chancellor Waddell's response signaled the continuation of the University's all-white status, where the minimal presence of black bodies in the domain of Ole Miss came in the form of paid servants, groundskeepers, and, much later, Federal troops stationed in Oxford.[9] Perhaps more importantly, the Chancellor's sentiments, and the activities of students—such as the black-faced white students performing annual "Negro minstrels" ("Negro minstrel given by 'M' Club," 1921c, p. 1) to the delight of the all-white student body—sketched a parochial outline of the supremacist racial intolerance of the institution's power elite.

New heights of the ultra-supremacist atmosphere of the University of Mississippi emerged in the 1920s and 1930s, and coincided with elevation of the local chapters of the Ku Klux Klan. In a striking article disseminated on the campus—and produced fifty years after Waddell's declaration—*The Mississippian* writers praised the work of the Ku Klux Klan in its efforts to preach the "gospel of pure Americanism and love of home and country" ("Ku Klux Klan reorganized," 1921, p. 1). The article went on to laud the white supremacist organization, suggesting that it was the opinion of *The Mississippian* that, "if the work of this organization is carried on in a conscientious and systematic way, some wonderful and gratifying results can be obtained" ("Klu Klux Klan reorganized," 1921a, p. 1). Later in the year, the newspaper again used its pages to promote the cause of the KKK (this time using the correct spelling), citing the "vindictive Northern Congress" as the source of America's social ills, and the Klan as an oppositional, and

---

9. The presence of black troops is in reference to the integration of Ole Miss in 1962, which "provoked only occasional and usually minor altercations" between white students and black soldiers (Sansing, 1999, p. 119).

"absolutely necessary" organization to combat the autocratic takeover by "scalawags, carpetbaggers, and . . . the wild Negro savages of Africa" ("Mostly politics: Old Ku Klux Klan an absolute necessity," 1921, p. 1).

The juxtaposition of anxieties toward 'outside' politics of race and 'insider' imaginings of whiteness—which became the focus and modality of ideological indoctrination at Ole Miss following Reconstruction—continued through the following decades. The presence of the Klan and other racist organizations became commonplace during regular on-campus celebrations which linked the directives of the University to the solidarity of Confederate whiteness. Throughout the period leading up to, and through, the Civil Rights Movement, the Ku Klux Klan held a number of rallies and membership drives on the Oxford campus—and in instances such as the rally in the fall of 1922, the "University students were very well impressed" ("The Ku Klux ably defended," 1922, p. 1). The growth of the Klan in the Dixie South benefited from sizeable enrollment throughout the state of Mississippi, and especially in northern Mississippi (Chalmers, 1981). Considered by the FBI to be "the most violent Klan in history" (Sims, 1996, p. 207), the White Knights of Mississippi actively pursued the students at Ole Miss, hosting on- and off-campus meetings and recruitment fairs throughout the Twentieth Century (Wade, 1998).

During this era, student and campus leaders adopted a number of symbols from which a system of signification could be constructed—one which would represent the visible center, and interpellate the 'traditionalist' bent of the reinvented, 'New South' genteel class. By mobilizing a white supremacist discourse, arbiters of the political stature of the University were able to both *keep out black students* and *hail the separatist sensibilities* of the white Dixie South collective. In turn, during the first half of the Century, the university became of locus of white exclusivity. From 1900 to 1950, enrollment nearly tripled at Ole Miss—whereby university activities and classes brought together Mississippi's largest [exclusively] white, and most invariable, social congregation (Cabaniss, 1971). To keep 'undesirables' out, campus administrators created a public sphere of hate and isolation, marking the imagined and physical Ole Miss spaces off as exclusive property of Mississippi's white elite (more on this in Chapter 4).

Throughout the period which later came to be known as the 'Second Reconstruction' (1950s-1960s), the popular mediations within the University space echoed the hyper-racist carriage of the broader Dixie South racial division. For example, during the late 1950s an underground white supremacist publication, the *Nigble Papers*, was produced by students and circulated throughout the campus. The satirical, yet sardonic, tone of the publication unabashedly transposed the 'threat' of integrating the 'Scotch-Irish' menace with 'true-blooded' Americans. Perhaps a premonition of late-twentieth century angry white retributionists, the *Nigble Papers* couched a gravity of insolence against racial difference in a distinctively caricaturized levity and calloused intertextuality borne of the three part recipe of: white superiority, black mockery, and racial intolerance. The *Papers*, purportedly organized by the "United Sons and Daughters for Segregation" (obviously referring to the groups of similar name devoted to preserving the Confederate cause), called for "complete segregation" (Viau, 1956, p. 1) of the 'white races.' The publication's primary aim, as was described in the May 18, 1956 issue, was "to ponder, promulgate, and propagate the true southern principles, vulture, traditions, and as many of the dear old southern customs as the law would allow. . . . [and] that we are interested in segregation but only in-so-far as it is a trusted and revered side of our southern way of life" (Morrison, 1956, p. 3). However, the mordant tone of the *Nigble Papers* was perhaps more exemplary of the ignorance and intolerance of the admonished 'Other,' and the psychosis of protecting the privileges of white discourse and white space.

The influence of the Klan and the public discourses distributed via the *Mississippian* and the *Nigble Papers*, and later the Citizens Council (during the 1950s and 1960s) and the Southern Nationalist Party maintained the episodic culture of segregation throughout the higher education system of Mississippi. Organized around visions of reinventing a supremacist South, the postbellum University of Mississippi, as well as the rest of the state's higher education institutions, remained hierarchically, as well as pheno-typically, segregated[10]—with increased opportunities for black students, but limited to all-black schools such as Alcorn College, and later Shaw, Rust, and Tougaloo. At the 'black schools' the quality of education was purposively inferior; a curricular product of systematic ideological repression cultivated around edicts such as the 1940 attempt by legislators to strip the state's black schools of any and all textbooks with reference to democratic polity, in fear black students might revolt against the white supremacist power structure (Sansing, 1990).

Alcorn and Toogaloo, the only two state-sponsored colleges in existence in the early 1900s, were specifically designed to produce graduates whose newly acquired skills were limited to agriculture. In creating separate institutional spaces, state politicians hoped the alleviate pressure from the federal government to create equal opportunities for all its citizens, while at the same time preserving the racial hierarchy within Mississippi's culture of segregation. As then Mississippi Governor James K. Vardaman proclaimed: "God Almighty intended for [the black man] to till the soil under the direction of he white man, and that is what we are going to teach him down there at Alcorn College" (quoted in R. S. Baker, 1964, p. 248). Governor Vardaman's vision of New South race relations was further postulated in his declaration that "the black man [was] a lazy, lying, lustful animal which no conceivable amount of training can transform into a tolerable citizen" (quoted in Silver, 1966, p. 19). As a consequence of Vardaman's ideologies and like-minded political leadership throughout the reconstructed New South, funding and resources allocated to black schools were well below the national average, resulting in much lower graduation rates at Mississippi's

---

10. In fact, Mississippi was the last state in the country to surrender to the Federal laws of complete desegregation.

black schools, with Tougaloo averaging only two graduates per year from 1901-1931 (Sansing, 1990).

Many white leaders in Mississippi feared that too much education for newly freed slaves might catalyze an implosion of the Old South plantation hierarchy. The more overtly racist among Mississippi's white elite disparaged the state's black men and women as "not having the ability to learn" (Cohodas, 1997, p. 14). But the more privately expressed concern was that "blacks would learn too much in school, not too little—and what they learned might make them dissatisfied and more likely to challenge the status quo" (Cohodas, 1997, p. 14). One of the University's well-regarded professors, Thomas Pierce Bailey,[11] later described the epistemological divisions of the early Twentieth Century this way: "White people want[ed] to keep the negro in his place . . . educated people have a way of making their own places and their own terms" (Bailey, 1969, p. 278). Whereas in the social strata of the antebellum Dixie South, the presence of black bodies typically reinforced the racialized power dynamic of the plantation economy, following the war, constructing the foundations of Dixie South whiteness at the University of Mississippi meant acknowledging the black bodied 'Other,' negotiating the portents of a coming 'race problem,'[12] and redefining the practices and discourses of prevailing whiteness as both physically exclusive and metaphysically superior.

New South-Old Habitus

It would be wrong to assume that the politics of exclusion, and the cultures of segregation, were confined solely to race-based ostracism and separation. In fact, the regionally-proffered critique (from the prevailing white media) of the University during the era of Reconstruction was not one of a 'race problem,' but rather one concerning the intermixing of social class groups. After the war, the University of Mississippi was infamous for being "a party school for rich kids" (Sansing, 1999, p. 175), and thereafter was regularly chided for being "a rich boys' school" (Sansing, 1999, p. 133)—reviving the sentiments of the antebellum principles upon which the institution was constructed. The Civil War had altered the state economy, and thus the University's student body. Before the war, the per capita wealth in Mississippi was higher than in any state in the Union (measured exclusively on the wealth of the states white 'citizens'). As such, before the fighting, University of Mississippi students were almost "exclusively the sons of wealthy white

---

11. Bailey also later went on to become the Speaker of the House of Representatives for the State of Mississippi.

12. Prior to the Emancipation Proclamation, there was not a 'race problem' in the most parts of the South because there was no struggle for power based on discourses of race. It was only when black men, and later black women, gained access to some of the same markers of social distinction, did the racialized 'Other' present a threat to hegemonic whiteness.

parents" (Cohodas, 1997, p. 12). However, after the war Mississippi's wealthiest students, according to the University's official catalog, were "the sons of parents who had been wealthy but whose wealth had been entirely swept away" by the Civil War (*Catalogue of the officers and students of the University of Mississippi*, 1884, p. 38).

However, what Mississippi's white aristocracy lost in economic capital during the war was soon replaced by other forms of distinction: namely what French social theorist Pierre Bourdieu (1986a) refers to as social (the social economy of who you know), cultural (the value of cultural tastes and preferences), and symbolic (representational and signified) capital. Within the remedial economy of the New South, the University's mission was to normalize and codified the codes by which these forms of capital were given currency. In the wake of war and dispossession, the University brought to life what Bourdieu (1985) might describe as formations of elite Confederate 'habitus' that could be thusly avuncularly mobilized within postbellum discourses and practices of economic, social, and political power. Bourdieu (1977) theorized the complexities of such a 'habitus' in this way:

> ... *capital* (economic, social, cultural—each of which is transferable to the other) is the source from which social status is gained, and the *field* is the complex discursive network where the exchange of capital through social relationships takes place (the transfer of capital). The habitus is the connector within the equation—the 'durably installed principle of regulated improvisations.' (p. 78)

Writing about his experiences in Twentieth Century France, Bourdieu (1986a) implicates the educational institution as a central engine for the creation and reproductive nature of class-based habitus. In the context of the New South, the project of the University of Mississippi was to create an elitist habitus whereby the student subject was instilled with seemingly natural or instinctive responsiveness to discourses of culturally, economically, and socially unique webs of power-knowledge and systems of status.

In the Reconstruction Era Dixie South and beyond, a degree from the University of Mississippi served as a signifier of New South gentility. To elide potential students of an inferior 'pedigree' from enrolling at Ole Miss, the University required "Certificates of good moral character . . . for all candidates [seeking] admission not personally known to members of the faculty, and if the candidate comes from another college this certificate must show that he was honorably discharged" ("The University of Mississippi," 1912, p. 6). Considered "the last bastion of the old aristocracy" (Sansing, 1999, p. 152), the significant voice on the Ole Miss campus during the period of Reconstruction was that of Chancellor Alfred Hume. Hume's commitment to class- and race-based separatism was perhaps surpassed by no other campus leader in the history of Southern universities. During his tenure (c. 1924-1930, 1932-1935), Hume neglected the upkeep of current buildings, rejected proposals for new structures (in spite of a qualitative need), and purposefully failed to pursue academic or athletic excellence. Instead, it was his view that the University of Mississippi should devote all its resources to creating "a citadel for the state's white elite, a place to build their moral character, the better to preserve their heritage" (Cohodas, 1997, p.

23). As such, it was during the post-depression era of Hume's regime that the University came to be known by both students and local media members as the 'University of the Old South' (Dodson, 1997).

Hume's efforts were primarily oriented toward maintaining exclusionary admission standards and committing the university's limited Depression Era resources of enhancing the cultural programs and pedagogies that would best mould the Delta's young white elite. During Hume's tenure, enrollment dwindled, which the administration cited was a result of the University's inability to board the entire student population. However, a writer for the *Port Gibson Reveille* had a different hypothesis: at a time when the wealth gap of the New South was revealing itself in turpid ways, the University's selectivity kept the enrollment low in an effort to maintain the school's "indoctrination of Mississippi's elitists" (Sansing, 1999, p. 155). The process of *ingratiation sans integration* thus excluded the 'vernacular' customs and bodies of the impoverished white South, and promote the physical, spiritual, and logical 'system of acquired schemes' to reproduce Dixieland exclusivity. Such schemes functioned as "categories of perception and appreciation, so that they act in a practical sense by organizing action as well as classification" (Mahar, 1990, p. 35). Moreover, the right to exist in that space, to obtain an education at the University of Mississippi, became an act of signification; of membership into the upper echelon of New South wealth and power. The student subject was thus *classed* and *classified*—an inheritor of both the social and cultural capital afforded by the university's closed network and of the pedagogies that they could thereby mobilize to reproduce the conditions of production which allowed Mississippi's young elite to congregate at Ole Miss in the first place.

Within Hume's University, this idealized habitus became entangled in the machinations of a closely monitored Greek system, exclusive Literary and social societies, and tight controls over admission—whereby the university became a place to learn to be wealthy and white (also see Chapter 5), to mobilize the various forms of capital accumulated upon its grounds, and to hold fast to the structures from which this status and power could be wielded. In short, the University infused a class-based Dixie South habitus onto the privileged white bodies of the Delta—a course of human activity "spontaneously inclined to recognize all the expressions in which [individuals] recognize themselves, because they are spontaneously inclined to produce them" (Bourdieu, 1996, p. 144). The well-trained, white-bodied University student subject thus understood the language of hierarchical Mississippi, and internalized the pedagogies for mapping a constellation of discursive empowerment.

Dixie Darlings

While architects of the social infrastructure of the University of Mississippi were able to maintain its elitist exclusivity and racial homogeneity throughout much of the postbellum era, in 1882 the interjection of a new 'interloper' disrupted a near half-century-long homogeneous bodily continuity of the University of Mississippi. After nearly twenty-five years of debating the issue, the Board of Trustees finally relented their position that a woman's "reasoning powers . . . can not sustain long and intricate trains of thought" (Sansing, 1999, p. 137) and 'allowed' women into the school. However, much like the foundational principles of Alcorn College in relation to black Mississippians, the liminal autonomy of the feminine student's curricular structure perhaps served to reinforce, rather than subvert, Dixie South patriarchy. In lobbying for the inclusion of women at the University, activist Sallie Eola Reneau accommodatingly proposed:

> We are not teaching women to demand the 'rights' of men nor to invade the place of men. The conditions are supplied here for the higher training of the mind, of the sensibilities of her aesthetic faculties, of the moral and religious parts of her being, which fits her for the ways of modest usefulness, for works of true benevolence, and which invests her with that true womanly character and those beautiful Christian graces that constitute her the charm of social life and the queen of the home. (quoted in Berry, 1987, p. 33)

Thus, while women gained admittance into the University, they did so under a guise of inferiority and subservience. Women students were not permitted to live in the dormitories on campus (*Catalogue of the officers and students of the University of Mississippi*, 1884). And although many women occupied desks next to their male counterparts in academy classrooms, University of Mississippi coeds were generally channeled into isolated disciplines of 'home economics,' 'needlework,' and 'spinning' (Cabaniss, 1971). Rather than equal treatment, University of Mississippi women "were to be protected, sheltered, and revered,"—translated into campus life this meant, among other things, "a curfew for female students and a dress code. Young women on their way from the dormitory or sorority house to their tennis classes, for example, were not permitted to cross the campus in shorts" (Cohodas, 1997, p. 95).

Part social concession, part economic necessity,[13] it can be argued that the admission of women into Mississippi's chambers of higher education was a matter of incursion through inclusion—transposing a masculine regime of power onto the feminine subject by bringing women into the campus space. The University limited the number of women enrollees to no more than thirty during the latter part of the 19th Century. The University hired a Dean of Women in the early part of Reconstruction to ensure the 'proper training' of newly admitted women students. With low enrollments, Ole Miss's women's academic programs were much more vocational, rather than epistemological, in those early years. The women's curriculum was largely modeled after neighboring Mississippi Industrial Institute and Col-

---

13. As Mable Newcomer (1959) observed, the "decline of enrollment combined the severity of the Civil War weakened the resistance and led to the opening of instruction to women in a number of universities during or immediately following the war" (pp. 12-13).

lege for White Girls (founded in 1885), whose founding statement of purpose read:

> The purpose and aim of the college is the moral and intellectual advancement of the white girls of the state by the maintenance of a first-class institution for their education in the arts and sciences . . . and also in fancy, general and practical needlework, and such other industrial branches as experience from time to time, shall suggest as necessary or proper to fit for the practical affairs of life. (*Sixteenth annual catalogue of the officers and students of the Industrial Institute and College of Mississippi, 1900-1901*, 1901, p. 35)

In sending their daughters to college, Conrid Berry (1987) later wrote, Mississippi parents felt the students would be taught "the proper moral, ethical, and intellectual subjects necessary to develop a cultured young woman" (p. 51).

And the gendered pedagogies of the University changed very little in the decades that followed. A report of Mississippi's public education system published in 1925 outlines the 'four objectives of education for women at the University' during the early part of the Twentieth Century were: 1) "teach every school girl how to cook and sew;" 2) to "universally . . . determine the school girl's place in society;" 3) develop "vocational efficiency;" and 4) training young women to "beautify the interior and exterior of the home" (M. O'Shea, 1925, pp. 238-241). As such, it can be argued that this institutional version of Dixie South 'emphasized femininity' (R. W. Connell, 1990) further subordinated the 'place' of women—incessantly relocating the feminine body within the domestic sphere—while repositioning masculinity at the fore of the 'public sphere.' Part domestic subject, part beguiled object, the discursive governance of Dixie South femininity located women in a pedagogical prison of second-class citizenship within these iterations of New South 'inclusivity' (Evans, 1989; Scott, 1989).

The inclusion of women into the University of Mississippi also hatched a long-standing culture of objectification within the campus space. Rather than contemplative equality, the bodies of Mississippi 'coeds' were often mediated as corporeal discourse and object of an infantilized masculine gaze. For example, the "Pretty women" competition— whereby Ole Miss men selected the 'most beautiful woman' on campus—became an "Ole Miss tradition" in 1909 (Sansing, 1999, p. 160). Beginning in 1918, the campus yearbook, the *Ole Miss*, annually celebrated the university's 'Dixie Darlings' in a section titled: 'Parade of Beauties.' William Faulkner even contributed a poem to the 'lovely ladies' of the Oxford campus in the 1920 yearbook (see Sansing, 1999, p. 160). *The Mississippian* featured a 'Coed Page' starting in the late 1930s that reported on all of the social events from the previous and advertised the upcoming activities on campus for women. In 1943, the page was renamed "Social Miss," a title more befitting the purpose of its existence. Moreover, Ole Miss students were often assumed to be attending the university not to get an education, but to 'find a good Southern man.' In describing the role of women at the University of Mississippi, the Dean of Women in the 1960s described the purported 'domestic urges' of campus women: "women often go to college expecting to find someone to marry.

Very few girls will admit this public, but in talking with girls I find it is at least in their realm of thinking" (Simmons, 1963, p. 5).

Women seen as too outspoken, or operating outside the 'campus cutie' mould, were often treated as 'suspect or unwanted' (Cohodas, 1997). As women became more centrally integrated into campus, the public concern was that co-educational environments such as the University produced 'educated women [who were] more sexual' and that they were more likely to feel "desperate and empty," because they were unfulfilled by their domestic roles upon receiving an education. Educators felt that as women learned more about the world, they would "also get false approval, which could cause problems in the marriage" (Shearer, 1963, p. 5). The prevailing ideologies about the domestic urges of women at Ole Miss, and their role in society upon graduation, became a foundational axiom upon which hegemonic masculinity could be reclaimed.

By defining the gender roles at Ole Miss, New South patriarchs were effectively able to dictate the context upon which women would construct, and perform, 'their gender.' For example, as part of the strategies for Ole Miss women set to implement their "Man trap," *The Mississippian* offered a "girl's guide to football," which detailed the strategic, yet feigned curiosity a woman must express during Rebel football games. In the article, Author Gwendolyn O'Shea (1964) directed young campus women to keep "one eye on the ball, one eye on the man, and both on the main chance" and suggested that having some knowledge about the sport would ward off any hint that "the girl is too interested in the boy" (p. 3).

In the decades following the passing of the Nineteenth Amendment—which effectively granted American women the rights of suffrage—the symbolic and pedagogical systems at work within University of Mississippi spatial discourses maintained, if not reinforced, the objectifying processes acting upon these 'ornamental women.' This mediated governmentality was brought to life in the form of *The Mississippian's* featured weekly 'campus cuties' and the campus yearbook's parade of beauties, as well as social clubs and Greek sororities which functioned for the promulgation of a contextually specific preferred femininity—and an increased emphasis on eliciting national renown for the Ole Miss 'belles' through beauty pageants and national circulars. In 1933, the University began featuring in its annual *Ole Miss* publication twenty-five "young ladies who received the most votes from the student body on the grounds of charm, beauty, personality, and popularity" ("Personnel of annual style show is released by 1934 'Ole Miss'," 1933, p. 1). A 'Style Revue' was held each fall throughout most of the Twentieth Century, whereby the 'lovely ladies' of the campus were paraded about for the voyeuristic masculine gaze. While the beauties were selected by a campus vote, such was a method of limited democracy as only male students were allowed to partake in the selection process (Russell, 1935).

The promotion of this emphasized femininity—often referred to as "the Ole Miss look" (J. Smith, 1963b, p. 7)—was further illustrated in the reverie reserved for Ole Miss women who won national recognition for their aesthetic qualities. The specters of disciplined femininity materialized in a

Magnus opus of subjected objectivity: the "Miss Ole Miss award"—the highest honor of Ole Miss womanhood. The images of Miss Ole Misses were profligately distributed throughout advertisements of local Oxford businesses, and the women became the iconic embodiments a parochial femininity. The communication of preferred femininity was but part and participle of a broader discipline of gendered subjectivity (money discipline versus bodily discipline). As a matter of considerable local pride, the University produced of three woman graduates who during their time in Oxford won the title of Miss America.[14] Further, a number of women's magazines visited the campus throughout the 1960s and 1970s to report on the famed beauty of Ole Miss coeds. *Mademoiselle*, for instance, came to the campus in the early 1960s to recruit 'talented' young women to be featured in the magazine and possibly work for the publication (Latham, 1962).

Finally, a 'Charm School' was instituted at the University to further regiment the codes of deportment and hygiene acting proscribed to campus women. This Charm School (later renamed 'Personality Development School') opened on campus in 1964, with classes in "modeling, charm, graceful walking, standing, sitting, and all the other social graces." The head of the School, Jan Nelson, posited that "femininity is a woman's greatest charm," and that the school would "analyze your assets and liabilities, eliminate the negative and accentuate the positive. Beauty is a woman's birthright. Learn the rules for perfect posture, figure poise and bodily grace, and the priceless ingredient of self-confidence" ("Charm school opens today," 1964, p. 6).

In sum, the docile, attractive, preferred femininity fostered within the confines of hierarchically gendered Dixie South ideology and strategically curved Ole Miss physicality evolved into a celebrated space of exclusivity, performativity, and [hetero]normativity. By propagating the discursive formations of emphasized femininity (and the imaginaries of 'campus cuties,' Miss Ole Miss,' and Miss Americas), crystallizing the separate spheres of Mississippi's domestic women and public men, and concretizing preferred feminine gait (Charm School), the hegemons of Ole Miss integrated the genders of the Dixie South, but most certainly on their terms.

Dixieland, Reconstructed

To summarize, during the Reconstruction Era that followed the Civil War—from the epoch which saw the emergence of the 'New South' well into the middle part of the Twentieth Century—the vigilant occupation of the Mississippi's government was to redistribute the economic and cultural wealth of its white citizenry by way of re-institutionalizing the norms of social hierarchization. To do this, lines of demarcation were drawn, in the form of *visible*, corporeal, and cultural practices and pedagogies. Under the

---

14. Mary Ann Mobley won the first Miss America for Ole Miss in 1958. Lynda Mead followed by winning the award in 1959, and Susan Akin won it a few decades later in 1985.

guise of religious entitlement, the state's political leadership mobilized a number of apparatuses to lead the reconstruction project. A principle institution in recreating this culture of segregation was the University of Mississippi, which purposively embarked on an indoctrination project which spanned the era and which circulated the ideologies of separatism and supremacy to the state's young white gentry. However, more than ideology, the demarcation of Dixie South whiteness was as a measure of symbolic fixtures—a brushstroke of physicality and pheno-typicality on a discursive canvas. The preferred text in the language of Dixie South identity politics thus became constructed out of difference—the bifurcation of a preferred white, genteel masculinity discourse situated against an oppositional (racialized, classed, and gendered) 'Other.'

In developing a preferred meaning set behind the semiotics of identity politics, the administrators and cultural intermediaries of the University transformed into administrators and arbiters of signification—embedding a preferred bodily hexis on the pliable student body. Through a rigid indoctrination project of mind (coursework, literary societies, etc.), spirit (hyper-religious tenets of university conduct), and body (muscular Christianity and the orthodoxy of a sport culture), the University became an armature of the broader body politic of the Dixie South, and the cultural practices therein became a petrified extension of the intolerance of the non-normative human subjects operating that space. One student critic from Iowa would later refer to the "ostrich-like attitude" on the Ole Miss campus, whereby the emphasis on "beauty pageants" and football games were tantamount as organizing activities and critical thought over local, regional, national, and international was negligible (Perkins, 1963). Thus, the function of Ole Miss during the era of Reconstruction was not to debate the teleological philosophies of the academy, but rather to expand the power of the visible center through self-reproducing discourses of Dixie South whiteness. Tiffany Atkinson (2005) writes that within such contexts, bodies as culture—and cultures of 'bodiliness'—are 'plunged into' the "particulars of gender, race, age posture and so forth" (p. 3).

For instance, here we might surmise that a distinctive masculinity emerged from the context of a reconstructed Dixie South, one which was a product of triplicate reincarnations of the 'Lost Cause,' the 'Southern eth(n)ic'[15] which Confederates fought to defend, and the gentility of the Old South plantation political economy. In other words, both the internalized and inseparably celebrated (ideal) articulations of intersectional masculinity and whiteness in postbellum Dixieland repositioned Ole Miss as the domain of uncontested white male hegemony—a representative polity reflective of the antebellum order of things. The residues of the Old South reconstituted the narrative structures and the social practices of this new Dixie South whiteness, one which privileged the 'traditional,' parochially mas-

---

15. I will often use the double meaning of 'eth(n)ic' to refer to the conflated logics of Southern morality and racialized politics of individuality which have come to take on an indiscernible discursive quality in the Southern popular.

culine qualities of: physical strength, safeguard from interloping aggression (in the paternal defense of the maternalized South; the South against unionization, the defense of white people against integration, and white Southern women against the newly empower black savage), and the clean-line ultimatums of economic wealth and access to distinctive forms of social capital. More empirically, the two definitive sites for expressing and performing the politics of this singular masculinity became the romanticization of the 'Lost Cause' which prompted the Civil War and the return of Mississippi's post-plantation prominence through a new forum: college football (Guttmann, 1978). More than parallel spaces of boorish catharsis, in each defenders of the Solid South came to define the solidarities and continuities of white masculine power in the logical flows of a centralized imaginary (Oriard, 1993). As the principle sites for the expression and promulgation of this imagined (and lived) white, masculine return conquest of the Dixie South, these soldiers of the Civil War and the gridiron both repudiated, and simultaneously resurrected, the hyper-masculine elocutions of an Old South whiteness and 'hegemonic masculinity' (cf. Messner, 1990). In the defense of an antiquated 'way of life,' of the politics which privileged white masculinity and the adoration of the imaged 'Southern ethic,' the University of Mississippi's posthumous and sporting combative heroes became fixtures within the symbolic economy of a re-imagined Dixie South.

Technologies of the South

"Mississippi is the decisive battleground for America. Nowhere in the world is the idea of white supremacy more firmly entrenched, or more cancerous, than in Mississippi" – Civil Rights activist Andrew Schwerner, 1964, only weeks before he was murdered in Northern Mississippi

The University of Mississippi emerged out of the post-war era as a dynamic, yet recalcitrant, cultural space; a disjunctural political and social institution at once wrestling with the changing racial politics of the US South and cultivating the backlash politics of a recoiling, hostile *white center*. As Civil Rights counter-hegemony gained momentum in Mississippi throughout the 1950s, the residues of antebellum and Reconstruction era authoritative control and corporeal apartheid—emblazoned with a fixed and stable power structure oriented toward a prevailing Dixie South whiteness—reformulated around the post-New South body pedagogics of the University (Brattain, 2001). While other universities throughout the US were integrating, what 'diversity' that did exist at Ole Miss came by way of class plurality; expressed in the narratives of a more economically-diverse Dixie South whiteness. While state and institutional strategies of the Reconstruction Era focused on reestablishing the University as a cathedral of elite whiteness for the state's genteel class, such efforts were usurped by the swell of working-class veteran enrollees following WWII and the Korean War. Like most publically funded colleges and universities at the time, the University of Mississippi experienced unprecedented mid-century expansion due to a more accessible public higher education system. In 1900, the state of Mississippi's collegiate enrollment was estimated at two percent of the college-age population; by 1950, it was nearly 15 percent. The total number of students enrolled in Mississippi higher education went from ten thousand in 1940 to seventy thousand in 1970 (D. G. Sansing, 1990).

The post-WWII enrollment boom brought on by the creation of the G.I. Bill[1] fashioned a more economically diverse white student populace at Ole Miss than had been there in generations prior. The opening of the University to a broader class-based constituency, and the reticent autonomy of the institution's newest women members, translated into an artificial condition whereby institutional affiliation signified only one final band of exclusion: that of racial homogeneity. As such, according to Nadine Cohodas (1997), the University's *final chapter of exclusion* would be one of belligerent "white supremacist orthodoxy" (p. 48)—of controlling the conditions and the discursive formations of Dixie South identity politics around an imaginary whiteness which was supremely antithetical to emergent forms of blackness. While the Civil Rights Movement was gaining momentum in many regions throughout the North as well as the South, the University became dialectically immersed in the polemics and social conjectures of the separatist cause.

As a producer of supremacist discourse, the institutional power elite's forthright mantra—demonstrated through both policy and rhetoric—was that "if the blood of our white race should become corrupted with the blood of Africa, then the present greatness of the United States of America would be destroyed and all hope for the future would be forever gone" (Silver, 1966, p. 24). Segregationist ideologies permeated all vectors of what bell hooks (2003) might refer to as the Ole Miss *white supremacist capitalist patriarchy*, as students "felt they too had a duty to protect their school and, by extension, the culture that supported it" (Cohodas, 1997, p. 34).

The initial reaction of controlling Ole Miss intermediaries to the 'threat of intermixing' was exemplified by campus leadership's refusal in January 1948 to join the National Student Association because they believed it to be a "suspiciously leftist organization, with an announced aim they found unacceptable: 'the eventual elimination of all forms of discriminatory educational systems anywhere in the United States. There can be no compromise with segregation'" (quoted in Cohodas, 1997, p. 34). This, as well as many of the instances that I offer in the pages that follow, bring into relief the

---

1. An important development for colleges during the post-war era was the provisions of the Serviceman's Readjustment Act of 1944, or what is more commonly known as the G.I. Bill. The measure set aside billions of dollars in federal aid for returning servicemen and servicewomen who wished to pursue college educations (Lucas 1994). Soldiers returning from both World War II and the Korean War took advantage of the G.I. Bill, as large numbers of veterans and military personnel enrolled in colleges and universities nationwide. The influx in student population at some major universities resulted in a need for increased campus housing, classrooms, and other facilities. One result of the G.I. Bill was that by the end of mid-1960s, more than 40 percent of all young men in America were enrolled in an institution of higher education (Jencks & Riesman 1968).

degree to which the prevailing attitude at Ole Miss in the years leading up to desegregation changed from systems of conformity, sovereignty, and homogeneity to *resistance* and [self-]*persecution*; resistance to Federal intervention on local social inequities based on race, and a mentality of persecution organized around the self-victimization of 'retaliatory' equalizing measures. Importantly, within this context distinctive, localized "new technologies of the self" (Foucault, 1988a, p. 45)[2] for Mississippi's white power elite were thus organized around, identified as, and authorized through a symbolic and hyperbolic 'autonomous state' of monolithic whiteness. In other words, I follow Foucault in rethinking how the Southern white 'self' was constituted within the context of the Civil Rights South—and interrogate the methods and techniques by which individuals and groups constituted themselves under the body pedagogics of white supremacy. In this way, the relationship between pedagogy and the body becomes powerful; in that "all knowledge is body-mediated, . . . all learning is primarily somatic" and thus "the act of knowing is largely a form of corporeal shaping" (McLaren, 1999, p. x).

I argue that much like Michel Foucault's notion of 'technologies of the self,' these contextually-specific *technologies of the South* produced subjects and subject positions.[3] Foucault's concept of 'technologies of the self' concerns 1) the relations between the self and other self(s), 2) the links between the self and the society upon which that self-hood is created, and most importantly, 3) the processes by which the individual self is subjected to, and simultaneously understood through, the structures of power and knowledge that frame the 'truths' within those subjective relations. In such an order, those subjects dialectically [re-]produce the discursive formations of which the subject is only one part. My purpose here then is not to deviate from Foucault's metaphysics, but rather to suggest that in the spirit of radical-contextualism, the Civil Rights Era US South offers an important, and unique, set of social and structural formations upon which the subject is dialectically bound. As I illustrate in what follows, those macrological 'truths' of Civil Rights subjectivity emerge out of the intersection of (binary, scientific) race-based techniques of order[ing] and representations of selfness incontrovertibly ensconced in the *langue* of difference; and thus any

---

2. Near the end of his intellectual career, Michel Foucault re-conceptualized his notion of 'technologies of the self' toward a more structurally-determined interpretation of the ways in which institutional forces capture the discursive imaginations of the individual. My use of the term here is a slight reprise from my use of the term in Chapter Two, oriented more toward Foucault's later formulation, whereby the collectiveness of a resistive whiteness interpellated the agents acting within this context. In other words, the normative nature of segregationist ideologies transposed onto Southern white bodies acted in this context as a means for expressing and promoting racist politics with the collective and individualized politics of the individual.

3. Foucault's definition of subject position highlights the productive nature of disciplinary power—how it names and categorizes people into hierarchies (of normalcy, health, morality, etc.).

readings of cultural anatomy and agency thereof can only be understood as participle of the histories and systems of governance operating therein.

At Ole Miss, whiteness came to be defined not only by the axioms of social praxis within the economically-disparate white Dixie South, but also as a 'new' collective *meme* of 'obedience' and 'sacrifice' (Foucault, 1988) for the sake of maintaining and reproducing the prevailing race-based social hierarchy. Ironically, the discursive formation of white resistance, or what might be referred to as the new discursive technologies of the [resistive Civil Rights Era, white] South, became the rudimentary and fundamentally inalterable inspiration upon which segregationist avocations were organized during, and unfortunately long after, the heights of the Civil Rights Movement. As such, these new technologies of the self—and the hierarchical structures which identity politics were constituted out of during the Reconstruction Era and beyond—came to look very much like those which preceded. A slight reprise from the Old South technologies of the representative self, the new Southern politics of representation located power in the discursive and physical boundaries of the visible center and located the individual within the collective imaginary of an oppressive cultural economy.

The Second Reconstruction

It would be hard to argue that the materializations of the Civil Rights Movement brought about a sea change in the paradigmatic and lived experiences of both white and black Dixie Southerners. Rather, the racialized 'body/subject' became the site of inter-subjective exchange; what Merleau Ponty (1968) describes as the 'threshold of experience.' The mid-Century stridency of Southern blackness meant the dissipation of a long residual equation of productive black bodies rendering white social, cultural, and economic capital (hooks, 1992). An intensified Civil Rights Movement brought about an emergent, contested 'political anatomy' of a Dixie South cultural economy—one which disrupted the continuities of the existing white body politic as hegemonic political discourse. As black bodies began infiltrating the 'clean edifice of white supremacy' (Gilroy, 2005) during the Civil Rights Movement—a movement that riot police, attack dogs, and fire hoses could not wash away—the corporeal canvas of Dixie South identity politics, and the power-knowledge hierarchy imbedded therein, was for the first time contested and contestable (Stowe, 1996). Though the discursive formation of whiteness had stood unopposed prior to the Civil War, and as a visible, monolithic center of identification and representational power during the first half of the Twentieth Century, the hegemony of identity and culture within the Dixie South was now contested (Skerrett, 2002).

However, for Mississippi traditionalists, rather than acknowledging the iniquitous realities of Mississippi's longitudinal racial hierarchy and negotiating the identity politics of the emergent 'Other,' there could be "no real debate on issues [of race] for the *there was no issue beyond the supremacy of the white man*" (Silver, 1966, p. 20, author's italics). As such, rather than framing the Movement as the accumulated inevitability in the shift toward equal human rights, the arbiters of Mississippi's 'closed society' disengaged the idioms of broader Civil Rights Era cultural and political economies by: 1) reformulating racist binaries in a logic of scientific discourse; 2) rearticulating the separatist *modus operandi* within a vernacular of 'Federal intrusion on states' rights'; 3) juxtaposing the suffering endured by many Southern blacks onto a newly self-victimizing whiteness through the rhetoric of advantageous integration; and 4) cordoning off and preserving distinctively white spaces and practices of privilege through the racist signifiers (and signification) of a collective Southern traditionalism. Through these dual practices of *authorization* and *spectacularization*, the political kinesis of preferred Dixie South whiteness was thus further made visible to white and black Mississippians, as well as spectators outside the realm of Dixie (W. C. Ayers, 1997).

Ipso Facto Body Science

The first *pièce de résistance* in the cornucopia of defensive dealings to preserve the hierarchical centrality of whiteness in the Dixie South came by way of an emergent scientific discourse on 'race' and 'natural' physiological and biological difference (Shuey, 1958). During the Civil Rights Era, leaders of Southern states authorized a lengthy 'racial study' which explained that structural differences in the brain caused "Negro inferiority" and concluded that "the Negro had smaller frontal lobes than the whites" ("Racial study completed," 1962, p. 1). The report stated that differences in brain structure existed because the Negro was "200,000 years behind the white man. The developed mental retardation suggested by the structural differences is confirmed by recent discoveries of fossil man indicating that the Negro is about 200,000 years behind the white race" ("Racial study completed," 1962, p. 1). The 'scientific data' rendered for this 'sociobiological' (Shilling, 2003) analysis was actually based on the records of racially-coded individuals inducted into the armed services in the first and second World Wars and from elementary and high school aptitude tests—each of which reflected the educational and cultural experiences of black and white individuals rather than biologically or genetically determined difference, as the study had concluded. The flawed logic of the study evaded the skeptical gaze of the Southern scientific community, and instead became the 'evidence' by which the specters of Jim Crow segregation were perpetuated.

As an ideological apparatus for the imagined post-Confederate state, the public education system of Mississippi surfaced as a *principal* medium by which scientific racism was conjured up, legitimated, and indoctrinated in the body pedagogic sphere (Irons, 2004). The educational system of Mississippi promoted a culture of segregation and white supremacy through a 'scientific pedagogy' of intolerance—a state-sponsored rhetorical campaign which started with Mississippi's elementary programs and continued through the University and into the public sphere. As an example of the political divisiveness of segregationist schooling, Mississippi's fifth and sixth grade children were required to read a state-produced manual on 'race relations,' by which a pseudo-scientific discourse of racist ideology was perpetuated in excerpts such as:

> No other part of the United States is more American than the South. America was built by white men. King George wanted his merchants to make money. So the Americans were made to buy Negro slaves. Americans did not want slaves. Americans never did like slavery. They would like to have helped the Negro build his own country. The Negro is happy among his own race, but two races feel strange around each other. Russia has white slaves today. . . . The Negro is not just a sun-burned white man. Famous scientists say races are very different. The white man is very civilized, while the pure Negro in Africa is still living as a savage. (quoted in Silver, 1966, p. 68)

By the early 1960s, students entering the state's institutions of higher education such as Ole Miss had been subjected to the scientific theory that postulated: "When races are mixed in school, the white children do not get as much education as they usually get. The whites have to wait for the Negroes to catch up" (quoted in Silver, 1966, p. 69).

The injudicious science of racial inferiority penetrated the University of Mississippi through a number of treatises on inherent white supremacy. On the Ole Miss campus, a publication distributed across campus, *Instauration,* featured a 'scientific analysis' of theories of race and intelligence by 'expert commentator' Henry E. Garrett, whereby the professor argued that intellect was determined by genetics, and "Black and white children do *not* have the same potential. They do *not* learn at the same rate. Environment is *not* the sole—or even the major—cause of underachievement" (Garrett, 1973, p. 5). James Silver contended that as a vessel for the state, Ole Miss became an instrument of totalitarianism which "imposed on all its people acceptance of an obedience to an official orthodoxy" (quoted in J. Smith, 1963a, p. 4). In a supplementary section to *The Mississippian* titled "The Rebel," Ole Miss Anthropology Professor Robert Rands expounded on the theories of race and reason by positing that the "backwardness of African culture [was] proof that the Negro was inferior to the white" (Rands, 1963, p. 4). Rands (1963) further argued upon his thesis by promoting the notions of 'plasticity' and 'inelasticy,' or the inability of Negro Africa to change in response to a cultural environment.[4]

These are but a few samples of a pervasive racist bio-science that plagued the mid-Century Ole Miss campus. The racist 'bio-power' of the academy stretched beyond the classrooms and newspapers of the Oxford campus and into the public sphere, as Rands and a number of his colleagues in the 'natural sciences' offered 'expert' opinion of natural racial superiority in many of Mississippi's legislative and media outlets (Cabaniss, 1971). This localized, hyper-racist body 'science' expanded upon existing logics of Social

4.Rands and his colleagues within the scientific community at Ole Miss often referred to Herbert Spencer's notion of social Darwinism to distort the realities of racialized experiences within the Delta South (Cabaniss, 1971).

Darwinism popularized by scientific racists of the 20th Century (Garrett, 1964; Kilpatrick, 1962; R. T. Osborne, 1960). Echoing the affective logics of Carolis Linnaeus from more than two centuries earlier, the 'scientific' articulations made use of racial categorization to further authorize prevailing white supremacist ideology and the anti-pluralist technologies of Dixie South identity politics—thus resulting in a delineated racial classification system based on examinable phenotypical dissimilarities and stereotyped cultural qualities thereof (Gregor, 1961).

The Dixiecrat Prologue

Much like the forays into the hyper-racist scientific discourse of the Civil Rights Era, Ole Miss students and faculty were subjected to racialized ideo-scapes of the political sphere during the lead-up to the Civil Rights Movement. As prologue to integration, perhaps the occurrence which best illuminates the didacticism of the Dixie South separatist cause—and the close proximity of the prevailing Ole Miss attitude to that cause—occurred during the lead-up to the 1948 Presidential election. After the Democratic Party adopted an unyielding civil rights platform and nominated Harry Truman as its presidential candidate at the Philadelphia convention in July of 1948, Southern delegates abandoned the party and reconvened in Birmingham, Alabama. In Birmingham, the separatist bloc formed the States' Rights Democratic Party (the Dixiecrats) and nominated South Carolina Senator J. Strom Thurmond for President and Mississippi Governor Fielding L. Wright for Vice-President (Frederickson, 2001). The catalyst and dividing principle between Dixiecrats and northern Democrats was the conservative South's motivation to restore a public polity and popular discourse "in the interest of white supremacy" (Sansing, 1999, p. 132). While in most Southern states secession from the Democratic Party was a gesture of only the most radical of separatists, in Mississippi the "color line was drawn . . . and membership in the [Southern] Democratic Party was expected of all white Mississippians" (Sansing, 1999, p. 132).

When word of the splintering faction reached the Ole Miss campus in the second week of July, numerous Ole Miss students immediately set-out in an eleven-car caravan to attend the separatists' convention (Frederickson, 2000). Their 'exuberance' for the Dixiecrats' cause became the stuff of both infamy and legend—leaving an indelible mark on the discourses of Southern mid-century politics and the University. Media accounts of the event reported that upon arriving to the convention site, Ole Miss students exultantly marched into the convention hall waving a large Confederate flag and wearing Confederate-style hats (Dubois, 1948).[5] Upon their return, Ole Miss students organized the 'Ole Miss State's Rights Democratic Association,' electing Rebel quarterback John "Buddy" Bowen as the chairman of the organization. Bowen publicly praised the efforts of Ole Miss students a week prior in Birmingham, stating:

> Never have I been prouder of Ole Miss than last Saturday at Birmingham when I saw a splendid group representing our great University. Your presence at this meeting was inspiring to me and every other Mississippian, and, I am sure, others participating in that all important and historic convention. When I witnessed the enthusiasm displayed by you Ole Miss students and the display and orderly manner in which you conducted yourselves, way (sic) I repeat, it was most inspiring and encouraging to know that our young men of today, our leaders of tomorrow, are so awake, patriotic and determined to stand by our cause and fight for fundamental principles of American government. ("Campus States' Righters elect Bowen as leader," 1948, p. 4)

Modeled after Dixiecrat edicts created a few weeks earlier, the Ole Miss States' Rights organization adopted eight 'guiding principles.' The first three resolutions dealt with their intentions to preserve and uphold the constitutionality of states' rights. The final two resolutions returned to issue of autonomous local governance. The fourth, fifth, and sixth resolutions, cited below, perhaps most clearly illustrate the segregationist politics at Ole Miss—and the importance of maintaining the status quo in order to uphold the prevailing 'social, economic, and political life of Southern people':

4. We stand for the segregation of the races and racial integrity of each race; the constitutional right to choose one's associations; to accept private employment, without governmental interference, and to earn one's living in any lawful way. We oppose the elimination of segregation, employment by federal bureaucrats called for by the misnamed civil rights program. We favor home rule, local self-government and a minimum interference with individual rights.
5. We oppose and condemn the action of the Democratic convention in sponsoring a civil rights program calling for the elimination of segregation, social equality and federal fiat, regulation of private employment practices, voting and local law enforcement.
6. We affirm that the effective enforcement of such a program would be utterly destructive of the social, economic, and political life of Southern people, and of other localities in which there may be differences in race, creed or national origin in appreciable numbers. (Sweat, 1948, p. 2)

Interestingly, though in reality dealing in the linguistic currency of an 'artificial construct' (Lopez, 1998), campus leaders repeatedly returned to the 'hard science' of racial difference, and the rhetoric of 'scientific evidence' to support the segregation and prevent the 'miscegenation' of Mississippi's various races. And while it would be imprudent to generalize that the white

---

5.Details of the Ole Miss student role in the events at the States' Rights Party Convention have been disputed, but the possession of Confederate garb and flags is evidenced in archival photos at the University of Mississippi. The students did take the flags into the convention, and were photographed with the Governor of Mississippi in Confederate hats with a large Confederate flag as the backdrop.

supremacist position of the Ole Miss States' Rights organization was representative of the entire campus populace, a campus poll suggested that *twelve out of every thirteen* students on the Oxford campus favored the Dixiecrat cause, and the "defense of white supremacy" throughout the South (Turnage, 1948, p. 4).

Indeed many Ole Miss students held fast to the appendages of Old South polity embroiled by the Dixiecrats, and political leaders of the state in turn invested significant resources in maintaining the University's centralizing function during the early part of the Civil Rights Era. White Mississippi's power elite viewed the seemingly inevitable transformation, not as an outcome of historical shifts, but rather a criminal conspiracy against the South's "sanctified institutions" (Silver, 1966, p. 3). Constructed to educate Mississippi's young white elite, the University had become the central artery for the flow of hegemonic whiteness and hyper-racist ideologies in the state—both the inward flow of authoritarian control from the capital in Jackson and the outward flow of graduates into the white controlled territories of industry, commerce, religion, and education. In the case of the former, the state and its monolithic ideological vision actively meddled in the affairs of the University. By the late 1950s, state leaders began reconstructing and re-centering the symbolic and material institutionalism of the University program around new formulations of Civil Rights Era white orthodoxy.

With the residues of Dixiecrat fervor still shaping the political activities in Jackson, and in an attempt to preserve the all-white status of their sanctified institution, the Mississippi Senate and House of Representatives concurrently passed a resolution on February 29, 1956, stating "The State of Mississippi declares emphatically that the sovereign states of the Nation have never surrendered their rights and powers to control their public schools, colleges and other public institutions." Therefore, the legislators continued, "when an attempt is made to usurp these powers, the people of Mississippi object and refuse to be so deprived, reminding the Congress that the preservation of the Union of States, as the compact intended it should be, depends upon the preservation of the sovereignty of states" ("State of Mississippi; House and Senate Concurrent Resolution," 1956, p. 3). State Representative Edwin White of the States Rights Democratic party, speaking to his constituents during the heights of the Civil Rights moment, redefined the 'bedrock principles' of the state's flagship of whiteness (Ole Miss) this way:

1. A belief in God, the accuracy of the Bible, and the immortality of souls.
2. The sovereignty of states and their right, among other powers, to operate public schools and regulate marriage, and the primacy of the Constitution over the Supreme Court.
3. A belief in the ethnological truth that where races of different color mix with each other socially that inter-marriage inevitably results and that we have the obligation, and the inalienable right to preserve the identity of the white race.

4. The right of private ownership of property and "the right to profitably engage in private enterprise" (Silver, 1984, pp. 66-67)

The cause of segregation and the activities of the University had become so indivisible by the early part of the 1960s that many commentators began to refer to Ole Miss as the 'University of the Old South.' Against the threat of government imposed integration, and to conserve and promote the 'ethnological truths' etched in the fabric of Ole Miss culture, Mississippi's state legislative bodies, on a number of occasions, proposed to privatize Ole Miss—and thus proactively subvert forthcoming federal integration laws.[6] The all-white student population held rallies in support of segregation through privatization, and a number of local and state segregationist organizations relocated their effort to Oxford in an attempt to marshal the escalating groundswell of support in the area. Through public demonstrations, sign-adorning shop windows in the Square, and other remonstrations of lynch mob activism, one thing was becoming clear: Ole Miss would not let the politics of the Jim Crow South go quietly into the good night (Sansing, 1999).

Whiteness, Interrupted

Everything changed for Ole Miss in 1962. The active creation of disciplined, white student subjects and the quest for embodiments of a preferred, hypermasculine Southern ethos during the Civil Rights moment brought forth numerous challenges to the unyielding political project of the University. At Ole Miss, the fluidity of a draconian 'Southern ethic' became unsettled, if not fundamentally altered, by challenges to white normativity and the interjection of black bodies in the exclusively white space. Nearly one hundred years after the Emancipation Proclamation, the uncontested corporeal exclusivity on the University of Mississippi campus evaporated in an instant. In the fall of 1962, white Dixie Southerners at the University—and particularly the traditionalists on campus—were forced to acknowledge, and contend with the physical existence of a black-bodied 'Other' within the all-white campus preserve.

If, as James Silver (1966) argued, the all-pervading doctrine of the University up to that point had been "white supremacy . . . achieved through slavery or segregation [and] rationalized by a professed belief in state rights and bolstered by religious fundamentalism" (p. 6), then the social recourses of the equal rights pursuits of James Meredith served to dissolve such a pre-

---

6.Interestingly, the state of Mississippi still has more registered Democratic voters than Republican voters (although the trend is a slow migration to the new Right), although the Presidential election and most local elections fall to Republicans. This in part due to the changing nature of the Democratic Party in mid-century toward a Civil Rights platform. When "the Democratic Party was becoming the party of blacks," says veteran Mississippi journalist Bill Minor, "the whites switched" (qtd. in Weeks, 1999, p. C1).

vailing racial fundamentalism. Meredith's black body in theretofore exclusively white educational space meant that Ole Miss traditionalists would be forced to confront the fissuring possibilities of a new Dixie South power structure. For many, paraphrasing Paul Gilroy (2004), the infra-human body of the would-be black interloper, rather than the body of the sovereign white Southerner, more acutely [re]presented the discomforting ambiguities of the Dixie South's painful and shameful history. Since much of the status and wealth which impelled the institutional propagation of hegemonic whiteness evolved from the circulation of 'old money'—or familial social economics—and cultural capital accumulated during the heights of plantation prosperity, the prospect that ancestors of former black slaves and sharecroppers would now be operating in the same social spaces as affluent white students (whose wealth was directly related to the former's historical oppression) became more than disconcerting for Ole Miss's controlling power elite. To flip Brian Fay's (1987) argument slightly upside-down, we might say that oppression leaves its traces not just on the muscles and skeletons of the sufferers, but also on their minds (p. 146).

One other attempt had been made by a black individual seeking admission into the University prior to James Meredith's enrollment in the University in Mississippi in 1962. The first effort to integrate the University of Mississippi came in 1958 when Clennon King, a one-time professor at Alcorn College, notified the Executive Secretary of the Board of Trustees that he planned to apply for admission into the Law School on June 5 of that year (Lord, 1965). When King arrived at the Lyceum to register, he was taken to a 'holding room' where he was left alone for several hours. Fearing that he was in physical danger, King began shouting for help and pleading for someone to save him. When the Governor—who had stationed himself in nearby Batesville in preparation for the event—was made aware of King's desperate pleas, "Help! Help! They are going to kill me!" (quoted in Sansing, 1999, p. 277), he instructed the highway patrol to take King to Jackson for 'psychological examination,' at which point he was declared 'insane' and committed to the state's mental institution (Lord, 1965).

After King's enrollment attempt, University officials installed a comprehensive plan of action to curtail 'Negro enrollment.' It became common practice at Ole Miss in the late-1950s and early-1960s to arrange for eight guards to be stationed outside the Lyceum at the beginning of each semester with orders to escort any dark-skinned individual attempting to register off the campus. In spite of these exertions and many others on the Oxford campus, as well as the legislative attempts in Jackson to thwart the enrollment of a black student into the state's flagship university, the definitive flashpoint in the history of the University of Mississippi's race relations came on January 21, 1961, twenty-four hours after the inauguration of President John F. Kennedy.

On that date a black Mississippian, James Howard Meredith, submitted the preliminary application materials to the University. Meredith, who was fully aware of the magnitude and revolutionary consequences of his endeavor, chose the University of Mississippi specifically in an attempt to disrupt the educational hierarchies in the heart of the Dixie South. In a let-ter to Thurgood Marshall of the Legal Defense Fund (who later became the first black US Supreme Court Justice) describing his plan to enroll at—and transfer credits earned at the University of Maryland and Jackson State College to—the University of Mississippi, Meredith proclaimed that he had always been a "conscientious objector" to his "oppressed status," and concluded by exulting that he was making this move in the "interest of and the benefit of: (1) my country, (2) my race, (3) my family, and (4) my-self" (J. Meredith, 1966, p. 56). Upon receiving his application materials, Ole Miss administrators created a series of obstacles to subvert and pro-scribe Meredith's admission. First, the Board of Trustees increased the re-quisite of two letters from responsible citizens to five—all of whom had to be white. Second, the University's Registrar, Robert B. Ellis, dismissed Meredith's application on the grounds that he inaccurately declared his county of residence—a selective interpretation which suggested that Meredith demonstrated malfeasance on his state voter registration inform-ation because he declared himself a resident of the county he lived rather than a county in which he owned property (R. H. Barrett, 1965).

These initial responses to Meredith's application, according to Nadine Cohodas (1997), were indicative of the 'racial caste system' abounding throughout Mississippi politics and education through the middle of the 20th Century. To further obstruct Meredith's pursuit of equal rights in higher education, the state legislature put into law a provision whereby any person 'who has a crime of moral turpitude against him' was not permit-ted to enrollment in any state institution (Meredith, 1966). The terms of this law allowed those convicted of manslaughter by way of drunk driving to enroll, but 'crimes' such as registering to vote in one's home county, not where one owns land, were seen as warranting proscription (Barrett, 1965). A local judge immediately put the plan into action, sentencing Meredith to one year in the county jail and $100 in fines for false voter registration in Hinds County—an extraordinarily long sentence for the alleged violation (Barrett, 1965).

With help from legal council appointed by the NAACP,[7] Meredith was able to circumvent the sentence for falsification on his voter registration and resume his pursuits for an education at Ole Miss. However, during the summer of 1962, Registrar Ellis, working as a minion of the Board of Trust-ees, launched a sharp and divisive muckraking campaign which depicted Meredith in the popular press as a 'troublemaker,' arguing his character was the sole determinant for denial of admission, and that his "race or color had no influence on the decisions" (Lord, 1965, p. 111) made by the University to block the black man's entrance. Circuit Judge Sydney C. Mize buttressed

---

7. Meredith's cause was greatly aided by the efforts of Constance Baker Motley. As a prominent civil rights attorney, Motley won nine of the ten cases she argued before the U.S. Supreme Court, including the 1962 case in which James Meredith won ad-mission to the University of Mississippi. In 1966 she became the first black woman to become a federal judge.

the University's position on Meredith's enrollment when, in delivering his opinion on the matter of Meredith's admission, he countenanced that the "proof shows, and I find as a fact, that the University is not a racially segregated institution. . . . Plaintiff [Meredith] was not denied admission because of his race" (Meredith, 1966, p. 133-134). Mize's ruling was twice overturned in appellate courts, with each ruling accompanied by scathing opinions referring to Judge Mize as 'obtuse' and citing the University's unwillingness to abide by the *Brown versus Board of Education* decision as unacceptable.

While the court cases were jostling back and forth between Oxford and Jackson, Governor Ross Barnett was beginning his crusade of public opinion through mediums such as popular Jackson newspapers and local television. In a television appearance on September 13, Governor Barnett vehemently proclaimed "We will not surrender to the evil and illegal forces of tyranny . . . No school will be integrated in Mississippi while I am your governor" and called upon the doctrine of interposition to blockade any Federal intervention in what he viewed to be 'Mississippi's problem' ("We will not surrender," 1962, p. 1).

As the fall semester approached, the meditation of state-sponsored resistance to the enrollment of James Meredith at the University of Mississippi quickened. The power of Mississippi's body politic, and the white hegemons which the order of things served, was perceived to be under siege from Federal imperatives to interject in what traditionalists and separatists perceived to be the state of Mississippi's issue. The overriding voice in the effort to assail the black interloper was that of Governor Barnett, who maintained that "It [was] against the public policy of the State of Mississippi as well as its laws for any colored person to be admitted as a student to said institution and his [Meredith's] enrollment and entry therein would be in direct violation of the laws of the State of Mississippi" (quoted in Barrett, 1965, p. 106). Many political leaders of the state viewed Meredith's attempts to desegregate Ole Miss as the catalyst to a broader compliance of Federal mandate for equal rights in government, business, religion, and other social spheres. Furthermore, a growing faction positioned the attempts by Civil Rights activists to gain equal access to the state's education institutions as a signal of the forthcoming plight of Mississippi's white race, arguing that the 'injustices' *they were about to experience* were equal to, or even more unjust than, those they had historically imposed (E. B. Brown, 2000).

The earliest attempts to physically integrate Ole Miss came during the first enrollment session of the fall semester of 1962. James Meredith arrived on the Oxford campus just before 5 P.M. on September 20 to a chorus of jeers and epithets from students and white Oxford residents—chanting such as anthems as "We want Ross" and such scurrilous appellations as "Go home nigger". Interestingly, the most oft-recurring chant during the demonstration was the Ole Miss sporting fight song:

Hotty toddy, God A'mighty
Who in the hell are we,
Flim flam, bim bam,

Ole Miss, by damn!

Both a symbol of pride and resistance, the Ole Miss fight song, most often evoked during home football contests, served as a spoken marker of obfuscated detritus and cohesive congregation within the all-white imagined and physical space. The song was fulminated to create a climate of vigilantism for the imagined white South, and of intimidation for the unwanted black 'intruder,' while at the same time serving as a technology of collective identity—a symbol of prideful scorn, and of scornful pride.[8] Upon his arrival, Meredith was instantly turned away from the University Continuation Center; with Governor Barnett emerging from the building shortly thereafter and triumphantly inveighing: "The only comment I have to make is that the application of James H. Meredith has been denied," which incited a celebratory roar from the fervent throng (Barrett, 1965, p. 108).

The Editor of the *Mississippian*, Sidna Brower, watched the racial tensions on the Ole Miss campus fester day-by-day in late September, 1962; chronicling the events in the student newspaper, and offering a voice of forlorn detraction along the way. In the September 21 issue, Brower extolled a group of Ole Miss students for their efforts in thwarting the attempts of an "angry thong" gathered near the Circle to replace the American flag with the Confederate flag (Brower, 1962a, p. 2). However, the peaceful, albeit scornful, exhibition of racist resistance on September 20th was supplanted by a more vicious and forceful version upon James Meredith's return to Ole Miss a few days later. On September 26, Meredith was escorted onto the Ole Miss campus by Federal marshals, only to be physically turned away Lieutenant Governor Paul Johnson and a band of local officials (Brower, 1962b).

One of the more important[9] occasions in the series of events in the fall of 1962 came three days later during a football game in Jackson between Ole Miss and the University of Kentucky on September 29. For white Mississippians, in this moment of hegemonic uneasiness, football became the conduit which linked ideology and spirit to practices of the bigoted folderol. As Derek Catsam (2003) later postulated, "during the Ole Miss crisis, football served as a sort of white supremacist anchor, mooring white supremacy with the values that too many white southerners held dear." (p. 1). He continued "Ole Miss, it was famously said, used to be known for three things: A rambunctious style of campus politics dominated by equally boisterous fraternities and sororities; Beauty Queens—Ole Miss used to redshirt Miss Americas; and football" (Catsam, 2003, p. 1).

The sporting spectacle of defiant whiteness thus took form on that fall afternoon, as the stadium in Jackson was "a sea of Confederate flags that

---

8. Chapter Seven will offer a more in-depth analysis of the symbols of the Confederacy acting upon the Ole Miss body politic.

9. Coach Jon Vaught would later title a chapter in his memoirs "Football Saves a School" in retelling the impact the game had on the 'crisis' at Ole Miss in the fall of 1962. The 1962 team did outperform any before and any since, going undefeated and untied in winning the National Championship.

were waved with special defiance during the playing of the national anthem" (Cohodas, 1997, p. 83). At halftime, to a chorus of "we want Ross" (Brower, 1962c, p. 1), Governor Barnett appeared to a mid-field stump post, and roared through the loudspeaker "I love Mississippi. I love her people—her customs! And I love and respect her heritage" (Barrett, 1965, p. 121). The response, which Russell Barrett likened to Nazi rallies from three decade prior, was both boisterous and energetic ("Defiant Barnett hailed at game," 1962). The crowd then joined in a (retrospectively prophetic) disobedient ditty, one which stood in direct violation of court orders:

Never, Never, Never, No-o-o Never, Never Never

We will not yield an inch of any field,

Fix us another toddy, ain't yieldin' to nobody

Ross's standin' like Gibraltar, he shall never falter

Ask us what we say, it's to hell with Bobby K,

Never shall our emblem go from Colonel Reb to Old Black Joe

The racist, symbolic, yet triumphantly obstinate dialogue between Barnett and the game's attendees during that intercollegiate football contest matriculated into a material, physically violent confrontation on the Ole Miss campus the following day (W. Doyle, 2001).

In one of the more hellish convulsions of the US Civil Rights Era, the University of Mississippi campus was turned into a battlefield on the night of September 30th. James Meredith was scheduled to arrive on the Oxford campus that evening, and register for classes the following day. Following a series of non-concessionary exchanges between Governor Barnett and then Attorney General Robert Kennedy, in which Barnett failed to assure the Attorney General that Meredith would be safely escorted into the University by state officials, Federal troops were ordered to secure the university space for Meredith's arrival (W. Doyle, 2001).

At the urging of General Edwin Walker—who had been an important figure in the integration efforts at Central High School in Little Rock, Arkansas five years earlier—hundreds of angry white traditionalists descended upon Oxford to figuratively, and eventually physically, confront the efforts by Federal marshals to integrate Ole Miss. From his command post near the monument to the Confederate war dead, Walker implored the riotous mob to remain rancorous in their protest. The initial "boisterousness" of the protesters included chants such as: "Why don't you go to Cuba, nigger lovers?" and signage that read "Yankee Go Home" (Humber, 1962, p. 1). However, as Governor Barnett was appearing on local television early that night to preach what amounted to defiant acquiescence (per the results of a threatening dialogue between he and President Kennedy), the campus mood turned more violent, as the Ole Miss grounds became "awash in gunshots and flames and then shrouded in tear gas, fired as a protective measure by the outnumbered [federal] marshals" (Cohodas, 1997, p. 85). The report of the incident by *Time* magazine read as follows:

> The crowd in front of the Lyceum had grown bigger and uglier. First it turned on newsmen in a face-punching, camera-smashing frenzy . . . Eggs came flying toward the marshals, then rocks. Out of a gathering darkness hurled the length of a metal pipe . . . When a group of students drove the campus fire truck up close and loosed a stream of water at the Lyceum, a band of marshals charged the truck. . . . Around 11 p.m., the attackers brought up a bulldozer, attempted to batter their way into the Lyceum. ("Though the heavens fall," 1962, p. 20)

As the campus was soaked with hostility and bloodshed, student and non-student vigilantes—who later likened themselves to Hungarian freedom fighters—charged through the tear gas fired by Federal marshals and hurled Molotov Cocktails, brickbats, and lead pipes at the officers (Silver, 1966). In what one observer exclaimed to be an "echo of the Civil War's last battle" (quoted in Sansing, 1999, p. 303), a number of automobiles were set ablaze, and by the time the violence had subsided, two individuals had been fatally wounded (Doyle, 2001). Whereas *Mississippian* Editor Sidna Brower was satisfied with the behavior of most students on September 20, she was embarrassed, if not mortified, by the insurgents "who started out yesterday by shouting slogans of pride in Mississippi and ended up with nothing to be proud of" (Brower, 1962d, p. 2).

A number of reports out of Mississippi in the weeks following September 30, 1962 suggested that the Federal marshals had 'incited' violence in what would have otherwise been a peaceful protest. This claim was debunked by members of the University of Mississippi chapter of the American Association for University Professors, who unanimously signed into resolution a declaration stating that while "some news media in Mississippi [had] entertained irresponsible and second-hand stories in distortion of the facts . . . [and attempts] to place all the blame for the riot on the United States marshals, [such reports were] not only unfair and reprehensible, but also completely false" ("Profs sign statement on recent happenings," 1962, p. 1).

Despite the violent efforts by segregationists on that late September night, James Meredith began his studies at the University of Mississippi a few days later. The existence of Meredith's black body within the homogenous campus space which had been preserved for Mississippi's white elite signaled a turning point in Mississippi's racially-encoded educational hierarchy. Interrupting the "unity of discourse" (Foucault, 1976, p. 32) within the racist educational power dynamic of Mississippi, Meredith's black body as corporeal signifier disrupted the universality of whiteness within the spaces of privilege in Mississippi's flagship university.

James Meredith's *entrée* into Ole Miss was a significant moment in the Civil Rights Movement—part of a larger contentious conjuncture of racist white social conservative ideologies and an emerging black empowerment in the South. Numerous instances during the time span of Meredith's enrollment contributed to a bellicose atmosphere in the US South. In 1963 in Birmingham, Alabama, Police Commissioner Eugene "Bull" Connor violently employed the use of water hoses and dogs against civil rights protesters, many of whom were children, to thwart a 'civil uprising' in that state (Eskew, 1997). On June 11, 1963, Medgar Evers, Civil Rights advocate and close friend to James Meredith, was shot and killed in Mississippi (Sessions, 1963). In spite of these setbacks, the Civil Rights Movement gained momentum, and reached its climax in August 1963 with a massive march on Washington, D.C.—as Martin Luther King, Jr. led activists in a protest of racial discrimination and demonstration supporting major civil rights legislation that was pending in Congress (Klarman, 2004).

In early June 1964, a busload of black Mississippians went to Washington, D.C., to testify publicly about the daily violence and the dangers facing the volunteers coming into Mississippi. Nearly two weeks later, three civil rights workers—James Earl Chaney, a young black Mississippian, and two white volunteers, Andrew Goodman and Michael Schwerner—were murdered near Philadelphia, Mississippi at the order of the Grand Wizard of Mississippi's chapters of the Ku Klux Klan (Cagin & Dray, 1988), demonstrating the ominous nature of the student entreaties, as well as the ruptured relations between black and white Mississippians. The sway of brutal segregationists unrelentingly persisted, as in September of 1966, black schoolchildren trying to attend class in Grenada, Mississippi were severely beaten by local officials following attempts to integrate a local grade school ("Intruders in the dust," 1966). Such violence and intolerance toward equal rights became the signature of mediated Mississippi, as these instances and numerous others littered local, national, and international media sources for the remainder of the decade.

On the day of his final examinations, having been eyewitness to the many of the seminal moments of white supremacist backlash against integration, Meredith wore a lapel pin that was popular amongst white students during the weeks leading up to his arrival on campus. The pin was inscribed with the word "NEVER" in white ink against a black background. During the ceremony Meredith wore the pin upside down to signify conquest over the resistance he encountered, as well as to celebrate the austerity and conviction demanded during his interruption of the fluid white hegemony of the Ole Miss campus (Cohodas, 1997). However, in spite of Meredith's intervention at Ole Miss, the sanctioned and sanctimonious nature of the power-knowledge dynamic at work in the university space was far from unlocked by the corporeal presence of James Meredith.

James Meredith's incursion on the chaste white spaces of the University of Mississippi did not create a multi-racial merger of oppressor/oppressed, nor a synthesis of antithetical cultural discourses on the Oxford campus. Rather, the black bodied interloper on white supremacist turf stimulated the steadfast faculties of a prevailing Dixie South 'binary system' (Foucault, 1978, p. 83). Unlike the colonization projects of the gendered and classed student bodies during the period between the first and second Reconstructions, the ideological and physical responses to the presence of a black student were not those of adaptation, but of demarcation and repudiation. The 'intermixing' of races on the Ole Miss campus did nothing to subvert or disengage the existing segregationist binary system. Rather, through an intensive campaign of hate against James Meredith, the lone campus black body, and those black students who followed, became the object of ridicule, alienation, and exclusion. In anticipation of Meredith's enrollment, on September 18, 1962, antagonists to the integration of Ole Miss distributed a *Liberty Bulletin* throughout the campus, urging students to refrain from violence until called upon by the Governor, and to resist the intimidations of "leftist administrators and officials." Reestablishing the linkages between the schools spirit symbols and the Lost Cause[s] of segregation and slavery, the notice was concluded with the salutation: "MAY GOD BE WITH US ALL! – 'The Colonel'" ("Liberty bulletin," 1962, p. 3). During the first week of October, numerous malicious leaflets were circulated throughout campus, each advising a directive for the maltreatment of the University's newest student. One handbill instructed students to "Ignore the nigger with vigor" and other depicted an angry bulldog set to attack a black-faced minstrel, with the caption "Sic 'em WHITE FOLKS" (Cohodas, 1997, p. 88).

Once the prospects of Meredith's enrollment were realized, the student-led campaign of hate against Meredith deepened. First, a number of Ole Miss students organized the Rebel Underground, a non-affiliated conservative advocate group united in the resentment "for the Negro, James Meredith being forced into our University by Federal might" and who viewed his admission as "only the beginning of organized aggression to bring about Negro political domination and racial amalgamation throughout the South" ("Rebel underground," 1962, p. 1).[10] To assuage the racial complications brought about by Meredith's (often referred to as "the Darkie") presence, in the second issue of their signature publication, the *Rebel Underground*, writers claimed that their primary objective was to "encourage James Meredith to transfer to some college where he would be welcome . . . There [were] many Yankee colleges which would eulogize him and make him 'Tar Baby' of the campus" ("Rebel underground," 1962, p. 1). Such an attitude toward racial diversity within the university space prompted the *New York Times* to decree that University of Mississippi students lived in "profound isolation" and that the range of political and social attitudes among the students was "from Y to Z" ("Ole Miss," 1962, p. 20). In a *Look Magazine* interview, James Meredith referred to the 'ostracizing campaign' which had effectively quelled any social relationships that he might have been able to forge on campus (see J. Meredith, 1966). In defense against accusations that the majority of the student body had activated and organized an ostracizing campaign against Meredith, the newly elected Vice President of the student body declared in *The Mississippian*: "There is no organized ostracism campaign against Meredith . . . He has been ostracized because almost every individual at Ole Miss has been repulsed by his presence," he continued, "Meredith has naturally been avoided by thinking people . . . because of the

---

10. The activities and opinions of the Rebel Underground student group were reported in the publication of the same name, and distributed to the campus students free of charge.

element he represents" (Lawrence, 1962, p. 4). The Vice President's comments are suggestive of the contested juxtaposition of corporeal blackness operating in discursively homogenous spaces of Dixie South white empire. Furthermore, the backlash against Meredith is suggestive of the re-creation of technologies of Dixie South identity politics around the discourses of assimilation and difference—particularly the ways in which depriving the lone black Ole Miss student of social capital, while fostering a preferred intra-discursive strategy amongst white students, became a meaningful practice within Ole Miss social spaces.

The unfettered irrationality of the Ole Miss racist contingent sweltered, as yet another circular was distributed throughout campus in the fall of 1962, titled the *Rebel Resistance*. The pages of the *Rebel Resistance* encouraged students to banish Meredith to a state of social *incommunicado*: "Let no student speak to him, and let his attempts to 'make friends' fall upon cold, unfriendly faces. In addition the students should banish him from their midst ANY white student" who opposed of failed to render this directive (quoted in Barrett, 1965, p. 197). Eventually, the softer forms of symbolic violence against Meredith were displaced by more physical measures. A group of white students chose to have supper with Meredith one fall evening, and for two of them the price of the kind gesture was high. The students returned to their dormitory room to find it "in shambles—books, records, and clothing scattered all over and next to the door the standard epithet printed crudely with black shoe polish: 'Nigger Lovers'" (Cohodas, 1997, p. 94). On October 29, a group of insurgents attacked Baxter Dormitory, hurling 'cherry bombs' toward the window of Meredith's dorm room and shouting racial epithets (E. Williams, 1962, p. 1). A few months later, on January 10, 1963, while trying to eat dinner in the campus cafeteria, Meredith found himself under siege by more than four hundred white students, chanting: "Go home, you nigger" ("Chancellor blames disturbances on news conference," 1963, p. 1).

If these segregationist practices of the University leading up to and during Meredith's enrollment were a reflection of, if not dialectically enmeshed in, the broader ideological formations of a conservative postbellum Southern cultural economy, and abjections to integration during the Civil Rights Era were indicative of a recoiling Dixie South body politic, the most wretched articulations and altercations related to the racialized dyadic body at Ole Miss occurred in the years succeeding desegregation. Following Meredith's graduation, having enrolled in the Law School in the summer of 1963, Cleve McDowell became the only black student on the Ole Miss campus. However, McDowell's stay in Oxford was brief, as he was eventually expelled from the University for bringing a firearm onto the campus (Corlew,

1963).[11] During the investigation, Oxford Sheriff Joe Ford, President of the Oxford-Fayette County Citizens Council, held McDowell in police custody, all the while vowing to keep the student away from campus "as long as we can" (quoted in "Sheriff Ford remains calm and restrained," 1963, p. 3). The news of McDowell's dismissal was greeted in the *Jackson Daily News* by the celebratory declaration: "McDowell Expulsion Erases Only Mixing Blot in State" (quoted in Barrett, 1965, p. 224). And so by the fall of 1963 Ole Miss had returned to all-white status, back to the comforts of an unchallenged white hegemony from which social relations were constructed, power formations were formulated, and [corpo]realities remained unfettered.

As public discourse, the longitudinal dealings of several hundred Ole Miss 'antagonists' helped sketch the most conservative side of the spectrum of Ole Miss race politics. According to Sidna Brower (1962e), the repeated efforts to perpetuate a climate of hatred further contributed to Ole Miss students as being depicted as "ignorant savages," and "rural, isolated, and uneducated" (p. 2). In other words, the practices of the body constituted discursive formations unto themselves which affectively centralized whiteness and alienated Meredith's lone bodily signifier of blackness. This culture of *segregated desegregation*, or the physical and psychographic segregation in the era of integration at the University of Mississippi, prolonged well into the 21st Century and continues to inform such a popular opinion concerning the University. The racialized social practices within the university space became the stuff of insolence for Civil Rights activists, and the peg upon which Southern traditionalists could hang their racist caps. In the following years, Ole Miss became the preferred destination for stalwarts of the Confederacy to send their degree-seeking children. By way of these and other spectacles of white power, separatist idioms were *marked* through the student body, creating an institutional identity and an institutional space which iconicized and parochialized the symmetry (and anti-symmetry) of race, space, and the body.

PM

In what came to be known at Ole Miss as the "post-Meredith" (or, more commonly referred to as 'PM') era, the university soon lagged behind its state-sponsored neighbors in the enrollment of black students. After Meredith finished his education, and following Cleve McDowell's expulsion, the University returned to all-white status for nearly one full year. Further, enrollment of black students was negligible during the remainder of the decade—with only a few dozen black students enrolled in any given year through the end of the 1960s (Fair, 1970b; New misery at Ole Miss," 1968).

The campus's return to [near] racial exclusivity allowed for the resurrection of a hyper-racist public vernacular wrought with corporeal expressions

---

11. Which, McDowell contended, was necessary for his protection—namely in response to numerous threats he received during his time at Ole Miss.

of unabashed Dixie South white supremacy. As an example, Stunt Night '64 featured comedic performances by fraternities and sororities reenacting significant moments in the history of the Dixie South. Kappa Delta sorority performed a play entitled "The South Shall Rise Again," in which the actors dressed in Confederate military garb and swashbuckled their way to victory in a latter day Civil War. Kappa Alpha fraternity used the event to reenact James Meredith's Ole Miss encounter, with one white student dressed in blackface as Meredith and a mob of white students mockingly caricaturizing the speech and gestures of the University's first black student. Phi Delta Theta fraternity's entry into the competition featured two members covered from head-to-toe in black paint reenacting a famous Sonny Liston versus Cassius Clay boxing match ("Stunt Night '64," 1964). Campus leader John Klein captured the endeavor to return to these simpler, less messy, white traditions of Ole Miss and the distance between the institution and racial equality by declaring: "Ole Miss students have made sincere if not desperate attempts to avoid further national scrutiny and return to the good ole days of party, football and beauty pageants" (quoted in Perkins, 1963, p. 3).

Those few black students who dared to follow Meredith were persistently terrorized by subject-vigilantes of the visible center. The first black student to enroll following the dismissal of Cleve McDowell, Irvin Walker, arrived on the Ole Miss campus in late 1964. During his first semester in Oxford, a white student reportedly attacked Walker, spitting in his face and calling him a "black bastard" ("Fight erupts between Negro and classmate," 1964, p. 1). In the summer of 1965, the University of Mississippi admitted its first black woman, Verna Bailey. Upon her arrival, Bailey was greeted in the cafeteria with a barrage of foodstuff projectiles and the singing of "Here comes the nigger, here comes the nigger" (to the tune of 'Here Comes the Bride') (quoted in Cohodas, 1997, p. 124). She also received harassing phone calls to her dorm room, mostly from white men[12] who told her, "Nigger bitches don't belong here. Nigger bitches belong in the cotton fields" (quoted in Cohodas, 1997, p. 125). The enrollment of Walker and Bailey signaled the end of a dying hope amongst traditionalists that Ole Miss could sustain a long-term return to white exclusivity. As such, symbolically, the 'clean edifice of white supremacy' would forever be 'darkened by the presence of black bodies.' However, the presence of black bodies did not quash the unyielding articulations of white supremacist ideology and corporeal expressivity on the Ole Miss campus; perhaps only offering an oft-maliced counterpoint upon which white supremacist body pedagogics could be articulated.

While black bodies had pierced the seemingly impenetrable fortification of university admission, the University of Mississippi remained an "enclave of white privilege" (Cohodas, 1997, p. 133) throughout the remainder of the

12. The assumption that these callers were white men was made by Verna Bailey during a personal interview with Nadine Cohodas. If nothing else, this speaks to the panoptic nature of terrorist whiteness for many assailed black woman students on the Ole Miss campus in the latter part of the Twentieth Century.

Twentieth Century. In spite of attempts by campus progressives to offer equal opportunities to black and white students—or what the *Clarion Ledger* condemned as an effort to "negroize Ole Miss" (Cohodas, 1997, p. 118)—the social and spatial accessibility for black students was limited, if not restrictive. The Board of Trustees passed a new set of rules in the fall of 1964 confining the use of college facilities to students, faculty, staff, and alumni. The measure effectively eliminated the presence of a black body in the privileged spaces of campus, sans but a few ostracized black students. Not coincidentally, the rule was first implemented during the home football weekend against rival Memphis State University. To prevent the black players of 'Tiger High' from 'darkening' the spaces and spectacle of Ole Miss sporting whiteness, players from the Memphis team were restricted from eating in the campus cafeteria, and black family members were prohibited from entering the university commons altogether on that Saturday (Sansing, 1990).

As the black student population grew in the 1970s—a trend which paralleled the increased exercise of 'good ole boy' power on the Ole Miss campus (see Chapter Five)—the chasm between the black campus experience and white campus experience became more evident, as college life in Oxford presented limited social opportunities for black students in the years following integration. *The Daily Mississippian* ran an introspective piece on black students at the University on February 13, 1970 in which the student newspaper's Editor interviewed two prominent black leaders on campus. The purpose of the article was to quell the fears of many white students on campus who expressed trepidation over the confrontational nature that the Equal Rights Movement had taken in the public sphere. With the increased relevance of the Black Panthers nationally, and a more militant blackness locally, campus whites feared that physical altercations might supplant the symbolic protests which had been waged since Meredith's enrollment.

The interviewer framed the black students' demands for social justice by spinning the plight of black students into a self-victimized cacophonic trope framed around the underprivilege of campus whites: "This week is Black History Week: What would be the black student's reaction toward a white history week?" A prominent black campus leader, Brian Nichols, responded to the inquiry in this way: "We have White History Week 52 weeks out of the year. And some history courses you are constantly taught what the white man has done, never the black man" (quoted in Fair, 1970a, p. 5). *The Daily Mississippian* was blunt in addressing these prevailing sentiments, inquiring "What stand do you take on militancy?' A figurehead of the Black Student Union (BSU), Jesse Dent, responded by stating that:

> People misuse the term, and anything that deviates from the parental type of action is considered militant. I do believe that the majority of the blacks on this campus are militant, but that doesn't mean that they go out and burn, break windows, and shoot people. I think that militancy is good, and that any political organization must be militant before it can be successful. (quoted in Fair, 1970a, p. 4)

Throughout the dialogue, the two interviewees went on to expound upon their ideals of militancy, and how the campus should respond to requests by black students for a more fair and equal learning environment. Citing in-equitable treatment by instructors, the fact that there were no black mem-bers of the Ole Miss faculty, and the notion that the Board of Trustees were "a bunch of ignorant people" who failed to structure the University in the interest of all its students, Dent and Nichols, along with other members of the Black Student Union, formulated a set of demands for equality on cam-pus (Fair, 1970a).

On the night of February 24, 1970, on the same day the list of demands devised by the BSU was presented to Chancellor Porter Fortune, a number of black students organized to protest their educational conditions in the cafeteria, listening to the music of B. B. King and burning a Confederate flag (Kriehn, 1970a). A small group of white students gathered outside the Student Union in counter-protest, only to have all the congregations broken up by campus police before violence erupted (Kriehn, 1970a). The next day, eighty-nine black individuals, not all of whom were students of the University, were arrested following a protest outside of Fulton Chapel dur-ing a concert. The protestors were charged with "inciting a disturbance" and "trespassing" and were held on bonds ranging from $50 to $500 (Kriehn, 1970b, p. 1). The student editor of *The Daily Mississippian* scornfully at-tacked the protestors actions, citing "People have been bending over back-wards trying to give students a fair shake with their 'rights,' but when these 'rights' start infringing upon others' 'rights' and causing disorder, its time to call a halt" (Fair, 1970b, p. 1). Interestingly, the hypercritical text offered by the Editor situated white students as the generic pronoun "people" and then hyperbolically conflated black students' *unfair demands* against white students' 'rights'—privileges which were being unfairly taken away. The charges were eventually dropped against the student protestors (Brumfield, 1970), and despite public statements to the contrary, Chancellor Fortune ultimately supported and instituted most of the demands filed by the BSU ("Cheerer reform, race bill passed," 1970).

Subsequently, black students organized their own Greek organization in the early 1970s, as Omega Psi Phi became the first black fraternity on cam-pus in 1973, and the first black sorority followed two years later. Within the following decade, the University would institute an 'Afro-American Studies' program and increase the number of black faculty to reflect the racial make-up of the student body (which was still predominantly white). However, while the conquest of resources and carving out of the campus power struc-ture by the BSU resulted in a banal re-territorialization of the campus as a predominantly white, but alternatively black cultural space, the measures taken by the BSU which were met by the visible center with a multifari-ous, hyper-mediated counterattack simultaneously repositioned masculine, white identity politics at the fore of Ole Miss subjectivity and further dis-empowered the marginalized 'Other' by way of reinvigorated externaliza-tion and representational relegation.

Dixie's Last Stand

With the unanimity of Ole Miss's racial cohesion and identity politics seemingly behind it, the University emerged from the Civil Rights Era primed to enter into an era of post-hegemonic whiteness. Unfortunately, rather than fulfilling the promise of an integrated collective, University stalwarts of the conservative cause rearticulated the Southern cause into what amounted to a battle cry for "Dixie's Last Stand" (Meyer, 1962, p. 441)—mobilized and motivated by the transience between a divisive educational system and its corporeal signifiers. The most pervasive, if not invasive, medium for rearticulating Ole Miss as a sanctimonious Southern space was in the discursive plasticity found throughout the University's sporting pastimes. Through the discursive formations of nostalgia and traditionalism, sporting Ole Miss was transformed into a political creature of the resilient Dixie South Right. In particular, during the post-Meredith era, the Ole Miss Rebel football team became the symbol of resistance to Federal dictums mandating integration in the schools, and a counter narrative to the diversification of Mississippi's power structure. The Rebels came to exemplify the transitory Dixie 'Southern Ethic' which had become such an integral part of Ole Miss social and corporeal identity politics. The *Ole Miss* yearbook likened the team to the revered war heroes a century earlier: "Amidst a sea of Rebel flags waving to the strains of 'Dixie,' these Confederate Soldiers fight for the Gallant Cause. . . . The Soldiers know that the Cause is not Lost . . . [each victory means] the Confederate troops rise again" (Cohodas, 1997, pp. 193-194).

To disrupt the obsequious tenor of hyper-racist performative whiteness within the Ole Miss football spectacle during the late 1960s and early 1970s, black students would attend football games and conduct 'their own ritual protest.' In this protest, black Ole Miss students would sit together in the end zone of the stadium and deliberately cheer for the opposing team, "ever more lustily when a black player [from the other team] made an outstanding play" (Cohodas, 1997, p. 169. The German scholar Peter Solterdijk (1987) refers to this type of bodily "cynical resistance" as "kynicism." For Solterdijk (1987), the oppositional body in this way comes to life through the:

> . . . urge of individuals to maintain themselves as fully rational living beings against the distortions and semi-rationalities of their societies. Existence in resistance, in laughter, in refusal, in the appeal of nature and a full life. It begins with plebeian 'individualism,' pantomimic, wily, and quick witted. (pp. 217-218)

The students, at great risk to their own safety, "refused to stand up for the alma mater of 'Dixie.' Occasionally someone from the group would hold up a banner: 'Racist Athletic Department' or 'Ole Miss Racism'" (Cohodas, 1997, p. 169). In one sense, these and other acts of 'spatial resistance' affectively disrupted the historically normalized spatial arrangements and practices within not only a football context, but in the hyperbolic South more generally.

More consequentially, we might also surmise that while this form of protest shook the previously uninterrupted organization of sporting whiteness as spatial practice, it also created a new architecture of racial segregation. In their collective configuration, situated within and against a more prolific configuration of spatialized Dixie South whiteness, the black students were marked as oppositional (and in so doing re-marked the visible center and its power-knowledge extensions). As I explain in more detail in the coming chapter, this geometric binarism at once contested the order of things in the newly desegregated university and at the same time recreated a new, micro-proximally insider segregation. Through this contact, the stalwarts of the Old South re-envisaged a dominant identity politics and a *louder* whiteness than that which had pervaded the campus prior to integration. Even more important, perhaps, the athlete on the field became a site onto which these Civil Rights Era racial tensions could be projected, contested, and made powerful. Under the mark of the Confederacy (the incessant waving of the Southern Cross throughout the stadium), the black-bodied 'student-athlete' at once became an instrument for propelling the heights of Southern delights (and sporting anxiety) and a reminder of the structural hierarchies and segregated spatialities they had usurped by existing there, on the field.

The decisive and divisive moment in the not-so-tumultuous history of the Ole Miss football came in the early 1980s, just as the *assemblage* (Deleuze & Guattari, 1983b) of symbols and imagery related to the Civil War and the Confederacy were regaining momentum as cultural signs. For more than a century these signifiers had been woven into the textual fabric of Ole Miss—from the stained glass window honoring the University Greys to the memorial to the Confederate war dead to the Confederate flag and 'Dixie.' Each was a "reminder of how the past shaped the present. The football team, in particular, served whites as a powerful link to bygone years" (Cohodas, 1997, p. 193). In the fall of 1979, for instance, the senior class elected to purchase a horse to represent the University as a mascot during home sporting events. The horse, which was named "Traveller" in honor of Robert E. Lee's favorite steed, became a source of contention as Civil Rights activists took notice of the increased connection between the University's athletic symbols and the Confederacy (Robinson, 1979).

While the athletic teams were integrated by the early 1980s, there was still a "reluctance to elect blacks to positions that went to the core of the Old South pageantry so much a part of the university's ethos" (Cohodas, 1997, p. 196). One such example came by way of the university's first black cheerleader, John Hawkins. Hawkins was a product of a Mississippi public school system which was, by his estimation, best described as "integrated but segregated," but one which he felt helped prepare him for his time at Ole Miss (Cohodas, 1997, p. 197). In 1982, he was elected to be the first black cheerleader on the Ole Miss campus, upon which he was asked if he would execute the tradition of carrying out the Confederate Battle Flag onto the field at the start of the game—a request which he refused. After repeated attacks against his personal belongings, his dorm room (which was set on fire), and his personage (constantly being called 'nigger' via harassing telephone calls and death threats), Hawkins spoke out to the local and national media: "While I'm an Ole Miss cheerleader, I'm still a black man. In my household I wasn't told to hate the flag, but I did have history classes and know what my ancestors went through and what the Rebel flag represents. It is my choice that I prefer not to wave one" (quoted in Rawls, 1982, p. 6). Hawkins assayed that "The Rebel Flag is the only thing separating blacks and whites at Ole Miss" (quoted in Dumas, 1982, p. 1). Instead of allowing the conquest of the black body through orthodox symbolic assimilation, Hawkins' refusal *for the first time* contested the discursive control of black deportment in spectacular white spaces.[13]

In the middle of the controversial football season of 1982, the Ku Klux Klan decided to stage a demonstration and recruitment drive in Oxford during the last week of October. The white supremacist group paraded through the Square in full regalia—wearing hoods and white robes, and carrying Confederate flags—with some 450 students and townspeople watching and listening to Grand Dragon Gordon Galle supplicate whites to unite, send black Americans back to Africa, and discontinue school integration: "I'm talking about whites dominating not Oxford, not Mississippi, but the world," Galle seethed (Stead, 1982, p. 1). In describing the events of the 1982-1983 school year, essayist Willie Morris posited in the year-end *Ole Miss*, the University "is a subtle blend of everything the Deep South was and is"—romanticizing the Confederate flag, celebrating the coming-of age of young white sorority girls. All of this, he said, "is the best and worst of the older South which has survived into a new age. Many of the white students live the most sheltered lives. Their proximity with the young blacks of Ole Miss seems both mystifying and exhilarating. . . . [a place where] much remains the same" (Morris, 1983, p. 4).

In the spring of 1983, a petition drive was undertaken to formally require the University to recognize the rebel flag as the school's official spirit symbol. The resolution asked that the Confederate flag, the mascot Colonel Rebel, and 'Dixie' remain "endeared traditions until the stones crumble from the buildings and Ole Miss is a mere whisper in history" and its proponents argued that "a University which betrays its traditions is a University not worth the respect of its students, prospective students or former students" (Cassreino, 1983, p. 1). Black students on campus were outraged by a pictorial essay in the 1983 Ole Miss which featured images from the Ku Klux Klan rally of the previous October in the "Themes" and "Issues" section of the publication (Freeland, 1983a). According to *The Daily Mississippian*, a number of black students from the BSU planned to 'protest' the symbolic oppressiveness of the KKK feature in the *Ole Miss* as well as the use of the Confederate flag at sporting events by demanding a refund for their

---

13. Hawkins' refusal to carry the Confederate flag onto the football field, and the controversies which arose from that act of protest, are more thoroughly developed in the section pertaining to the Confederate flag as Southern signifier in the next chapter.

student fees (D. Turner & Nettleton, 1983). As part of their protest, black campus leaders formulated a set of 13 demands for a better learning environment of the Ole Miss campus—most of which echoed the specters of a generation before, calling for the hiring of new black faculty and administrators and expanded cultural programs (D. Turner & Nettleton, 1983).

Upon hearing of the proposed protest from black students who felt disenfranchised by the University and its policies, carloads of white students 'waving Confederate flags' drove through the campus on Friday, April 15, shouting, "Save the flag" (Freeland, 1983b, p. 1). On the following Monday, more than fifteen hundred white students gathered in front of the Lyceum in their own protest, shouted racial epithets and chanting "Hell no the flag won't go" and "Hotty Toddy;" and then proceeded to march toward the black fraternity house of John Hawkins[14] chanting "We want Hawkins" (Raines, et al., 1983). As an act of defiance, many white students again clad themselves in the accoutrements of the University Greys, as a demonstration of Southern solidarity and as a tribute to the heritage culture which many so dearly revered, and performed various ceremonies throughout the campus to re-assert the hegemonic whiteness upon the campus space. The sentiment of many white students on campus resonated in Richard Benz' comment which captured the prevailing campus attitude in that moment: "What started the whole controversy? John Hawkins' refusal to wave the flag. What finally prompted the KKK to march? James Meredith's ultimatum to Ole Miss. If we need to throw out the KKK pictures, we also need to throw out the picture concerning Meredith and Hawkins" (Benz, 1983, p. 2).[15]

On April 20th, Chancellor Fortune somewhat quelled the volatile emotions on both sides by acknowledging the important role of the flag to Mississippi's 'shared heritage,' but declaring that the symbol was no longer formally associated with the University. In describing this 'shared heritage,' Fortune intimated that both black and white Mississippians shared a 'common history' (D. Turner, 1983). While perhaps this assertion is true, it in no way addressed the deep cultural divide from which the flag controversy sprang. As a half-hearted solution, the Chancellor's called for the installation of a set of rules that banned the distribution of flags in the stadium during football games and disallowed student cheerleaders from running onto the field with the Southern Cross (D. Turner, 1983). Black Student Union President Lydia Spragin immediately rejected Fortune's solution, citing that the organization's request for the abolition of the playing of 'Dixie' and the mascot Colonel Reb had not been met, neither had the terms of the 13-point resolution which the BSU had passed a week earlier (Nettleton, 1983). That fall, the first pep rally of the football season saw "more Confederate flags

---

14. John Hawkins was elected as BSU President in April of 1983, succeeding Lydia Spragin (Tullos, 1983a).

15. James Meredith had offered his opinion of the controversies at Ole Miss only a week earlier, publicly supporting the demands of the BSU.

than usual" (Tullos, 1983, p. 1)—a defiant response to the threat of dissolving the heritage of a supremacist, symbolic Southern shadow which cast its racist austerity over Ole Miss sporting traditions.

As a further complication in race relations, during their fall recruitment efforts, Pi Kappa Alpha fraternity was reported to have communicated to potential members that to enter the fraternity, they "would have to fuck a black woman . . . black women are the best because they move good" ("Pike's, E's: Abusive?," 1983, p. 1). This caused a great deal of commotion on the Ole Miss campus, but ironically not primarily because of the racist practices of the organization, but rather because of the violation of an unwritten ascetic code by the student newspaper when using the word 'fuck' in reporting the incident. Also in the fall of 1983, less than a week after the University had established a 'biracial task force' to address the growing divide between black and white students on campus (Bibbs, 1983a), *The Daily Mississippian* reported of a Chi Psi fraternity party where the attendees were dressed up like Klansmen (Bibbs, 1983b). The University's affirmative action officer, Erie Jean Bowen, responded to the exhibit by stating that "she was not shocked at the 'display'" and BSU President John Hawkins stated that "some of the people in these outfits harassed black students as if they were trying to intimidate them" (Bibbs, 1983b, p. 1).

These responses are further illustrative of both the intolerance with which alternative politics were engaged by the visible center from the Civil Rights Era forward, and the programmatic assimilation into the boundaries of Dixie South whiteness which is expected from racialized outliers coming to Ole Miss. As the surly environs of the South's most Confederate-inflected university became more racially divisive, new black student enrollment took a decided downturn. Following the tumultuous 1982-1983 academic year, for example, the total black student enrollment at the University of Mississippi fell from 715 that year, to 656 in the fall 1983, to 536 in 1984 (Gooden, 1985). Bowen, the University's Affirmative Action Officer for much of the 1980s—commenting on the "history of racial prejudice in the state and university," lamented that for many, the role of Ole Miss in creating and reproducing Mississippi's power structure during the 1970s and early 1980s was viewed "as one step shy of the Klan" (quoted in Cohodas, 1997, p. 205).

The John Hawkins 'controversy' is but one example in a contiguous series of post-Civil Rights Era tumult around race, 'place,' and Ole Miss sporting traditions anchored to symbols of the Old South. Take, for instance, the backlash aimed toward four African-American students' refusal to play the song 'Dixie' at Ole Miss sporting events in the early 1990s. 'Dixie' was written in 1859 by a white playwright for a blackface minstrel performance (Stanton, 2005). The song became enormously popular in the North and South during the antebellum and Civil War years, and eventually became known as an unofficial anthem for the resistive cause of the Confederate states. The original lyrics to the blackface hymnal carry both the mood of Southern lore and the dialect of Southern black slaves:

I wish I was in the land of cotton,
old times there are not forgotten,
Look away, look away, look away, Dixie land.
In Dixie land where I was born in, early on a frosty mornin',
Look away, look away, look away, Dixie land.

Old Missus marry Will de Weaber, Will-yum was a gay deceaber,
Look away, look away, look away, Dixie land.
But when he put his arm around her,
smiled as fierce as a forty pounder.
Look away, look away, look away, Dixie land. (Chorus)

Dars buckwheat cakes an' ingen batter, makes you fat or a little fatter,
Look away, look away, look away, Dixie land.
Den hoe it down and scratch your grabble to Dixie's land
I'm bound to travel,
Look away, look away, look away Dixie land. (Chorus)

Then I wish I was in Dixie, hooray! Hooray!
In Dixie land I'll take my stand, to live and die in Dixie,
Away, away, away down south in Dixie,
Away, away, away down south in Dixie. (Emmett, 1893)

This version of 'Dixie,' which originated in 1893, became the post-war signature sonnet of the New South. While the words to the hymnal are not necessarily "demeaning to blacks," wrote David Sansing, its problematic nature lies in the use of "the black dialect (of the original words). It is one of subservience and a song of deference to blacks" (quoted in Cleveland, 2003, p. 19). The version which became popular during the Reconstruction, and from which the Ole Miss anthem was created, more indiscreetly summoned the slave vernacular as a means of linguistic conquer.

The singing of Dixie during Ole Miss sporting events began in the fall of 1948, the same year as the first use of the Confederate flag and the rise of the Dixiecrats. By the mid-Twentieth Century, 'Dixie' was the 'anthem of the white south,' as "the song and the flag by now were inextricably linked to segregation and white supremacy, not just school spirit" (Cohodas, 1997, p. 162). The Anglo-Saxon-ized version, which can be heard bellowing from the white spectating collective of Vaught-Hemmingway Stadium on football Saturdays, marks the reterritorialization of the black vernacular, as well as the celebration of a heritage culture from which the minstrel song sprung:

O, I wish I was in the land of cotton
Old times there are not forgotten
Look away! Look away!
Look away! Dixie Land.

In Dixie Land where I was born in
Early on one frosty mornin'
Look away! Look away!
Look away! Dixie Land.

Old Missus marry Will, the weaver,
William was a gay deceiver
Look away! Look away!
Look away! Dixie Land.

But when he put his arm around her
He smiled as fierce as a forty pounder
Look away! Look away!
Look away! Dixie Land.

His face was sharp as a butcher's cleaver
But that did not seem to grieve her
Look away! Look away!
Look away! Dixie Land.

Old Missus acted the foolish part
And died for a man that broke her heart
Look away! Look away!
Look away! Dixie Land.

Chorus:
O, I wish I was in Dixie!
Hooray! Hooray!
In Dixie Land I'll take my stand
To live and die in Dixie
Away, away,
Away down south in Dixie!

'Dixie' has become a symbolic mainstay for the racial problematic of Ole Miss sport and physical and cultures. "Any black coming to the University, particularly anyone thinking about playing sports, had to realize he would be confronted with these symbols day in and day out, and not solely in the athletic domain" (Cohodas, 1997, p. 162).

While most other Southern universities broke ties with 'Dixie' as a sporting anthem during the latter part of the Twentieth Century, the relevance of the minstrel song became intensified at the University of Mississippi. For example, Roger Dancz, the University of Georgia's bandleader in the 1970s, ordered that the band at that school stop playing 'Dixie' in 1974. He based his decision on the growing animosity the song created among the university's black student populace (Borucki, 2003). However, following the banning of the Confederate flag in 1983, Chancellor Fortune was asked if he would curtail the use of 'Dixie,' to which he responded in the negative citing 'freedom of speech concerns' (McWhite, 2002, p. 342).

Nearly a decade earlier, a *Clarion Ledger* writer predicted that as long as "the real Ole Miss anthem is 'Dixie' . . . There will be no Negro flashes in the Ole Miss backfield, or lightening-fast black flankers in the flats or tough Negro troopers in offensive or defensive lines so long as the Stars and Bars of the Confederacy remains the true standard of the school" (Kanengiser, 2003a, p. 2F). Again citing the close relationship between the song/flag combination and Ole Miss racism and isolationism, the introspective tack of the visible center understood the song not as an obstruction to social progress, but rather as a hindrance to the aspirations of the visible center. And so the song remains an uncontested marker of [white] Dixie Southern solidarity and the associational ties between the Old South and the University of Mississippi. However, much like the flag and Colonel Reb, a transitory consideration of the appropriateness and appropriations of the song materialized, only to be met by the recoiled backlash of the visible center.

In the winter of 1993, as the student band prepared to strike up 'Dixie' during an Ole Miss home basketball game, four black students in the University's band, affectionately known as the Pride of the South, put their instruments down and stood in silent protest. The group's leader, Tim Jones, cited his uneasiness with the song and its racist intonations—particularly how the song had been used in the past by members of the Ku Klux Klan and the Southern Nationalists in efforts to preserve the vestiges of slave based racial hierarchies ("Students protest 'Dixie' at Ole Miss," 1993). A heated dialogue ensued in the pages of the *Daily Mississippian*, with one writer from the visible center slathering:

> We have got to draw the line somewhere of there will be nothing left to re-mind us what a spirited and traditional school is like. If you take away 'Dix-ie,' then what's left? Johnny Reb? Then what have we got to call ourselves? As for the African American Mr. Jones, who said the song offends him and his people, I tell you that I am very offended as a white Southern-American that you would come to the University of Mississippi and try to take something away from it that creates so much pride and spirit to our sports programs. (Weeden, 1993, p. 2)

As a former member of the campus band, the author instructed Jones to "play your part likes it's written—*Play Dixie Damnit*" (Weeden, 1993, p. 2). Another commentator scathingly protracted: "If ignorant minorities can't read well enough to learn history correctly, they have no place at Ole Miss. . . . perhaps our motto should be 'Get your heart in Ole Miss or Get Out'" ("Angry reaction," 1993, p. 3).

Brave New Whiteness?

In the year 20 PM (1984, 20 years after Meredith graduated from Ole Miss), the University appointed new officers with the purpose of 'guiding Ole Miss into the next century,' readied to face the challenges of a more diverse and changing Dixie South. In an evolution which mirrors the theme of Aldous Huxley's *Brave New World*, what followed over the next two decades was a discursive union of public opiates, reestablishment of a [clearly] demarc-ated caste system, and, much like in George Orwell's *1984*, an over-reliance on the centralizing appurtenances of distributional [white] power. Ironic-ally, it was in 1984 when newly appointed Chancellor Gerald Turner's pro-claimed the beginning of a new era at Ole Miss in regard to race: "This is the University of Mississippi for all Mississippians—white, black, brown, red. . . . If you as alumni are not ready for this to be, get out of the way" (Cohodas, 1997, p. 222).

Ushering in a period of *veneer multiculturalism* and the *façade of equal op-portunity*, Turner's publicly-stated goal was to make the campus 'psycholo-gically accessible' to Mississippi's prospective black students. In spite of his best intentions, Chancellor Turner's maneuvers were not received favorably by many of his white constituents. In fact, the initiatives to create expan-ded opportunities for black students were met with considerable hostility and various forms of public detritus. One group started its own publication, the *Ole Miss Review*, modeled after the conservative publication from Dartmouth University. The *Review* documented the impinging accommodations offered to black students, and how such measures threatened to undermine "the anchor of the Old South [that] many of these students were looking for in Ole Miss. Further, *Review* writers admonished the University, stating that attempting to "curb displays of the Confederate flag or silence 'Dixie' was [an effort] to diminish the college experience they had expected" (Cohodas, 1997, p. 224).

In Huxley's brave new world, human agents over-relied on *soma*, a drug-like opiate, to rid society of pain and anguish. At contemporary Ole Miss, that opiate is the discourse of disadvantage, which not only masks the iniquitous social relations of the present, but erases the historical biography of the University and the Dixie South which led to the present circumstances of racial iniquity. In this brave new world, much like in Huxley's, citizens have no awareness of history except for a vague idea of how different things were before the inception of the present society.[16] In his book, Huxley tells of a common practice in his brave new world, whereby crowds gathered and chanted 'Orgy-porgy'—a sensual hymn used to generate a feeling of oneness. Ole Miss Orgy-porgy, one might argue, has over the past few decades materialized through the cultures of embodied spectacle (or spectacles of embodiment). Merleau-Ponty (1945/2002) explains the trans-corporeal politics of such expressions cultural embodiment in this way:

> The body is our general medium for having a world. Sometimes it is restricted to the actions necessary for the conservation of life, and accordingly it posits around us a biological world; at other times, elaborating upon these primary actions and moving from their literal to a figurative meaning, it manifests through them a core of new significance . . . Sometimes, finally, the meaning aimed at cannot be achieved by the body's natural means; it must then build itself an instrument, and it projects thereby around itself a cultural world. (p. 146)

Through a panoply of *bodily spectacles* not unlike those faced by James Meredith (in political intent of corporeal cartography) that came to proliferate across the Ole Miss campus during the latter part of the Twentieth Century, the arbiters of racial privilege therein created a series of iconic, symbolic, and practiced pedagogical configurations (which I discuss in more detail in the second half of this book)—a core of new significance—linking the biological world (and human bodily praxis) to the cultural world of Dixie South whiteness.

In these unsettled times, that projection of whiteness came as sharp contradistinction to the egalitarian myths often projected onto, and throughout, the 'post'-segregation South. Consider: As a response to staunch criticism concerning the Ole Miss fight song and use of the Confed-

---

16. In the following chapters, I aim to deconstruct the discourses of racial privilege operating with contemporary Ole Miss, and how clandestine racism and white empowerment are coded in the unique language of Ole Miss spectacle whiteness.

erate flag, *Daily Mississippian* Editor of 1987, Frank Hurdle (1987), baptized the opening that fall's football season with the following remarks: "Wave a flag, drink a pint and yell a cheer . . . The Rebel flag is still the official flag of Ole Miss as far as the students are concerned, and it always will be," he wrote during homecoming week. He continued, "If you are against the flag, go to hell. Because my preacher told me that heaven was full of the things we love, which means it is full of Rebel flags" (p. 2).

And indeed, Frank Hurdle and his compatriots soon had their way. Despite a series of chaotic passages and incendiary controversies during the Civil Rights Era, generally speaking things went *back to normal* at Ole Miss in the years following the integration 'crisis.' By restoring *order* and getting back to *normal*,[17] most University constituents believed that the institution could 'clean up the messiness' that had defined the Civil Rights Era. As a 1969 *New York Times* article suggested, by decade's end the University of Mississippi had "returned" to being "little more than a party school attended by the empty-headed offspring of planters and bankers" only a few years after James Meredith temporarily 'broke up the party' (quoted in Cohodas, 1997, p. 129). For most of the campus's white students, this meant the recommence of the 'order of things' that had predominated social life in Oxford: a steady routine of white-bodied dominance in lectures, at pep rallies for the football team, fraternity parties, and afternoon strolls through the Square. Conversely, black students were now included in the academy, yet excluded from many of its various extramural social spaces.

In her book *Volatile Bodies*, Elizabeth Grosz (1994), following Nietzche, offers an important interpretation of the how 'co-ordinated' corporealities, collective ideas, and relations of power such as those at Hurdle's Ole Miss coalesce around 'bodily strategies':

> Bodies construct systems of belief, knowledge, as a consequence of the impulses of their organs and processes. Among the belief systems that are the most pervasive, long-lived and useful are those grand metaphysical categories—truth, subject, morality, logic—which can all be read as bodily strategies, or rather resources which co-ordinate the will to power. (p. 124)

In Hurdle's imaginary, Ole Miss is reflective of a broader salience of whiteness and spectacular dispensation. In Huxley's world, *normal* behavior is to be highly sociable, engage in promiscuous sexual activity, avoid negative thoughts and feelings by regular consumption of soma, practice sports and, in general, be good consumers (see Featherstone, 1982). This hyper-normative sociality is reinforced in the novel by the characters' frequent repetition

---

17. In the decades since, things have indeed by-and-large returned to normal at Ole Miss. Debates concerning 'reparations' for past acts of exploitation and oppression have been trivialized or out-right dismissed—as to do anything else would mean acknowledging the graduated systems of economic and social oppression, and the legacy that passing through the generations. One might argue that to the contrary, the University has more consequentially returned to the business of protracting the cultural privileges of whiteness and the economic wealth of a post-plantation economic system.

of populist mantras such as 'Everyone belongs to everyone.' In this world, it is socially unacceptable to spend time alone, to be monogamous, to refuse to take soma, and to express opinions which conflict with those taught during conditioning. In Hurdle's new post-segregation world,[18] as we will soon see, the spectacle of Dixie South whiteness at Ole Miss parallels Huxley's world with uncomfortable exactitude. The bodies of everyone belong to both the social formations of the present and to those bodily pedagogics of the Confederate, segregated, and Civil Rights Era South. As I make clear in the second half of this book, through spectacles, myths, heroes, fetes, and signs, Ole Miss's symbolic and physical cultures continue to fall under the sway of what Merleau-Ponty (1968, 1993) might describe as techniques of *intercorporeal* governance (see Weiss, 1999). Through the strategic arrangement of celebrity, space, symbols, and spectacles, Ole Miss re-emerged out of Civil Rights tumult as a pedagogical nexus for promulgating a new set of Old South identity politics; a thirdspace that synthesizes the dreamworlds of Huxley and Hurdle.

---

18. Let me be clear in saying that my use of the term 'post-segregation' in this instance and in those that follow is in no ways meant to suggest a period 'beyond segregation.' Rather, the prefix 'post-' in this and other instances throughout the text to connote a linking of the social formations (in this case segregation) of the past to the formations of the present (think: post-industrial, industrialism still holds influence in society, but under shifting conditions).

A re-enactment of the University Grey's 'Charge on Manassas' from 'Dixie Week,' 1948. Reprinted with permission from Special Collections, University of Mississippi.

'The World's Largest Confederate Flag' being unfurled at an Ole Miss football game during the Dixiecrat Era. Reprinted with permission from Special Collections, University of Mississippi.

James Meredith, accompanied by US Marshalls, in route to his enrolment at the University of Mississippi in 1962. Reprinted with permission from Special Collections, University of Mississippi.

The vitriolic mob that assembled outside the Lyceum on the Ole Miss campus awaiting James Meredith's attempts to enroll at the University of Mississippi. Reprinted with permission from Special Collections, University of Mississippi.

THE COLORED GENDER.

Minstrel performance by members of the Ole Miss student body during 'Stunt Night, '64'. Reprinted with permission from Special Collections, University of Mississippi.

Ben Williams and Barbara Biggs

In 1975, 'Gentle' Ben Williams, the first black football player at Ole Miss, was elected the prestigious title of Colonel Rebel—the first black man to so be honored. Barbara Biggs was elected Miss Ole Miss that year. Reprinted with permission from Special Collections, University of Mississippi.

A Confederate re-enactment from Dixie Week,1983. Reprinted with permission from Special Collections, University of Mississippi.

An image from of a Ku Klux Klan rally on the Ole Miss campus during the 1982-1983 academic year. Reprinted with permission from Special Collections, University of Mississippi.

The University of Mississippi's 'signature' building along its administrative axis, the Lyceum. Photograph by the author.

The Trent Lott Leadership Institute at the University of Mississippi, named after the university's famous alumnus and Senate Majority Leader Trent Lott. Photograph by the author.

Memorial to the fallen soldiers of the Confederacy sanctioned by the United Daughters of the Confederacy and erected on the Ole Miss campus. Photograph by the author.

A 'Seven-Gun Salute' during the procession of the 2005 Confederate Memorial Day Parade in the center of the Oxford Square. Photograph by the author.

Military re-enactment during Confederate Memorial Day festivities. Photograph by the author.

A woman attending the Old South Lawn Party, held by the Ole Miss chapter of the Kappa Alpha Order, in 2006. The fraternity members in the background are dressed as Confederate soldiers. Reprinted with permission from William Albert Allard/National Geographic/Getty Images.

Rebel tents in the Grove prior to a football game in the autumn of 2004. Photograph by the author.

The tailgating spectacle 'The Grove' prior to the 2003 Ole Miss-LSU football contest. Reprinted with permission from Scott Burton/WireImage/Getty Images.

Part II
Archeology of Neo-Confederate Whiteness

The Good Ole Boy, Solemnized

"We are who we are, but we're not who we were" – Ole Miss Chancellor Robert Khayat, prior to the US Presidential Debate in Oxford, 2008

In his bestselling sojourn, *Confederates in the Attic: Dispatches From the Unfinished Civil War*, Pulitzer Prize-winning author Tony Horwitz[1] (1999) offers a timely journalistic anthropology of a contemporary US South still wrestling with the last vestiges of an antebellum-borne, Jim Crow-era-refined, and segregationist-practiced social and cultural history. Making use of sharp prose and an exhaustive sociological fascination, Horwitz guides his readers through the negotiations and contestations of everyday life within the region—stopping along the way to mediate on both the enchantments of a charming regional vernacularism and the specters of recalcitrant racism and hyperpatriarchal sexism that still haunt the life experiences of many Southerners. Perhaps most importantly, *Confederates in the Attic* offers inspection—and to some degree, introspection—of the ways in which the spaces (many of which remain segregated), symbols (such as the Confederate flag), identities (located in the discursive disgorges of terms such as "redneck," "nigger," "hillbilly," and the like), and histories (both recovered col-

---

1. Although confessing his "non-Southern roots," Horwitz's (1999) rigor and reflexivity take on a deeply invested perspective of a self-professed 'non-Southerner' who nonetheless identifies with the cultures of the region. Furthermore, he maintains a reflexive voice throughout his travels and writings on "the South" and the people he meets.

lective memory and revised traditionalism) of the Old South incontrovert-ibly constitute the region's current cultural and political economies.

The principal objective of Horwitz's (1999) book, since followed by a growing quantity of like-themed manuscripts that have made their way to press in recent years (cf. Blight, 2001; Goldfield, 2002; J. M. McPherson, 2007), seems to be fixed on illuminating the 'meaningfulness' of Southern identity and the reemergence of what the author refers to as a 'neo-Con-federate' Southern eth(n)ic. This strand of neo-Confederate recalcitrance is thrust forward it two parts: (a) as a reclamation of masculine White privilege resuscitated in imaginaries of a modern-day supremacist Southern faction; and (b) as a much softer romanticization of Southern "tradition," the gen-tility of plantation life, and, to quote from the slave minstrel "Dixie," 'old times there not forgotten.'

As I have labored to make clear thusfar, the racial politics with undergird the history(ies) of the Confederacy has always been fixtures in the consci-ence of Ole Miss; always been at the fore of its directives and its problems. No other public institution in US society is more self-conscious about race than Ole Miss, and certainly few have endured the intense internal debates and external scrutiny. And yet no public institution, anywhere in the US, so steadfastly celebrates its Confederate allegiances of both past and present. In this chapter, I aim to illustrate the disjunctures of symbolic and lived experiences of neo-Confederate Ole Miss. For to this day, there is a deep-seeded "chasm fueled by that dichotomy between a shared history and a di-vided heritage" (Cohodas, 1997, p. 259) that splits the human agents acting within the campus space.[2] It has been repeatedly proffered, after classes conclude for the day, there are 'two different campuses at Ole Miss'—one for white students and one for black students.

Whereas the homogeneity of white bodies prior to integration dialectic-ally infused an institutional wholeness over the all-white student populace, the existence of *bodies of difference* after Meredith at once activated sub-jectivities of sameness and difference and stimulated racialized-, classed-, and gendered-binary schisms therein. Gilles Deleuze (1988) suggests that this symbiosis of subjectivity and power can perhaps best be framed as 'the double.' 'The double' is for Deleuze a negotiation of 'the inside' and 'the out-side'; whereby subject positions are constructed out of normative and dif-ferential processes, and the active, fractious structures of identity discourse and politics. In this way, identification becomes a process of "interioriza-

2. Much like his predecessors, Chancellor Robert Khayat's inaugural speech was high-lighted by a spirited contention that "We are one—we must be one—regardless of our role, race or gender, economic status, religious affiliation, or political persuasion. We are one people" (Khayat, 1996, p. 1). In a visit to campus to participate in a town hall meeting conducted by the President's Initiative on Race, the chairman of the organizing committee declared, after being away from the campus for thirty years, that the university had undergone a "complete revolution," so encouraged by what he saw the chairman affirmed "we don't have quite as far to go as we thought we did" (quoted in Sansing, 1999, p. 315). In spite of the rosy rhetoric from this and other campus leaders.

tion of the outside" (Deleuze, 1988, p. 98); the connection between the external discourses of identity and the internal definitions of the self.

In overly simple terms, Deleuze (1988) is suggesting that we come to understand who we are by locating our-selves against that which we are not. In the case of desegregated Ole Miss, we might ask: what was really at stake in the unsettled Meredith days?; and more importantly, for whom did this return to normalcy most benefit? The answers to the both questions are interconnected. Just as James Meredith's 'black body' had become a unwanted reminder for the University's traditionalists of what the institution *was not*, the bodily practices and representative embodiments of a preferred Dixie South whiteness served to re-mark what the University *was*. In turn, the bodies and bodily practices of the 'offspring of planters and bankers' were centrally re-placed, and thusly re-inserted, at the center—the 'inside' corporealities and discursive formations of Dixie South whiteness. In turn, these binary logics (black/white, outsider/insider, etc.) of subjectivity translated body pedagogic human action into the concurrent, metonymic circuits of representation and mediation floating about the public sphere. Against these logics of 'the double,' the bodily practices and mediated imaginings thereof on the University of Mississippi campus became more than a celebration of 'white reign.' Rather, the amalgam of white bodied privilege and desegregated bodily segregation (in the stadium, in the classroom, in the cafeteria, in the dormitories, and so on) rendered a coalition of both racialized, corporeal pubic pedagogy and syntagmatic repositioning of the pasts' normative gaze onto the present.

In this chapter, I denude the flesh politics of this new order of *integrated segregation*; revealing the cultural politics and structures of power articulated through those most-reified, most-fetished, and most-celebrated corporealities of an institution that seems to be stuck in a *constant state of duality*. At Ole Miss, as in other socio-cultural contexts, celebrity culture and the cultures of celebrity act in symbiotically reciprocal ways—both as products of the sociopolitical and economic world and existing to reproduce (through embodiment, narrative, and other textual forms) existing social formations. Celebrities as discursive formations, Pramod Nayar (2009) notes, both "circulate as images in everyday life and public space" and "thrive on the response these images invoke and circulate even more as a result" (p. 2). And indeed what becomes less relevant in our study of the celebrity cultures of Ole Miss is the actual body, and the agency of the *somebody* who is being celebrated, than do the popular discursive formations brought to life in meaningful and political ways. For these bodies are made meaningful as what Donald Lowe (1995) describes as "the body referent" (p. 5), whereby the actual human corpus is thrust into the realm of representation (and in these cases mass mediation), and thus the 'body/subject' as polyvalent text usurps, or stands in place of, the lived body. Thus, celebrity is not "a property of specific individuals. Rather, it is constituted discursively, by the way in which the individual is represented" (G. Turner, Bonner, & Marshall, 2000, p. 11). As Richard Dyer (1979) careful explains in *Stars*, celebrities are semiotic systems layered with cultural meanings to be actively decoded and interpreted by audience members. In this way, the celebrity body [re]presents a new system of power-knowledge—whereby discursive encoding and meaning-making processes formulate and engage the cultural imaginaries that hold sway over the lived experience.

As the first foray into the 'archeological' aspect of this study (subsequently followed by chapters on space, spectacle, and symbols), this chapter offers a cultural forensic of the celebrity cultures that influence(d), and are influenced by, the formations of Dixie South whiteness at Ole Miss. Whereas the previous chapter focuses on the tensions and contestations emerging out of integration's bodily disjunctures, in this chapter I examine how mediated bodily praxes of past and present sit as the locus of the politics and privileges of the 'inside' at Ole Miss. Marshall (1997) reminds us that it is here, in the diologics of the *inside*, where:

> the types of messages that the celebrity provides for the audience are modalised around forms of individual identification, social difference and distinction, and the universality of personality types. Celebrities represent subject positions that audiences can adopt or adapt in their formation of social identities. Each celebrity represents a complex form of audience-subjectivity that, when placed within a system of celebrities, provides the ground in which distinctions, differences, and oppositions are played out. The celebrity, then, is an embodiment of a discursive battleground on the norms of individuality and personality within a culture. (p. 65)

I follow a number of scholars who have fixed their critical gaze on the celebrity system not as an amalgam for hagiographic fetish (D.L. Andrews & Jackson, 2001b; Ang, 1989; F. Bonner, 2003; Boorstin, 1971; De Cordova, 1990; Dyer, 1979, 1986; Gamson, 1994, 2001; Gitlin, 2001; Gledhill, 1991; Hartley, 1999; Klein, 1999; Miller, Govil, McMurria, & Maxwell, 2001; Rojek, 2001; Rowe, 1995; Schickel, 1985; G. Turner, 2004; G. Turner, et al., 2000; Whannel, 2002), but as a culturally significant feature of broader [mass-mediated] power relations existing within contemporary society. I connect those most emphasized physicalities within the Ole Miss celebrity system to the subject positions, and forms of audience-subjectivity, from which individual and collective expressions of power-knowledge are bound.

I start by interrogating the stars of the 'good ole boy network' that emerged out of the Meredith Era; and the epistemes for educating and empowering a generation of post-Civil Rights young, white, wealthy men the South therein. As observers of the current regional and national politicoscape can attest, the university has in recent decades 'produced' legions of genteel statesmen—from US Senator James Eastland to former majority leader Trent Lott to John McCain Sr. (grandfather of 2008 US Presidential nominee John McCain). A vast majority of the Mississippi's most influential business and civic exponents claim Ole Miss as their alma mater as well. More specific to our purposes here, I investigate the systems by which social and 'physical capital' (Bourdieu, 1986b; R. Connell, 1983; Shilling, 2003) have been accumulated on the Ole Miss campus in the age of integration.

That section is followed by a series of episodic readings of those most lionized embodiments of 'good ole boy' subjectivities in the post-segregation era: former Ole Miss football coach John Vaught; the University's most heralded athlete, Archie Manning; the complicated racial politics of Ole Miss's first black football player, Ben Williams; and the more recent appellations of Southern sporting whiteness brought to life through the media[ted] politics of Super Bowl winning quarterback, 'Son of the South' (and Archie), and former Ole Miss 'All-American' Eli Manning. As an important space for social relations and cultural representations, sport, and specifically the athletic sporting body, became the definitive space for constituting, and reconstituting, dominant post-segregation identity politics in the Dixie South (Friend & Glover, 2004). As such, I trace how at Ole Miss these celebrities come to embody, by way of strategically manipulated representations and corporealities, the *preferred* cultural politics of this new economy of socio-cultural power.

While there is "no guarantee that celebrities will be consumed in the manner intended by those orchestrating the manufacturing process" (D.L. Andrews & Jackson, 2001a, p. 5), I suggest that these celebrity discourses actively and importantly inform understandings of the post-segregation 'Southern self.' More than 'signs of the times,' these political and footballing hero-figures fuse together a mass-mediated, collective, and normalizing 'technique of government' around which contemporary identity politics often coalesce (Foucault, 1982a, p. 19). I conclude the chapter with a brief discussion on how these practiced and mediated body politics have more recently been articulated with(in) the conjunctures of 1) white backlash toward US multiculturalism, Affirmative Action, immigration, and most recently the election of Barack Obama (and the recent upsurge in white supremacist hostility across the South); and 2) the cultural economy of 'conservative' neoliberal transference—whereby the body politics of Dixie South whiteness infer, if not confer, consent for Ronald Reagan's, to a lesser extent Bill Clinton's, and certainly the Bush family's free-market body politic.

Of Fraternal Ingenuity

It has been argued that this 'insider' normativity was principally organized for, and around, the University's established 'good ole boy' network (Weeks, 1999). This intraspatial (Brattain, 2001) conglomerate has been described as "statewide network of money and influence that began at the University of Mississippi in the late 1950s and early 1960s" (Weeks, 1999, p. C1)—one which was both exclusive to white men, and which fostered the antiquated subjective politics of the Old South. Most governors, state senators, and national political figures have come from Oxford's 'Mississippi Mafia'—a "loosely formed yet tight knit brotherhood. This is the Good Ole Boy network you've always heard about—mostly white, mostly middle-aged men" (Weeks, 1999, p. C1).[3] During the late-1960s through the early 1980s, virtually all student government leaders and print media intermediaries were sponsored and elected as correlative to their standing in the Greek system.[4] For Mississippi's power elite of the late Twentieth Century, the school's knowledges and networks reproduced the conditions upon which cultural and social capital, to borrow from Pierre Bourdieu (1986b), could be created, accumulated, and mobilized. For while class politics are often reduced to economic matters, in the Dixie South bourgeoisie distinction is both performative and connective.

Those who came to the university with a habitus refined around, and moulded by, these systems of capital have in years since sought to guarantee their continued power, wealth, and status through association with Ole Miss—and the relationships developed in the halls of exclusive Greek organizations such as Kappa Alpha, Omicron Delta Kappa, and the other high profile social organizations on campus. As Nadine Cohodas (1997) later suggested, it was well known that the "key to a successful social life at Ole Miss was to be in a sorority or fraternity" (p. 130). From the dress and behavior at football games, to the standards of patriarchal social decorum, the Greek system has become a regulatory extension of the antebellum ideologies of race and Southern life. A University appointed task force on minority participation in campus life cited fraternities and sororities as 'cogs in the racist machine,' stating that they played a significant role in "institutionalized racial separation" (S. Mason & Yarbrough, 1989, p. 1).

Those individuals whose social existence lacked secret handshakes and pillared-fraternity residence were often pushed to the margins. In an article featured in *The Mississippian* during the fall of 1964, student writer Nancy Mason discussed the place of alterative, and 'beatnik,' forms of culture; proffering that such an alternative sociality was adversative, 'unwelcome,' and 'unappreciated' within student life in Oxford. The author suggested that Ole Miss was "not Bohemian enough to support a beatnik society," and that in Oxford a 'quiet rebellion' would consist of overstepping the expected behaviors on the campus by dressing even more professionally, adding creativity to athletic cheers, and asking profound questions in class (N. Mason, 1964, p. 5).

---

3. The exclusivity and divisiveness of the Greek system at Ole Miss, and specifically the men's fraternities, has been the subject of scrutiny and debate for more than a century at Ole Miss. Non-fraternity students began to protest the exclusivities granted Greek organizations as early as 1905, when the repeated clemency given to wrongdoing fraternity members brought about the publication of two virulent student diatribes: *The Facts About the Troubles of the University of Mississippi: The Jim Crow Laws Against Whites at the University* and *The Mud Beneath the Whitewash*. The former publication was intended to bring attention to the perceived class-based preferences given to the University's wealthy students, and the latter was particularly aimed at motivating legislative action against the University, its Chancellor, and its Board.

4. A Greek Hall of Fame was established at the University of Mississippi in the early 1960s to celebrate the more "outstanding" Greek students on campus ("Outstanding students selected to '69-70 Greek Hall of Fame," 1970c, p. 1)

Moreover, the Ole Miss Greek system has, and continues to be, almost wholly racially-exclusive and segregated. *Daily Mississippian* columnist Jay Oglesby (1989) postulated that the problem of racism was not confined to one house but was system-wide. "The thinking in too many houses," he wrote, goes like this: "'I may not be better than anybody else and minorities may have every legal right that I do. But I never will let a nigger be my brother.' This racism, devoid of a shred of logic, is the worst form of the disease and to say that it does not exist in our system is simply naïve" (p. 2). Furthermore, the large number of Ole Miss students who are members of Greek social organizations on campus and the almost total lack of multiracial chapters suggests that "the Greek social organizations are discriminatory and do not promote participation by minority students" (Cohodas, 1997, p. 246). Despite the fact that the University of Mississippi's Greek system was finally integrated in December 1988, when Kappa Alpha Psi, a black fraternity, admitted two white members, there have rarely been black students invited to join white fraternities over the past twenty years.

In the closed halls of their fraternity houses, these men of campus power shape the social livelihood on campus. On football Saturdays, Ole Miss fraternity men are clad in khakis, button-up shirts, and ties. They occupy tents which identify their fraternal allegiance by way of their banners; while inside these 'men of the South' lounge around consuming foods and beverages prepared either by servants, caterers, or the chapter chef (depending on the epoch). Surrounded by a phantasmagoria of Confederate whiteness, these men of the South were "more like spectators than active agents, occupying roles assigned to them in a state of passive contemplation" (Pinder, 2000, p. 362). These men share a unity in dress, deportment, gait, and behavior; one that stirs the hierarchical echoes of their predecessors' purview. Following Chris Rojek's (2001) taxonomy of celebrity forms, then, we might surmise that as these spectacles of *passive habitus performativity* come to flourish within local, national, and international media spheres through the Old South stylings of Trent Lott and his 'brothers,' their soft, white, contemplative, relaxed disposition articulates an *ascribed* celebrityhood. For Rojek (2001), the ascribed celebrity is that icon figure who 'commands automatic respect and veneration' based on their 'biological descent' (p. 17). In other words, these men of the South come to embody not only the status afforded them by their symbolic capture of Dixie South whiteness, but also of an inherited whiteness that seemingly *comes naturally*.

As Homi Bhabba (1994) has argued, ambivalence is at the epicenter of such a social structure. Through the uncritical reification of a nostalgic and uniformed acculturation of preferred Old South deportmental whiteness, evoked through gait, dress, and practice, engagement with these spectacular practices links the individual to the spectacle (both the local fraternal spectacle and the broader spectacle of Dixie South whiteness) (Debord, 1990). This unwritten language of control is extrapolated and expounded upon throughout *The Society of the Spectacle* as the means by which the spectacle reproduces itself (Debord, 1994). In this instance, the spectacles of class-, gender-, and race-hierarchy are, much like Bourdieu's (1984) notion of habitus, made to be seemingly natural by the mystique, and lack of mystification, within the gait, posture, and dress. Perhaps this 'good ole boy' deportment can best be described in this way: Ole Miss is like a Confederate Ball,[5] as the men and women of the campus dress in their best attire promenade in a spectacle of conspicuous gentility.[6] The student subject as spectator is thus transformed into both a conduit of embodied politics of the hierarchical body politic, and the imagined representational space of corporeality which reaffirms the impulses of such a hierarchy.

That embodied 'good ole boy' habitus has long been inseparably soldered to the performative politics of an imaginary conservative consensus. Social distinction—and social and cultural capital of Mississippi's white, ruling elite—has thusly been bound to the formulaics and pedagogics of what some scholars have referred to as patriarchal, white, 'paleo-conservatism' (Newman & Beissel, In Press). Ideologically, the 'good ole' in 'good ole boy' is etymologically anchored to idioms of the social-political status quo of the Old South.[7] Generally speaking, these paleo-conservative political sensibilities are syllogistically located within traditionalist, Biblicalist, masculinist,[8] sometimes racist, anti-Federalist ideologies usually opposed to social change and especially government intervention to bring about that change. Unlike 'neoconservatism,' which tends to be more focused on free-market economics and what critics have referred to as the state-fashioned 'American empire building project' (more on the amalgamation of the two at the

---

5. Which is an actual event on the Ole Miss campus, hosted bi-annually by Kappa Alpha fraternity.

6. In a *Sports Illustrated On Campus* article (2003a) entitled: "The 100 Things You Gotta Do Before You Graduate (Whatever the Cost)," number three on the list was "Tailgate in the Grove at Ole Miss, the 10-acre, debutante-stacked meadow on campus" (p. 4).

7. In other words, Ole Miss men—and particularly Ole Miss fraternity men—have developed a reputation throughout Mississippi for their paradoxical bodily aesthetic of one part disheveled patriarch (untidy hair cuts, unshaven facial hair, etc.) and one part regimented genteel bodily adornment (shirt-and-[bow]tie to football games, loafers, etc.).

8. My use of masculinity here draws inspiration from the work of Antonio Gramsci (1999) and his theorizing on 'hegemony,' or the contested nature of meaning and representation and the ability of the ruling class to gain consent for an iniquitous social order: one in which power is unequally distributed—and in which the oppressed members of that society contribute to, and are complicit in, the reproduction of these hierarchies. Using the precepts of Gramsci's theory of distributional power, Robert W. Connell (1990) layered the complexities of a empowering gender binary upon the Italian Marxist's understanding of social authority, and in doing so formulated a heuristic for interpreting the hypermasculine nature of modern social relationships in Western society (and beyond). Connell (1990) defined 'hegemonic masculinity' as "the culturally idealized form of masculine character" (p. 83), whereby 'traditional' markers of masculinity such as aggression, volatility, and rationality hold sway over a marginalized femininity and an ostracized alternative sexuality (outside the hetero-norm).

end of this chapter), paleo-conservatives typically seek to uphold 'tradition-al values,' reject state and Federal intervention in domestic and intersocial affairs, and protract a jurisdiction regulation of both the body politic and the politics of the body.

For instance, while most American colleges had formed, or were in the process of organizing campus Republican and Democratic societies, the Ole Miss students created their most popular non-Greek student organization around political bent rather than affiliation. The Conservative Students As-sociation hosted an number of political rallies and sponsored on-campus presentations and orations, including the hallmark political event of the mid-1960s when the students brought Ross Barnett back to speak at Ole Miss in 1965 ("Barnett urges stand," 1965). Such a rigid climate of segrega-tionism on campus motivated a number of faculty members to resign from the University, many of whom specifically cited the racial apartheid on cam-pus as the reason for their departure ("A new dean at Ole Miss," 1969).

Perhaps more than any other 'Good Ole Boy,' the archetypical paleo-conservative 'Southern Man' on the late 20th Century Ole Miss campus was (US Senator) Trent Lott. A staunch Democrat until the mid-Century Dixiecrat secession, Lott's conservative social politics and racial ideals loc-ated him at the center of a polemical segregationist backlash Ole Miss dur-ing his undergraduate days:

> Senate Majority Leader Trent Lott helped lead a successful battle to prevent his college fraternity from admitting blacks to any of its chapters, in a little-known incident now four decades old. At a time when racial issues were roiling campuses across the South, some chapters of Sigma Nu fraternity in the Northeast were considering admitting African-American members, a move that would have sent a powerful statement through the tradition-bound world of sororities and fraternities. At the time, Lott was president of the intra-fraternity council at the University of Mississippi. When the issue came to a head at Sigma Nu's national convention—known as a 'Grand Chapter'—in the early 1960s, 'Trent was one of the strongest leaders in res-isting the integration of the national fraternity in any of the chapters,' recalls former *CNN* President Tom Johnson, then a Sigma Nu member at the University of Georgia. (Tumulty, 2002, p. 16)

Following his days at Ole Miss, Lott emerged as the figurehead of the Mis-sissippi Republican party; and with one of the Senate's 'most conservative' voting records, Trent Lott's 30 years in public office became some of the most influential, and consequential, in US politics over the last half-century.

Lott's became a significant voice in US politics, particularly during the George W. Bush Presidency, when he became majority leader of the Senate and one of the most visible figures in the US 'Conservative Movement.' As homage to his life's work, the University of Mississippi created the Trent Lott Leadership Institute. However, shortly after the Institute opened, the Senate Majority Leader came under heavy scrutiny within the national me-dia in December of 2002 after he declared that his state was 'proud to have voted for Strom Thurmond's segregationist ticket' in 1948 (the year of the Dixiecrats). In remarks at Thurmond's 100th birthday party, the celebrity-like political elephant postulated that "if the rest of the country had followed our lead, we wouldn't have had all these problems over the years either" (Tumulty, 2002, p. 16). And this was not an isolated incident or a slip in rhetoric. Lott also incurred the wrath of the critics in 1993 following reports that he held close ties to leaders of a local white supremacist group (Weeks, 1999). Despite, or some might argue because of, these and other signposts of his overt racist leanings—or for that matter many of those of his Southern legislative brethren such as Strom Thurmond, George Allen, and more recently Joe Wilson—Lott remains a hero figure on the Ole Miss campus. Moreover, as generations of Mississippi's 'leaders' make their way through the spatial and pedagogical domains of the University Leadership Institute, they do so very much under the specters of not only the University's namesake 'Good Ole Boy,' but the cultural politics he spent his career promulgating.

Dixie South Whiteness, Enfleshed

Trent Lott's emergence as the political paragon of post-segregation Dixie South paleo-conservatism can only be understood as part of a broader, more longitudinal Dixie South celebrity culture. While Lott's political cocksureness exemplified a conservative genteel pragmatism, the superior cultural physicalities of the white South were, in the minds of men, confirmed through the pugilistic exploits of Ole Miss's master footballing tacticians and protagonists (P.B. Miller, 2002). At Ole Miss, the less pronounced tribute to the warrior-like servitude of the Greys and the preponderance of Old South, demarcated masculinity emerged over time in the discursive reveries of performative footballing bodies. Like many sporting forms in the US South, Ole Miss football came to epitomize the hierarchical structure of gendered and racialized social relations in the post-Civil War Era (Martin, 2002). Through football, idealized masculinity in the New South became grounded in the common tropes of calculated recklessness, stoic instrumentation, corporeal sacrifice, and familial allegiance. A consistent narrative in the mediated celebration of football heroes of Ole Miss' located the combative white body as an *instrument of the Dixie South*, a site of praiseworthy Southern stock and imaginary racialized genetic superiority (Cobb, 1999; A. Doyle, 2002b; P. B. Miller, 2002).

From the 1950s and through to the late 1960s, Ole Miss football players came to be known as 'Mississippi mules' (Vaught, 1971)—a reference to both the environmental prowess and physical superiority of the state's white gentry pedigree. Willing to surrender their bodies in defense of Dixie's past glory and future perfect, the racialized chaste-missiles of the University of Mississippi came to symbolize the Dixie South's return to magnanimity and the proliferation of a 'Southern mystique' (Vaught, 1971, p. 8). The media descriptions of Ole Miss players during the team's heyday typically engaged a narrative thematic similar to the portrayal of All-American George Kinard, one of Ole Miss' most heralded performers, who was depicted as "a six foot, one inch, brown haired, brown eyed, 190 pounds of human dynamite" (Brownstein, 1940, p. 8).

In the context of a soon-to-be integrated University, mediated *sporting embodiments* became the visceral link to the appurtenances from which new gesticulations of preferred whiteness could be formulated, marshaled, and mediated against the anxieties and perceived inferiorities of the 'black-bodied' footballing Other. With the specters of integration looming, there was no more poignant *tabula rasa* to celebrate the storybook stylings of rugged Dixieland [white] masculinity than through the gridiron narrative. For the Ole Miss white supremacist faction, the legendary feats of hard Southern men such as Archie Manning (and later his son Eli) and John Vaught at the dawn of the Civil Rights Era reaffirmed both the superiority of the race and the necessity for its preservation and purity. Likewise, after integration, the emphasized 'docility' of the University's black athletes such as Ben Williams reaffirmed the 'place' of the 'New New South's' racialized athlete. In sum, the composite story these icons of Dixie South sport culture tell is one of [parochial] bodily and rational excellence at a time when the idioms and physicalities of white supremacy were coming unraveled against the tensions of a Civil Rights equality movement.

The Southern Sporting Logician

Leading the conglomeration of corporealized neo-Confederates, the commander of Ole Miss's most successful football army was Johnny Vaught: the cerebral, calculating, stoic patriarch of the seminal institution in Mississippi's version of the new sporting South. During his tenure (1947-1970, 1973), the University's football squad compiled a record of 190 victories, 61 defeats, and 12 ties, including three national championships, six conference championships, and eighteen bowl game appearances (R. W. Baker, 1989). His enduring legacy is cemented in the imaginations of sporting adherents throughout the South. As rival coach Bill Battle of the University of Tennessee lauded:

> Few men have had as much an impact on modern collegiate football as John Howard Vaught of Mississippi. His Ole Miss teams always set the trends toward new, progressive offensive formations and techniques. His great won-lost record and his phenomenal bowl record only begin to reflect the influence he had on Southeastern Conference football. He will be remembered as one of the giants of his profession. (quoted in Vaught, 1971, jacket flap)

Vaught was the quintessential celebrity figure for the visible center of Dixie South whiteness in the post-Emancipation generation and the lead-up to the turbulent Civil Rights years: instiller of Southern values, extractor of white physical excellence, and commander of the perfect sporting apparatus (A. Doyle, 2002a). As Porter Fortune, Chancellor of the University of Mississippi during Vaught's tenure exclaimed: "The years take away the snap from a passing arm and the spring from the legs; but courage, endurance, self-reliance, alertness, steadfastness, teamwork, loyalty—these things which Johnny Vaught has taught his boys last for a lifetime" (quoted in Sorrels & Cavagnaro, 1976, p. 140). Vaught's new science of footballing excellence was not only constructed out of and defined by the logics of white supremacy; his team became the last bastion of an exclusively white monolithicism. The team came to be known not just as the last hope of the Southern white Right, but as a symbolic configuration of resistance to integration (A. Doyle, 2002b). Vaught himself confessed that "after 1954 white Mississippians tried to preserve the caste system they inherited" (Vaught, 1971, p. 7), and his team became the emblematic army of that racist caste system. Just like General Robert E. Lee before him, and Dixiecrat leader Strom Thurmond during his time, Vaught's celebrity was erected as the discursive figurehead of Ole Miss' visible center—the iconized embodiment of supremacist values and whiteness as *par excellence*.

First, the narrative structure of John Vaught's mediated celebrity at Ole Miss was constructed out a recurring thematic of his ability to exhibit the rationalized calculability of late modern industrial America (P. B. Miller, 2002; Watterson, 2000). For Vaught's 'industrious' footballing mind came to symbolize New South ingenuity in the greatest period of industrial expansion in the Mississippi Delta region (Todd, 1951). Just as the academy and business sectors of the region became entrenched in the fetish logics of [*post facto*] industrialism, and the core principles of rationalization and specialization, football culture had itself been rationalized, specialized, and perhaps more importantly, spectacularly commercialized. As the performative and strategic dynamics of intercollegiate football changed during the middle part of the Twentieth Century, and the game 'opened up' and tactics and preparation took on newfound import, Vaught became the archetypical figure of industrial Old South [white] ingenuity (Borucki, 2003). Dialectically, John Vaught's celebrity discourse came to be moulded out of these prevailing attitudes, and thus the Ole Miss football coach became the iconic figure of late industrial Southern rationality and footballing cerebralism: "Vaught was nothing if not innovative" (Cleveland, 2000, p. 9), later wrote one local journalist. Another commentator identified the specific aspects of Vaught's style, claiming that the Ole Miss head coach "was an innovator who in many ways was ahead of his time. He was the first coach in the Southeastern Conference to hire a full-time recruiting coordinator. . . . He was also a genius at tinkering with offensive formations to capitalize on weaknesses in the opposition's defense" (Baker, 1989, p. 43).

The celebration of Vaught's intellect was emblematic of the 'managerial coalescence' of media-sport intermediaries of the mid-century, as the burgeoning sport content of print and radio new media echoed the preponderance of an American celebrity culture (Riesman & Denney, 1970). New cultural technologies not only contributed to the expansion of Vaught's iconicity across the Dixie South, but his ability to mobilize these technologies became part of his legend: "In his coaching days at Ole Miss Vaught studied football game film and scouting reports with the dedication of a 12th century monk putting together a religious tract. For Vaught it was a sin to field a Rebel team uncertain about its toughness and the tendencies of the enemy" (Sorrels & Cavagnaro, 1976, p. 136). The modern technologies of late industrial era cerebralism and 'toughness' conjoined at 'one dimensional' (Marcuse, 1964) masculinities of the changing South; and infused the discourse with a *turn time technologies of the self* which valued whiteness and reinvigorated the mind/body, white/black dualism further cemented the celebritization of coach Vaught at Ole Miss. At the end of his career, Vaught's analytical prowess was reflected upon in this way: "Vaught's Rebels won big because he considered football a science. . . . Vaught had a head full of common sense" (Sorrels & Cavagnaro, 1976, p. 137).

As the economic rationalities of modern industrialization soon became unsettled by the cultural commotion of the Civil Rights Era South, and efforts to integrate the Dixie South's exclusively white institutions intensified in the late 1950s and early 1960s, the fixtures of celebrity became important sites for reconstituting the politics of white supremacy. The categorical pantheon of celebrated masculinity took many forms, as Southern men such as the emotional persona of Mississippi Governor Ross Barnett, the indefatigable supremacy of Dixiecrat Presidential nominee Strom Thurmond, and the quiet confidence of University of Alabama head football coach Paul Bryant. However, in the face of the race tempest that inundated the Mississippi Delta, more than any other, the symbolic fortitudes of John Vaught's celebrity helped to assuage the anxieties of the visible center: "Vaught was far from the fiery, emotional leader. Indeed, he rarely changed expressions on the sidelines" (Cleveland, 2000, p. 9). Vaught stood as the physical embodiment of a broader formation of poised white resistance to integration. "Ole Miss football is a tradition which has weathered the wind and rain. Rebel coaches, players, and fans are a special breed, whose image was created in the post war years" (Collins, 1970, p. 255).

That 'special breed' of Ole Miss whiteness was secured by the fact that Vaught's coaching pedagogies were limited exclusively to white Mississippians. *All his players were white*,[9] as were the fans, students, and affiliates of the institution which his team represented. Ole Miss boycotted play against teams with black players in Vaught's early years, and later banned parents of opponent black players from entering the campus Circle prior to Ole Miss home games. While coach Vaught's techniques proved successful during his tenure, they were performed by "a relatively narrow band of the state's population. Ole Miss recruited almost exclusively for the young, white, Mississippi-born male. The situation was very much a family affair that worked to the University's advantage for years. . . . Vaught ruled recruiting in Mississippi like no other coach before him or after him" (Baker, 1989, pp. 34-35). As such, on the field, Vaught's disciplinary stoicism served to temper the emotional impulses of footballer and segregationist alike, so-

---

9.Actually, Vaught returned to coach an integrated Ole Miss football team for part of the 1973 season. That team had black players, but those players were recruited by Vaught's successor—as the team integrated almost immediately following his retirement in 1970.

lidifying the resistance of integration and disciplining this 'special breed' of whiteness.

As an intermediary of local whiteness and masculinity, Vaught was both symbol and arbiter of white exclusivity and white supremacy in the mid-Twentieth Century. His stoicism meant calm in the face of a Civil Rights storm, as Vaught "did not lose his temper and rarely showed emotions on the sideline during a game. He was stern with his players, but could show compassion with their personal shortcomings" (Baker, 1989, p. 42). His reassuring presence further symbolized the efficacy of Dixie South whiteness in the context of desegregation and modernization. His successes on the field presented a fulcrum of white sporting prowess and physicality for Dixie Southerners. Further, the isolationist carriage of Coach Vaught's teams symbolized the separatist posture of the institution and its followers in the pre-Meredith days: John Vaught's was recognized and lauded as "the leader of a closely-knit, quality organization" (Collins, 1970, p. 254) built on the foundations of familial ancestry and white exceptionalism.

Southern Man[ning]

> Dad's days at Ole Miss were life-shaping. For me, they were magical. If I could, I'd want to go back to when he played. I'd have loved to make an entrance into a fraternity party on one of my linemen's shoulders the way he did after a big game. I'd love to have played a game where I got hurt in the second quarter and then came back and won it in the fourth like he did against Georgia. I wanted all the things my dad had. I wanted to have the girls look at me twice and walk through campus and have people I didn't know smile and say hello. I'm not sure you could ever again completely experience what he had then. It was a different time – Peyton Manning (quoted in Manning, Manning, & Underwood, 2000, p. back cover)

John Vaught's most heralded 'student-athlete' was unquestionably a 'red-haired, freckle-faced' native of the nearby Delta town of Drew named Archie Manning. "One of the last true Southern icons" (Barnhart, 2003, p. 1E), Archie Manning was not only superstar but folk hero: "I don't think I could describe how big he was," one teammate marveled (quote in Calkins, 2003, p. D1). His popularity in Mississippi was captured in the opening gambit of a *Sports Illustrated* article titled "Archie and the War Between the States": "Mississippi is the place where a doctor hangs up a picture of Archie Manning and then wonders: 'Is it wrong for a 40-year-old man to be in love with a 21-year-old boy?'" More than any other athlete before or since, Archie embodied the cultural politics of the [imaginary] isolationist white South. Under the celebrated discourses of 'Manning Mania,' the post-segregation imagined community of the visible center could reunite every Saturday and glorify the sporting prowess of the white Dixie South's thoroughbred.

It has been argued that Ole Miss football in the era of Archie Manning took on a new life, as white Dixie Southerners congregated at the on-campus football temple to pay homage to the sporting icon, and to the resurrected glory of Southern white corporeal solidarity (Breed, 2003). In the era of Archie Manning, the Ole Miss football program became:

a white man's haven, a place for the young, the strong, the committed—boys like Archie—where a victory on the football field in front of thousands of adoring fans could stand for more than just a notch in the win column. It was another reassertion of southern pride and a victory on the cultural battlefield. For four months every year, football was the university's secular religion, and as one astute observer put it, 'If you were not waving a rebel flag, then you were not part of the congregation.' (Cohodas, 1997, p. 166)

Put simply at a school where football remains a quasi-religion, quarterback Archie Manning was 'a god' (Breed, 2003). As the phantoms of race riots from five years earlier haunted the Ole Miss campus, and the residues of a tarnished national reputation constrained the identity of the University, Archie emerged as the central figure in the lexicon of requiting white subjectivity.

Songs were written about Archie Manning during the heights of his playing days; songs which celebrated his athletic exploits and his parochial ways. A University of Tennessee linebacker, when asked by a reporter if he 'feared' Archie Manning in an upcoming game, snidely replied, 'Archie who?.' Following that footballing contest against Tennessee, which resulted in an outcome of 38-0 in favor of Ole Miss, a local songwriter composed a song in honor of the 'red-hared hero' of the neo-Confederacy titled: "The Ballad of Archie Who" (Gildea, 2002, p. D1). 'The Ballad of Archie Who'[10] was one of many tributes which glorified the exploits of Archie, and sold thousands of copies in 1969—with one line summing up the magnitude of the 'the red-haired bomber's' (Kriehn, 1970c) celebrity: "They try to make a tackle, they wonder where he went . . . Archie Super Manning should run for President" ("'Archie Who' could be state's top seller," 1969, p. 7).

More importantly, the song located the 'red-haired' quarterbacking hero as a distinctively white celebrity—a popular figure in the rebuilding of a 'Southern Ethic' which reserved adoration for the likes of General Robert E. Lee, Jesus Christ, and Ross Barnett. During his college career, more than 20,000 'Archie' buttons were sold, along with 12,000 buttons which read 'Archie's Army' (Sorrels & Cavagnaro, 1976). 'Archie's Army' continued to grow, and in 1970 the University organized a campaign to promote his candidacy for the Heisman Trophy, college football's most coveted award—and the distinction reserved for the nation's best all-around player. While intermediaries wrote songs and parishioners named children in the honor of Archie Manning throughout the course of his playing career at Ole Miss, his visibility as the star of the 'new New South' meant more than simple sporting adoration.

In early September of 1970, *Sports Illustrated* featured Manning in an article entitled "And the best of them all is . . . Archie." Archie was named the Oxford campus's 1971 Colonel Reb, the highest honor for any male student during that time. Archie 'Super' Manning, who writer John Grisham

---

10. The song was sung to the tune of 'Folsom Prison,' was written by a postal clerk from a small Mississippi town, and was sung by Mississippian Murray Kellum ("'Archie Who' could be state's top seller," 1969a).

described as "a legend larger than life" (Manning et al., 2000, p. 3), bestirred an exclusively Dixie Southern celebrity discourse, a strategically encoded byproduct of the reclamation of white authority. In a place that 'redshirted both all-Americans and Miss Americas,' Archie Manning emerged as *the* contextually-important, hyper-mediated representative of the Old South hierarchical logics of race, gender, and sexuality. Positioned at the center a local Mississippi mediascape that had, for some time, held as a chief exercise the manipulation of white iconography—constructing the social ideologies for its constituents through a calculated mosaic of half-truths and deified venomous ideologues—Archie was the sporting savior of the post-segregation failed Old South.[11] For the *Clarion-Ledger*, as well as local radio and television producers, Archie was the embodied redeemer of the Lost Cause: "Archie came to Ole Miss at a very critical time," noted David Sansing, "Archie was a wonderful and pleasant distraction from our everyday trouble" (Gildea, 2002, p. D1). In the context of home-spun mediations and recompensatory luminaries of the local, Archie was leveraged as the homegrown [white] 'Southern boy' made-good in the face of an assailing federal government and antagonistic national media.

More importantly, Archie Manning's *stature* as sporting icon and champion of the white Dixie South[12]—constructed out of a two-part narrative of a white-stock physical prowess (and sacrifice) and a distinctively Southern trope of native instincts and unassuming diligence—transmitted a glorified technology of the New South sporting self. This 'bonafide southern football idol' (B. Gutman, 1975, p. 7)—defender of the visible center—was persistently located in the narrative structures of divine [Anglo] physique and the resurrected visions of corporeal machinations and of primordial language: relays, extensions, and media-mediators of a 'natural' manifest destiny of idealized Old South deportment. The essential performative white Southern sporting body, Archie's athleticism was described by rival University of Georgia coach Harry Mehre, who lauded:

> Manning is so elusive and so dangerous as a runner that he breaks down any pass defense. He motors backwards, sideways, and upwards. When you're close to him he finds someone open and lets go. He creates this situation, and

---

11. For instance, when Byron de La Beckwith, son to an established Deltaland family, who despite being born on the west coast had lived the previous 38 of his 42 years in Mississippi, was apprehended and accused of killing civil rights activist Medgar Evers in June of 1963, The *Clarion-Ledger* of Jackson offered the imaginative headline: "Californian Is Charged With Murder of Evers" (Lehew, 1963, p. 1). Similarly, the only pictures of the August 28, 1963 Civil Rights March on Washington, D.C. offered by the *Clarion-Ledger* showed the trash left behind after by the swells of protestors. The caption to a report of the events read: "Washington Is Clean Again With Negro Trash Removed" (Silver, 1966, p. 32).

12. As an insight into the relevance of football and Southern pride during Archie's term at Ole Miss, prior to the start of the Southern Mississippi game in 1970, one Ole Miss player said, "to control the Confederacy, we have to start by controlling Mississippi" (Anon, 1970b)

then eats it up. He's got to be the best quarterback I've ever seen in the SEC (Southeastern Conference). (quoted in Gutman, 1975, p. 15)

The physicalities of a contextually-specific Dixie South whiteness afforded cultural intermediaries of Civil Rights Era Mississippi entrée into the con-joined politics of: whiteness as intellectual capacitance (the white = cerebral/ black = unintelligent trope); whiteness as inherited assiduousness (i.e. the white-diligent/black-lazy trope); and the return of athletic gait as symbolic discourse of Southern [white] sacrifice. The physical capital constructed out of, and performed within, the discourses of Archie Manning were, in the first instance, embodiments of newly articulated whiteness in the chan-ging climate of the desegregated South. The politics of Archie Manning's athletic body extended into the politics of race, as the all-white team Man-ning played for become the last symbol of segregation in the climate of the integrating South. While other football powers in the region were integrat-ing their teams, Ole Miss stood vigilantly in opposition of integration. Thus, Manning and his all-white teammates resuscitated a counter-narrative to in-tegration—a symbolic, mass mediated discourse of resistance and reaffirma-tion. Further, Manning's accomplishments against integrated teams further cemented the corporeal merits of Ole Miss football within the white Sport-ing South soon imaginary.

Concurring with the Georgia coach on the superlative nature of Man-ning's abilities, Ole Miss head coach John Vaught extolled that: "Archie's got it all. Not only is he blessed with a strong arm but he has another in-valuable asset. After one step he's under full throttle. He can really take off. Combine that with a great football mind, which he has, and you've got your-self an A-1 man" (quoted in Gutman, 1975, p. 16). In a famed quote from his coach, Manning was praised for the 'seemingly-natural' union of intel-lect and physical prowess: ". . . in the spring drills I saw how quickly Arch-ie could read defenses and come up with an automatic way to exploit it" (John Vaught, quoted in Sorrels & Cavagnaro, 1976, p. 252). In the custom of an idealized, genteel Southern Man, the technologies of Archie Manning's celebrity discourse engaged the Southern cerebralism in the mould of Wil-liam Faulkner or John Vaught, as well as the traditionalism of an imaginary parochial 'Southern ethic':

> Archie Manning deserves a special note for his performance and leadership on the field which has won him much national acclaim and above all for his mod-est acceptance of the honors he has received. This red-headed quarterback is adored by every football fan in the South, mobbed by every kid that sees him play, and placed in high regard by the students at Ole Miss. (Collins, 1970, p. 252)

The *reaffirmation of Southern Manning* through public discourse thus trans-lated into a reaffirmation of Dixie South whiteness. The politics of the mind/body consummation leveraged within the Archie Manning celebrity discourse during his playing career at Ole Miss recentered fleeting white-ness at the core of identity and representational politics on the campus and beyond.

As the iconic embodiment of Southern white excellence in the era of seemingly ephemeral white power, Manning became the archetypal incarnation of the reclamation of exemplary whiteness in the late Civil Rights moment. His commitment to his craft became another central element in the discursive constitution of the Archie Manning celebrity. One teammate famously described Manning's work ethic this way:

> He worked harder than any guy on the team. The thing about Archie was watching him practice. The way he could throw harder running to his left than anybody else running to the right was unbelievable. And the reason he could is because he spent 30 minutes a day down on one knee throwing passes. That's how dedicated he was (quoted in Sorrels & Cavagnaro, 1976, p. 250)

During his senior season, Archie suffered a broken bone in his arm during the Southern Mississippi contest. In the tradition of corporeal sacrifice for the Confederacy, Manning's mediated persona (often pictured in the infirmary with a Confederate Battle flag as the backdrop during his rehabilitation) took on the popular position of fallen footballing soldier—hero figure who sacrificed his body for the betterment of the solid South. The media hailed Manning as the 'captain of the Confederacy,' the leader of a sporting army who, in the defense of Mississippi's honor, forfeited his wellbeing for the greater good of the Old South. Upon his return to the battlefield, Manning was lauded as the unyielding champion of the white South:

> It would have been easy for Archie to just stop right there. But he didn't! He kept himself in shape despite a heavy cast on his arm, and when the cast came off four weeks later, he insisted on getting right back into the action. He did, with a steel pin inserted in his arm and a cumbersome brace almost immobilizing the injured appendage. Yet he led the Rebels to a postseason bowl bid for the third straight year. That's the kind of guy Archie is, the reason there have been songs written about him, parties given in his honor, and legends spread around like wildfire. (Gutman, 1975, p. 8)

And thus Manning's stature as sporting icon of the Dixie South whiteness was constructed, crystallized, and solidified through the popular mediations of his sporting profile. Amidst the backlash discourse of white entitlement, whereby black civil rights activists were assailed in the media as lazy, philanthropy-seeking vagrants, Archie's celebrity came to be fashioned as an idealized version of whiteness: hard-working, cerebral, 'naturally' gifted with pure-pedigree physicality, and leader of the new Army of the South.

'Gentle' Blackness

> We got to make him a nigger first. He's got to admit that he's a nigger – William Faulkner, *Notes on Virginia*

If the central embodiment of Dixie South whiteness in the late/post-Civil Rights Era on the Ole Miss campus appeared in the narrativized physicality of Archie Manning, the first important black celebrity figure on the Ole Miss campus arose from the bodily discourses of Ben Williams. Williams was the first black athlete to play football for the University of Mississippi, arriving on the Ole Miss campus in 1972. Williams was recruited to Ole Miss by John Vaught's immediate successor,[13] and chose to attend and play football for the University not as an agent acting to catalyze social change, but rather to serendipitously abide by the prevailing racial politics of the institution in the post-Civil Rights Era. Williams recalled a few years after his career at Ole Miss:

> I came to Ole Miss because it was a challenge for me, and I liked a challenge. Also, I was recruited by Coach Junie Hovious, and I admired him a lot. He helped me make up my mind, plus I felt like I could make a contribution at Ole Miss. As far as what had gone on before—in terms of race—my attitude was that I couldn't change history. All that had already happened before I came to Ole Miss. If I couldn't deal with that, I shouldn't have come. (quoted in Wells, 1980, p. 136)

After arriving at Ole Miss, Williams quickly emerged as the best player on the post-Archie Manning squads of the early 1970s. Subsequently, as his role on the team expanded, his celebrity in the imagined football community of Ole Miss fandom swelled. Williams eventually took on the nickname 'Gentle Ben,' which he was afforded due to his 'savage-like disposition' on the field, and 'gentle mannerisms' off the gridiron. Williams' placid blackness, as opposed to the more virulent activism of members of the BSU during that time period, became a symbol of 'advanced, progressive' race relations at Ole Miss. In numerous commentaries in the *Mississippian*, white student subjects interjected that Williams' ability to work within the normative social relations of the University was 'a welcome reprieve' from the more strident efforts of many 'campus blacks.' Thus, Ben Williams' complicity, or the public persona constructed for Williams, served to reinforce the hegemonic norms of Dixie South whiteness and the authorization of preferred sterile blackness.[14]

In the fall of 1975, Ben Williams announced his candidacy for heralded post of Colonel Rebel, an honor bestowed on many a football player before, but never a black man. To the surprise of reporters from the *Mississippian*, Ben Williams won the award that spring semester. The awkward juxtaposition of a black man occupying the profile of 'Colonel Reb' in the imaginations of Ole Miss student subjects was soon displaced by a more discernible image, that of the 1976 yearbook which featured Williams and 'Miss Ole Miss' Barbara Biggs positioned with farmland as the backdrop, with the black man and white woman separated by a fence. Whereas the tradition had been for most popular campus coeds to interlock in the pose for the *Ole Miss*, this picture signified the separatist ideals regarding race at Ole Miss—the fence almost acting as a metonym for the separatist divisiveness of social attitudes within the institution. The inclusivity awarded Ben Willi-

---

13. Vaught never recruited a single black player to play for any of his Ole Miss teams, and thus his team were always and unequivocally racially-exclusive to white players.

14. Similarly, the University's most high-profile black running back in recent years, Deuce McAllister, donated $1 million to the University after his graduation as a gesture of 'appreciation' for the 'opportunities afforded him' at Ole Miss during his playing career.

ams for his service to the University (and its football team) was thus usurped by the segregationist posture employed against the black body of Williams and the white body of Biggs. Rather than challenge the normalized racial hierarchy of the Dixie South, Ben Williams's celebrity iconography promoted "integration without equality, representation without power, presence without the confirming possibility of emancipation" (Wiegman, 1995, p. 41). It can thus be argued that symbolic configurations of Williams' celebrity discourse, and the closeness of his sterile, 'gentle' blackness to the preferred blackness of an antiquated, hegemonic Dixie South social hierarchy, afforded him entrée into the symbolic universe of Dixie South whiteness, but only under *pretenses of submission*, rather than equality.[15]

Another significant figure in the black Ole Miss sporting iconography was Roy Lee 'Chuckie' Mullins, a defensive back for the Rebel football team in the late-1980s. While his accomplishments on the field were not as distinguished as Archie Manning or Ben Williams, Mullins has been posthumously memorialized as a seminal figure in the heroic Ole Miss sporting lexicon. In a nationally televised game, Mullins was paralyzed after making a tackle during the October 28, 1989, contest against Vanderbilt. When the severity of his injuries became clear, members of the University community came together to raise money to help the fallen athlete's family meet his medical expenses and continue his education. A few years later, Mullins passed away from complications resulting from the injury and surgery. Subsequently, his legacy as a gladiator of the highest order became further embalmed in Ole Miss lore—as well as inscribed into a memorial outside the Vaught-Hemingway stadium wall.

The more critical observers of the Chuckie Mullins trauma have posited that the philanthropical bent which motivated Ole Miss supporters to assist Mullins was suggestive of the pattern of 'white paternalistic behavior' common in the Old South's slavery days. In other words, some commentators have suggested that this post-facto egalitarianism too closely resembled the ambivalent humanitarianism of slave-era race relations, whereby the athletic black body only became humanized after suffering injuries while rendering services for the white power elite. Subsequently, such charitable actions did not offend the racial status quo of the Old South, but rather reinforced the iniquitous, patriarchal power relationships in which whites from posi-

---

15. As a further example of post-Meredith sporting servitude and preferred blackness, in 1979 Rose Jackson, an accomplished student and All-American basketball player for the Ole Miss women's team, elected to attempt to become the first black 'Miss Ole Miss.' However, her efforts were met with a great deal of resistance, as her campaign posters were defaced with by scribbles of the word "nigger" and many of her white classmates suggested to the Ole Miss senior that while they respected her, they could not support a black woman. Whereas Ben Williams was more easily accepted because of his athletic prowess and acquiescent personality, Jackson was perceived to be both too strident in her blackness, too rigid in her academic pursuits, and too masculine in her sporting femininity (Cohodas, 1997), and thus, while she was a much more qualified candidate than Williams, her mediated persona eclipsed the preferred intersections of sterile blackness and servile femininity.

tions of privilege bestow their benevolence on a particular black individuals in need—only to the effects of reinforcing the 'hierarchized racial code' (Mouffe, 1992). As King and Springwood (2001) suggested, by the latter part of the century at Ole Miss, this type of "racial paternalism was manifest as a patrician, Southern whiteness which, when mapped onto the newly racialized collegiate sporting world, turned on the assertion of difference, supremacy, and generosity" (p. 154).

Southern Man[ning], Redux

> *The ball is on the 50,*
> *the down is third-and-10.*
> *Some 30 years have slipped away,*
> *we don't know how or when.*
> *A Manning still under center,*
> *what other could it be?*
> *The best dad-burn quarterbacks,*
> *Ole Miss will ever see.*
> *The ball is snapped to Eli,*
> *the down it is the last*
> *he throws it to the end zone*
> *and what shall come to pass?*
> *A glorious win? Atlanta bound?*
> *Or a loss to LSU?*
> *Either way, they're father-son,*
> *Two legends, cast in blue.*

- 'The Ballad of Eli Manning' (quoted in Calkins, 2003, p. D1)

The University 'suffered' more than a few setbacks on the gridiron in the post-Vaught/Manning year. Throughout 1980s and 1990s parishioners of the 'Old South's football team' endured numerous mediocre seasons—which begat a renewed longing for favorable turn in their oblong-shaped fortunes. That figurative savior of the white sporting South soon came to Oxford in the reincarnate flesh. The Manning legacy first re-materialized on the Ole Miss campus in the form of Cooper Manning, Archie and Olivia Manning's oldest son, who briefly played on the Rebel football team in the early-1990s before his career was cut short by injury. Following Cooper's injury, expectations grew rampant in Oxford as the king of Ole Miss football was set to send his second son, highly-regarded quarterback Peyton, to Ole Miss. However, following an exemplary senior season at his high school outside New Orleans, Peyton chose to attend and play football for the University of Tennessee. While Peyton's accomplishments at Tennessee have become the stuff of legend, his 'betrayal' of the anticipatory heritage culture which he abandoned at Ole Miss fueled both 1) an ill-will toward the future Hall-of-Fame player and 2) the intensity with which his younger brother, Eli, was recruited to play football for the University of Mississippi.

Following an equally illustrious high school career, Eli chose to follow father and oldest brother, and fulfill his destiny as the hero son of the neo-

Confederacy. When Eli arrived at Ole Miss in the fall of 1999, he did so with "the fanfare expected of being Manning, a brand name in Southern college football" (Higgins, 2003, p. M3):

> Eli could be the family's best, and that's saying a lot since Peyton was the NFL's co-MVP, along with Tennessee's Steve McNair, last season, and Archie is still a legend in the South. Say 'Archie' almost anywhere south of the Mason-Dixon Line and you don't have to utter a last name. To understand Eli, you have to understand the Mannings and what they have meant to football in the South, particularly at Ole Miss. University chancellor and former NFL kicker Robert Khayats called the Mannings 'the DiMaggios of the NFL.' (Blaudschun, 2004, p. E3)

The room where Eli usually performed his weekly media interviews at Ole Miss was named 'The Archie Manning Room,' a space which featured memorabilia from his father's career and where his image dominated the interior decoration (Altavilla, 2004).

Accompanying the expectations of a return to the golden age of Ole Miss football which the 'Manning name' conjured up for many Ole Miss supporters, Eli brought with him a diachronically informed-celebrity canvas from which new articulations of celebrity whiteness could be formulated and mobilized. In a Machiavellian sense, the prince was empowered by, and counternarrative to, the king's elocutions of power:

> Talk about bloodlines. Archie was the second pick in the 1971 draft. Peyton was the first pick in the 1998 draft. And Eli figures to go No. 1, maybe to the New York Giants, if you believe the latest trade rumors. He's smart enough to say he doesn't care. 'I can't worry about it,' said the 6-foot-4 3/4-inch, 221--pounder who [emerges] as the most famous Mississippi quarterback since, well, Archie. (Blaudschun, 2004, p. E3)

During his career, Eli Manning rewrote all of the Ole Miss records for passing, replacing many standards which were set by his father in the early-1970s. More importantly, Eli became the acculturated embodiment of idealized sporting Dixie South whiteness in the era reclamationist white elitism. As the University 'celebrated' its superficial pursuits of racial diversity by rescinding many affirmative action opportunities for students and faculty, citing a 'lack of interest' from the black community, Eli emerged as the physical reincarnation of white entitlement and hereditary solipsism.

Eli's celebrity discourse thus became a story of devotion and destiny. Under the hyperreal auspices of familial inheritance and ascendancy through genetic dispositions for 'hard work' (think: George W. Bush as determined political figure, rather than product of systemic exploitation), Eli's physical prowess was celebrated as an effect of his father's meritocratic investments in physicality, rather than the successor of a distinctive Southern socio-economic stature. Perhaps more than coincidence, as the Junior Bush's ascendancy to power gained momentum in the South—and the wave of public attitude in Mississippi supporting the abolition of 'hand-outs' in the form of social welfare, eradication of public works for minority and women's projects, and lowering subsidies for Americans experiencing unemployment (Whiteside, 2003) intensified—the Junior-most Manning's iconage was similarly feted as a product of Southern individualism rather than stratified manifest destiny.

The vast majority of rich, white Mississippians—many of whom themselves were inheritors of 'old money' (in the form of plantation wealth)—had become mystified by the convictions of the dominant [white] Mississippi majority (and its politico-practitioners such as Trent Lott and Haley Barbour) and its newfound, post-Dixiecrat affinity for imaginings of the neoliberal self. That subjectivity was fashioned out of the fundamental belief that individual freedom can only be achieved through unfettered economic/market relations. Much like the antebellum political structures that contoured democratic governance around the interests and voting rights of the white majority, the neoliberal ethos on offer by Dixie's free-market reformers and their Chief Officers presented the plantation wealth inheritors of the region a feasible, and increasingly popular, system where they might seize a familial legacy while caricaturizing the politics of race and social class, the access afforded rich whites and denied poor blacks, and the racist histories which both were forged under.

While grossly under-theorized in the academic literature, this relationship between the cultural politics of race and the political economics of free-market hegemony are not loose ones. As Christopher Robbins (2004) explains:

> The cultural logic underpinning justifications of racism and racial inequality bear an uncanny resemblance to the economic practices and cultural politics that have emerged under the authority of neoliberalism . . . as contemporary racist practices and structures of inequality are now coupled with the authority of neoliberalism, which has so dangerously emptied the social and privatized vocabularies, neither racism nor racial inequality can be systematically contested or transformed unless the power of neoliberalism is simultaneously contested. (p. 1).

While Robbins quote speaks specifically to neoliberalism's systematized racial logics, it could be argued that racialized praxis and neoliberal polity share more than just an 'uncanny resemblance.' For both are structural formations that at once caste systematic inequities onto the individual whilst simultaneously reproducing a cultural economic order that assures power is unevenly distributed. In George W. Bush's 'Southernized America' (discussed more in the coming chapters), the postulations of the conservative Right for a return to individual wealth and end to social welfarism tethered the security of wealth and opportunity to those with capital and simultaneously cast the inequities of the system onto the imaginary failing of the racialized- and gender- individual (H.A. Giroux, 2004; H. A. Giroux, 2006).

At Ole Miss, Eli Manning came to signify a localized symmetry of wealth and inheritance veiled in this parallax of social conservativism and economic individualism. Decidedly, the fruits of Eli Manning's parochialized, politicized import were not a matter of accident, but rather:

> In following the father to Ole Miss, Eli is envisioned returning the school to its golden age of football, which ended more than 30 years ago with Archie.

> The son has created expectations that broil like the summer sun. They would smother him, surely, if it were not for the fact that he is Eli, meaning that in addition to his physical stature—6 feet 4, 215 pounds—and natural quarterbacking ability and all that he has been taught both by Archie and older brother Peyton, the Indianapolis Colts quarterback, he possesses a God-given knack for letting nothing faze him. Or so it would seem. (Gildea, 2002, p. D1)

The 'god-given-ness' of Eli's sporting prowess echoed Archie's corporeal superlatives, and connected the 'times not forgotten' to the new politics of Southern representation from which is celebrity sprung. Much like Archie, Eli's complimentary set of natural physical attributes and innate intellectual abilities was subjected to intense media adoration:

> Eli had a private tryout for scouts at the Saints' training facility over the winter, and the feedback was positive. 'Excellent size, good fundamentals and leadership skills,' read one report. 'He is intelligent and makes good decisions. He has an outstanding arm and can make all the throws. He has good vision of the field and the defense, and is very accurate with a nice touch.' (Blaudschun, 2004, p. E3)

And much like Archie's neo-confederated hero trope, the Eli-as-local-hero-figure narrative was constructed in the mass media out of the complimentary characteristics of 'dignity,' diligence, and deservingness. As a product of "the dignity and poise Eli has displayed in staring down what could have been an impossible legacy" (Drape, 2003, p. D1), the native son's public persona was both a product, and reproducer of, the former Manning's centrality as the seminal figurehead of Dixie South whiteness.

During his sons' days at Ole Miss and beyond, Archie actively marketed and manipulated Eli's position in the Southern celebrity vernacular to insure he received the fruits of his father's social and economic capital investments. The "son of Archie and brother of Peyton took the Fightin' Secessionists" (Hummer, 2003, p. 3F) to new heights of national notoriety during the era of sporting hyper-media, as most Ole Miss football contests were circulated through national television outlets and attendance and merchandise sales skyrocketed. Archie was typically featured on Ole Miss programs, and was often brought in as a 'guest commentator' during telecasts of Eli's games at Ole Miss. Following his graduation, Archie notified the National Football League's San Diego Chargers that if the first pick of the 2004 Draft were spent on Eli, the Ole Miss quarterback would sit the year out, and thus demanded that the quarterbacking son be traded to a more high-profile team if they were to use the pick on Eli. Archie Manning cited the lack of comfort he and Eli had with the Chargers front office as the reason for the demand, a move which drew heavy criticism in the national media. Most media commentators proffered that the real reason for the hold-out was that Archie had been in contact with the New York Giants, who were interested in attaining Manning's services. Those critical of Archie suggested that the elder Manning wanted to capitalize on his son's popularity in the more lucrative market of New York:

> The Mannings were characterized as manipulative crybabies before the draft when they informed the Chargers that Eli would sit out the season rather than play for them, forcing the trade to the Giants. . . . He came off as a real Little

League father in April, a characterization he detests, but he knew what he was doing. (Myers, 2004, p. 116)

Archie's careful stewardship of the early stages of Eli's early professional development has thusfar eventuated in a successful career, as the Ole Miss alumnus quarterbacked the New York Giants to victory in the National Football League's 2008 Super Bowl (and like his brother Peyton the year prior, was named that game's 'Most Valuable Player'). In that instant, the otherwise introverted Ole Miss alumnus was immersed in a frenzied media machine that saw him appearing on popular late night television shows, meeting President George W. Bush at the White House, and featured in various advertising campaigns throughout the New York metropolitan and US national media markets. Up to this point in his career, it would be hard to argue against the notion that Eli Manning has become Ole Miss's most successful professional athlete. In 2009, Eli signed the most lucrative contract in National Football League history, making him the highest paid player that sport has ever known.

Back in Oxford, Eli is celebrated as a 'native son who made it big'—an embodiment of Deep South corporeality done the right way. Whereas black athletes such as Eli's Rebel quarterback predecessor Romero Miller or successor Michael Spurlock (who also has gone on to play professionally in the NFL) were publically remonstrated throughout their careers for 'lacking the know-how' or 'discipline' to guide the Ole Miss offense, Eli has become the contemporary archetype for what many regard as his superior 'leadership abilities,' 'toughness,' 'command of the game,' and 'pedigree' (a discourse echoed in the plaudits now afforded current Ole Miss quarterback Jevan Snead). More critically, we might surmise that for many Mississippians, Eli's celebrity was one part reprise from Archie's heroics, one part mirror of his father's iconage, and one part crude poetics of late capitalism. Eli's celebrity skin was moulded out of a narrative defined by his 'close-cut brown hair,' [decidedly white] phenotypical profile, and parochial vernacularism as expressed in the imaginary and spoken 'drawl' (Gildea, 2002, p. D1); and thus he came to signify the return to a unique expressivity of whiteness and a power elitism structured around Old South lineage and 'new New South' problematics.

At the intersection of white privilege in the hegemony of *faux* egalitarianism, the hereditary politics of individualism in the South, and the drug-like enchantment with subversive iterations of Dixie South whiteness, Eli Manning's celebrity discourse links agents of the dominant faction to both the past (through the superior fertilization of Archie and his neo-Confederate stardom) and to the synchronic politics of exclusivity, 'angry Southern white male' ideals, and a colonizing Bush-era cultural economy of 'heritage' and 'lineage.' Consider: by inheriting the social, economic, and political capital to create his own conditions of labor (to not play for San Diego, a smaller media market and a team with a history of not awarding large contracts to its players), Eli was able to optimize the conditions of his labor. He was able to control his working situation so that he could maximize his exposure and potential success. Whereas an elite college football player with less capital would lack the capital to create such demands, Eli was able to achieve 'freedom' through his ability to exercise his inherited capital. Even more problematically, as Ronald Bishop (2009) has argued, whereas Eli was mediated as a 'gifted athlete' just trying to get what he deserved, African American players who were similarly attempting to wield some degree of autonomy is determining their labor condition within the NFL cartel structure were depicted as "moody adolescents" motivated "greed" and "their own self-interests."

Much like entrepreneurs in other sectors of US capitalism, Eli had 'taken the risk' (of playing in the NFL), but controlled for that risk by transforming accumulated capital into optimal conditions for accumulating power (and additional capital). Within the 'neoliberal doctrine of personal uplift,' writes Robbins (2004):

> ... citizens are responsible for their fates, the state is whittled to the protection of free markets and the policing of individuals inassimilable to the new logic. Put differently, as the state disinvests in the protection of citizens against the vicissitudes of the labor market as it is further deregulated, individuals, in particular those subject to the legacies of racism and racial inequality, are subjected to redefinition as expendable, dangerous, or personally responsible if they are found on the losing end of the new public pedagogy of neoliberalism or, in current parlance, if they fail to 'pull themselves up by the bootstraps.' (p. 3)

Antithetical to his 'greedy' gridiron compatriots, Eli Manning's ascent through the footballing ranks thus became symbolic of this de-historicized, anti-dialectic *bootstrap fortitude*. For his has become an *iconoclast of neoliberal autonomy* without the acknowledgement of how that autonomy came into being; inheritor of his father's whiteness, his brother's prowess, the Dixie South's fortunate son. As such, his is a body that confirms popular neoliberal tropes of hard work=success without complicating the equation by interrogating how that working body was conditioned for practice.

It could be argued that in the momentary Bush-bliss of [racialized/classed] market-based individualism, Eli Manning's touchdown toss ascendancy typified, and indeed personified, the body politic of contemporary Southern society. Even more critically, one might suggest that to embrace Eli Manning as anything else, or under any other pretenses, would deceive both the overt paleo-conservative ideologies floating about the mindspaces of the Dixie South capitalist class and, more consequentially, betray the structural histories by which his iconage has been fashioned. He embodies the modes of capitalist desire which contribute to what David Michael Levin (1987) refers to as "a reduction of human beings to the dual states of subjectified privatized egos and subjugated, engineerable objects" (p. 486). Thus, Eli perhaps embodies a more attractive paradigm for Mississippi's white elite: that strange amalgam of 'Libertarianism,' individualism, and social conservatism. Within the overlap of these three ideologies lies a common ontology that individual life chances, experiences, and outcomes are ante-structural; and that in the egalitarian 'new New South' the past is ostensibly past (and structures of privilege, wealth, inheritance, and so on do not matter).

On Rebel Anti-Dialecticism

These rhetorical and ideological moors mirror more popular mediated stylings of neoliberal/paleo-conservative Southern political figures such as Trent Lott, Joe Wilson, Ron Paul, or Rush Limbaugh. In turn, Eli's celebrity flesh can thus be read as a denial of the individual's inherited cultural, economic, and social capital (or lack thereof) and rejection of the historical and structural processes upon which these inequities are produced, and reproduced. As I have argued up to this point, corporeal whiteness in the South is both unique and contextually specific — one part access to orthodox power, one part visible materialization of what Alejandra Marchevsky and Jeanne Theoharis refer to as the 'racialization of entitlement.' Such "visibility," Sean Redmond and Su Holmes (2007) note, "increasingly functions as a way of ordering the world: to be in the media frame is to be at the centre of things, an idea so heavily naturalized that it often, paradoxically, seems difficult to *see* (through)" (p. 5).

The decidedly virile nature of sporting practice and proliferated sport discourse created a popular sporting realm at Ole Miss which has been, and continues to be, 'isomorphic' with racialized, masculine power (Miller, 2001). In other words, the dialectic of post-segregation sporting stardom activated the spectator sensibilities of a distinctive, contextually-specific Southern masculinity. Recent postulations concerning the patriarchal politics of sport, and the fluidity of masculinized, heterosexualized, and racialized sports stars, have turned toward contextually-contingent understandings of celebrity discourse as active product and producer of regimes of representational power. This trajectory of theory emanates from the notion that within the 'sign culture of celebrity' (McDonald & Andrews, 2001), discursive [sport] iconographies are encoded in the language and imagery of traditional regimes of power, and yet because of the superfluous nature of modern (and postmodern) identity and commodification thereof, the social knowledges constructed out of those discourses are, following Foucault (1977b), up for grabs, or 'free-floating.'

Borne of modern formations of power (see B. Carrington, 2001) which were inculcated with masculine, heterosexual, and white, identity politics imbedded in the celebrity texts of Ole Miss's most high-profile sports icons echo the specters of subjectivity and the systematized discourses of the Old South traditions and the politics of the visible center. The singularity of Dixie South whiteness as inscribed in the prevailing celebrity discourses of Manning further situated, and continues to situate, the visible center at the core of this parochial hierarchy and insulated the homogeneity of racial and gendered power-knowledge relations. Kaja Silverman (1988) details the affective qualities of such discursively constituted bodies on real human action in this way: "not only is the subject's relation to his or her body lived out through the mediation of discourse, but that body it itself coerced and molded by both representation and signification. Discursive bodies lean upon and mold real bodies in complex and manifold ways" (p. 59).

And so following the impetus for critical readings of white masculinity put forward in *Revealing Male Bodies* (Tuana, Cowling, Hamington, Johnson, & MacMullan, 2002), we can see how the public pedagogies of embodied celebrity articulate the gestic-ular, testicular, celluloid politics of preferred Dixie South whiteness. Rephrasing Andrews (1996a), the binary-reinforcing industrial era body pedagogies of Ole Miss's calculative football general John Vaught, the imaged persona of the most famed quarterback of the neo-Confederacy, Archie Manning, and the faux 'alternative' celebrity-hood of Ben Williams each offer an important passage in the mediated Ole Miss popular in the post-segregation era—and the problematic, yet celebrated discursive spaces in which preferred racial ideologies and representations are *publicized* and *authorized* in the language of a monolithic Dixie South whiteness. In this way, as McLaren suggests, "the body/subject becomes *both the medium and the outcome of subjective formation*" (p. 61, author's emphasis). Within distinctive contextual moments of post-Meredith Ole Miss, each of these *selfsame sporting symbols* captured, and indeed defined, the narratives and imagery of Dixie South masculinity as dialectically celebritized within the cultural economy of the visible center. These were not the only bodies that mattered in Ole Miss's Dixie South context; but as those most lionized, most omnipresent of bodily texts therein, they were mediated as to ensure that *they mattered most*.

From those pedagogies, the broader Dixieland constituency was paradoxically thrust into *the new logics* of *old racial hierarchy* in post-segregated South and the harmonious, *normal* race relations therein. In this way, the pedagogical formations of John Vaught, Archie, Eli, and other icons of Ole Miss [white] individuality at once re-write and erase history. Each inscribes into the collective consciousness the body politics of what Russell Ferguson (1990) describes as the 'phantom center'; at once *making visible* the corporeal-cognitive plaudits of whiteness (and thus displacing oppositional race-tetherings onto the 'Other') and *making invisible* the histories by which structures of racialized (and patriarchal) power have synchronically interfaced with those binary logics from which that power is made real (Kristeva, 1980). These stories of white achievement have "laid the foundation for the formulation of White power" (C.R. King, Leonard, & Kusz, 2007, p. 6).

Writing in George W. Bush's America, Christopher Robbins (2004) describes the contextually-important conservative ethos this way, "In this instance, *racism is reduced to a consequence of . . . personal 'taste'* and, consequently, is displaced entirely from the realm of history, cultural practices, and social relations of power" (p. 2). In recent decades, the measures taken by the University administration to provide greater access to the institution for Mississippi's black high school students has often been met with cries of 'reverse discrimination' by many campus whites. For example, in a preview for the 1990s backlash against affirmative action and equal opportunity, many white students publicly decried the measures taken by the University to make an education at Ole Miss more accessible to the state's poor black high school students. On July 10, 1984, the Gannett Foundation pledged $100,000 to help 'minority students' seeking an education at Ole Miss (Moore, 1985). Columnist Robert McLeod despondently scathed: "If you are a white male, look out . . . There are countless organizations, scholarships, and grants for everybody, but white males." McLeod's angst continued, "I am tired of working. I'd like some of that scholarship money, but I have something wrong with me. I'm white" (McLeod, 1985, p. 2).

The logic in this and other outcries was this: the over-representation of white men at Ole Miss was a product of hard work, industriousness, and agency; whereby white men simply worked harder than their black or feminine counterparts, thus deserved the opportunities and fruits provided them upon arrival. Following this logic, those individuals outside the University were excluded not because of the structural privileges brought to life by Ole Miss's admissions policies (e.g. standardized test scores and grade point averages that were guaranteed to be higher for white applicants), but because those outsiders were 'lazy' and looking for 'hand-outs' (Ferber, 1998b). Rhetoric of a disadvantaged, angry white male recurrently permeated the editorial pages of *The Daily Mississippian* throughout the 1980s and 1990s. The longitudinal proclivity of this crisis of white male hegemony typically incited one of three themes: anti-affirmative action, victimization of the hegemonic center, and defense of an imagined Confederacy. Some twenty years after McLeod's tirade, the Editorial Board of *The Daily Mississippian* offered a similar interpretation of the effects of greater opportunities for black students in the Ole Miss Law School:

> . . . one of the most negative impacts that these scholarships may have is that of diffusing incentive among black students who are aspiring to law school Undergraduates who plan to enroll in expensive graduate programs have a great incentive to work hard and remain academically competitive in order to get scholarships for these programs. If you tell any group that they don't need to do anything in order to qualify for substantial scholarships, it will certainly decrease their incentive to perform to the full extent of their abilities in their undergraduate programs. (E. Carrington, Scovel, & Salu, 2005, p. 2)

In spite of the fact that these scholarships are very competitive, these acolytes of ahistorical, anti-dialectic whiteness returned to the tropes of a perceived stultification of *their* privilege (as well as the overly popular 'lazy black' figuration). The racialized 'other' is in this way atomized and detached from the structures of economic and social hierarchy and at the same time generalized and demonized as part of, and situated within, the collective configurations of race.

This is Eli Manning's new Ole Miss—an institution where the "talk of race 'went underground' after the 1960s," and the white power elite turned toward a "more subtle and invidious rhetoric about 'qualification'" (Brattain, 2001, p. 243) in order to deny black individuals access to public power and employment opportunities—and thus entry into the 'Good Ole Boy' network. University administrators have suggested that the intermingling of racialized bodies has spawned "new, progressive race relations," as the Associate Commissioner of Higher Education for Mississippi proclaimed when speaking about the "new Mississippi" (Cook, 1988, p. 1)—a more racially tolerant and diverse state and University (Gurner, 1988). In much the same rhetoric vein as more popular axioms of a 'post-racist America' where merit is quantifiable and life chances are determined by a classless and raceless meritocracy. Under such a paradigm, the architectures of economic and socio-cultural privilege have collapsed as capital now over-determines all aspects of social order. Under this Milton Friedman-inspired ruse, all human activity is a market activity, and thus interaction becomes transaction—supposedly divorced from the historical and socio-political structures from which the transactional encounter occurs. Zygmunt Bauman (2002) explains this turn toward market individuality *sans* history:

> The subjects of the contemporary state are individuals by fate: the factors that constitute their individuality—confinement to individual resources and individual responsibility for the results of life choices—are not themselves matters of choice. We are all today 'individuals *de jure*' (p. 69)

Oher

At the impasse of anti-Affirmative Action hostility and the iconography of white excellence (sporting or otherwise) that came to define race politics on the Ole Miss campus during the George W. Bush years, we find perhaps the institution's most prominent pedagogic body: that of Michael Oher. Oher was a top offensive lineman on the Ole Miss football team from 2005 to 2008. The story of Oher, as we came to know through Michael Lewis's (2006) best-selling book *The Blind Side* and the Hollywood blockbuster by the same name (starring Academy Award winning Sandra Bullock) is this: Oher was one of twelve children born to Memphians Michael Jerome Williams and Denise Oher. His mother became addicted to crack during Michael's infancy, an Michael struggled through school (repeating the first and second grades) in part due to an 'unstable' home life (Oher's estranged father was murdered while he was a senior in high school). During his adolescence, Michael grew into a very football-productive frame, and was transferred out of Memphis city schools and into the private Briarcrest Academy so that he might bring his grade point average up enough to capitalize upon his growing football physique and reputation. With the help of Briarcrest teachers and through a few 10-day-long Internet-based courses from Brigham Young University (where he was able to replace Ds and Fs earned in earlier school classes with As earned via the internet), Michael was able to gain eligibility to play NCAA Division 1 football.

It was also during this time that Oher met the Tuohy family from Germantown, Tennessee (an affluent suburb of Memphis). As the film and book describe in detail, the upper-class family (the family's patriarch is a successful businessman who owns more than 80 restaurants and is a broadcaster for the National Basketball Association) shepherded Oher's development into both a successful student-athlete and part of the Memphis social elite. As Melissa Anderson of the *Dallas Observer* suggests, the film version of Michael Oher's life "peddles the most insidious kind of racism, one in which whiteys are virtuous saviors, coming to the rescue of blacks who become superfluous in narratives that are supposed to be about them. . . . The filmmakers would like to lull you to sleep with this milk of amnesia, hiding behind the fact that this bewilderingly condescending movie is based on an actual person—but one who you end up knowing almost nothing about." Film critic David Fear went even further, stating that the film displays "blinkered middle-class pandering at its most shameless." And while most white commentators (eg. Barbara Walters) in the US mediascape lauded *The Blind Side's* 'color-blindness' in representing the Tuohy's role in Michael Oher's life, many black media personalities (such as Vanessa Williams) criticized the paternalistic tone of the book and film. As the *Huffington Post's* Mark Blankenship wrote, Lewis's story "begs us to feel sorry for black people and feel grateful that there are white people in the world who can take [care] of them."

Perhaps more problematic is how Oher came to attend the University of Mississippi. At the urging of Ole Miss alumnus Sean Tuohy, along with that of Oher's high school coach Hugh Freeze, Oher accepted a scholarship to play football at the University of Mississippi. Soon after his signing, Freeze was offered a job as Ole Miss's assistant athletic director for external affairs (twenty days after Oher signed a letter of intent with the school). Upon suspicions that the Tuohys had taken in Oher in order to secure his services as a player for their favorite college, the NCAA launched an extensive investigation into the Oher case (one they have yet to close).

Herein lies the Ole Miss 'post-race' paradox. As I have attempted to detail in this chapter, the men of the 'good ole boy' network and icons of Dixie South whiteness emerge out of various historical moments always already bound to economic, socio-political, and institutional chains of interdependency; chains which link each—whether through a shared physicality, cerebralism, or genealogy—to the knowledge-power formations of Dixie South whiteness. And yet in recent years, and particularly in the context of a neoliberal individualist hegemony, men of the South such a Trent Lott, Archie Manning, and Eli Manning have come to re-emphasize not those structures from which their intersectional positionality is made relevant, but their individuality and individual accomplishment. These are the heroes of structural absolution; icons of a 'new New Southern' whiteness somehow detached from plantation-accumulation and segregation-privilege.

Corporeographic Whiteness

"It took getting away to appreciate Oxford and Ole Miss. I went to Alabama my fresh-man year. I couldn't get into the Roll Tide. It's not as traditional as Ole Miss is. Ox-ford itself is so traditional. It is a small, quaint hometown that becomes students' new homes." - Ole Miss student

"Ole Miss is an intangible experience rather than just a place. It is the beauty of the Grove, the sound of 'Dixie,' and the charm of Oxford itself." - Ole Miss student

In 2004, the University newspaper solicited Ole Miss students to describe their various affinities for the institution; to describe 'what makes Ole Miss special to them.' The responses, some of which are offered in the epigraph above, often referred to 'Ole Miss' as both a physical place and as an imaginary space existing beyond the trees of the campus Grove, the mortar of the Lyceum portico, and the architecture and geography of the geometric space in Oxford. For many, that imagined space of Ole Miss transcended the geometric features of the campus in a dreamworld of Southern hospitality and gentility; of 'intangible experience' and 'tradition' rather than lecture auditoria and coed dormitories. These quotes echo the sentimentality etched into the minds of many Ole Miss undergraduates, as well as the famous central wall of the Student Union: 'The University is respected, but Ole Miss is loved. The University gives a diploma and regretfully terminates tenure, but one never graduates from Ole Miss.'

In this chapter, I explore the 'signifying system' (R. Williams, 1981) of Ole Miss representational and identity politics and the 'continuities' across space, body, and history. This chapter complicates the spatialized Ole Miss body pedagogic and the interface between space and race therein. More specifically, I aim to elucidate the strategic use and manipulation of spatial aesthetic and infrastructure to examine the portents under which bodies operating within Ole Miss [imaginary and built] spaces are reformed and contoured through the progression of a Dixie South universalism—unified through both the centralizing function and race- and class-infused habitus created within the institution. Through a series of interviews with significant intermediaries of the cultural spaces of Ole Miss (architects, physical plant managers, and campus master planners), I engage the social constructs within, and social construction of, geometric space within the Ole Miss empirical—investigating how physical Ole Miss space organizes somatic and ideological conjunctures of the embodied (and the interplay between aesthetic, bodily, and imaginary spaces of the campus) and the disciplined (the conscience of a governing center, which 'one can never graduate from').

Theorizing the Corporeographic

Throughout this chapter, I synthesize a multifarious and occasionally contradictory *body of theory* on 'physical' and 'mental' space to develop a sociological interpretation of the empirical complexities at work within formations of discourse at Ole Miss. In so doing, I follow Vicky Kirby (1989) in explicating the 'corporeographies' that suture the politics of bodily practice to spatial arrangement. In particular, this 'spatial analysis,' or "the effective critique of representative and normative spaces" (Lefebvre, 1991, p. 356), will engage the work emanating from debates on late modern space as conceptualized by French social theorists Henri Lefebvre and Maurice Merleau-Ponty. I will also utilize the vocations of Walter Benjamin, Michel de Certeau, and Michel Foucault to expound upon the relationships between the body and competing and complementary physical and ideological spatialities within the institutional formations of Ole Miss. Acknowledging the multifarious, eclectic, and perhaps incompatible nature of such a vast corpus of literature, I first want to preface such an open-ended theoretic project with a few provisos.

First, my appropriation of, and engagement with, this diverse theoretical corpus is not merely a matter of conceptual reposition or juxtaposition (one upon another upon another), but rather a fusion (grafting the best of each) of a complex interpretive lens from which to best make sense of the phenomenon under investigation. For instance, while many cultural geographers, especially those theorizing from a Lefebvrean perspective, have identified critical contradictions between Lefebvre and Foucault citing "deficiencies in Foucault's spatial imagination" (van Ingen, 2004, p. 209)—I prefer to explore how Foucault's conceptualizations of governance and disciplinarity make Lefebvre's theory of space more incandescent, more empirically luminous. This prevailing critique of Foucault's space is that his theory fails to address the complexities of human agency in the production of social space. As Smith and Katz (1993) argue:

Foucault's pervasive substitution of spatial metaphor for social structure, institution and situation continues to elide the agency through which social space and social relations are produced, fixing these instead as the outcome of juridico-political forces (p. 73)

While this sentiment falls in line with broader critiques of poststructuralist thinking—whereby deconstructionism is misread as abstractionism—it fails to acknowledge that Foucault (1980), in the latter stages of his career, reflected on his own thinking about space and 'geography' in relation to discourse and formations of power in this way:

> . . . geography acted as a support, the condition of possibility for the passage between a series of factors I tried to relate. Where geography itself was concerned, I either left the question hanging or established a series of arbitrary connections. The longer I continue, the more it seems to me that the formation of discourses and the genealogy of knowledge need to be analysed, not it terms of types of consciousness, modes of perception and forms of ideology, but in terms of the tactics and strategies of power. Tactics and strategies deployed through implantations, distributions, demarcations, control of territories and organisations of domains which could well make up the sort of geopolitics where my preoccupations could link up with your methods. (p. 77)

Chris Philo (2000) has suggested that 'Foucault's geography' is more implicit in his archeology of discourse, and space as productive discourse is overpronounced while the production of social space is underdeveloped. The active agent is there in Foucault's theory, and if anything his theory seeks to strip back anti-agentive forces (Bratich, 2003). As such, my use of Foucault's archeology of discourse and Lefebvre's 'spatiology'[1] of more concrete forms is not intended to be read as an amalgamation of irreconcilable perspectives, but the synthesis of two heuristics, or inspections, converging upon the same set of cultural phenomena.

A second provision that must foreground this analysis is the penchant for ruptured appropriations of theory that the reader will no doubt find apparent in the following passages. It is my intention to vacillate between the poststructuralist abstractions of Foucault and de Certeau, and the more agentive (and cognitive) conceptual frames of Merleau-Ponty and Lefebvre—juggling the imaginative and cognitive with the signified and abstract. For each theorist offers a radical conceptualization of *body works as/are dialectical*: constitutor of space and constituted by space.

The convergence of *spatial physicalities* and *temporalities of space* (see Fielding, 1999) is perhaps best conceptualized in the phenomenological acumen of Maurice Merleau-Ponty. Merleau-Ponty (1945/2002) locates the origins of space within the movement(s) of the body, which he regards as holding a productive functionality in space. Further, Merleau-Ponty locates the body/space conundrum within two essential features of *embodied mobility* (mobilization of the spatialized body): expressive movement and bodily orientation—each of which results in interaction between the spatial and the corporeal (Kelly, 2002; Kujundzic & Buschert, 1994). The dialectic orientation

---

1. I will develop Lefebvre's notion of spatiology and its relevance to this analysis more in the coming pages.

of the spectacular (somatic, readable, signified, textual) body is not a consideration of solitaries; not as the body as it in fact is—or as a thing in objective space—but as a system of possible actions, a virtual embodiment with its contextually phenomenal possibilities. Thus, Merleau-Ponty (1945/2002) warns against isolating the body from space, as momentary producer or singular product of space, and rather petitions us to consider the ways in which body inhabits space—the body combines with space, includes space, and unifies space.

Henri Lefebvre (1991), in his seminal work *The Production of Space*, develops a similar framework for theorizing the complexities of space and embodied social discourse. He organizes his conceptualizations of space around a 'spatial triad' in which three conjunctural moments of dialectical simplification are identified: *representational space, representations of space*, and *spatial practices*. These three 'moments' of social space "are inseparable from one another and each involves, underpins and presupposes the other" (Van Ingen, 2003, p. 202). In Lefebvre's work, the body occupies, and is organized in, space; the body is space; the body produces space; and the body exists both within spatial configurations and the spatial imagination. For Lefebvre (1991), the body is the most imperative of spaces in the social/spatial conundrum:

> ... social practice presupposes the use of the body: the use of the hands, members and sensory organs, the gestures of work as an activity unrelated to work. This is the realm of the *perceived* .... Bodily lived experience, for its part, maybe (sic) both highly complex and quite peculiar, because 'culture' intervenes here, with its illusory immediacy, via symbolisms. (p. 40)

Hence, the body does not act in autonomy, but rather "the body is a composite and hierarchized space which can be invaded from the outside" (Augé, 1995, p. 61). Such an 'invasion' belies the externalities acting upon the body; and the power dynamic between temporal space, physical space, and the intercession of the two (corporeality). Space itself becomes a disciplinary technology which acts upon the body, as—through normalizing judgments and ideological imbeddedness—rationalized space converges on spectacularized physicality. Lefebvre (1991) describes the body/space relationship in this way: "all 'subjects' are situated in a space in which they must either recognize themselves or lose themselves, a space in which they may both enjoy and modify" (p. 35). The body is a stitch in the spatial fabric, the embodied conduit of imagined space and the representative locus of social politics (Casey, 1997). The corporeal subject, for both Merleau-Ponty and Lefebvre, acts within the realms of conception, perception, and spatial experience, vacillating between the ideological and the 'concrete' (Kelly, 2002).

Borrowing from the best of both Merleau-Ponty and Lefebvre, my intent is to develop a sociology of spatial ideology, as transposed onto and materialized by corporeal gesticulations and physical spaces which comprise imaginary and lived experiences at Ole Miss. The recent trend within contemporary social theory has been to conceptualize the active formation of space and the interrelatedness of space, place, ideology, and social praxis in the theoretical framework of 'spatiality.' Spatiality refers to more than the socially produced spatial configurations of social activity, to a stronger conceptual framework regarding the inherently spatial constitution of social relations (Giddens, 1984, 1990, 1991; Harvey, 1989a; E. Soja, 1989). In what follows, I map the articulated dialecticisms of the preferred meanings written into campus spatialities, the active body as a site for governance by the prevailing power structure, and the politics of whiteness which pervade and unite each under the imagined spaces of a collective consciousness of the Ole Miss imaginary. The interplay between physical space, corporeality, identity politics, and unifying discourse acts in consequential ways upon the lives of individuals within the society of Dixie South whiteness, and I aim to disrupt, if not implode, the perfunctory power structure embedded in this social and institutional dynamic.

At the collision of the 'juggernaut' of late capitalism as context (see Giddens, 1990; Jameson, 2001; Mandel, 1975) and post-positivism as paradigm (Lincoln & Guba, 2000), one of the more substantial contributions to the conceptualizations[2] of 'space' and 'place' was formulated by Michel de Certeau, who imagined a distinguishable, yet unified relationship between the two. According to de Certeau (1984), the former can be understood as a kind of locus, specifically as "a plane which is the order in accord with which elements are distributed in relationship of coexistence" (p. 117). Place is the cognitive, dynamic, representational, codified, and signified mechanism of meaning in practice. For de Certeau (1984), "place is constituted by a system of signs" (p. 117). In navigating the relation between place and space, de Certeau locates the notion of space as a frequented system of the experienced, mobilized by and understood as an "intersection of moving bodies" (see Augé, 1995; Certeau, 1984).

Space is a physical and imagined geography constituted by dynamic elements which meet, intersect, unite, cross each other, or diverge. Or, as de Certeau (1984) argued, "Space occurs as the effect produced by the operations that orient it, situate it, temporalize it, and make it function in a polyvalent unity of conflictual programs or contractual proximities" (p. 117). Perhaps the relationship between space and place can be described in this way: place is a "fixed position," and space is a "realm of practices" (Crang, 2000, p. 138). In other words, *"space is practiced place"* (Certeau, 1984, p. 117, author's italics). Space is the dominion of fluid exchange — exchange of practices, conceptions, and discourses of the products, and the producers, of lived experience therein. Place is fixed, bound to a particular location within discourse, while space is "composed of intersections of mobile elements" (Certeau, 1984, p. 117).

Following Maurice Merleau-Ponty (1945/2002), de Certeau likens his notion of 'place' to Merleau-Ponty's notion of 'geometric space,' or "a homogenous and isotropic spatiality" (p. 24). Geometric space is constructed out

---

2. Henri Lefebvre's *Production of Space* was printed in 1974, but the first edition to be translated into English came in 1991. Michel de Certeau's *The Practice of Everyday Life* was first published in English in 1984.

of the material world, and the language used by human being to locate fixed objects in the realm of the imagination. By way of distinction, Merleau-Ponty's notion of 'anthropological' space is reconstructed in de Certeau's work to refer to the dreams and perceptions defined out of, and by, distinctive spatial experiences. For de Certeau, an "anthropological, poetic, or mythic experience of space" (Certeau, 1984, p. 117) differs from the built environment or physical geography most commonly referred to as 'space,' as anthropological space is situated within the complexities of interpretation. De Certeau theorizes that place involves a varying level of perception, in that anthropological space is defined out "of the journeys made in it, the discourses uttered in it, and the language characterizing it" (Augé, 1995, p. 81).

This relationship between space and place is at the heart of the Ole Miss problematic, as the signifying processes acting upon Ole Miss subjects to demarcate Ole Miss spaces from Ole Miss places, or more importantly those which construct Ole Miss as collective 'place,' activate sensory nodes and cognitive experiences and the collective conscious of the institution and its members. This process is further detrimental when those symbols of Dixie South whiteness, and those practices of ocular racism, organize the signified constellation under which this unity in spatial discourse is constructed. Such an anthropological space, as utilized in the theorizing of Henri Lefebvre, has been described as "organic and fluid and alive; it has a pulse, it palpitates, it flows and collides with other spaces" (Merrifield, 2000, p. 171). As Lefebvre (1991) postulates:

> Every social space is the outcome of a process with many aspects and many contributing currents, signifying and non-signifying, perceived and directly experienced, practical and theoretical. In short, every social space has a history, one invariably grounded in nature, in natural conditions that are at once primordial and unique in the sense that they are always and everywhere endowed with specific characteristics (site, climate, etc.). (p. 110)

The spatial imaginations of Ole Miss subjects are dialectically intertwined in the 'perceived' and 'experienced' possibilities of the signifying system from which the University as 'place' is immersed.

Kristen Ross (1988) suggests that space "is not an immutable thing. It is made, it is remade, every day" (p. 91) through social practice. The interactions of the body, or embodied practice, and anthropological space thus create an aura of 'place,' a sense of representational location grounded in the logics of white-bodied collectivity, black-bodied ostracism, and iniquitous antiquities. Ole Miss space becomes a discursive formation which mobilizes a post-plantation aesthetic and operationalizes conduct therein to create a sterilized, strategically intermediated ether of solidarity under the arches of Dixie South whiteness. As such, in this analysis I will alternate between abstract space (discursively informed spaces of the imagination) and concrete space (material, lived spaces of the Ole Miss campus) in an attempt to illuminate the taciturn, yet congealing forces which constitute iniquitous social relationships within the contemporary Ole Miss empirical.

My central interrogative lies in the cross-examination of bodily signifiers floating throughout the various spaces of Ole Miss, excavating the oppressive articulations between triumvirate processions of signification, representation, and identification. Lefebvre (1991) refers to such a critical analysis of spatiality as critical 'spatiology'—an interpretive rapprochement between physical space (nature), mental space (formal abstractions about space), and social space (the space of human action and conflict of 'sensory phenomena'). Through an analytical triangulation of corporeality (the body in space), ideology (spatial imagination, or the cognition of place), and spatiality (the complex arrangement of discourse), the following analysis will illuminate the spatial constellations and discursive practices of empowerment within the logical and physical expressions of Dixie South whiteness at Ole Miss.

Of Phantasmagoric Kudzu

> *The lovely school is built in concentric circles, ever spiraling outward from the Circle. About a thousand yards to the east, some 700 of the Civil War fallen . . . are buried. William Faulkner walked the paths here. So did Willie Morris and John Grisham. History still overwhelms this campus like kudzu. The streets are named Confederate Drive and Magnolia Lane. The students are called Rebels.* – Linton Weeks (1999, p. C1)

Over the course of the long Twentieth Century, the physical spaces of the Ole Miss campus underwent a series of 'metamorphic' changes. Due to unprecedented growth in the student population, the first metamorphic phase (from the mid-1930s to the end of the late-1960s) brought about an expanded topographic radius and a doubling of the number of buildings on the campus. Unlike in prior generations, the buildings and campus spaces designed during this era exemplify a noticeable break from the original architecture woven through older campus buildings such as the Lyceum and the 'Y'. Function over form was the logic of the day, as these newer buildings were designed for their utility—bringing students onto the campus space and organizing their conduct once there. During this era, the Old South 'feel' of older buildings such as the Lyceum and the Chapel gave way to a more functional, 'brick box' style such as that of Bishop Hall, the Student Union, or Guess Hall.

In the second phase of campus metamorphosis, roughly from the 1970s through the 1990s, architects refocused the constructed, material spatialities of the Oxford campus (and those which I focus most on here) not just on institutional utility, but linking the symbolic and aesthetic qualities of the campus spaces to the ideals and ideologues of the Old Dixie South. During this period, the property (at least symbolically) and the produced (those bodies which had been operationalized over time within that space) took up an imperceptible likeness.[3] Through the reinvented similitude between the university geometric space developed during the era, and the embodied Old

---

3. Let me, for a moment, refer back to the first half of this project, and the genealogical analysis of deportmental transposition—the layering of a preferred masculinity onto the student body.

South signifying system of institutional neo-Confederates, an antiquated aesthetic re-emerged in the built spaces of the campus. For example, the Grove was cordoned off, and the football, baseball, and basketball arenas were constructed or remodeled to promote the burgeoning 'Rebel-esque feel' of the University. In this stage of metamorphosis from functional space to imaginary place, the fusion of symbolic space, physical space, and bodily space created a hyperbolic *mélange* of cultural isolationism, governance over the student subject, and spatial and ideological homogeneity.

Through a strategically contrived aesthetic and a tactically organized topography, the spatial landscape which now constitutes the Ole Miss campus is now undergoing a third phase of metamorphosis; whereby the semiotics of perceptible spatialities which *outline* and *define* the ideological possibilities produced within that space. Buildings created in the middle part of the Twentieth Century are now being retrofitted and re-aestheticized to accommodate the Old South 'feel' of the campus, as one campus architect explained to me: ". . . but mainly the changes to the exterior appearance of the building [are done] because it's not a style that's generally compatible with most of the other nicer buildings" (Personal Interview). That Old South uniformity, comes to life in and through various design features of the campus built environment. As this long-time Ole Miss planner suggested, even the most specific details such as the color of the bricks used in the buildings is carefully selected to 'fit' in the style of the 'nicer buildings':

> We do have a standard brick now that we try to use now whenever we can. If we're renovating an older building obviously we can't go and stick in a brick, a different brick on it, you know. But in some cases we'll try and match as close we can the old brick but, we have developed a standard brick that we try to use in every instance that we can. We started that with the athletic department, actually, when we did the baseball field, and we were looking for brick. We thought, well, you know, orange brick is not particularly good. At which most brick tends to be kind of orange, not particularly good for Ole Miss since we're red and blue, and athletic department in particular tries to have a lot of red and blue things in the buildings and such, particularly in the baseball field we were going to have red and blue elements all in that. So, we tried to get a brick that was basically red, and this one that we picked actually, it's a basic red brick that has some blue highlights in it, so the red and blue relates well to it, and everybody kind of liked that. So we kind of adopted it as our standard brick and we use it whenever we can on campus. (Personal Interview)

From the brick color to the nearly $3 billion in renovation projects undertaken over the past decade—particularly the restoration of the Chapel and Lyceum and the construction of new buildings such as the Ford Center for the Performing Arts—the University of Mississippi geometric spaces in this third phase of metamorphosis have been erected in the tradition of Old South nostalgia and symbolic collectivity.

A campus planner who originally hailed from outside Mississippi explained the linkages between the built environment and the 'Southern ethic' this way:

So, that brings us back to Ole Miss, which is to say that it is a very, very specific campus. And it does bring you back to the other thing that it has, which is this, this Southern tradition. And, it's going to take a huge amount of study to understand what that means. Some of it's nostalgic, I can speak of that as being an outsider coming in. Southerners like to think of themselves in a particular way. And I can say that without offending them because English people like to think about themselves in a particular way too. I think that I've been able to see how Southerners perceive themselves, probably, as well as most because I'm an outsider (not from the USA). I think that enables you sometimes to see things, maybe more clearly. (Personal Interview)

We might surmise from this quote that as a cultural 'outsider,' this individual can at once recognize the unique qualities of the campus space (while the cultural insider might only see those 'normal' Dixie South spatialities) and distinguish the particularities of the spatialized university that often coincide with the distinctive nuances of Dixie South identity politics.

This final metamorphosis of Ole Miss spatialities can perhaps best be framed within a synthesis of Walter Benjamin's interpretations of the early modern Parisian Arcades and Foucault's (1977a) (by way of Bentham) notion of 'panopticism' (see Buck-Morss, 1991). Much like the Ole Miss integrated spatiality, the architectural, ideological, and habitus-based interworkings of Parisian spectacular space is developed in the work of Walter Benjamin. As a politicized "phalanstery"—a dream world of utopian form and function (Benjamin, 1999, p. 5)—the Ole Miss campus, much like the Arcades, forges the prevailing logics (capitalism for the Arcades, Dixie South whiteness for Ole Miss) with the spectacular geometric spaces of the institution. In such a politically incorporated space, the property of symbolic universes is limited in that it constitutes a means of recognition, rather than knowledge, for those who have inherited them. Such spaces form "closed universes where everything is a sign; collections of codes to which only some hold the key but whose existence everyone accepts; totalities which are partially fictional but effective; cosmologies one might think had been invented for the benefit of ethnologists" (Augé, 1995, p. 33).

In his work on the physical spaces of the Arcades, Benjamin (1999) situates the blurred dyadic of material and ideological spaces within the notion of 'phantasmagoria.' For Benjamin (1999), the phantasmagoria is a collection of "rapidly shifting scenes of real or imagined things" (p. 9); forever swarming, constantly charming, always interpellating. Within the Arcades, the spectacularized space is layered onto the visceral geography, forging an inseparability that "beckons the flaneur" into the phantasmagoria—phantasmagoric space appears as both an open opportunity and an enclosed restriction, "now a landscape, now a room" (Benjamin, 1999, p. 10). Benjamin's interpretations and logics of the Arcades can be similarly applied to the physical spaces of the Ole Miss campus, moulded into a spatiology of the imaged, imagined, and the aestheticized.

Based on my extensive discussions with campus planners and architects, and a broader historiographic reading of various design and master planning materials, in what follows I offer a taxonomy of the phantasmagoric possibilities and phalansteric enclosures of the Ole Miss campus. This taxonomy will be divided into three parts: The first part, following Benjamin and Foucault, is an examination of the forms of governance woven into the architectural aesthetic of the Ole Miss campus, and how this 'representational space' allow for, and in some ways perpetuates, a 'cult of the ephemeral'—the ghostly landscape of Confederate pleasures, professions, and power relations within this context. The second part turns toward spaces of the imagination; toward the construction of an idealized spatiality existing somewhere amidst and between the borderland of physical space (monuments, tombs, symbols) and temporal space (the imagined 'Southern Ethic'). Finally, in the third part, I map the politics of spatial organization; and how, much like in Benjamin's Arcades or Bentham's prison, the physical spaces of the Ole Miss campus direct and *conduct performative conduct* therein. In form and function, each of the empirical illustrations which follows is not archetypically singular in its design, purpose, or interpretation; and each (i.e. the Lyceum, the streets on campus, and the Grove) can be read as constitutive of more than one of Lefebvre's spatial triad (*conceived* space, *perceived* space, and certainly *lived* space).

Old South Aesthetic(s)

Visitors to the Oxford campus quite frequently extol its 'strikingly beautiful' fascia: a fusion of classical and neo-classical cenotaphic buildings and a multihued montage of floral accoutrements bound to a geographically expansive and historically antiquated Old South gentility. The aestheticization of the Ole Miss campus, and the hallowed inscription of Old South gentility into that built space, did not come into being by happenstance. After careful consideration, according to an Ole Miss administrator, University officials commissioned the Fredrick Law Olmstead firm to create a master plan for the campus in the middle part of the century (Personal Interview).[4] A prominent firm noted for its members' contributions to the art of interweaving built space with green space (Rybczynski, 2000), Olmstead's group successfully conjugated the antebellum structures of the University with the prevailing magnolias and native shrubs to create a phantasmagoric Dixie South campus aestheticism. For Olmstead's firm, Ole Miss was one of very few encounters[5] in the architectural landscape of US universities, as the renowned architect usually worked with parks (such as Central Park in New York City and the U.S. Capital Park in Washington, DC) and estates (such as the Biltmore Estate and Gardens in Asheville, NC) (Rybczynski, 2000).

The process of creating a strategically-contrived aesthetic within the campus topography of Ole Miss initiated by Olmstead's master plan conformed to a long-standing celebration of 'Old South' stylization, one that

---

4. Chancellor Williams contracted Olmstead Brothers of Brookline, Massachusetts, in September of 1947, to construct a 25-year campus master plan.

5. Olmstead also developed a master plan for Stanford University in Palo Alto, California.

was metonymically intertwined with the plantation cultural economy of the Cotton South. Incorporating elements of the local and historical, Olmstead's vision[6] for the University was to develop an imaged space consistent with the early American architecture traditions of Greek revitalizations while maintaining the bountiful and lush greenery of the campus. Recognizing that the built environment of the Ole Miss campus was founded upon the classic Greek architectural influence seen in many plantation-style Delta South homes and buildings of the antebellum and Reconstruction eras, Olmstead seized the campus geography and reinvented it as *a living museum to early American South reinventions of classical architecture.*

Borne of the 'classical language of architecture,' the Ole Miss campus resonates the aesthetic logics of distinctive early American appropriations of Greek construction and style. The oldest, most prominent buildings on campus are crafted out of the Ionic order, which is a stylistic and chronological compromise between the earlier Doric[7] or later Corinthian[8] Greek styles, a synthesis which appears as both decorative and masculine in form (Chitham, 2004; Tzonis & Lefaivre, 1986). In the context of an emergent plantation cultural economy of the middle part of the Nineteenth Century, the Ionic order was popularized in the built environment of domestic (plantation homes), governmental (court and state houses), and public (universities) spheres (Lane, 1993). More importantly, throughout the Cotton South of the 1800s, the classic Greek language materialized as signification and signifier of the Old South political economy of genteel expressionism and aesthetic habitus of the plantation bourgeoisie (Hoelscher, 2003). In Mississippi, the spatial 'tastes' of the wealthy white were manifested in the convergence of a colonial style popularized in the early 1800s overlain with a layer of signified wealth expressed in the subtleties of the Ionic Greek order (Aiken, 1998). In revitalizing the plantation aesthetic from a century earlier, Olmstead, and his succeeding architectural exponents, protracted the imagery of the Old South colonial/classical architecture and the 'richness' of the campus fabric as defined through its connections to the antiquities of an imagined and perceptible plantation gentility.

The results of the Olmstead master plan, of which many are still in the making, are a multifarious geometric space—from the administration buildings and fraternity houses to the strategic campus-wide use of shrubbery and florally infused color schemes—which visually discharges a commit-

---

6. Following Olmstead's death, which actually occurred prior to the administration of the master plan, Ardemus Richardson of the Olmstead office in New York took over the Ole Miss project, and designed the campus space until his death in the early 1990s.

7. The Doric order is very plain, but masculine, or 'powerful-looking,' in its design. Doric, like most Greek styles, works well horizontally on buildings, and compliments the long rectangular buildings made by the Greeks.

8. The Corinthian order is the most decorative order of classical Greek architecture. It emerged much later than the Doric and Ionic orders, and features more curvature and tapestry.

ment to a socially and historically distinctive post-plantation aesthetic. In their design and manufacture, each building is calculatingly planned to incorporate various elements of style, texture, and color to correspond with, and complement, existing structures. When asked to describe the 'Ole Miss aesthetic,' a campus architect explained:

> I think it's both classical and colonial in nature. I think that non-architects with their nostalgic view of the University, and who may have been here as undergraduates or graduates years and years ago, have a fondness for the University. And I think if you would ask them to sketch on a napkin what their image of Ole Miss would be, I think they would probably draw columns. . . . So, in their subconscious they know that it has classical characteristics. [The University] is based in the classical language, which in turn goes back to ancient Rome and Greece. And when this nation was founded, the founding fathers saw that as a very stable image from which to found the Republic. They were very attractive images and that's where the classical language of architecture really captivated people in this country. And so when you come to the 1850's, you've already got a hundred years of architecture under your belt in terms of classical buildings and so it isn't surprising [this campus is designed in this style] (Personal Interview)

At Ole Miss, physical spaces are encoded in an overarching language of 'classical and colonial' architecture that enlivens, if not transmits, an Old South aesthetic—evoking both colonial (symbolizing the new-gentility which occupied plantation wealth in the period of westward expansionism and the university's founding) and early modern American classical regimes of architecture (the Grecian built environment as signifier of wealth and privilege).

Most of the celebrated buildings on the campus grounds, such as the centerpiece of the campus space, the Lyceum, have common aesthetic qualities, those of this 'classical and colonial' tradition. As such, the physical spaces of the campus are understood in the idioms of the imaged past and the visceral, habitus-based taste for the aesthetic. The first portent of Lefebvre's (1991) 'spatial triad' speaks to the aesthetic implosion of the ideological (perceptive space) and the physical (perceived space). Lefebvre's notion of *representational space* offers heuristic to:

> directly *lived* space through its associated images and symbols. . . . This is the dominated—and hence passively experienced—space which the imagination seeks to change and appropriate. It overlays physical space, making symbolic use of its objects. Thus representational spaces may be said, though again with certain exceptions, to tend toward more or less coherent systems of non-verbal symbols and signs. (p. 39)

The affectivity of *representational space*, or what Lefebvre interchangeably refers to as *lived space*, lies in the active construction of social solidarity and spatial unity (or normative interactions with that space) and through the value system assigned to the particularities of the signifying system.

In the first instance, this solidarity is formulated through the construction of a *unified spatial discourse*. At Ole Miss, the solidarities of space are constructed through the formulaic materializations of a common 'classical and colonial' architectural design. As one representative of the University noted:

Now we're trying to relate more to the original buildings on campus in which you get a collegiate style that was pretty much classical, or neo-classical . . . So we want our overall campus theme to be sort of, [or] at least relate to, classical. It doesn't have to actually be classical, but like the Natural Products Center, so it's got the columns on it, it's, uh, connects to Pharmacy and up to Chemistry. Between those two buildings with connectors to both of them. But it's a fairly new building, and while it's not what you would call classical style, it relates to classical style. It's got the little pavilion the out front with columns, and it's kind of stylized columns on the building itself that looks kind of, uh, what's done in there is cutting edge technology. . . . It looks more like, instead of the Lyceum, it looks a little more like a science type building, but it relates . . . So we're trying to make everything relate. (Personal Interview)

In trying to 'make everything relate', the arbiters of Ole Miss spatial discourse are placing value on the Old South aesthetic inscribed in the campus's signature buildings such as the Lyceum.

The 'building code' at once creates geometric homogeneity and in turn a codified scheme for resurrecting plantation South architectural habitus-based taste. Problematically, value is assigned to the aesthetic, and thereby the process of valuating the representational spaces on the Ole Miss campus frames notions of 'beauty' and normativity in the spatial discourses. The significance of that classical/colonial style was defined in the era of slavery, and mobilized by slave-owning bourgeoisie for the ocular expression of their economic, cultural, and social wealth and power (which was a product of racialized inequities within the region). By rearticulating antiquated regimes of such an aesthetic, the institution both locates itself within the imagined space of the Old South, and revitalizes the class- and race-based problematic of built environment a hierarchical signifying system. As an uncontested, [time-]honored system of signs, the Ole Miss spatial landscape organizes the spatial imaginations of its hegemons, whereby the population of "absolute space" by political forces (Lefebvre, 1991, p. 48) further weaves Dixie South identity politics into the discursive fabric of the institution.

Following Lefebvre (1991), such an absolute space, "religious and political in character, is a product of the bonds of consanguinity, soil and language, but out of it evolved a space which was relativized and historical" (p. 48). This 'relativized' space thus dialectically informs the present by articulating the past to the active formations of lived experience within the confines of the institutional geography. The Ole Miss lived space is both oppressive and enabling, constrictive and open-ended. Lived space[s] of Ole Miss is oppressive in that it can become "the site of discriminatory practices such as racism, sexism and homophobia and is where marginalization is produced and enforced" (van Ingen, 2003, p. 204). At Ole Miss, the unity in spatial discourse brought about by collective configurations of a 'classical and colonial' aesthetic imaginaries reconstitutes an aura of plantation privilege which harkens back to the slavery politics upon which the university was founded.

Consequently, the representational spaces of Ole Miss are enabling for the controlling intermediaries of the Dixie South social hierarchies of race, gender, and social class. In describing the unity of spatial discourse on the

Ole Miss campus, a campus planner outlined the strategic management of
the aesthetic in this way:

> You know we're trying to make all the buildings classical or neo-classical be-
> cause our best buildings are ... pretty much classical design. [These are] really
> nice buildings with *a good people kind-of-feel* to them. It's a good kind of human
> scale that relates to the feeling, makes you kind of want to be in the building
> or go in the building or at least appreciate the size and scale of it—a scale that
> relates to people that makes you want to go in the building. (Personal Inter-
> view, italics added)

Much like the plantation homes built during the same era as the classical
structures on the Ole Miss campus, the symbolic import of the designs and
designations and 'good people' aestheticization of the institution do not extend very far beyond the power-knowledges of the visible center.

By embalming, or resurrecting, Old South representational spaces, campus intermediaries deploy the *strategies* of spatial organization, encoded in
the politics of race and class based distinction and burden on the student
subjects operating within the ephemeral situation. De Certeau refers to
the notion of 'strategy,' which is suggestive of the "imposition of power
through the disciplining and organizing of space" (Crang, 2000, p. 137). The
control of representational spaces shapes the perceptions people can have
about that space, which in turn generates a normalizing function, as "space
is fundamental in any exercise of power" (Foucault, 1984a, p. 254). Thus, the
spaces of the imagination, and the discourses which dialectically engage collective memory, become both important and significant and the physical
space becomes that node which activates those affective responses.

Environmental elements such as light and architecture have been vital
to the implementation of self-disciplinary mechanism in geometric space.
Tony Fabijancic (2001), referring to the Parisian Arcades theorized by Benjamin, described the relationship between aesthetic and geographic elements in this way:

> Fortuitously for the builders and entrepreneurs, though it was not deliberate,
> providing aesthetic pleasure was also a method of control, initially working to-
> ward an entrenching affluent nineteenth century subjects' reified vision by re-
> directing or refining their intellectual or cognitive awareness about the crass
> commercialist reality in arcades, transforming the actual orientation toward
> profit into a cultural experience. (p. 143)

Within the social spaces of Ole Miss, the strategic management of physical
space leads to a secretion of normalizing judgments from within the physical
and ideological collective, as the embodied cohesion between mental space
(attitudes and appreciations for the aesthetic) and physical space (the aestheticized spatialities of the campus) operationalizes, narrows, and nor-
malizes. In simpler terms, white bodies operating within geometric
spaces—purposefully created and managed to promote an Old South orientation—redistribute the marginalizing forces of ancestral privilege in the
phalanstery of Dixie South whiteness.

The veiled *politics of representation* enlisted by *representational space* (and
vice versa) lead to the politicization of the aesthetic, and the aestheticiz-

ation of political. As such, it can be argued that each of these elements contribute to a racialized, spatialized signifying system coded in the prevailing logics of social relations within the region. And while the various spaces of Ole Miss are contested, the *prevalence of these codes* activates the power-knowledges of 'the double,' as the normalization of space creates normalizing judgments and thus normative practice—marking the territories of whiteness and the exteriorities of the 'Other.' Such a signifying system, since the days of slavery, has long granted affirmation and licensure to a code of racist praxis and social inequality. One critic has gone so far as to suggest that "for many whites in the state, the University of Mississippi isn't so much a school as a kind of secular temple" (Nossiter, 1997)—a temple which is secularized by the representational politics imbedded in the stylized spatial framework on the built environment.

Spatial Fabric of a Memorialized South

> *At the University of Mississippi, the past clings to the campus like kudzu. It's in the face of the marble Confederate who stands over the entrance to the famed Circle. It's in the Lyceum's bullet-scarred columns, enduring reminders of the school's bloody 1962 integration.* - (Breed, 2003)

The strategic construction and aestheticization of space on the Ole Miss campus is more than a prosaic tutorial in Old South architectural history. There is a hierarchical overtone amidst the pronounced Ole Miss aesthetic woven into the architectural fabric of the university's institutional spaces. The placid spatialities of the institution give way to ideological and physical appellations of 'place' which supports, if not promulgates, the diachronic ideological chains bound to the systematic reconstitution of a fusty 'Southern Ethic.' Returning to the epigraph and the placation of an embalmed Ole Miss spatiality, Ole Miss spaces ignite the obtuse (and obtrusive) sentimentality of a distinctive Old South populism. In other words, what makes Ole Miss a 'place' for many individuals is the symbolic, aestheticized spatial fabric of a geographic traditionalism in the order of the Old South.

Lefebvre refers to this form of space as the second construct in his 'spatial triad': *representations of space*. In the most generic sense, the notion of 'representations of space' refers to "conceptualized space, the space constructed by assorted professionals and technocrats" (Merrifield, 2000, p. 174). Representations of space, or 'conceptualized spaces,' are "tied to the relations of production and to the order which those relations impose, and hence to knowledge, to signs, to codes, and to 'frontal' relations" (Lefebvre, 1991, p. 33). For Lefebvre, conceptualized space "is the dominant space in any society" (Lefebvre, 1991, pp. 38-39), strategically constructed around discourses of a prevailing signifying system.

If, as I have suggested up to this point, the overarching utility of the University is to produce a dominant form of Dixie South whiteness through the human modalities of representational power, then the codified spaces within the campus serve to organize, if not make coherent, the logics of

this project. This type of social space "always remains imagined and is constructed through discourse . . . the kinds of social spaces that we engage
in through our thoughts, ideas, plans, codes, and memories" (see E Soja &
Hooper, 1993; van Ingen, 2003, p. 203). In other words, in representations
of Ole Miss space, physical space (the aesthetic of the built environment)
gives way to conceptions within the spatial imaginary. Representations of
space create a spatiality which is "*conceived*, and invariably ideology, power
and knowledge are embedded in this representation" (Merrifield, 2000, p.
174).

At Ole Miss, the social construction of representations of space is exfoli-
ated through the systematic signification of semiotic physical spaces. Over
time, the campus space has become a *museum of Dixie South whiteness*, a trib-
utary of the longitude of oppressive forces acting on the subjects of the
institution. The permutations of this "ideological blanket" (J. Baudrillard,
1983b, p. 25) reach far beyond the aesthetics of the campus space, beyond
even the inscribed history of the built environment, into history itself, into the diachronic imagination, retelling and rebuilding the myths of an imagined South. As Edward Soja (1996) argues, such a pervasive social order "is
constituted via control over knowledge, signs, and codes: over the means of
deciphering spatial practice and hence over the production of spatial knowledge" (p. 67). The arbiters of physical discourse at Ole Miss have created a
wonderland of the "Confederate myth"—a romanticized phantasmagoria of
"the South as a humane society risen in spontaneous self-defense of its sanctified institutions, its family and country life, against wonton northern aggression" (Silver, 1966, p. 150).

As counter narrative of social vagrancy, this universe of 'wish symbols'
(Benjamin, 1999), dispersed by those in control of production, serves as a
collective expression of the ethereal in tangible, monumental memorials. As
Debord (1997) argues, the degree of aesthetic success and conceptual perpetuity "is measured by a beauty inseparable from duration, and tending
even to lay claim to eternity" (p. 90). Through these symbols, physical space
becomes mythologized space, which promotes the ideological products of a
prevailing "wish imagery," whereby "the collective seeks both to overcome
and to transfigure the immaturity of the social product and the inadequacies
in the social organization of production" (Benjamin, 1999, p. 4). Mythologized history (collective memories of the center) is authority at Ole Miss,
and collective solace becomes knowledge and thus power, distributing privilege through the nodes of a collective conscience.

At Ole Miss, strategically conceptualized physical spaces alert the senses
to a liminal vista, collapsing the distance between physical space and imagined place. Through the consecration of symbolic artifacts, memorialized
monuments, celebratory encomia, eternalized interments, and semiotic
statues, these representations of space unify signifier and signified, as the

contemporary (experiential now) with the historical (discursive then).[9] The campus buildings, by dictum of campus administrators, were to remain "consistent in form and style to the existing structures and built on site within the campus proper" (Sansing, 1999, p. 265). More importantly, the visual accoutrements of power written into the newly formulated spatial texts mobilized the power dynamic of space, creating a geography of knowledge and a topography of imagined entitlement. The intermediaries of the campus space thus constructed a semiotic-burdened layout defined by commemorative decorum, an imaginary infrastructure, and terrestrial monuments.

The effect, as one student commentator recently noted, is that the spaces of the Confederacy on the Ole Miss campus serve as divisive markers and demarcations of neo-Confederate racialized spaces within the university:

> The university has a Confederate cemetery, a Confederate monument, a stained glass window honoring Confederate soldiers and a street named Confederate Drive. Even Colonel Reb, the nickname 'Rebels' and the words 'Ole Miss' are wistful reminders of Mississippi's pro-slavery and anti-minority past. ("UM should honor Black History Month with diverse monuments," 2000, p. 2)

This constellation of signified spaces act in concert to create a stratosphere of discourse—whereby space and identity actively interchange, and the celebrated politics of Dixie South whiteness permeate the pliant bodies partied (apartheid) to this oppressive imaginary. I will now, in turn, offer a brief introduction to these discursive sites which comprise such constellational *spaces of representation*, and thus constitute the spatial fabric of the memorialized Dixie South on the Ole Miss campus.

Firstly, one of the University of Mississippi's most 'picturesque,' and certainly most pictorialized, buildings is the centrally-located (connecting the Grove and the Circle) Ventress Hall. The building has served as the University's main library, and the home for the College of Liberal Arts. Ventress Hall, the first building constructed on the Ole Miss campus following the Civil War, has undergone a number of cosmetic changes over the last century. A campus architect described the building in this way:

> ... it's more playful, and it's got the little turrets, the little towers, and is highly attenuated, it's having more fun. The Lyceum is a very serious building. It would be extremely uncomfortable if, for instance, you move those two buildings, if you put Ventress at the end in that prominent place at the end of the Circle, and the Lyceum on the side, everybody would understand even if they'd never been to an architectural lesson in their life, they may not know what it is, but they'd know there was a hierarchical problem, and that this,

---

9. Not coincidentally, a majority of the hyper-symbolic spaces were developed within the Ole Miss campus during the post-war period of intensified collectivity and US nationalism (see Chapter 3). The influx of post WWII student enrollment served as a catalyst for the addition of several new buildings on campus. This expansion of the Ole Miss built environment was part of a strategic plan to install new physical spaces to accommodate the growth of the University populace in lieu of the G.I. Bill.

this buildings the boss, sitting down there, and then off to the side it needs to be, put right where it's on the axis. And so Ventress, in the cast of characters is a supporting character. Although it's got significance in its own rights, of course. (Personal Interview)

In addition to the towering turret, castellated walls, expressive Romanesque arches and lintels of stone and concrete, and the two-level attic which rises skyward under the steeply-sloped roof, there are two features for which the architectural showpiece is best known.

The first is a fine stained glass representation of the Confederate Grays heading off to war, which is located on the northern face of the building's central stair hall. The window commemorates the many students who joined the Confederate cause at the onset of the Civil War. Linking collective space to imagined place, the stained glass embodiment of diachronic physicality as instrument of the machinations of ideology reinforces the configurations of power-knowledge which permeate the campus space (see Zizek, 1989). The body layered onto geometric space serves an encapsulating function, uniting the politicized corporeality of warring militia (the instrumental corpse as extension of a Confederate ideological corpus) with the spatialized and stylized discursive formation of the built environment. As further linkage to the past, students at the university have prolonged a tradition of inscribing their names, dates, and hometowns onto the walls of the second floor of Ventress Hall, and thus symbolically etching the individual subject onto the collective body, the attitude of an entity within an imagined totality. The University Museum's graphic designer explained:

> Legend has it that a Confederate veteran signed the staircase wall first. We found several names, but one—J.R. Anderson—caught our eye because of his handwriting, this old-fashioned script. And it was in the middle of a cluster of names from the 19th century. (quoted in Houston, 2004, p. 1)

And through the legend of J.R. Anderson, and the specters of the 'Lost Cause,' the traditional rites of exodus become symbolic gestures of the Confederate collective.

Further, the walls of Ventress Hall act as an expression of the intersectional hegemony of: communal cognitive space, transpositions of the active physical being layered onto the geometric canvas, and the active relationship between spatial practices and spaces of representation. As one campus planner described:

> it's one that when the art classes go draw something, that's the one they draw. So it's probably the most photographed and drawn building on campus. But it's an interesting style with the spires and the stained glass window in there commemorating the University Grey's and all that kind of thing. It's got a lot of history in the building itself. And the tower of the spiral staircase that goes up has signatures from students from the early 1900's on. So we've several governors and senators and folks like that that have signed the stairwell in there. So it's an interesting piece of campus. (Personal Interview)

The charming and 'playful' nature of the building gives Ventress Hall is location within the aesthetic imagination, while the symbolic layers of commemoration give the building its identity within the pantheon of Ole Miss spaces of representation. In other words, the aestheticized built environment alone stands as an awkward, yet well-received juxtaposition of style and function in the central space of campus, while the spatial narrativization of the building, that which gives it an assonant quality in the imaginations of the Old South, is bound to the traditions of the University Greys and the rites of the institution's degree-holders.

Secondly, the dual functionality of campus streets and buildings (organizing the flow of traffic; symbolizing the lifeblood of the institution) is an interesting, if not important, element in the social production of *différance* (the social creation of cultural difference) and *communitas* (momentary collectivity, the transient space of the imagined communal) and thus the spatial politics of the Ole Miss campus.[10] The infrastructural 'labyrinth' of paved streets, paved sidewalks, and barren pathways, acts as a system of vessels through which human capital flows, connecting the main arteries of the campus and connecting transportation-oriented spaces to symbolic and imaginary spaces. The vascular nature of the campus infrastructure is perhaps only superseded by the signified relevance of these conduits of symbolic resilience and the ideological, trans-historical collective. Rephrasing Walter Benjamin (1999), I argue that no less important than the symmetry of the campus's layout is the unconquerable power in the names of the streets, squares, and theatres, a power which persists in the face of all topographical displacement (p. 516).

With regard to the naming of streets, the cultural intermediaries of Ole Miss have created a topographic web of glorification and memorialization of the Old South. Through the strategic naming of streets, the campus has been transformed into a "linguistic cosmos" (Benjamin, 1999, p. 522) whereby the ideological spaces of the Confederacy intercept, and intersect, at the junction of such roadways as Rebel Drive, Confederate Drive, Jeff Davis Drive, and Lee Loop. To the delight of the Old South sensibilities, the classification system of traffic routes has taken on a "peculiar voluptuousness" (Benjamin, 1999, p. 517), as street names become symbolic of the broader *communitas* (Alderman, 2000). The passage through campus takes on an imaged life unto itself, as individuals are confronted by a dominion of representational space and spaces of representation. As Benjamin suggests, "street names are like intoxicating substances that make our perceptions more stratified and richer in spaces" (Benjamin, 1999, p. 518). Collective Confederacy of the logics of an imagined Ole Miss community is thus not only inscribed in the linguistic cosmos of street names, but the act of transport on these symbolic spaces becomes that spatializing action which concretize the bond between the active body and representational space.

The celebration of a 'Southern ethic,' and the homogenization (or unification) of a racialized collective conscience, is cemented in the representa-

---

10. In the next section I will further discuss the organizational infrastructure and the organization of space as disciplinary apparatus, but here I want to briefly flesh out the titles of Ole Miss campus streets and buildings as a further stylization of hegemonic (entitled) Dixie South whiteness.

tional network of signposts and pavement which meanders throughout the campus physical space. The further embodiment of that 'Southern Ethic,' as inscribed into the celebrity discourses of Ole Miss sporting icons, is transfixed onto the streets through naming practices and symbolic overtones (Alderman, 2000). For example, the commemorative signpost at the entry point to Poole Drive reads:

> Poole Drive honors the legacy of the Pooles of Ole Miss, who stand proudly as one of the shining cornerstones in the history of the University of Mississippi athletics. This one family—beginning with the fabled trio of brothers Buster, Ray, and Barney Poole—were the first of many Poole student athletes at Ole Miss. It is an athletic lineage like no other at the University. Buster's son Jim, and Ray's son, Ray, Jr. suited up for the Rebels as did cousins Fleming, Phil, Jack, Oliver, and Leslie Poole. Reggie Robertson and Joseph Robertson, whose mothers were Pooles, and nephews Paige Cothren and Robbie Robertson. Among this extraordinary family, a total of 47 athletic letters were earned. From the sandy banks of the Homochitto River in northern Amite County, the Poole family members have left their indelible mark on the pages of the record books and in the memories of Rebel fans. They will forever be remembered as one of the greatest families in the history of intercollegiate sports in America.

This recounted genealogy of the Poole family, and their impact of the sporting imaginations of the Ole Miss spectator, cuts a historicized, unidirectional line through perceived sporting space much like the linear design of the passageway which bears their name crosscuts the geometric campus space. The celebration of Ole Miss sporting celebrity as an extension of embodied ideological space is further represented in the signposts which authorize acceptable speed limits throughout campus. While American regulation of the speed of vehicular transportation is almost always organized in increments of five miles per hour, the speed limit throughout the Ole Miss campus is "18" miles per hour. The extraordinary spatio-temporal regulatory symbolic is commemorative of the university's most esteemed sporting icon, Archie Manning. During his playing career at Ole Miss, Manning wore the number "18" on the back of his jersey (a jersey which as since been retired).

Thirdly, the naming of campus buildings holds a similar utility in the promotion of unified spaces of representation at Ole Miss (see Hale, 1999). Through the narrative of the built environment, disparate campus locales become a unilateral campus text, upon which a thesis of hyper-masculinity, Old South conservativism, and the politics of Dixie South whiteness is transposed. Through a geographically and aesthetically expansive collection of buildings, such as Vaught-Hemmingway Stadium (the physical materialization and iconic commemoration of the legendary football coach's contributions to the University), Paul B. Johnson Commons (celebrating the life's work of former Governor and Lieutenant Governor who physically blocked James Meredith's admission attempts in 1962), Bondurant Hall (honoring the University's first head football coach), Lamar Law Center (in memoriam of the secessionist politician and University professor), and the Trent Lott Leadership Institute (in tribute to the [formerly] segregationist U.S. Senator from Mississippi). Each of these buildings is immersed in the structural impetuses of campus life: both the need for physical structures in the development of the campus space, and the 'mental' structures of spectacularized Dixie South masculinity which comprise a panoply of separatist space. These legends of white accomplish, and the commemoration of their efforts through the naming of buildings, further cements the relationship between the ideological and the spatial (Fusco, 2005, 2006).

While students of the University likely traipse though the halls of buildings named for Johnson, Lamar, and Bondurant with no historical grounding of their separatist doings, Lott's more contemporary neo-segregationist profile is prevalent in the political imaginations of American political spectators. Regardless of its inhabitant's political and historical awarenesses and sensitivities, by naming a building in Lott's honor, and in the honor of Johnson, Lamar and the others, campus edifices are transformed into meaningful spaces of representation—bound to the Old South logics of privilege and separatism. In conjunction with the naming of streets bound to the same logics, the geography of Ole Miss constitutes a contemporary plantation-like space of reverie, tradition, and imagined configurations of the confederate collective.

Fourthly, the most pronounced nostalgic creation of the parochial geometric landscape of the Ole Miss campus is comprised by the configuration of four homag[inations] to soldiers of the 'Lost Cause.' A monument in the campus Circle commemorating fallen Confederate soldiers serves as the centerpiece of what Fredric Jameson (1984) refers to as the "aesthetic of cognitive mapping"; whereby fragmentations of the social body create the need for a recognizable discursive constellation that "enables a situational representation on the part of the individual subject to that vaster and properly unrepresentable totality which is the ensemble" (p. 90). The ether of a Confederate ensemble is comprised of: the monument in the center of campus, a monolithic shrine in the Grove, Confederated, flag-pierced phallus erected in the center of the Circle, and a cemetery behind C. M. "Tad" Smith Coliseum where "several hundred Union and Confederate soldiers who died while being treated in the university hospital are buried in unmarked graves" (Sansing, 1999, p. 111).

The Confederate monument in the Circle is perhaps the most conspicuous of campus edifices. Its central locale allows the gaze of extolled soldier perched atop the memorial, peaking above the tree-line, stretches across the vast campus space (and perhaps more importantly, so the campus inhabitants can readily gaze back). Also holding a central position in the geometric campus space are the Class of 1986's monolith which petitions for Ole Miss students to "Preserve our Heritage" and flag garden directly outside the Lyceum which hosts the modified banner of the Confederacy—the Mississippi state flag. Lastly, the most revered space of representation on the Ole Miss campus, the Civil War Cemetery, sits atop a hill on the northern edge of campus. The central marker of the cemetery functions in a Tolkien-like double spatial consciousness, a second tower from which the flows of Old South power can oscillate from and between. The diffuse symbolic power emanating from the structures of the built environment are in some ways the lifeblood of a prolonged Confederacy, as the spaces of representation consecrated around the lifeless body (such as those depicted in the stained glass representation in Ventress Hall) act upon the living body in meaningful ways. As Marc Augé (1995) posits, "the mummification of a body and the erection of a tomb completes the transformation of the body into a monument after death" (p. 62). That transformation, from living to dead and back, fossilizes in perpetuity the connection between the physical spaces of Ole Miss, the imagined spaces of its constituents, and the identity politics which shape hyper-conformity at the University.

Southern Synoecism

Lefebvre's (1991) spatial analysis takes a number of detours through both time and space, perhaps none more useful to our purposes here than his study of Theseus and Roman synoecism. By gathering village folk into one city-state to form a more integrated political power, Roman leader Theseus proscribed a new distribution of space, power, and lived experience—the synoecism. In turning his attention toward spaces of lived experience, Lefebvre points to the synoecism and the modern regimes of control through the organization of space. The third installment in Lefebvre's 'spatial triad' contemplates the political function of spatial management, what he refers to as *spatial practice*. Spatial practice, for Lefebvre, "embraces both production and reproduction, and the particular locations and spatial sets characteristic of each social formation," as "spatial practice ensures continuity and some degree of cohesion. In terms of social space, and of each member of a given society's relationship to that space, this cohesion implies a guaranteed level of *competence* and a specific level of *performance*" (Lefebvre, 1991, p. 33, author's italics).

Spatial practices could thus be defined as "conception and execution, the conceived and the lived, [which] somehow ensure societal cohesion, continuity, and what Lefebvre calls a 'spatial competence'" (Merrifield, 2000, p. 175). This conceived space, as Edward Soja (1996) explains, is "the process of producing the material form of social spatiality, [it] is both the medium and outcome of human activity, behaviour and experience" (p. 66). Spatial intermediaries configure social space in a calculated orchestral of human activity and performativity. As such, the orchestration of spatial practices becomes both a medium and means of social control. Drawing on the work of Foucault, Clive Barnett (1999) argues that in this way the body is constantly subjected to:

> new forms of discipline that are precisely calculated to regulate the movements, gestures and attitudes of the bodies of its subjects . . . disciplinary power is exercised through the spatial distribution of individuals in order to subject them to various modes of surveillance and monitoring. (p. 378)

The diffusive nature of this form of governance infiltrates the perception of physical or material space, as spatial practices "involve the use of an estab-

208

lished spatial economy characteristic of each social formation (place) and demonstrate the ways in which bodies interact with material space" (van Ingen, 2003, p. 203). Interactions within space are bound up in "an economy of representation and difference" (Crang, 2000, p. 142).

In the spatial practices of the institution, where "representations of space and representational space, though they do not coincide, are harmonious and congruent" (Lefebvre, 1991, p. 247), the lived spaces and the conceived space converge into a sophisticated "body schema" (Simmel, 1918/1971) of spatial disciplinarity and individualized governmentality. While Lefebvre argues that to empiricize spatial practice one must conduct individualized accounts of the routines of human agents acting with space, he also suggests that the politics of spatial design[11] work in tandem with social practices to create a cohesiveness between the logical and the spatial, as the spatial practice of a society "is revealed through the deciphering of its space" (Lefebvre, 1991, p. 38).

To understand and critically engage the spatial practice at Ole Miss, I will offer a synthesis of Benjamin's spatial poetics and Foucault's hermeneutics on governmentality. In Benjamin's Arcades, the topo-geometrics of spaces of consumption are first organically, then strategically, organized to promote the ideals of hyper-consumerism. The panoptic relationship between carceral disciplinarity and disciplined bodies found in Bentham's panoptic prison setting could be translated (as Foucault suggests) to the order and discipline of everyday life (Foucault, 1977). In modern Western spaces of representation such as the Arcades of Paris or the campus of Ole Miss, discipline has been "centered on a motivation or even a visceral need among conservative governing elites with aristocratic pretensions to control [public] space" (Fabijancic, 2001, p. 142).

The organizational infrastructure of the University of Mississippi was described by a longstanding campus architect whom I spoke with as a 'spine,' a linear configuration which distributes power along an x-axis of historical and spatial linearity. His description is worth quoting at length:

> I would say it's [the campus] laid out along a spine. An east-west spine that begins at the Square, which is non-university property, of course. It may even begin at the Square, but I think that's where it's most noticeable. It moves west from the Square along University Avenue and then onto campus: University Avenue crosses the threshold between the main entrance to the University, actually around about the M House. And then, there is a, what I think of as a, preliminary kind of portal or gate into campus, and you now pass the new forts enter on your right hand side which is the north, and goes forth to the south which is a less significant building. And then the Ford Center. And then critically you pass over, truly what I believe is the threshold which is the rail, the old railway bed known as Hillgard Cut. That's traveled the busiest and the

---

11.Lefebvre refers to motorways and the strategies for organizing air transport as sites for understanding the complexities of spatial practice. These and numerous other synoecistic apparatuses in modern society act to control activity, regulate the flows of humanity, and create a universal governmentality bound to the spatial logics of the dominant regimes of power.

north south direction. You pass over that and you find yourself at the Welcome House, or the Guard House. It depends on how you view the security, which is a little wooden shack, and which is traffic control. The road past is Oak. In a westerly direction or east-west direction as far as the war memorial, which is right at the entrance to the Circle. The Circle's well known. We talk about key objects along this east-west axis but then the Lyceum which is the first significant building to sit on the axis, it was recently renovated. Now Longward has recently undergone restoration, not renovation. Moving all the way through the Lyceum you come to a library which has had a key addition placed on it's west side. You're still on this east-west axis moving west, you can go all the way to the library, you come out at the other end and you find yourself in the new quadrangle still moving east to west. The quadrangle is terminated on it's east side by a library that you just walk through, and on it's west side by the new chapel. Then the, the spine, the actual spine, we can say that it ends at the Chapel. But if you stand on the west side of the Chapel on axis, you can see all the way up to Dyson Hall, so that the axis gets weaker as it continues all the way up to Dyson. (Personal Interview)

Within the Ole Miss 'axis' of spatial power, buildings are organized within the significant 'syntactic codes' (Eco, 1986) of this 'spine,' which extends to both the eastern and western ends of the campus boundaries. From this linear power formation, discipline can be distributed outwardly to the reached of the university grounds. Whereas in the panopticon described by Bentham, and later Foucault, surveillance of the prison guard evoked self-discipline by the imprisoned, in the panopticon of the Ole Miss campus, the eternal gaze of the dominant ideologues and the osmosis of a phantasmagoric phalanstery serve as the disciplinary mechanisms.

At the fulcrum of the 'axis' lies the aforementioned Lyceum. The Lyceum, the oldest building on the Ole Miss campus, was constructed from 1846-1848 by a local contractor. William Nichols[12] was chosen by the Board of Trustees as the architect by a vote of five to three, in part to his commitment to a traditional style of the Greek tradition. It has been suggested that the exterior of the building "still preserves the dignity and tradition of the Old South" (*History of the Lyceum*, 1952, p. 1). The building is constructed of brick, with a portico in front, "resting six columns, of the Corinthian order, finished in a plain, neat and substantial manner" (Walton, 1995, p. 4). Styled in the Prostyle tradition, having a heastyle portico on the front entrance, the proportions of the columns and entablature of the portico "are taken from the Grecian Ionic Temple on the Illyssus near Athens" (Walton, 1995, p. 3).

The adoption of a Greek aesthetic, in the era of university expansionism, signified the cultural politics of Classical intellectualism, as well as similitude of the imagined American *universitas*. The building also features a memorial clock, sanctioned by the Class of 1927, as well as a bell, where the ringing of which symbolizes athletic victory or celebration of some other sort. Beyond the documented and aesthetic accounts of the university's cornerstone structure, the symbolic history of Ole Miss, and of Dixie South

---

12. The Trustees choice of Nichols was informed by the work he had done at the University of Alabama and the University of North Carolina (Walton, 1995).

regional politics, is written onto the Lyceum walls and accoutrements and reads like a recalcitrant dictum of the 'cooperations and tension' of cultural and spatial politics at the university. To understand the political function the Lyceum plays, one must look no further than the historical marker in front of the building, which reads:

> The Lyceum, which opened for the first University of Mississippi class in 1848, symbolizes the origins, endurance, and triumphs of higher education in Mississippi. During the Civil War, the building served as a hospital for Union and Confederate soldiers. In 1962 it was the scene of a major event in the Civil Right Movement. After a night-long riot, the University's first African-American student, James Meredith, enrolled in the Lyceum. An extensive structural renovation was completed in 2001.

The landmarking of the Lyceum can be read in two ways: the first is the preferring meaning, which tells the story of the space which has endured and overcome adversity; while the second, a *détournement*[13] of sorts (see Debord & Wolman, 1981), recounts the physical space as a site for triumphing against diversity. The preservation and persistence of the physical space gives way to the perseverance of the ideology from which it originated, and for which it symbolizes. As the campus's "main edifice," the Lyceum has symbolically systematized the power-knowledge relationship between the politics of representation and access to the university space. One campus architect described the symbolic function of the Lyceum in this way: "The Lyceum sets the standard for the architecture of the University. It's image is everywhere. You see it on this table,[14] you see it in the Ole Miss logos, there it is, it's the 6 column, um, pediment, classical pediment, ionic" (Personal Interview). As a symbolic and administrative gateway into the University, the Lyceum is that physical apparatus which mitigates the 'repetition' of an inclusivity/exclusivity dyad of the University's "dominating-dominated rhythm" (Lefebvre, 2004). It symbolizes the endurance of the institution and the institutionalism which prevails over campus bodies; the *entrée* into the history of racialized politics at Ole Miss and the medium for allowing entrée into the halls of the academy.

We might surmise that the power relations acting upon the regulated human bodies starting from the Lyceum are diffused as they work outward. The 'concentric circles' referred to in the epigraph of this section offers description of the geometric map of the campus, and how over time the various sectors of the campus space flowing outward from the central axis have taken up identifiable, if not unique, aesthetic and disciplinary functions. The spherical orientation of the 'Circle,' within which the six original cam-

---

13. For Debord's Situationists, the practice of *détournement* served as a means for rearranging the praxis of the spectacle, and to create 'situations' rather than serve the overarching aim of the spectacle—reproduction. These situational *détournements* were a principle element in the application of Situationist political perspective.

14. Here the interviewee is referring to the table at which the interview was conducted. In the center of the table is the mark of the University, which features six columns modeled in the image of the Lyceum columns.

pus buildings and early campus social life were organized around, has operated as both central locus of control, encompassing the main administration buildings for the majority of the university's history.

In the earliest years at Ole Miss, Chancellor Fulton labored to maintain a high aesthetic standard throughout the campus. The centerpiece of his endeavors was the land area to the east of the newly constructed library (which was located around the Circle). He planted ornamental shrubs and blossoming trees in the area, and cordoned it off with privet hedge—establishing the geometric space which generations that followed have embraced as their celebrated 'Grove.' If the Circle is where the brainpower of the campus lies, then the Grove is the university's heart. A campus planner described the Grove this way:

> The Grove is kind of the heart of campus, I guess you could say, particularly for athletic events. You know it has become kind of famous—most to the magazines and so on that come to write about it say they haven't seen anything exactly like that. . . . What is it? Georgia and Florida have what they call the 'largest cocktail party' or something in the country. But you know most of that's all on parking lots and such so we've got a fairly, maybe not unique, but it's close to unique situation here. We have that available area in the center of campus which it adds a lot of ambience during just the regular period to the campus. It's a nice place for students to walk through, and just hang out in. (Personal Interview, 2004)

The cultural center of the Ole Miss campus, the Grove is the manifest destination of Old South social and ideological expansionism. Tailgating, concerts, theatrical and filmic presentations, and occupy the Grove space from early spring through the end of fall (Frederick, 1999).

The spatial practices within the Grove are often regulated by and through bodily contact and the spatialization of Dixie South whiteness, from the Dixie Week events of mid-century through the tailgating *fêtes* of a more contemporaneous texture. As such, one could find in this type of geography a "good example of a discipline which systematically uses measure, inquiry and examination" (Foucault, 1980, p. 75). In the Grove as well as the Circle, ideological mystification turns these landscapes into spectacular spaces, whereby the natural topography of trees, shrubbery, and flowery are augmented (if not supplanted) by Confederate memorial erections, scars of desegregation, and celebratory inscriptions of the rigidity of a preferred and performed whiteness. Spatial governance within these spectacular spaces (detailed more thoroughly in the following chapter) organizes the student subject as performer of Dixie South whiteness within the regimes of solidarity, hyper-normativity, and collective conscious. Panopticism in this instance creates governmentality, as the neo-Confederates operating within these carceral spaces are transformed into discursive cells, agents of the body politic. The 'dominating-dominated rhythm' becomes unidirectional, emanating from the visible center in a multitudinous gleam of refractory corporeal subjectification and unification.

If the land and buildings which occupy the center of campus in the Circle and the Grove are the main organs of the campus spatial body, then perhaps the terrestrial arteries which best exemplify the extension of ideological and representative power of the visible center of whiteness at Ole Miss can be located in its Greek armatures of power-knowledge: namely the westward flanking fraternity houses and contiguously northward sorority houses (a spatial axis of gendered power relationships?). Lefebvre (1991) might suggest that the spatial arrangement and symbolic functionality of the geometric space of the Ole Miss Greek system organize bodies within space in a manner in which those with less power are relegated to less desirable spaces; as socially constructed difference of race, class, gender, and sexuality come to life in these social spaces. Because of the historical develop of the campus space and social hierarchies, black fraternity and sorority houses on the Ole Miss campus occupy the outer 'margins' of the campus space. This ideological and physical [infra]structure can be identified by as a product of epoch or function—the former referring to the eras in which Greek life swelled on campus; the latter to an iniquitous system of hierarchal affirmation which situates white masculinity at the core of concentric spheres of social power.

In the first instance, the Greek fraternity and sorority houses on campus were constructed as domestic spaces for the campus students involved in these organizations. A number of these Ole Miss fraternity houses were razed during the era of Greek expansion on campus (early 1900s), The aesthetic elements woven into these structures are symbolic of an elite artistic habitus borne of an appreciation for Classical architectural antiquity popular during the era. The Ole Miss aesthetic domicile, is bound to, and descended from antiquity, a "conceptual framework which gives practical direction to our commerce with the arts" (H. Osborne, 1970, p. 16). The artistry of the built Greek structures on the Ole Miss campus reverberate the antebellum era styles and tastes of plantation elites: the common aesthetic elements shared throughout many of the older houses on Fraternity Row resonate the preferred stylization of the antebellum era—large porticos with sizable pillars at the front entrance, layered with elements of a plantation aesthetic shared by the Lyceum and many of the campus's other older buildings.

The dual formations of ocular governance and geometric segregation reinforce the spectacular nature of physical spaces within the Ole Miss Greek system. First, the perceptible differences between the wealthiest white fraternities and sororities and those of middling wealth signify an embodied politics of privilege. This politics of privilege is trumped only by the noticeable variations between the architectures of white fraternities and black fraternities, and more so by the grandiosity of white sorority houses versus the meagerness of black sorority houses. For instance, during my time in Oxford, I was made aware that it is common parlance amongst many Ole Miss students to refer to the two of the black sorority houses on campus as the 'slave quarters.' At Ole Miss, such a meta-territorialism acts in meaningful ways, beyond built environment as artistic transponder of taste, toward a restrictive regime of hyper-normativity which regulates the social actions of the participants within the spectacularized space. The language of space is representative of the broader topography of power at Ole Miss, as the

Greek system organizes and distributes power across the vectors of campus intermediation. Spatial practices of dominator/dominated create a hyper-disciplinarity in which a third space, a space of contestation and contest-ability, is rationalized and subsumed into the ideological formations of tra-dition and 'place.'

In other words, the spatial power-play encoded into the structural lan-guage of the Greek buildings is representative of a broader cultural politics of the institution and region, whereby inclusion of black bodies in the academy of the visible center is a function to redistribute notion of 'place.' Black students learn their 'place' through segregation from exclusive white spaces (such as Trent Lott's Sigma Nu house), but are insufficiently 'in-cluded' in the system as a means of social control. For instance, each black Pan-Hellenic student organization must be 'registered' with the University, yet the diachronic distribution of social and economic capital is apparent to any visitor on the Ole Miss campus. The grandiose plantation-style white Greek houses anchoring both Fraternity and Sorority Rows locate the do-mestic and social center of campus life, and stand in spatial opposition to the underdeveloped Pan-Hellenic houses located 'on the other side of the street'–thus symbolically reinforcing the fact that black Greek organiza-tions exist on the Ole Miss campus, but not with the same economic and social authority as their cross-street neighbors. As a symbolic discourse, the diametric polarity of black/white, privilege/underprivilege, subject/object, and center/margin are encoded into the built spaces of the campus Greek system. Further, the existence of an aesthetically hierarchical geography further crystallized Dixie South whiteness at the core of social and spatial relations on the Ole Miss campus.

Bodyscapes of the New Confederacy

Within the Ole Miss collective consciousness, the geometric environment is reconfigured into an illusory space of unification and alienation; whereby Ole Miss is distinct from—and made meaningful by that distinction—the University of Mississippi. 'Ole Miss' articulates the solidarities of meaning, space, and whiteness (as a locus of representation) and in so doing trans-poses the ideological onto the physical. Consequently, there is an inter-esting, if not problematic, interplay at Ole Miss between spaces of the representational imagination, the physical spaces of the campus setting, and the lived experiences that connect the imaginary and the spatial. The historically-nuanced reciprocities and animosities collide on the Ole Miss campus, where: the buildings are scarred by both the *first act* of rebellion against racial equality (the US Civil War) and the *second act* of resistance to integration (James Meredith in 1962); the campus space features a torrent of Confederate memorials paying homage to those who 'sacrificed' for that 'Cause'; and the streets and walkpaths regulate human activity in such a way as to bring those human agents acting within the campus environ in direct contact with these and other (aesthetic and physical) neo-Confederate symbols and idealized spaces.

In this way geometric space—and particularly discursively constituted space (and spatial discourses)—becomes that interpretive sphere upon which meanings are affixed. David Harvey (2001) suggests that through these types of relational manifestations of space and place, intermediaries and agents acting therein *make space place*: discursive regimes of power which are mobilized through space to construct the lived realities unique to that space. The interplay of place and space is an important site for understanding modern formation of power, and also for interpreting the conjunctures of ideology, discourse, and agency (Harvey, 1989b). Much like Harvey (cf. 2001), for Lefebvre (2004) space is neither fixed nor is it neutral. Space operates on the everyday experience of human agents, often in productive *and* oppressive ways (Lefebvre, 1991a). Following Foucault (1984a), the "construction of a collective infrastructure" (p. 239) at Ole Miss became a technique of normalization over the performances within that spatiality. As such, here I have sought to make the case that the spaces of the Ole Miss imaginary and the material have been conjoined through a space/race collective consciousness, whereby spatial formations of symbolic discourse organized the oppressive politics the Old South are emblazoned upon the spatial linguistics of, and performative embodiment in, the University of Mississippi campus.

To a great extent, Lefebvre's theorizing on space was developed in the company of the Situationists,[15] and thus our concluding discussion here might benefit from revisiting the conceptual dialogue between Lefebvre and Guy Debord. In particular, the ideological conscription provided in and by space in Lefebvre's theory is indebted to Debord's notion of 'psychogeography.' For Debord, in spectacular practices and the public spaces of spectacular society, the confluence of the lived and the imagined and the affectivity of power are made possible because of the interconnectivity and internalization of ideological chains shared by the 'atomized masses' (Debord, 1967/1994). As such, Debord implored that to understand the cognitive processes of the imaged spectacle, critics must engage "a study of the precise laws and specific effects of the geographical environment, consciously organized . . . on the emotions and behavior of individuals" (Debord, 1981d). Debord's psychogeography was a framework for resisting spectacular spaces as political armatures, extensions of the ideological police state. Manuel Castells would later outline the connection between oppressive ideological

---

15. The Situationist International was a group of young artists and social critics who enjoyed public attention in Paris during the late-1950s and 1960s. The group evolved from their Surrealist predecessors and formed the Letterist group, which eventually became the Situationists. Their most qualitative contribution to social theory is Guy Debord's The Society of the Spectacle, a complex set of theses on the effects of consumption, the mass media, and the spectacle on late modern society. While the SI never had more than a handful of members, their manuscripts had a rather significant impact, as some attribute the uprising in May 1968 to the Situationist.

space and ostensibly collective physical space in this way: 'social space produces spaces of hegemony' (Castells, 1985). For Debord, followed by Lefebvre and Castells, the aspirational and spectacular power of space thus lies in the formation of a 'unity of atmosphere,' a Debordian term referring to the collective consciousness amalgamated through, and organized within, space (Debord, 1990). In other words, unified space becomes a meaningful, and powerful social formation, as "the subject's freedom of movement is restricted by the instrumentalized image" (McDonough, 2002, p. 243). Unity of space creates codification through homogenization, and through the contextually-specific set of laws that govern ideology and practice within that space.

Contemporary *spaces of identity* within the Ole Miss vernacular and the popular have come to be understood through the intersecting discourses of: contrived physical space (aesthetics of the built environment); active 'embodied significance' (gendered, racialized, and classed physicalities of the Ole Miss spectator); and spatialized representational power (the semiotics of identity politics, and power-knowledge relationships therein). Rethinking Foucault's notions of panopticism and governmentality, we can thus understand the relationship between the productive, yet constricted interactions of the Ole Miss body in space in this way:

> Disciplinary power depends upon the creation of novel physical arrangements in which people can be monitored in the minutest details of their activities. It works by partitioning, enclosing and codifying space, enabling the detailed management and training of conduct by organizing the movement of bodies in space and through time. (Barnett, 1999, p. 378)

As a product of space, the body is the defining signifier of conformity (or contestation), adherence to prevailing polity, and the contestability of saturated ideology (Blum & Nast, 2000). Put in other terms, "starting from simple spatial forms, we see how the individual thematic and the collective thematic intersect and combine. Political symbolism plays on these possibilities to express the power of an authority, employing the unity of a sovereign figure to unify and symbolize the internal diversities of a social collectivity" (Augé, 1995, p. 62). In and through space, the body becomes both a unifying instrument and a unified object, a discursive axis of 'social collectivity' and representative affixture (K. Ross, 1988).

However, it would be myopic to consider the body as only a product of the spaces in which it exists. The corporeal space is both constituted by, and constitutor of, the physical and mental spatialities in which it resides (E. Soja, 1989). For the Situationists, individuals become part of what could be termed a *spectacular spatiality*, what Debord refers to as the *plaque tournante* (the revolving platform used to connect the tracks of a locomotive). Linking the segments of a 'psychogeographic map' (Debord, 1981e), yet always oscillating between the discursive pathways which have already been laid out, the active human subject becomes both that imagined and physical space for connecting discursive formations, as well as the conduit by which power relations flow. Joanna Latimer (2009) refers to these spatio-corporeal complexity as an 'assemblage', noting that in this way the body sits amongst "complex forms of relationality, wherein the powers accorded to flesh (and subjects) to engage in 'world-building' are decentered and kept symmetrical to other material forms" (p. 2). Further, perceptible, embodied space extends beyond the autonomous fixtures of physical and imaginary spatiality, toward a more involved synthesis of the productive forces and social product of the human body (A. Ross, 1988). In other words, "rather than define the body *through* space," we must investigate "how bodies create and *produce* space" (van Ingen, 2003, p. 202, author's italics). In Lefebvre's work we find recurring inferences to what Situationists refer to as "spatializing actions," or the physical performances of space, in space, which serve as gesticulations of spectacular society, either confronting or reinforcing the "certainties inscribed in the soil" (Augé, 1995, p. 119).

For Lefebvre (and Debord's Situationists), social practice constitutes and constructs space. The reconciliation of structuralist and poststructuralist over-determinism starts for Lefebvre with the reassertion of the spatialized body as active producer of social space. Space is first of all heard (listened to) and enacted (through physical gestures and movements), and the body is ensconced in the dual regimes of disciplinarity and intertextuality—operating as an active producer of discourse and governance (Vasterling, 2003). Furthermore, the spatial and dialectic centrality of the body in modern regimes of power work to reinvent and re-inscribe the prevailing logics of a spectacular racialized, gendered, and classed social hierarchy. As Marc Augé (1995) suggests, "the narrowness of the confines containing the sovereign figure, quite literally form a centre that underlines the permanence of the dynasty, and orders and unifies the internal diversity of the social body" (p. 63).

In summary, as a phantasmagoria of Dixie South whiteness, the spatial fabric of the University of Mississippi is interlaced with elements of: nostalgia for the Old South and the Confederacy which fought to preserve it, the preferred aesthetic of the contemporary post-plantation gentry, the normalizing functionality of the campus infrastructure, and the segregationist politics written into the geometric text. The collective, cognitive space of the University, defined by the narratives and imagery of a spatialized signifying system, both unite and divide the subjects operating in boundaries of temporal Ole Miss space. As Ernesto Laclau and Chantal Mouffe (1985) suggest, "a discursive structure is not merely a 'cognitive' or 'contemplative' entity; it is an articulatory practice which constitutes and organizes social relations" (p. 96). For the collective body of whiteness, Ole Miss space becomes meaningful place, and disparate agents are bound to the University, and united through its political discourses of 'topophilia,' or what John Bale (1994) refers to as their "love a place" (p. 120). Yi-Fu Tuan (1974), who originally authored the concept of 'topophilia,' described the notion as "the affective bond between people and place or setting" (p. 4).

The experienced, or embodied, spaces of Ole Miss create an austerity of topophilic response, whereby the student subject is immersed in the 'collective dreams' of a Confederate utopia (Buck-Morss, 2000) which influences, informs, and is materialized in the spaces of spectacle whiteness. The collective conscience becomes a device and medium through which layers of geometric signifiers coagulate, taking on cohesive, reified characteristics. For agents of the white center, paraphrasing Tuan (1974), the phalanstery of Dixie South whiteness offers a spectacle of topophilic space whereby a fleeting visual pleasure and the sensual delight of physical contact create a fondness of Ole Miss as physical and imagined place—it is home and incarnates the past, because it evokes pride in ownership of regimes of power within the racialized past and present (p. 247). Consequently, for the black-bodied outlier, the spatialities of the visible center at Ole Miss further shift blackness to the outside—to physical, imaginary, and symbolic margins of the lived, perceived, and conceived spaces of the institution.

A Neo-Confederate Sportscape

In a cultural moment when the red-state values of 'cowboy' politicians (e.g., George W. Bush), the 'redneck' balladry of country-western crooners (e.g., Gretchen Wilson), the blue-collar humor of Southern comedians (e.g., Jeff Foxworthy), and the hyper-white physicalities of the idealized Southern sporting Man[ning] (e.g., Peyton and Eli Manning) have come to dominate the public sphere, it would be hard to argue against the notion that the complex cultural economies of the American South have increasingly come to the fore of the popular realm. Some scholars have pointed to this trend as a 'Southernization of America' or a permeation of all things Southern into the mainstream (Egerton, 1974; Faust, 1988; Hale, 2000; Horwitz, 1999; Naipaul, 1989; Phillips, 2006; J. S. Reed, 1986; Rubin, 2002). While there are debates to be entertained with regard to this so called 'Southernization of America,' as well as alternative theories that suggest a cooptation of a Southern aesthetic for the purposes of grafting a representational lexicon of the "white right," what is becoming increasingly clear is that in American mass culture, the South is once again rising.

Just as these recent celebrations of the South have popularized local cultural wares and personalities, the same processes of mass 'culturalization' (J. Allen, 2002) have reinvigorated a number of debates relative to the region's persistently iniquitous social, political, and cultural configurations. The most polemic are those born out of a history of antebellum slavery, Old South patriarchy, Jim Crow segregation, Civil Rights Era lynching, and numerous other forms of oppression. In this chapter, I focus on the intersection of that history with its increasingly relevant sporting present. More specifically, I mediate on how the Confederate flag[1] has historically mobilized, and to this day continues to authorize, a meaningful conjuncture of the practices and discursive formations of sport spectatorship with the privileges of localized Southern whiteness formed under its banner.

Nearly 150 years after the Civil War, the flag and the cause for which it symbolizes are as contentious as ever. The Confederate flag has reemerged in the discursive machinations of the 'American' (sporting) popular by way of recent Hollywood mediations such as the *Dukes of Hazzard, Remember the Titans,* and *Talladega Nights: The Ballad of Ricky Bobby.* The flag has been simultaneously regenerated through its omnipresence in the South's most recognizable consumer and spectator spaces, such as NASCAR and intercollegiate football. This return of the consummate symbol of the South has brought with it polemic interdictions, backlash social commentary, and political activism. To such an end, the flag now symbolizes a contested discursive terrain defined by race and racism, nostalgia, power, and heritage culture—and one through which journalists, political officials (à la John McCain), religious leaders, and governing bodies have intervened in attempts to either reconnect or disconnect the flag's representational politics from the South's incendiary material history.[2]

One such intervention surfaced when the Black Coaches Association of the National Collegiate Athletic Association (NCAA) called for a ban on all postseason games in states where the Confederate elements (the "Stars and Bars") were still part of the state flag. In 2001, the NCAA announced a two-year moratorium on awarding postseason events to the state of South Carolina (where the Confederate sensibilities and state politics are still very much intertwined). In response to questions regarding the NCAA's stance on the flag, an NCAA representative stated, "I don't know that anybody is comfortable playing in a place where they fly the Confederate flag" ("NCAA might expand Confederate flag ban: South Carolina baseball, football may not be able to host postseason games," 2006, p. 1). The governing body has

1. Within contemporary discourse, *Confederate flag* is the popular term used to refer to the battle flag of the Confederate States of America, which was popularized during the Civil War. This flag is slightly different from the official flag of the Confederacy, which also features a cross emblazoned with stars, but in smaller configuration. For the purposes of this article, I refer to the Confederate battle flag as the Confederate flag, acknowledging its historical inaccuracy but locating the flag in its modern linguistic context.

2. For example, amidst a backlash against the Confederate elements embedded in state symbols, local governments in South Carolina, Mississippi, and Georgia have in recent years proposed changes to their state flags. In Georgia, a new flag was adopted by a vote of three to one, thus removing the signifying elements and ideological expressivity of the Confederate battle flag (Bonner, 2002). In 2001, Mississippians voted by a margin of two to one to retain the original 1894 state flag put in place by an all-White state legislature. The antiquated state symbol to this day still features the Southern Cross in the top right corner of the banner. Ironically, the margin of victory for supporters of the Southern Cross was nearly identical to the percentage of White residents (61) versus Black residents (36) living in the state at the time ("Why did Mississippi vote on state flag lose?," 2001).

continued the ban indefinitely, declaring in 2004 that significant change on the issue had not taken place in South Carolina. University of South Carolina head football coach Steve Spurrier, currently the state's most popular sporting icon, interjected, bluntly proclaiming that the flag "should come down" from the statehouse and that it is "an embarrassment to our state" ("Spurrier: Flag should come down from S.C. Statehouse," 2007, p. 1).

While the flag has long been a source of anxiety, pride, discrimination, and division, these most recent debates bring several issues into relief: Why is the flag so incontrovertibly bound to Southern sport culture? Can the cause be separated from the symbol? Who benefits from its public presence? How can sport, often viewed as a progressive social space, function for the privilege of some and the detriment of others? Why? Furthermore, as the flag's import has extended beyond American South and into the grandstands of World Cup matches between Spain and Tunisia or local Dutch pubs on the eve of English UEFA Cup fixtures, what is the degree to which symbol and practice unite under the discourses of a seemingly banal, yet insidiously divisive, Southern heritage–based sport culture?

In a poststructuralist sense, the flag as a marker of sporting territories is a "free- floating" signifier. Its meanings are up for grabs and both contested and contestable. The flag has at once, and throughout its history, been a source of pride for Southern heritage groups, a marker of identity for white supremacist organizations, and a symbol of racial oppression for the marginalized peoples of the South. However, in this chapter, rephrasing Adorno and Horkheimer (1979), I want to mediate on how the Confederate flag as cultural product signifies an overall organization of power brought to life through its relevance in public culture. The principal aim of this article is not to prove or disprove the meanings of the flag, nor to historically excavate the reasons for which the Confederate cause came into being (the slavery versus States' Rights debate). On the contrary, this article constitutes an interpretation of the signifier, the meanings extracted from it, and the race-based power dynamics it organizes. This is a study of the dominant readings (Williams, 1981), public pedagogies, and symbolic power of the Confederate flag—enacted in and through sport-related practices and discourses—and how those readings are leveraged to perpetuate an antiquated knowledge–power hierarchy within the region and beyond (see Foucault, 1976, 1982b, 1984b, 2001). Answering the call put forth by David Andrews (2006) for a critical study of sport formulated out of rigorous empiricism, diachronic historicism, and synchronic contextualism, this chapter problematizes the past and present relations of the flag and the political knowledge formulated from representation through praxis.

In some ways, then, this is a starting point toward a much broader contemplation of the symbol and its relation to racist practices within sport cultures of the South and beyond. While I focus on the flag's race-based politics at one particular sporting institution—that of the University of Mississippi's intercollegiate football team—it is my intent to open a public dialogue toward a more expansive discussion concerning the race, gender, class, heteronormative, generational, and geopolitical implications of the flag as a sporting symbol in the context of both the local and the global.

For as I have endeavored to make clear thus far, Ole Miss is not just another Confederate sporting institution. On the contrary, more than any other sporting apparatus, Ole Miss is symbolically, and perhaps symbiotically, bound to the Confederacy and its cultural iconography (Cohodas, 1997; L. E. Davis, 2005; D. Sansing, 1982). Today, as has been the case for more than half a century, attendees at Ole Miss Rebel sporting events are welcomed by a 'sea of Confederate flags' (Duerson, 2004), whereby thousands of Confederate symbols dominate the campus spaces surrounding the football stadium. Ole Miss football, perhaps more than any other sporting institution in the American South, remains a *Confederate preserve*—a social, ideological, and physical space marked by the flag and the ideologically formulated ethnocentric territories of the post-Confederate white South. In this Chapter, I locate the flag as an important symbolic formation that represents a much larger configuration of racial privilege and oppression from the context of Civil Right and post-Civil Rights Ole Miss to more contemporary iterations of the symbol and its uses as part of a broader anti-affirmative action, anti-immigration, post-September 11, 2001, paleo-conservative, Dixie South socio-iconography. Due to the depth and space such an analysis demands, I will only briefly canvass equally important, similarly oppressive aspects of the Confederate-sport dynamic, particularly those of hegemonic patriarchy or class-intensive hierarchy.

Informed by a cultural historiography of the sign and an ethnography of its contemporary uses in the context of sporting Ole Miss, I offer critical reading of the cultural locale of the signifier (the flag) in relation to the signified (those whose identities are grafted out of the cultural discourses of the sporting local). To do this, I (1) trace the practices and praxis of flag waving, flag adorning, and flag adoration at Ole Miss sporting events throughout multiple historical contexts; (2) examine such a neo-Confederate sporting condition through a series of observations and fieldnotes compiled while at major sporting events on the University of Mississippi campus; and (3) conclude with a discussion on the ways in which these spectacles of the neo-Confederate South now map sport as a territory of ethnic nationalism both in the American South and beyond.

To understand the powerful nature of the Confederate flag at Ole Miss sporting events, we must consider how the visibility of hyper-white identity politics and the marking of institutional space have reconstituted "a conceptual space for desperately clinging to the social relations of an imagined past" (C. R. King & Springwood, 2001, p. 154). As such, whiteness is not only performed at Ole Miss; it is spectacle. And sport has historically offered a popular public space through which to make visible the privileges of being white at the university and beyond. This spectacle of Dixie South whiteness, however, is not a natural extension of history. Rather, it is a product of social relations and semiotic leveraging enacted by, and empowered through, the preponderance of semiotic contestation (and lack thereof).

From the Battlefield . . .

There has been a substantive dialogue in the history literature regarding the cause for which the flag[3] has come to represent. A majority of scholars and historians agree that the foundational principle of the Confederacy, indeed its primary reason for secession (and thus fighting the war), was a state's right to maintain the institution of slavery (Hale, 1999). "There is no reputable historian anywhere in America that will say slavery was not the cause of the war," declared University of Mississippi historian David Sansing (quoted in Baldwin, 1993, p. 2). While the flag has come to represent the fallen Confederacy, perhaps more important, the entanglement of the flag in the prevalence of white supremacy (i.e., the use of the flag by the Southern Democrats, or "Dixiecrats," during the era of integration) has further cemented the close symbolic ties of the cause to the sign.

The flag's incessant reappearance at pro-segregation meetings of the Civil Rights Era, political gatherings of the Citizen's Council after the *Brown versus Board* decision, voracious Ku Klux Klan rallies from the Jim Crow days onward, and Nationalist Party meetings throughout the second half of the 20th century—as well as persistent cross burnings, lynchings, and other spectacles of race-based malice during the same period—have concretized the symbolic import of the flag with a cause even further removed from 'States' rights' (Mcwhite, 2002). While the history of the flag has been sterilized over the past few decades, the uses of the flag continue to resuscitate it as a "living symbol" with a "potent ideology" (Coski, 2005, p. 291). That fluidity has evolved into a double-stranded, axiomatically discursive cultural helicon: one trajectory sanitizing the genealogy of the incendiary symbol, the second further propagating the racist ideologies imbedded therein.

. . .to the Ball Field

At Ole Miss, the Confederate battle flag—which is thoroughly absorbed in the contemporary discourses of an institutionalized 'heritage culture'—is a relatively new fixture. For the most part, the 'Southern Cross' did not follow the Confederate veterans back to the Ole Miss campus after the Civil War. In fact, the image of the flag was rarely seen on the Ole Miss campus before the late 1940s (L. E. Davis, 2005). According to research,

---

3. The origins and meanings of the Confederate battle flag have been debated among Civil War and Southern historians since the moment the fighting ceased at Palmetto Ranch (see Coski, 2005; Hunt, 2002). The Confederate battle flag—also referred to during the war as the Beauregard Battle flag, the Southern Cross, and the flag of the Army of Northern Virginia—did not become the official flag of the Confederate government during the war, but rather the symbol used by numerous regiments of the Confederate Army during battle (Coski, 2005). The symbol that now is generally identified as the Confederate or Rebel flag was actually popularized throughout the postwar years and identified in the public sphere with the Confederacy *post facto* (Bonner, 2002).

the "Beauregard Battle Flag" did not appear on campus until 1948, a date with double significance (Cohodas, 1997). During the University's centennial year, the Confederate flag was brought to life by way of that year's Dixie Week festivities: a campus-wide carnival of Southern whiteness that featured "slave auctions," reenactments of Civil War battles, and blackface minstrels that continued late into the 20th century. In the first instance, this spectacular prelude signaled the reemergence of the Confederate flag on the Ole Miss campus. Students included the flag in many of the marching activities honoring the University Greys (Ginn, 2003). More important, this was the same year the Southern Democrats, or Dixiecrats, abandoned the National Democratic Party over the issue of civil rights.[4] At about the same time when the Confederate battle flag was coming to be identified with "Southern resistance to civil rights and the Ku Klux Klan" (Sansing, 1999, p. 108), the nascent support on the Ole Miss campus for the Dixiecrat cause escalated, and thus the mediations of the moment further cemented the representational Dixie South triad of segregationist politics, Ole Miss, and the Confederate flag.

The flag cloaked the public spaces of Mississippi as the Dixiecrats and their isolationist politics gained momentum in the Dixie South. From courthouses and government buildings to commercial spaces and sporting places, the flag became a marker of white space and separatist ideology. The sovereignty of sign and space further crystallized through the symbolic symmetry of the wildly popular Ole Miss football team and its new proximity to the banner of the Confederacy (R. H. Barrett, 1965; Silver, 1966). In the 1950s and 1960s, two movements surfaced that further circulated the symbiotic ties between the Confederate flag and Ole Miss. First, as the Civil Rights campaign turned its focus toward the Dixie South, and specifically on the state of Mississippi, the University of Mississippi became a significant site for contesting segregation and resisting integration. Second, intercollegiate football became an increasingly relevant social space for expressing racial intolerance, particularly as the Ole Miss squad became a considerable football power during the era—attending 17 bowl games in 18 years (Baker, 1989). Conservative Southern politicians became habitual speakers on the midfield podium at halftime of Ole Miss home football games (Cohodas, 1997; Meredith, 1966). As a result, the flag became simultaneously identified with both the Ole Miss Rebels and the Dixiecrats. As historian Nadine Cohodas (1997) explained, "It was a happy marriage of politics and

---

4. The recently established Civil Rights Commission sought to bring sweeping change in Southern race relations. With the support of Harry Truman and the Democratic Party, the CRC alienated many Mississippians and their long-standing avocation of the party's race-based politics. Southern Democrats, upset with the party's support of the commission, abandoned the Democratic Party to start their own political group, what came to be known as the Dixiecrats. The party was openly opposed to civil rights legislation, as their leader, Strom Thurmond, campaigned almost exclusively on the platform of segregation.

school spirit, a way to celebrate white southern pride in the safe confines of the stadium" (p. 162).

The definitive moment of this hyper-white sporting conjuncture came during the football homecoming celebration of 1948. At that game, the Ole Miss band introduced a wildly popular halftime routine during which members marched onto the field and unfurled "the world's largest Confederate flag" to the stirring strains of "Dixie" (Sansing, 1999). Writers for the 1948 *M-Book* later mused over the gesture by explaining that giant Rebel flag was a symbol that announced to the non-segregationist world, "We do not want anyone telling us what to do" (p. 5). Spectators were given miniature Confederate flags to wave during each subsequent home football game, and cheers for "Ole Dixie" could be heard echoing throughout the stadium filled exclusively by white-bodied separatists (Cabaniss, 1971).

Rephrasing Rosemary Coombe (1998), one could argue that the symbolic properties of the Confederacy were evoked to represent the backlash politics of defiant early Civil Rights–era whiteness, and thus interpellated the white individual with a more visual orientation and with more corporeal desires. Those desires were met by both physical occupation (of the embodied neo-Confederate masses in exclusively white space) and symbolic consumption (of the flag). These corporeal responses to Civil Rights interloping included the introduction of a new tradition: Students began painting Confederate flags on their bodies and bore costumes and accessories that memorialized the "Lost Cause." For these neo-Confederates, this temporal moment and sardonic sway of the culture of segregation was realized through the unobstructed, trifurcated convergence of the mark of the Old South (the flag), the racist politics of the Dixiecrats and Southern segregationists, and the institution's sporting iconography. One local journalist observed, "More and more it looks like the confederates (sic) will rise again as Rebel boosters don their black hats, wave the southern flag and whistle 'Dixie'" ("Long live the Colonel," 1953, p. 1).

The persistence of the Ku Klux Klan in the public affairs at the university further obscured the meanings connoted by the flag, particularly as the Southern Cross became a permanent symbol for their cause and organization:

> On the news program each night there was the Ku Klux Klan waving the rebel flag, and on the sports program there was the Ole Miss football team with the same flag. Ole Miss and the KKK, using the same symbols, became identified with each other, especially after the resistance to admitting James Meredith in 1961 and '62. (Cohodas, 1997, p. 237)

The contextual symmetry of the sign and the ideological chains from which the flag drew meaning gained momentum in the lead-up to desegregation. The boiling point in the institution's social history came in 1962 with the arrival of James Meredith. As most historical accounts have documented, this pivotal moment demonstrated the malevolent auspices under which the "civilian army" of segregationists marched and that the Confederate flag came to mark the cause of separatism:

> Not only a common banner at KKK rallies but also at civil government build-
> ings and general protests against federal desegregation orders, the Confeder-
> ate flag was the choice symbol of those many citizens who gathered in Oxford
> during the weekend preceding October 1, 1962. (King & Springwood, 2001, p.
> 134)

Confederate flags littered the landscape of the campus in a spectacle of
symbolic (and physical) defiance as riots ensued in the hours leading up to
Meredith's Federal troop–aided admission into the University of Mississippi (Barrett, 1965). The flag was draped across the front porticos of many
of the fraternity houses on campus, and the American flag in the center of
campus was displaced in favor of the Southern Cross (Silver, 1984). Similar
to ways in which the Klan's appropriations of the flag were understood to
be representative of the white supremacist cause during the middle part of
the 20th century, the riots surrounding Meredith's admission galvanized in
the public discourse the notion that Ole Miss not only had symbols but was
itself a symbol. In the American popular, "the Rebel flag and 'Dixie' were
symbols of organized resistance to civil rights. . . . The nation was seeing
Ole Miss use its symbols in the act of denying a black man admission to the
school" (Lord, 1965, p. 18). Consequently, through resistance to integration
and civil rights, and under the banner of symbolic Old South "traditions,"
Ole Miss came to represent the avaricious politics of whiteness in the Civil
Rights Era Dixie South. The flag remained the uncontested symbolic fixture of white privilege at the University of Mississippi throughout the remainder of the 1960s and well into the following decade. In fact, it was not
until the early 1980s that the first serious challenge to the flag's supremacy
was formulated.

On April 22, 1982, the student body elected John Hawkins as the first
Black cheerleader in school history. It was assumed that the first Black
cheerleader in school history would "honor the tradition" in which every
male cheerleader carried a large Confederate flag onto the football field for
the start of every Ole Miss home contest (Cohodas, 1997). After Hawkins
was elected, however, the *New York Times* reported that he would break
with the tradition:

> While I'm an Ole Miss cheerleader I'm still a black man. In my household I
> wasn't told to hate the flag, but I did have history classes and know what my
> ancestors went through and what the Rebel flag represents. It is my choice
> and I prefer not to wave one. (Rawls, 1982, p. 6)

Hawkins continued, "I am a black man and the same way whites have been
taught to wave the flag I have been taught to have nothing to do with it"
(Rawls, 1982, p. 6). With the exception of two Black student journalists who
wrote, "For the blacks who make up about 35% of our state's population,
the flag stands as both a barrier and as a banner for Mississippi's racist past"
(Read & Freeland, 1983, p. 2), Hawkins garnered little support in the local
media and on the campus.

Not coincidentally, as Reagan-era anti–affirmative action backlash spread
in the American South, backlash against Hawkins grew on the Ole Miss
campus. According to most accounts, Hawkins was verbally and physically

harassed throughout the period leading up to the football season. As the flag issue heightened, many white students began wearing T-shirts with the symbolic letter X popularized by the late Civil Rights leader Malcolm X. Underneath the letter were the words "You wear yours . . ." and on the back were the words ". . . We'll wear ours" (with the latter decorated in the style of the Confederate flag). Other popular garb during this period included a T-shirt on the Ole Miss campus that read, "I'll give up this flag when you give up MLK Day." To temporarily quell tensions, as a "compromise," university administrators decided that flag toting was to be optional, as long as one flag was carried onto the football field (Nettleton, 1983).

Ironically, the 20th anniversary of integration at Ole Miss coincided with that same 1982 football season. To commemorate the integration of Ole Miss, the university invited James Meredith to speak on campus. In his speech, Meredith charged that the Confederate flag, Colonel Rebel, and "Dixie" "must be abolished as school symbols and songs," continuing, "There is no difference between these symbols and the segregation signs of twenty years ago such as 'white-Only Waiting Room,' 'Colored Drinking Water' . . . and so forth" (J. Meredith, 1982, p. 1). That fall, while the school's administration deliberated the flag issue and Meredith's appeals, the Ku Klux Klan organized a rally in Oxford in support of their signature symbol and its continued affiliation with the University of Mississippi (Stead, 1982). At the event, the Grand Dragon of the Klan stood in the middle of Oxford Square and declared, "The Rebel flag . . . is more sacred than anything else in the South." Many of the hundreds of spectators on hand applauded as the white supremacist leader, amidst a sea of Confederate battle flags, went on to proclaim, "Blacks should go back to Africa!" (Sansing, 1999, p. 327).

In the spring of 1983, a number of white students formed a Save the Flag movement. This Confederate calling of the white majority was surmised by a contributor to the *Daily Mississippian*:

> The Rebel flag is Ole Miss. Its tradition embodies this university. It IS Dixie, our pledge, our symbol. What would Ole Miss be without it? Just plain Miss, I guess. Certainly, with a name like that we would get even fewer recruits than we do with the flag. Granted, our racial dispute would probably be solved. But what would become of everything else? (Becker, 1983, p. 2)

Many white Ole Miss students, often numbering in the thousands, organized protests in front of the university's administration building, the Lyceum, one of which eventuated in a march on the Black fraternity house of John Hawkins (Raines, et al., 1983).

In response to the confrontational actions of what seemed to be a majority of the white student population, members of the Black Student Union (BSU) formulated a number of demands for social justice. One such demand from the BSU was that the Confederate flag be removed from all university-sanctioned events. In response to this request, on Wednesday, April 20, 1983, Chancellor Porter Fortune announced that the university was no longer "actively promoting" symbols of the Confederacy as part of signified Ole Miss. Fortune declared, "It is time that the University of Mississippi disassociate itself from the debate over what various symbols might mean to various groups and individuals" (D. Turner, 1983, p. 1). Almost sardonically, the chancellor demurred that the debates, rather than the symbols, were the "problem" of the university.[5]

While the flag debates of that academic year eventually dissipated, the venomous response of the visible center spilled over into the pages of the *Daily Mississippian* for the months and years that followed, invoking what has come to be described as "the longest running dialogue on the Confederate battle flag" (Mcwhite, 2002, p. 309) in American history:

> It looks as though Ole Miss has spawned yet another terrorist group onto the face of the planet [the BSU]. . . . Blacks have accomplished a good deal within the time they have been allowed at Ole Miss. They have succeeded in getting rid of the old Confederate soldier and his white horse. They have gotten the Rebel off the football helmets. They have been increasingly accepted in some white circles at Ole Miss. They would have eliminated the Rebel flag, the song "Dixie," and Colonel Rebel if they had been able to control themselves just a little bit longer. . . . Notice how many of these demands are "gimme demands." The writers of these grievances want things to be GIVEN to them (sort of like a Christmas list). They did not want to have to work for them—GOD FORBID. . . . Will these type of people ever realize that others have only so much Christian spirit and are tired of giving them everything that they want. I especially resent the fact that they say I owe them something because of their history. . . . If they really want these things, then they must prove it and stop acting like greedy, violent little children and more like mature adults. (B. E. Reed, 1983, p. 2)

The logic of this commentator's argument is moored in the traditions of an ultra-conservative white pathology: These Black students should be content in their oppression because their experience is better than those of their ancestors, and that strides toward humanity and equality have resulted in "unnecessary" concessions from the normative white center of power. Thus, in some twist of logic, white folks are themselves victims of a reverse form of inequality.

According to this solipsistic logic, the "invasion" of the white center by Black-bodied infiltrators is a two-part equation of "lazy, greedy" Black ingratiation to newly disadvantage "hard-working" whites and the ill-advised failure of Black students to conform to the racist norms of the institution. Another writer deployed an eerily similar argument:

> First of all, who are you to "demand" anything from anybody? Some of your demands are too ridiculous to even be considered. Why should the University create another department when it just did away with one? Provide a separate budget which is substantial for black cultural projects, which includes funds for black speakers and professionals? If this is not separatism and discrimination, what is? . . . As for banning the use of the Rebel flag, "Dixie," and Colonel Rebel, just try. These have nothing to do with academics and if you're here to get an education then ignore them and start studying. I guess the biggest ques-

---

5. That same year, the *Ole Miss* annual featured several pictures of the KKK during their demonstration on campus in the fall of 1982. In the pictures, the Grand Wizard is photographed amidst rebel flags, urging Mississippi's resistance to the surge of post-Civil Rights era challenges to White supremacy in Mississippi (Raines et al., 1983).

tion and the one asked most often is, "Mr. (or Mrs. or Miss) BSU member, if you don't get what you want, what are you going to do? (R. A. Hill, 1983, p. 2)

The author warns that the tolerance and goodwill of the visible center is limited, and these "separatists" seeking to undermine the historical priv- ileges of Dixie South whiteness will not succeed in their endeavors to re- shape the face of race-based access at Ole Miss. Another offering from the deluge of white backlash against the challenges to their beloved represent- ative symbol further illustrates the ideological chains operating within the racial politics of Ole Miss during the era:

> I am appalled at the lack of realism shown by the Black Student Union. . . . What started the whole controversy? John Hawkins' refusal to wave the flag. What finally prompted the KKK to march [in Oxford]? James Meredith's ul- timatum to Ole Miss. . . . If we need to throw out the KKK pictures, we also need to throw out the pictures concerning Hawkins and Meredith. (Benz, 1983, p. 2)

For this white Ole Miss constituent, and many of his fellow members of the visible center, the KKK ad the flag it bears served as a highly visible confed- eration of an aggravated white reaction to racial equality, and the seminal instrument that had to be deployed to stave off the "irrational" appeals for social justice from black Ole Miss students (Mcwhite, 2002).

Old Signifying Acts and New Cultural Racism

Capturing the incendiary tenor of an angry white backlash to the residues of the Civil Rights Era, the dualistic endeavor of repositioning the debate around democratic racism (retaining the privileges of the white "majority") and the victimization of the angry white male emerged as central tropes in the subversive prestidigitation and symbolic gesticulation of neo-Con- federate hyper-white orthodoxy. The former was fashioned under the co- alitions and attitudes of an insular reigning whiteness, an ideology and dis- course founded on a logic that went something like this: The campus was predominantly white, most white students found the flag's sporting presen- ce to be an endearing symbol of Old South traditionalism, and thus the de- mands of the minority were unfair because they threatened to undermine the axioms of the majority (and thus the precepts of democracy). The white majority was effectively "asking black students to surrender to the blatantly racist symbols and attitudes of much of the white Ole Miss student body. The logic of this argument is evident—Black people should not ask for so- cial justice because it will upset white racist traditions" (Alred, 1983, p. 2). Or perhaps more explicitly, the ideological bent of the white majority conjured up the residues of the Confederacy, and its cause to preserve the majority's democratic rights to preserve institutions of racism, oppression, and sym- bolic violence.

The latter surfaced in an imaginary civil rights for [pseudo self-victim- ized oppression of] Ole Miss's white faction. A signifying system marked historically by racial oppression was thus converted into a site for the preservation of the infiltrated white race. One commentator went as far as to suggest that the reified symbols themselves were tortured through this debate, somehow taking on human- like qualities and having nothing to do with the racist practices of the Confederacy or the Jim Crow South:

> As for the banishment of the so-called "racist symbols," does the BSU really feel that their removal would ease racism? I tend to feel that any removal of our symbols for the sole purpose of pleasing one group would merely result in increased tension directed toward that group. Is the BSU willing to make a martyr out of these symbols? These symbols do not possess mystical powers that cause all those who come in contact with them to become practicing bigots. Racism exists within people, and removing these so-called "racist symbols" would help end racism like removing the swastika would have helped to have ended Nazism (Peirce, 1983, p. 2)

Based on this reading of the emblematic impasse, challenges to the symbolic representations of Dixie South whiteness threatened the heritage culture of the plantation-wealthy white South, but falsely implicated the individuals who for nearly 200 years perpetuated the racist hierarchies for that the flag and its cause represented. The moribund autonomy of the Confederate sign was thus demonstrative of baseborn charges against the ethnic nationalism of the Dixie South whiteness, past and present.

Again, for many students and community advocates of the neo-Confederate–Ole Miss amalgamation, white traditionalists were the "real victims" in this dispute:

> The Black Student Union has no intentions of improving race relations at this school. Consider these actions by the [BSU President] and company: publishing an article in *The Daily Mississippian* in which she drags up every conceivable negative thing she can say about my ancestors; making an issue out of a simple symbol which causes no one harm; . . . then holding closed door, black only meetings, and inciting the members to hate, yes HATE anyone who disagrees with them, especially those of the Caucasian variety. . . . Let's be fair. Oust the BSU or install a campus chapter of the Knights of the Invisible Empire. (Henley, 1983, p. 2)

This self-victimizing trope of the visible center became a recurring narrative in the pages of the *Daily Mississippian* and other local media outlets for years to come. As the practices and signifiers of the hegemonic Dixie South whiteness were imploded by way of both national and local interrogation, the reflexive response of the visible center was to further expand the sovereignty of local symbolic power. With the endorsement and support of the Southern National Party and the KKK, protests continued well beyond the fall semester of 1983 (Cassreino, 1983).

In the post-Hawkins malaise, the visibility and ideality of the Confederate flag failed to fritter away, and instead took on a more "natural" existence. Well into the next decade, the flag persistently enveloped the geometric (and ideological) sporting spaces of Ole Miss. Upon visiting an Ole Miss home game in Oxford in 1989, conservative political commentator Lewis Grizzard (1989) surmised, "I lost count of just how many times the University of Mississippi band played 'Dixie' last Saturday . . . the number had to be in double figures . . . . There were 31,000 at the game. Everyone who wasn't from Georgia had a Confederate flag" (p. 2). The presence of the flag inside Vaught-Hemingway Stadium diminished in 1997 when the university passed a law banning poles in the stadium. Citing safety concerns, the administration and athletic department prohibited large flagpoles in the stadium and thus stunted the display of large flags that had become popular during the late-1980s and early 1990s. In November of 1997, Chancellor Robert Khayat applauded the Associated Student Body for voting to discontinue the display of the Confederate flag in the on-campus stadium, stating, "I have faith in the students of Ole Miss. They have courage to objectively review issues and the wisdom to make good decision" (Cohodas, 1997, p. 247). The response from the visible center was, however, quite less collegial.

After the removal of flag poles from the stadium, and the seemingly amicable response of the student body, an insert in the *Daily Mississippian* instructed students to "let a Sea of Stars and Bars Fill the Field on Saturday. . . . For we dare defend OUR rights and the rights of countless thousands who came before to our Ole Miss" (Malone, 1997, p. 1). Answering the call, fans witnessed a surge of new flags surrounding the stadium. To this day, and despite repeated pleas from various community leaders, university administrators, and even head football coaches, supporter groups and local leaders have ensured that the flag remains a central element of the symbolic and discursive texture of sporting Ole Miss. More flags than ever clutter the Grove and the Circle (the central campus spaces near the major sporting venues) during home football, basketball, and baseball games, as the symbolic territorialization by the old guard of the campus space continues to be demarcated by the cross-cutting lines of racial power and Southern Crosses.

Dispatches from the Land of Cotton

At these Ole Miss sporting events, contemporary performances of white power are constituted by a series of spectacles and conspicuous displays of Confederate- emblazoned whiteness. The visible center has successfully crafted a new cultural economy of symbolic violence based on the fetishization of symbolic and spectacular forms of racial representation. Through the modalities of adornment and deportment, and the display of Confederate signifiers, the reification of the racialized body politic is dispersed through, and onto, politicized and spectacularized space. As such, the symbols and ideals of the Confederacy are not only alive on the Ole Miss campus, but indeed are layered onto broader formations of sport culture and identities formulated therein. In particular, the conspicuous practices surrounding Ole Miss sporting events often provide a spectacularized space through which these expressions of visible Dixie South whiteness can be articulated, if not celebrated.

At Ole Miss home games in recent seasons, symbolic garments, branded tailgating tents, themed provisions, and a variety of Confederate signifiers dominate the green space in the center of campus on game day. My fieldnotes taken at a pep rally held on the Ole Miss campus before the first spring football scrimmage of 2005 suggest the spectacular nature of the Grove communal:

> Amidst the pom-poms and giant "M" signs, fashioned after the stars and bars of the Confederacy, the team walked through the Grove to the stirs of Dixie and the chants of "Hotty Toddy." The sprit of Dixie takes on a material form in the Grove, as witnessed by the proliferation of Confederate flags, the images of an Old South mascot, and a culture industry fueled by the themed commercialization of every aspect of the Grove space, all the way down to the "Hotty Toddy Potty" (the portable restroom situated on both the north and south sides of the Grove). (Fieldnotes)

In this type of perceptible world of neo-Confederate ethnic nationalism, best theorized by Henri Lefebvre's (1991) notion of perceived space, the white spectator mobilizes various signifiers within a representational lexicon of Dixie South whiteness.

Following Foucault (1977a, 1982b), it could be argued that the Confederate sign mediates the spectating panoptic, organizing and territorializing the ethnic[ized] spaces of Dixie South whiteness on and through local sport culture. The Confederate flag holds disciplinary sway over the contemporary Dixie South sport spectator by standing as the unchallenged, hyper-proliferated marker of space and the bodies operating therein. Moreover, much as incessant technological renewal (Debord, 1967/1994) shapes the eternal return of the consumer to the market, the incessant renewal of technologies of the self, embodied in the practice of reifying and consuming symbols of Dixie South whiteness, unremittingly conjoins the politics of identity to the ideologies signified in and through the practices of sport spectatorship (Foucault, 1977a, 1982a, 1982b). Further, perception itself acts as a form of governance, whereby each spectator within this spectacle of Dixie South whiteness, through surveillance and spectacular praxis (and surveillance of the spectacular), disciplines the alternating (normative and alternative) subjectivities operating within that space. The unity in symbol and subjectivity leads to the empowerment (actualization) of the signifier as panoptic currency—framed around the politics of a Southern ethic, imbedded in the deportment and praxis of a preferred whiteness, and reproductive of social hierarchies through engagement with the symbolic and the material.

Of Purity and Performance

To this day, the flag symbolizes, and simultaneously authorizes, whiteness at the epicenter of the politics of racial representation within the post-plantation Dixie South context. As a point of *entrée* into the spectacle of neo-Confederate whiteness—as enacted under the auspices of sporting Ole Miss—I offer a series of notes from ceremonies conducted by the Sons of Confederate Veterans in the spring of 2005 on the Oxford campus. The event, which was sanctioned by the University, was held in conjunction with an Ole Miss baseball game. The day's festivities began with a parade through the town of Oxford. Originating from the resting place of William Faulkner, the cavalcade of the Confederacy meandered through the streets of Oxford and eventually arrived at its first stop, the Confederate memorial statue outside the courthouse in the center of the Square:

> It was quite an astonishing procession, featuring: women dressed in antebel-lum costumes; men dressed in Confederate military uniforms and carrying rifles; younger boys serving as the color guard of the Confederacy (carrying Confederate flags, the state flag, and flags of local regiments); older men on horseback dressed in full commander regalia donning swords; and perhaps the most famed of post-bellum automotive television icons, the 'General Lee' from the popular television show, *The Dukes of Hazard.* The lattermost appar-atus carried Ben Jones, known on the show as 'Cooter'[6] (Fieldnotes).

The Confederate compatriots proceeded to perform a 'wreath laying' cere-mony to the delights of hundreds of spectators. Men dressed in military gar-ments then fired three shots in a salute to the fallen Confederate soldiers of the American Civil War. Next, almost in organic unanimity, members of the parade as well as its onlookers joined in singing a full rendition of 'Dixie,' the Confederate battle song and official song of University of Mississippi athletics. At the conclusion of the ceremony in Oxford's downtown Square, the re-enactors proceeded to the University campus (Fieldnotes).

Once the Confederate convoy had assembled at the front entrance to the cemetery on the Ole Miss campus, the official program of the memorial services resumed. Amidst a backdrop awash with Confederate imagery, and with a crowd of approximately one hundred 'spectators' looking on, the 'Commander' of the University Greys camp (the Oxford division of the Sons of the Confederate Veterans) began the proceedings with the Confederate Pledge of Allegiance: "I salute the Confederate flag with affection, rever-ence, and undying devotion to the cause for which it stands" (Fieldnotes). This collective performance of allegiance was followed by the reprise of the "Confederate National Anthem," 'Dixie.' Following the collective celebra-tion of these traditions, the Commander then introduced Ben Jones, laud-ing the *Dukes of Hazard* actor as a 'real treasure of the South.'

Ben Jones then offered a brief speech, in which he thanked the Sons of Confederate Veterans for their efforts to preserve a heritage culture, and implored the spectators to endeavor to "reestablish the heritage, symbols, and traditions of the South." The orator derided those in the media, as well as political and academic spheres, for contributing to a "bigoted" depiction of the Old South. Breaking from the conventions of Confederate logics, and the pledge which he had just recited, Jones then suggested that the symbols of the Confederacy "represent not the cause, but the efforts, the valor." He

---

6. The 'General Lee' was the name given the car driven by Bo and Luke Duke in the popular American television program, *The Dukes of Hazzard.* The bright orange ex-terior of the car is emblazoned with the Southern Cross atop the roof of the automo-bile, coinciding with the 'good ole boy' theme of the show. The show's protagonists, the Dukes, embodied a momentary celebration of rural Southern whiteness, in this instance closely allied with the imagery of the Confederacy. Perhaps the recent re-lease of a Hollywood reinvention of the *Dukes* is suggestive of the broadening import of the South in contemporary American popular culture.

then thanked the organizers of the event for their hospitality, and evoked the 'laudable' customs of Southern gentility and generosity he was afforded in "the tradition of Nathan Bedford Forrest"[7] (Fieldnotes).

Following Ben Jones, a local historian offered a background on the genealogy of the cemetery, positing that while a few Union soldiers had been buried on the campus grounds following the 'War of Northern Aggression,' their corpses had since been removed, and thus the burial ground was 'purified.' The spectacle of the Confederate dead concluded with a prayer lead by a local minister, in which the man of the cloth asked "God's forgiveness for [his] ill will toward those who stand against the Confederacy, against is symbols and ideals." He also asked forgiveness for the "anger" that sometimes overcame him when "people attempt to desecrate the legacy of his forefathers" (Fieldnotes). The minister then asked for the Lord's guidance for those Southern Democrats (Dixiecrats), and those "who have the audacity to call themselves Southern Democrats," who "stand in opposition of the appointment of people of good will and intention who are seeking appointment to the Supreme Court of the United States" (Fieldnotes).

The prevailing postulations and gesticulations of the visible center—diffused by way of *stars, bars, and logoed cars*—stand uninterrupted as the main artifices of Ole Miss identity politics. Not all spectators of the Dixie South spectacle imbibe the Confederacy as those I witnessed in early May 2005, but importantly, the pervasive presence of these symbols, and the ideologies for which they stand—paraphrasing Marx (1976)—constitute and reconstitute the actualized, material relationship between individuals that assume, in their eyes, the fantastic form of a relation between things. In other words, the Confederate flag and its presence at Ole Miss *reifies Dixie*, conjoining the fanatical practices of neo-Confederates at the Civil War Memorial or in the more subversive hegemonic relations of the Grove to the hegemonic position of whiteness at the center of Southern social relations. As the flag congests the symbolic spaces of sporting Ole Miss, it brings to life the power dynamics of the Confederacy, of those who constructed symbolic and material violence on the campus from its inception through to the days of Meredith and Hawkins, and of the 'order of things' that still operates on, and oppresses, non-white subjectivities throughout the Dixie South.

These spectacular performances of neo-Confederate subjectivity bring to life the culturally-integrated spectacle of Dixie South whiteness, replete with its conjunctural rudiments of: conservative ideology, symbolic spatiality, and signified corporeality. While for Debord (1990), such an 'integrated spectacle' starts with the encircling visions and fetters of an omnipotent nation-state, in the *integrated spectacle of the Dixie South* at Ole Miss,

7. Nathan Bedford Forrest is considered by many historians to be one of the most important military figures of the Civil War. He was a highly regard cavalry officer, as his guerilla tactics proved successful in battles won by the Confederacy. In the shadows of the war's end, Forrest became a founding member and eventually 'Grand Wizard' of the Ku Klux Klan, and firmly opposed Reconstruction-era attempts to desegregate.

power and authority are paraded about by the visible center, re-enchant-ing the spectator with stultifying splendor. In the spectacle of Dixie South whiteness, symbols of the Old South, of an imagined rationalized structure of Southern privilege, inform, constitute, and organize the monolithic tra-jectories of hegemonic whiteness.

Spectacularizing the Confederacy

Through the socio-cultural 'mystifications' of intercollegiate sport, a spec-tacular space is constructed and unto itself becomes the unifying principle upon which the integrated spectacle is organized. Thus, spectators' tend-ency to fetishize a hegemonic Dixie South whiteness, defined in both the Grove and the Memorial by a constantly rejuvenating historical adoration for the Old South, has led to an integrated spectacular system of laws "cor-responding to its needs and harmonizing with its own structure" (Lukács, 1971, p. 95). Ultimately, those empowered within hubristic institutions of whiteness such as Ole Miss must reconcile the problematic mobilizations of the sign. Indeed, the elimination of the Confederate symbol offers the first real step toward an emancipatory, progressive public pedagogy. Those em-powered by the signifier *do not* get to define its meaning for those who have suffered under its social and geographic territories—and if the University of Mississippi is to ever realize its promise as a 'Great American Public University,' then administrators, students, and supporters of its athletic program must break free from the shackles of iniquity which have long served to bind, and has equally long since been bound to, the institution.

These contemporary spaces of the Ole Miss sporting Confederacy are problematic in that they reconstitute a spectacle of historically constrained white power in the Dixie South. As the discursive stylings I have presented illustrate, the neo-Confederate sporting spectacles of Ole Miss activate conjunctural rudiments of conservative ideology, exclusive spatiality, and subjected corporeality. In this spectacle of Dixie South whiteness, symbols of the Old South, of an imagined, yet rationalized, structure of Southern privilege, inform, constitute, and organize the multifarious trajectories of identity politics under the dominion of a divisive sport culture. The prevail-ing postulations and gesticulations of the visible center stand uninterrup-ted as the main artifices constitutive of the Ole Miss fan experience. Not all spectators of Ole Miss sporting events imbibe in the Confederate symbols or ideologies to the extent of many of those I represent here. However, not once during my time in Oxford were these symbols, their presence at these events, or their dominion over the university space challenged or called into question. By way of its hegemonic posture, the symbol not only remains rel-evant, but it also maintains power.

Imagined space and physical space are sutured in and through the fan-atical practices of neo-Confederates spectators of today, the lynch mobs of the Civil Rights era, the pro-slavery faction of the Lost Cause, the segrega-tionist politics of the Dixiecrats, or the marauding Ku Klux Klan rallies. As

235

the flag congests the symbolic spaces of sporting Ole Miss, it brings to life the power dynamics of the Confederacy, of those who constructed symbolic and material violence on the campus from its foundation through to the days of Meredith and Hawkins, and of a racially oppressive order of things that still operates on, and oppresses, non-white subjectivities throughout the Dixie South (as witnessed by staggering disparity in race-based literacy and poverty rates, household incomes, incarceration rates, and enrollment figures at the state's most highly regarded institutions of higher education, such as Ole Miss).

More important, in recent years this local symbolization of neo-Confederate white sporting supremacy has taken on expanded import. While I may have focused on the flag as a symbolic fixture within Ole Miss sport culture, I would be remiss in failing to acknowledge the increased global import of the Confederate flag and other symbols of white supremacy. While for decades the Confederate flag has mainly acted as a symbol of spectator identity in the local sporting cultures of the US South, the sign has recently come to represent 'white reign' over international sporting spectacles. The Confederate flag can now be found in non-Southern sporting spaces worldwide, such as at British Nationalist supporter group gatherings, the South Island rodeo spectacles (loosely defined as such) of Aotearoa/New Zealand, and in the grandstands of Spanish national team matches. Just as German football fans of yesteryear or Croatian fans of more recent times have evoked the Nazi swastika (the latter in the form of a giant human swastika) as a symbolic gesture meant to both intimidate their opponents and mark racial solidarity, the Confederate flag seems to have emerged a new, softer symbol of racist ideology. While there is a dearth in the academic and popular literature devoted to the internationalization of the sporting Confederacy, it nonetheless points us in the direction of two concluding observations.

First, while the flag's meaning is contested and contestable, local intermediaries have been successful in stitching hyperracist meanings onto the discursive fabric of the Confederate marker. Taken out of its US South context, the Confederate flag as a marker of racist ideologies comes into much clearer focus. As the flag has remained a fixture at sporting events such as those I studied at Ole Miss, it has been given license as a symbol of broader idioms of white supremacy. Defenders of the flag are often highly critical of academics, commentators, and outsiders whom they argue are revising the history of the Civil War and the flag that has come to represent their place in that conflict. The transcendentalism of the signifier is perhaps better traced back to the labors of the local. At Ole Miss, the flag's singular sporting implication is bound to a trenchant lexicon of oppression, backlash, and power. This was history written from within. Racist praxis begot contestation or opposition. The flag has emerged from that history as exactly what many marching Klanswomen and Klansmen, University Greys, Citizen's Council members, Dixiecrats, Rebels, and other members of the white center intended. British Nationalists are simply extending the antihumane symbolic gestures that both white supremacists from the South and beyond have fought to preserve under its mark.

Second, Ole Miss spectators' tendency to fetishize the Confederate banner has enacted a more significant endorsement of a hegemonic whiteness. Defined in the Grove by a constantly rejuvenating historical adoration for the Old South and more generally by ideologues of a globalizing white right, the flag authenticates a double entendre of ownership: ownership of a privileged past (in the face of global mediations on Civil Rights, human justice, anti-apartheid, affirmative action, equal opportunity, and immigration and immigrant backlash) and ownership of the terms by which a contemporary sporting ethnic [trans]nationalism is formulated. Moreover, those racist ideologies that have taken a material form under the auspices of the Confederate flag are reconstituted as a "natural" extension of Southern identity rather than an artificial, reinvented articulation of what Henry Giroux (1994) refers to as *new cultural racism*. This new cultural racism enacted in and through the Confederate flag at Ole Miss sporting events carries with it a more subtle variety of the same malevolent discursive and material tendencies from the eras of slavery, Civil Rights, and 1980s white backlash through to the Dixieland's present and future.

Branded Sporting Dixie

Without symbols...social feelings could have only an unstable existence. . . . While emblematizing is necessary if society is to become conscious of itself, so it is no less indispensable in perpetuating that consciousness. - Emile Durkheim, 1912

In recent years, a number academic journals and other written outlets have comprised an important forum for discussing the meaningful exploits of racially divisive mascots by major American universities and professional sports franchises (Baca, 2004; Duncan, 1993; Farnell, 2004; C. Richard King, 2002; C. Richard King, Davis-Delano, Staurowsky, & Baca, 2006; C. Richard King & Springwood, 2000; C. R. King, Staurowsky, Baca, Davis, & Pewewardy, 2002; C. D. Pewewardy, 2001; Cornel D. Pewewardy, 2004; Sigelman, 1998; Springwood, 2004; Ellen J. Staurowsky, 1998; E. J. Staurowsky, 2001; E.J. Staurowsky, 2004; Ellen J. Staurowsky, 2004; E.J. Staurowsky, 2007; Strong, 2004). For many scholars and social commentators who have contributed to this well-considered castigation, these mascots remain troublesome in that each promulgates long-standing stereotypes and stimulates a course vernacular of surplus value for the sporting entities they signify (i.e., logoed and branded merchandise). As a composite evaluation, these interjections have been instructive in illuminating how the fetishization of Washington's Redskins, the emblematized save the CHIEF movement at the University of Illinois, and the vigilantism of uninformed casino tycoons and other alumni-bourgeoisie in perpetuating counterfeit histories of Native American genocide victims continue to marginalize and oppress various non-white subjectivities.

Interestingly, within these debates there is a paucity of critical discourse devoted to reconsidering, or unsettling, how the symbolic dimensions of ethnocentrically white mascots function in an analogously powerful way—positioning whiteness as the norm within these same cultural institutions (C. R. King & Springwood, 2001; K. Kusz, 2007; K. W. Kusz, 2001). The mascot as a caricatured symbol of sporting identities, as the Durkheimian epigraph suggests, not only grafts a discursive formation which functions to alienate and disenfranchise (as is the case with many Native American mascots), but also marks cultural territories representative of the ideologies (or what Durkheim might refer to as "consciousness") and identities of the dominant faction. My aim here is to bring into focus the latter problem—the normative identity politics that have been layered onto the bodily discourses of sport's most popular hyper-white mascot: the University of Mississippi's Colonel Rebel.

In the coming pages, I will draw on (a) a genealogy of the university's mascot, (b) a series of interviews with local cultural intermediaries, (c) fieldnotes from Ole Miss sporting events, and (d) a collection of relevant media texts to elucidate the complicated practices of fandom and spectatorship within Colonel Reb's sporting institution. I will argue that although the cultural seductiveness of Colonel Rebel as signifier is in the first instance rooted in the perseverance of unbending nostalgia for the Old South, for many, the academic institution and its most recognizable sporting icon have become inextricably linked to the broader idiomatic and symmetric formations of longitudinal racial oppression and monolithic Dixie South whiteness. Some scholars have gone so far as to say that University of Mississippi has strategically fashioned a symbolic "good ole boy" aesthetic that pays homage to, and locates the institution within, the "signs and symbols of the nineteenth-century Southern Confederacy" (King & Springwood, 2001, p. 130). Although it is more likely the case that the University's academic mission is to ensure that its graduates are anything but the next generation of racist automatons, the discursive formations activated in and through Ole Miss as a symbolic structure serve to substantiate such a claim by constructing an imaginary social institution occupied by ideals of supremacy, alienation, and oppression and made real by a history of segregation, racism, and intolerance. Through this reincarnation of an Old South symbolic system in the context of a post-plantation 'new New South' (Cobb, 1999), the Jim Crow identity politics and the white supremacist thrusts of the New South are updated, if not activated, within the contemporary moment. Rather, in the diachronic progression of the post–Civil Rights, Affirmative Action Dixie South, whiteness is performance—an overt *theater of white Power* brought to life in and through the discursive machinations and political stylings of normalization and identification.[1]

1.Much as the 1936 Olympic Games constituted a theater of power for expressing Aryan supremacy, solidarity, and political ideology, this theater acts to reinforce the normative nature of preferred Whiteness in the Dixie South context while simultaneously authorizing the practices of the oppressive center.

By rethinking the symbolic occupation of whiteness over the institution, and situating the discursive formations of Colonel Reb at the contextual intersection of corporatized public education and neo-Confederate identity politics, I assert that the pervasiveness and popularity of the Ole Miss sporting symbolic is a product of the dual processes of a *collective conscious* and *commodity racism*. In other words, I argue that as both a product and producer of a distinct cultural history—a diachronic dialectic of contestation, resistance, subjugation, oppression, and privilege woven through the material histories of slavery, civil wars, eugenics movements, segregation, civil rights, and new forms of racism—the symbolic system of Ole Miss is more than an imprint of the banal symbolic or poststructuralist fodder. Rather, it enacts an antihumane polity and ideology that to this day maps privilege and works to oppress the marginalized peoples of the region. I conclude by briefly discussing how Ole Miss is instructive in blurring the notions of spectatorship, consumerism, and identification.

Situating Colonel Reb's Whiteness

While attending an Ole Miss sporting event, and particularly a contest involving the university's championship intercollegiate football team, spectators are immersed in a universe of Old South symbols and signifying acts. On football Saturdays, the central campus space is transformed into a veritable modern day Civil War encampment, as tens of thousands of Ole Miss fans congregate amidst a sea of Confederate flags. This exclusively white imagined community adheres to a patriarchal, genteel Old South dress code as many Ole Miss men customarily wear collared shirts and ties and women spectators typically don formal dresses. These Ole Miss fans chant the fight song 'Hotty Toddy' in support of their Rebels—a resistance song that became popular on the campus during the resistance to James Meredith's integration of the school in 1962. During the opening processions of each game, the white spectating throng welcomes the footballing combatants, almost all of whom are Black, to the battle by singing the Confederate anthem 'Dixie'; whereas other Southern universities abandoned the song decades ago, it remains a fixture at Ole Miss contests. All of these signifying acts—each of which perpetuates the conspicuous affect of Dixie South hegemonic whiteness—is lorded over by the transcendental embodiment of sporting Ole Miss: the wildly popular mascot Colonel Rebel. More commonly referred to as 'Colonel Reb' or 'Johnny Reb,' the mascot features a cartoonish physique of a mustachioed "gentleman planter" slouched over a cane, as if leisurely overseeing his plantation. The Colonel is traditionally outfitted in the colors of the Confederacy and is often illustrated in accompaniment with the traditional Ole Miss script and Confederate-referent 'Rebels' moniker (Sindelar, 2003).

Contrary to popular convention, the "traditions" of symbolic Ole Miss, those of an evocative Old South and courageous Confederacy, are relatively recent allusions. Although each signifier of the Ole Miss sporting lexicon resurrects a romanticized vision of the Old South, each has been artificially constructed within the arcs of a contemporaneous signifying system. The flying of the Confederate battle flag and the singing of the minstrel song "Dixie" were adopted by the university in the late 1940s in response to national trends toward integration. On campus in 1948, exponents of a mid-century states' rights platform (popularly known as the "Dixiecrats") activated symbols of the Confederacy to promote their anti-integration polity (Frederickson, 2000, 2001) 'Dixie' became the 'official song' of the Dixiecrats, and the Confederate flag became the collective symbol for segregationist efforts and ideals (Sansing, 1999). To rally support on the Ole Miss campus, the Dixiecrats passed out small Confederate flags during home football games that year (Sansing, 1990). The reemergence and revivification of the Rebel flag at Ole Miss sporting events contributed to more than one bond between Ole Miss and the Confederate past, and the fact that it was an election year even further cemented the relationship between symbol and ideology. "The crowd in the stadium could not only cheer the Rebels on the field. They could also wave their flags and sing 'Dixie' for the insurgent politicians representing their cause and way of life" (Cohodas, 1997, p. 34).

In the year in which the university was celebrating its centennial anniversary, the 'Southern Cross' became a symbolic fixture on the Ole Miss campus, a representative marker of Old South 'heritage' and 'perseverance'—a banner of *credence* for its constituents and a territorial marker representing the cause for which they seemingly stood united (Collins, 1970). The symbolic construction of collective whiteness at Ole Miss through these symbols prompted one professor at the university to later suggest, "the song and the Confederate battle flag were adopted by the all-white university specifically as a gesture of white supremacy" (Lederman, 1993, p. A52). The regenerations of the flag and 'Dixie,' as well as the creations of caricaturized whiteness, thus gave corporeal credence to Dixie South whiteness, and further complicated an already complex interaction of the symbolic, the embodied, and the political.

The sporting mascot of the University of Mississippi has an equally problematic history with regard to signification and racism. A genealogy of 'the Colonel' offers a great deal of insight into the politics of representation and sporting iconography at Ole Miss. More importantly, the diachronic evolution of the Colonel into his role as the caricaturized embodiment of contemporary Ole Miss further complicates the already complex relationship of the university, the South, and racialized identity politics. The university's inaugural football squad, established in 1893 by Latin professor Alexander Bondurant, originally played under the colors red and blue. The football team subsequently adopted the nickname "The Red and Blue," as a symbolic moniker that remained until the late 1920s. Then, in 1929, the university sponsored a contest to rename the football team. The winning entry was the "Mississippi Flood," adopted in remembrance of the great flood of the Mississippi River that devastated the Mississippi Delta in 1927. "Mississippi Flood" was chosen over "Rebels" (second choice), "Democrats"(third choice), and "Ole Marsters" (fourth choice) ("'The Mississippi Flood' picked as name for athletes," 1929, p. 1). The nickname was not atypical for the period, considering the University of Alabama was known as the Crimson Tide and Tulane University was the Green Wave. But "Mississippi Flood," like "Red and Blue," would not last long. The nickname was deemed "inadequate [just as] the one before it . . . had been dumped for lacking that certain something" (Cohodas, 1997, p. 161), and so 7 years after the "Flood" was adopted, the team moniker was dropped for the name that has endured ever since.

The team nickname, "Rebels," was officially adopted in 1936 following a second contest sponsored by the student newspaper, the *Mississippian*. Of the 500 entries in a contest to choose a nickname, "Rebels" was narrowly selected over "Ole Massas," a term often used by Black slaves when addressing their white plantation masters in the era of slavery. The "Rebels," the *Mississippian* proscribed, was "suggestive of a spirit native to the Old South and particularly to Mississippi"("University adopts new nickname - Rebels," 1936, p. 1). Furthermore, in an explanation given to the *Mississippian*, the Confederate Army nickname was selected because Ole Miss Rebels was easier to say than Ole Miss Ole Massas ("University adopts new nickname - Rebels," 1936).

The visual presentation of Colonel Rebel emerged for the first time on the cover of the 1937 *Ole Miss*annual. The original image of Colonel Reb was that of "a southern gentleman in the image of a plantation master: flowing white hair, bushy mustache, wearing a long coat nipped at the waist, light pants, dark shoes, and a big broad-brimmed hat" (Cohodas, 1997, p. 161). The earliest iterations of Colonel Reb featured a caricature of a plantation owner representative of plantation culture and the Old South. Interestingly, this version of Colonel Reb featured no visible connections to the Civil War. There is a considerable debate as to the origins of the image. The Colonel Reb Foundation, an organization committed to "preserving the Colonel as the mascot of Ole Miss," contends that the mascot is molded in the image of "Blind Jim" Ivy, a blind Black man who worked on the campus until his death in 1955. According to the Colonel Reb Foundation:

> Jim Ivy became an integral part of the University of Mississippi in 1896. Born in 1870 as the son of African slave Matilda Ivy, he moved from Alabama to Mississippi in 1890. Ivy was blinded in his early teens when coal tar paint got into his eyes while painting the Tallahatchie River Bridge. Ivy became a peanut vendor in Oxford and was considered the university's mascot for many years. Ivy attended most Ole Miss athletic events and was fond of saying, "I've never seen Ole Miss lose." Ivy was very much a part of the Ole Miss scene in 1936 when the editor of the school newspaper proposed a con- test to produce a new nickname for Ole Miss teams, then known as The Flood. . . . According to [Ole Miss faculty member] David Sansing, 'If you look at the photo of Blind Jim in the three-piece suit, with the hat, there's a striking resemblance. The original Colonel Rebel emblem is a spitting image of Blind Jim Ivy, except for white skin.' ("Let's keep the Colonel at Ole Miss," 2004, p. 1)

Although this account has been questioned over the years, if accurate, the "whiting out" of Blind Jim is nonetheless problematic. One of a handful of Black individuals on the Ole Miss campus during his life, this posthumous recreation of Blind Jim represents the docile, subservient Blackness of the postbellum, Jim Crow era. His celebrity was constructed out of his non-threatening, accommodating "Otherness." In other words, if the embodiment of Colonel Reb was derived from Blind Jim Ivy, it was not done so as to signify the racial diversity of the collective institution, nor was it constructed out of tribute to the individual, but rather as a pedantic conquest of the servile Black body. One of the more public figures in the early days of the Colonel Reb Foundation reconstructed the cultural import of Blind Jim Ivy with the following description:

> He was the true Ole Miss mascot during that time. And I've had a lot of questions asked about why he wasn't Black. Well, students back then were all white, and why, I mean, do you not think that if a student body that was all white used a Black mascot, don't you think that would send people up in arms and get people upset because it's not well representing the university by creating a mascot of a Black man? But instead he simply created a white man but based him off of, of the Black man Blind Jim Ivy. And so they put it in the first edition of the yearbook in 1937. (Personal communication)

Thus, Jim Ivy presents those of a nostalgic bent with a cultural 'mystification' (Freire, 1970/2006) absolved of oppressive segregation and racial subservience, instead celebrating the "harmonious times" of the Old South; whereby an all-white student body exercised its dominance over subservient Blacks through an objectifying caricature rather than subjective social justice. Symbolically, the whiting out of Blind Jim's likeliness (whose dress, unlike Colonel Reb, was not emblazoned with Confederate military insignias) further emblematizes the invasion of downtrodden Jim Crow Blackness and its twin logic of co-optation of the oppressed 'Other.'

Over time, the Colonel came to be known by other names, including 'Johnny Reb' and 'General Nat'—with the latter a reference to General Nathaniel Bedford Forrest, Confederate war hero and founder of the Ku Klux Klan. In both instances, the causes of slavery and segregation were never too far removed from the symbolic physicality of Colonel Reb (Kanengiser, 2003b). In the years following the creation of the Ivy-allusive Colonel, the mascot was brought to life in the form of a student mascot dressed in a Confederate military uniform. The microphone-wielding student paraded down the sidelines exhorting the Rebel faithful to cheer for their team and their [lost] "cause." The popular pseudo soldier led the cheers of Ole Miss fans through the heyday of the university's football team, as the squad captured three national championships (1959, 1960, and 1962) and six Southeastern Conference titles (1947, 1954, 1955, 1960, 1962, and 1963) (Cleveland, 2003, p. 19). Interestingly, this reification of the Colonel Reb image corresponded with the reemergence of the Confederacy as a political counternarrative to the forces of desegregation—namely the *Brown vs. Board of Education* ruling of 1956.

The debut of the cartoon-like embodied mascot, a "huge, mustachioed headed" caricature with the wide brimmed hat, came in 1979 (Cleveland, 2003). Supplanting the preceding version, the garish incarnation of Colonel Rebel immediately became a symbolic fixture of the sporting Ole Miss signifying system. Colonel Reb could be seen all over Oxford and the Ole Miss campus, including several Southeastern Conference sporting tournaments such as Ole Miss football, baseball, and basket- ball games. To such an end, the mascot became the central element in the university's sporting identity both in Mississippi and throughout the country. More importantly, his physical characteristics, in the wake of the Civil Rights Era, gave credence to the dominion of whiteness within the campus spaces. As most other Southern universities' Old South signifiers were slowly petering out, the Colonel came to represent the post–civil rights, neo-Confederate articulations of a resistant, yet resilient, whiteness. The Colonel's presence meant the perseverance of 'tradition'—a tradition that in its most banal form represents Southern life, but in a more insatiable function is indivisible from the "simpler" times of the over-determined white authority imbedded in the systems of slavery and segregation. Put simply, in the 'land of cotton,' one person's 'tradition' is another's torture.

A Neo-Confederate Tribunal

In 1997, following the decision by the administration to do away with Confederate flags in the football stadium, the Chancellor was presented with concerns from alumni and students as to whether Colonel Rebel would remain the university's mascot. His reply was that "The University does not consider it 'racist' and will not discontinue its use" (quoted in Cohodas, 1997, p. 220). This declaration was extolled by booster groups and most supporters of the university, while simultaneously derided by civil rights groups and the NAACP (Coski, 2005). In 2003, as a response to growing criticism from the latter faction, the chancellor and the athletic director of the University of Mississippi announced the institution's plans to replace Colonel Reb. Failing to cite racist overtones of the Colonel's image and use, the Chancellor instead postulated that the "decision to update the mascot was based on the belief that a Disney-like elderly plantation person [was] not representative of a modern athletics program" (R. C. Khayat, 2003, p. 1). The more public rationale offered by pundits of the sporting South suggested that much like in the case of the Confederate flag, the problematic nature of the mascot had become a serious issue in recruiting top Black high school players to come to Ole Miss (Mcwhite, 2002).

In more critical terms, one might suggest that these concessions made by the university with regard to Colonel Reb were mere acquiescences to the following conundrum: "Ole Miss coaches have said for years that Old South symbols, such as the Confederate battle flag, the song Dixie and Colonel Rebel, have hurt in the recruitment of African-American athletes" (Cleveland, 2003, p. 19). One earlier report positioned the race/recruitment issue this way:

> Steve Sloan coached at Ole Miss from 1978–1982 and contends the university lacked a strong commitment to integration. Sloan is one of several former Rebel coaches contending that the racial history of Ole Miss dating back to

the Meredith crisis has damaged Ole Miss' ability to recruit quality black athletes in large numbers. He believes athletic symbols . . . significantly hinder
recruiting at Ole Miss [and thus] the university is immediately placed on the
defensive when recruiting a black athlete because of the school's racial history
and reputation. Coaches must spend valuable time with a recruit explaining
that these symbols 'aren't important.' (R. W. Baker, 1989, p. 36)

This viscous, selective "import" of the sign has continued to allow the white
politics of the signifier to evade the interpolations of critique while simultaneously propagating the ideological consternations of those in power.
Black students are thus repeatedly assured that these symbols 'aren't important' and are 'innocent' or 'harmless,' whereas a majority of white students vigilantly fight to preserve these symbols of "times not forgotten"—times when their white ancestors owned the land and ruled over the
great-grandmothers and great-grandfathers of their Black classmates. Ultimately, the problem with the mascot becomes conveniently simplified to
the negative consequences for those in power (poor performances of their
beloved Rebels) rather than any reflexive consideration of the oppressive
nature of the sign.

As was the case when the university suspended any 'official' ties with the
Confederate flag, the decision to replace Colonel Reb was met with a great
deal of hostility from the dominant faction of the conservative white center. Numerous supporter groups and other activist parties lobbied to retain the mascot, citing its significance in the nuanced social histories of the
school, its sports teams, and the region. During the 2003 football campaign,
when faced with the possibility of changing the school mascot to a more
contemporary, less racist iteration, a number of Ole Miss students, "Southern conservation" organizations (such as the Sons of Confederate Veterans),
and white supremacist groups (such as the Nationalist Movement) organized and protested outside the university's administration building (Kanengiser, 2003a).

In a campus poll taken in the early fall of 2003, almost 94% of students
voted to keep Colonel Reb as the school's athletic mascot (Bartlett, 2003).
The echoes of "reverse racism" and white disenfranchisement were stirred
about in the present-day public sphere—a central theme that directed students and alumni to prevent the Colonel from being replaced:

> This whole movement of "political correctness" is just a milder, more innoc-
> uous aspect of the same slop Mao and Robespierre tried to dole out. I guess
> the Ole Miss (excuse me, University of Mississippi) officials think retiring the
> Colonel will turn us into New Age Mississippians and better love our fellow
> man. (Emmerich, 2005)

Members of Kappa Alpha fraternity organized a Support Colonel Reb drive,
in which they encouraged students to protest the university's decision
through the popular print mediums of the region (Kanengiser, 2003a).
Meanwhile, administrators organized a contest in which students and community members were beseeched to submit renditions for the new Ole Miss
mascot. After reviewing hundreds of sub- missions, a large majority of which
were deemed "unacceptable for consideration" by the committee appointed

to review the entries (a decision that the *Daily Mississippian* speculated was a result of numerous racially insensitive sketches), the contest was scrapped and the university took the decision out of the students' hands (Sindelar, 2003). The ultraracist Nationalist Movement offered their own contributions to the discourse, publicizing a cartoon titled "The New Ole Miss Mascot" featuring a Black man with exaggerated facial features (enlarged lips and nose) portending "Ah Diss Dem Crackas An De' Lo, Too, Suckas . . . Ah' Bees De' Baddest Mascot" (Nationalist Movement, 2003).[2]

In the end, the entries were pared down to three options: "a bear, a horse, and a biker in the image of James Dean" (Burnham, 2003, p. 12). The lattermost option lost momentum in the lead-up to the vote, as the likeness to Dean brought into play the rumors of the film star's sexual preferences: "Would Ole Miss have a gay mascot if the rumors are true?" (Burnham, 2003, p. 12). To come to a decision concerning the new mascot, officials announced that students, faculty, and alumni would be eligible to select the new mascot by way of a popular vote. Despite the nearly $12,000 spent by the university to publicize the election, the search for a new on-the-field mascot was terminated in the fall of 2003, as university officials declared that following a preliminary vote to decide the new mascot in which only 2,400 of the eligible 40,000 voters cast a vote, the university would have no in-stadium mascot (Sindelar, 2003).

Citing "poor participation and no support for either mascot," the Chancellor determined that the matter was now closed and it was "time to move forward"(Sindelar, 2003, pp. 1–2). According to the *Daily Mississippian*, the low voter turnout was in part because of a boycott of the election called for by traditionalists within the Ole Miss community (Bartlett, 2003). It was rumored that of the 2,400 votes that were cast, a considerable number were "write in" votes for Colonel Reb. By "moving forward," the university effectively decided to discontinue the sanctioning of an on-the-field mascot. In other words, even though Colonel Reb remains a prominent fixture in the signified landscape of the institution, and generates millions of dollars in revenues through reproductions of his likeness on consumer goods, his persona is supposedly "banned" from the stadium during home football and basketball games. To this day, the Colonel's likeness is still a prevalent part of the Ole Miss sporting signscape. Although the Colonel's undying resilience is in part due to the neo-Confederate populism of the student body, another rationale could lie in the entrepreneurial forces that act on Ole Miss as a 'corporatized university.'

2.Richard Barrett, head of the Nationalist Movement, presented a supremacist-inspired speech on the footsteps of the Lyceum on October 30,2003,to the Ole Miss student body, a conclave which was "well-received" by a "number of Ole Miss students." Barrett has filed suit against the University of Mississippi for "unlawfully" disallowing the Confederate flag in public places. This lawsuit eventually went to the Supreme Court, where Barrett and his Nationalist lawyers lost their case.

The Corporate Haunting of an Undying Soldier

To a large extent, the controversies and debates surrounding Colonel Reb are incontrovertibly bound to, and by, the money disciplines of late capitalism and its subsidiary logics of quasi-professional college athletics. As Jonathan Rutherford (2005) poignantly posits, public education has become folded under the sutured axes of marketization and public service under the neoliberal condition: "The market imperative of optimal performance penetrates the university and carries with it the erosion of its traditional social and cultural mission" (p. 299). Building on Bill Readings's (1996) important work *The University in Ruins*, Rutherford argues that universities are encouraged to tailor their program's market needs, researchers are transformed into savvy grant-hunting venture capitalists, students are now referred to as "customers," and escalating tuition fees are invested in new football stadia. The subordination of public education to neoliberal market logics, coupled with the increasingly lucrative nature of intercollegiate sport, has resulted in a condition whereby the corporate thrusts of late capitalism now position universities not as centers for the construction and exchange of knowledge, but as highly marketable global 'brands' (M. W. Apple, 1995, 2001; Bok, 2004; Readings, 1996; Sperber, 2000).

In other words, we have seen an increased "marketization and commodification of higher education as indicative of the wider transition of previously public sector institutions as we move from the welfare state to the market state" (Canaan & Shumar, 2008, p. 4). The university campus is now dominated by corporate language such as 'networking,' "employability" (Ainley, 2004), 'workforce needs,' 'cost effectiveness,' and 'economies of scale.' Much like a corporation, the university now hires consultants to help control, or 'streamline,' variable costs such as faculty wages and 'production-related' expenses. Academic staff are disciplined by an intensifying regime of assessment of their teaching and research products. Those products—whether they be learner proficiencies (discussed later) or lines on a *curriculum vitae*—in some ways stultify the dynamism with which scholar-teachers can do their work. "Rather than a democratic discourse where all of an institution's citizens are involved in developing dispositional knowledge," write Tierney and Rhoads (1995), this assessment-protocol "has tried to create a sharper division between managers and workers and to reinforce norms rather than bring them into question" (pp. 109-110). Such a technocratic rationality "operates under very specific patterns aimed at the increase of production and prediction, the control of the economy, and the regulation of society" (Fernandez-Balboa & Muros, 2006, p. 199). Ritzer (1998b) describes the consequences of these rationalizing processes on what has later been termed '*McUniversity*': "Many students and faculty members are put off by its factory-like atmosphere. They may feel like automatons processed by the bureaucracy and computers or feel like cattle run through a meat processing plant" (Ritzer, 1993, p. 143).[3] In other words, Ritzer (1993) argues that much like a franchise link in the McDonald's restaurant chain, the production processes of the university has come to be defined by the precepts of efficiency, calculability, predictability, and control.

As social critic Noam Chomsky (2002) suggests, the democracy of the academic institution has been sacrificed by a privatizing impetus that now organizes all aspects of higher learning:

> There has been a general assault in the last 25 years on solidarity, democracy, social welfare, anything that interferes with private power, and there are many targets. One of the targets is undoubtedly the educational system. In fact, a couple of years ago already, the big investment firms, like Lehman Brothers, and so on, were sending around brochures to their clients saying, "Look, we've taken over the health system; we've taken over the prison system; the next big target is the educational system. So we can privatize the educational system, make a lot of money out of it."(p. 1)

In other words, the corporatized university has become a capitalist enterprise, and a generation of funding the activities in the university is now reduced to the profit-driven model of accumulation and commodification (Canaan & Shumar, 2008; J. J. Williams, 2001). Chomsky's (2002) contention echoes that of David Harvey (1998), who asserted:

> The hidden hand of the market distributes resources and rewards so as to ensure a proliferating freedom of market choices in higher education while denying the capacity to explore alternative values. Money discipline undercuts the freedoms of research and speech promised by tenure and threatens to be worse than McCarthyism in its effects on independent scholarship and critical thought. And it is far more insidious: there is no overt source of oppression to be identified and resisted. Even university presidents are caught within the logic, forced to raise more and more money or economize on costs by whatever means to meet the escalating financial needs of teaching and research. (p. 115)

To meet these escalating shortfalls, a number of North America's largest public universities have been forced to increase tuition by substantial increments over the past decade (H. A. Giroux, 2007). Corporate knowledges, those of the business sector and those that hold market value, are now privileged over those emanating from critical, liberal, humanitarian, or justice-driven modes of inquiry (Slaughter, 2006; Slaughter & Leslie, 2000; Slaughter & Rhoades, 2004). The tenure process has succumbed to the individual researcher's neoliberal imprint. Many schools have reduced the programs and services offered to students in a corporate 'fat-trimming' exercise heretofore unseen in American higher education (Henry A. Giroux,

---

3.Ritzer (1993) has drawn considerable criticism for what many regard as a hasty generalization of the current 'dehumanizing' climate of higher education. While it should suffice to say that Ritzer (1993) might have offered an overstated brushstroke of the current university environ, it must also be noted that his argument was formulated based on his own empirical observations formulated while working at the University of Maryland, College Park. As former graduate students at that university, while we agree that Ritzer (1993) might overzealously vilify life at the generic McUniversity (Ritzer, 1998b), none of the authors of this chapter would disagree with his assessment of the dehumanizing forces active within their *alma mater*.

2001). Conversely, those for- profit armatures of the institution have been extended at most public schools. "Development officers" and those charged with stimulating "partnerships and giving" have been shuffled to the top of most organizational charts. Indeed, solicitation and corporate groveling trump instruction and service in the functional order of most colleges and universities in North America (white & Hauck, 2000). More students than ever attend institutions that generate student fees not to enhance student learning, but to enhance stockholder portfolios (e.g., University of Phoenix, DeVry, ITT Tech, etc.).[4]

Of equal importance, public universities have turned to sport to further expand their capital accumulation efforts. Although they operate outside the organization structure of the [academic] university, and although the quality of academic programs wane, these athletic departments have been able to procure considerable funding from alumni, booster groups, mandatory students fees, and state initiatives to grow college athletics (Lamb & Sperber, 2000). Operating in the big-business context of the Southeastern Conference, the sporting ventures of the University of Mississippi have become the centrifugal force in meeting the escalating economics of the corporate/ institutional collective. To accumulate the funding necessary for academic and athletic activities, the university has capitalized on its football team as a cultural conduit through which booster, alumni, and corporations can ally themselves and forge an economic relationship with the institution (white & Hauck, 2000).

This form of collective identification is in part indebted to the purchase of Old South symbols such as Colonel Reb. According to a representative from the sports marketing division of the Ole Miss Department of Athletics, Ole Miss–themed merchandise generates between $4 and $6 million of capital inflow per year for the university (Personal communication). Unlike national collegiate brands such as the University of Notre Dame, the University of Michigan, or the University of Southern California, most of the commodities sold under the Ole Miss banner are consumed in the Mississippi Delta region—from Memphis to Jackson. Through creative partnerships with Nike, the Collegiate Licensing Company, College Sports Television (CSTV), and Barnes and Noble, Ole Miss has capitalized on the upsurge of interest in their brand. Furthermore, Ole Miss is "a Nike school," meaning that Nike has exclusive rights to produce, market, and sell apparel and footwear donning the Ole Miss Rebels logo.

The Collegiate Licensing Company (CLC) handles all the licensing agreements for the University of Mississippi, including player presentations on video games, the use of intellectual properties by third-party vendors, and other uses of the symbols and markers of the institution. The University

---

4. Indeed, we are in the midst of corporatization of the US university, whereby the classroom contemplations of civil society have been replaced by sidebar corporate sponsorships from intolerance-spewing profiteers such as Ann Coulter on the "academic" cyberspaces of the University of Phoenix (who recently expanded Coulter's exposure on the company's Web site following her antigay, "faggot"-laden tirade).

of Mississippi is currently working under a contract with CSTV, as the newest addition to the media–sport dais has the broadcast rights to many Ole Miss football, baseball, and basketball games via multiple platforms, namely broadband Internet feeds and cable and satellite television. Through an extensive contract with Barnes and Noble Booksellers, Ole Miss symbolic properties are sold via the campus bookstore and other on-campus retail spaces during the semester, and on game days (Personal communication). In total, these and other initiatives catalyzed by the university's athletic department have further expanded the economic and symbolic value of the Ole Miss brand, and the gestalt of signifying properties and practices have become further unified under the guise of the broader portents of Ole Miss as one part academic institution, one part marker of sporting solidarity.

Unlike many other universities, institutional allegiance at Ole Miss is closely bound to sporting extensions of a local *commodity whiteness*, materialized "in the form of an array of Jim Crow symbols, discourses of Southern pride and resistance, and an investment in victory" (King & Springwood, 2001, p. 141). As the figurehead of the Ole Miss sporting brand, Colonel Reb's command over the consumers of symbolic, sporting Dixie South whiteness encrust his image as a valuable commodity with layers of institutional 'pride and resistance.' Subsequently, any 'compromises' or concessions by the university (to those concerned with the Colonel's racist past) are made only under the pretenses that the Colonel remain in his liquid, transcendent, symbolic, and commodity form. As the academic programs at Ole Miss toil for economic support, the private logics of the branded academy cannot escape the grip of a corporatized neo-Confederacy, commodity whiteness, and the racialized sporting symbolic:

> Instead of reminiscing about some place that never existed outside the minds of men, the administration should attempt to distance itself from those things and allow students to gain the best education possible. The best educational opportunities are thwarted by the administration's overt attempts and drive toward emphasizing research and on-field excellence, not the quality of the undergraduate degree. (Niemeyer, 2004, p. 2)

The 'sign value' (J. Baudrillard, 1981, p. 65) of the Colonel Reb institutionalized image eclipses the traditional model of commodity exchange, and the active manipulation of both signifier and signified further expand the discursive affectivity of Ole Miss as a popular cultural form. Jean Baudrillard (1981) claims that within such a postmodern consumer society, commodity forms—such as those of the sporting Ole Miss brand—are exhibited and consumed more for the perceived sign value than for any utility-based "exchange value," and that the existentialism of the sign precludes any rationalized exchange value relative to contemporary consumer society. For Baudrillard, the entire society is organized around consumption and display of commodities through which individuals gain prestige, identity, and standing. In the Ole Miss signifying system, the accumulated value of the sign is thus transferred onto, and distributed throughout, the corporeal and corporatized materials of a branded sporting whiteness. In this way, commodity and white identit[ies] are folded into the same process, and the acceleration of capital accumulation is borne out of the subjectification of whiteness as semiotic declaration. In more concise terms, the act of consumption fabricates the [re]production of sign value and the lexicon of identification (see Baudrillard, 1981). To be an Ole Miss fan—and particularly to semiotically consume Colonel Reb's Ole Miss—is thus a signifying act which reconstitutes the power-knowledge spectra of the Old South.

Furthermore, the active creation and performances of signified Ole Miss create a locus of identity politics distributed through consumption, and the act of consuming gives life to the symbolic commodity. In other words, the faculties of the Ole Miss brand themselves only garner sign value in relation to the ways in which those signs are created, mobilized, and exchanged: "there is no symbolic 'value,' there is only symbolic 'exchange,' which defines itself precisely as something distinct from, and beyond value and code" (Jean Baudrillard, 1988, pp. 38-39). Following Baudrillard (1989), by locating the spectating body in the "ecstasy" of *dimensional annihilation*, whereby the complete immersion of the consumer in the universe of the sign connects the physical experience to the visceral nodes of identification, subjectification, and inculcation, the Ole Miss fan/consumer/subject incarcerates her or his body in *la langue* of a differential system of representation. In such a differential system of prestige and status, connection to the ideologies and structures embodied by the Ole Miss brand and branded onto the consuming bodies locates the consumer as an active agent in reproduction of a hierarchized symbolic exchange. In turn, Colonel Reb, as a symbolic commodity, contributes to a semiotic exchange rich in representational history, and wrought by the politics of oppression.

Redressing the Colonel

Following the administration's removal of the Colonel from Ole Miss home events, a group of students and alumni organized the Colonel Reb Foundation, a nonprofit association committed to "bringing the Colonel back to life" (Personal communication). A founder of the organization recalled the creation of the foundation in this way:

> It was the summer of 2003, and we had just gotten word that they were removing Colonel Reb from the field and from the sidelines. I went to a friend of mine who I was taking business calculus with and I said, "Man we're going to have to do something about this." And we got in touch with a couple alumni members. I knew one of them was big into Sons of Confederate Veterans and another one was a very big PR guy. . . . We got in touch with both of them and they helped us tremendously in trying to start up an effort to try and save Colonel Reb. Well, one of the first things that we started was in September, I think it was September the 4th right after the Vanderbilt game and right before the Memphis game. We had an interest meeting, we had a meeting to show that we are going to do something about it, and we're going to fight the administration to keep what we feel is a symbol of this university. That he is our mascot. Um, but not just that, the fact that they pretty much shoved it down our throats that we was never going to remove Colonel Reb regardless

of what the students, alumni, and the staff of this university want. (Personal communication)

The group's mission was to bring the Colonel back into Vaught-Hemmingway stadium: "He's a great mascot. He's the character we all relate to," said one of the group's leaders. "Colonel Reb is like our grandfather, or our old uncle" (quoted in Kanengiser, 2003b, p. 5). Although the founder's sentimentality and genealogy loses its residual effect on many of the Black students of Ole Miss, particularly those who fail to make the paternal connection and in turn see the Colonel as a symbol of institutionally sponsored white solidarity in the form of whiteness as hegemony, the command of the Colonel over the Ole Miss campus becomes a marker of power for the white majority.

In an effort to reinstate the Colonel to his post, the Colonel Reb Foundation passed out more than 125,000 lapel stickers to Ole Miss fans and attendees during the 2003, 2004, and 2005 football seasons. Each of the stickers featured a message consistent with the organization's position:

> We've had about five different stickers. The first one that we came up with was "Colonel Reb is my mascot." The next one was, "Pete Boone bring back Colonel Reb." And this year's was "For Pete's sake bring back Colonel Reb." And then the final was, "For Pete's Sake, Khayat Bring Back Colonel Reb."[5] (Personal communication)

Through these campaigns, the group raised enough money to create "Colonel Too," a nearly identical replica costume of the original Colonel Reb. The group used more than $25,000 in alumni contributions to have a North Carolina company reconstruct the Colonel Reb costume (Alford, 2005). As one of the foundation's organizers explained:

> The "Too" design, it's more of a Confederate uniform with stars, with the whole entire outfit. He's got the gold band around the hat, which Colonel Reb didn't have. He's got the blue stripe down the pants, which the Colonel didn't have. (Personal communication)

There are subtle differences between Colonel Reb and his "cousin" Colonel Too, namely in the latter's dress—a style more consistent with the military look of the Civil War era (Breed, 2003).

Again, the Confederacy re-emerges as a symbolic territory of the white South. Despite the interdictions against Colonel Reb in the stadium during games, Colonel Too has continued to showcase his Rebel pride at Ole Miss football, basketball, and baseball games, "waiting for his famous cousin to respectfully return to the Ole Miss sidelines" ("Let's keep the Colonel at Ole Miss," 2004). In response to the new embodied product of the Colonel Reb Foundation's efforts, which have included bringing the corporeal plantation simulacrum back into the stadium, the chancellor stated, "If the students want Colonel Reb in the seating areas, that's great. I don't mind" (Alford, 2005, p. A1). Consequently, Colonel Reb and his cousin continue to organ-

---

5. "Pete" refers to Pete Boone, the University of Mississippi's athletic director; "Khayat" refers to the university's chancellor, Robert Khayat.

ize social and symbolic relations around the embodied politics of the dominant, neo-Confederate center. As one of the central figures in founding the
Colonel Reb Foundation described, the role of the Colonel is to symbolically locate the institution in the realm of a collegial Dixie South whiteness:

> Colonel Reb, to many people, is a symbol of the good times that people have
> had. Ole Miss for many of us is a spot down deep in the South that anybody
> can come, where— it's kind of like a *Cheers* bar—everybody knows your name.
> And, it's a sacred place to many people. As the quote says: "One may for-
> feit tenure at the University of Mississippi, but one never graduates from Ole
> Miss." I mean you're always a part of Ole Miss, and that's very true, and be-
> cause you're always welcome back here. (Personal communication)

Those "good times" have not traditionally been shared by "everybody" or
"anybody," but by the dominant white faction that have, for generations,
constituted Ole Miss's formalized "good ole boy" network (Weeks, 1999).
As such, like the Confederate battle flag and the moniker "Ole Miss," the
Colonel symbolizes the non- reflexive epicentrism of the visible center
rather than the openness of one of the South's leading academic institutions. Furthermore, as the embodiment of Southern plantation gentility in
the postplantation era, Colonel Reb stirs the echoes of an Old South hierarchy and the deportmentalization of a racially-divisive 'Southern ethic.'

Revising the Present

As a fundamental element of local cultural discourse, Colonel Rebel embodies the governing trajectory of an interpellative signscape of Southern
identification. As a seemingly germane, spectacularized sport discourse, the
Colonel has come to transcend the educational institution in the cultural
imaginary of many white Dixie Southerners, and thus as a signifying system
has simultaneously placated the broader cultural anatomy of a social and
educational body and become a commodified, representative embodiment
of outdated cultural politics of the region. Conversely, the Colonel—not
so conveniently absolved from a history of slavery and oppression in the
South—means something quite different to those living on the margins. At
once the mascot is representative of a society that privileged white plantationeers (who looked very much like the Colonel) and white Confederate
soldiers (who looked very much like Colonel Too) and of the systems of
oppression from which bodies of difference suffered during that same history.[6]

As Cameron McCarthy (1998) suggests, the symbolic nature of public institutions such as Ole Miss act on behalf of the prevailing order within a racialized power-knowledge dynamic, or as:

6.As an important imaginary and signified locale, Ole Miss, much like other American
academic institutions, is bound to the hypernormalized order of discordant Whiteness as monolithic signifying praxis: "American colleges and universities, intercollegiate athletics, and sporting spectacles structure are structured by an insidious, if
largely invisible, white supremacy" (King & Springwood, 2001, p. 9).

... critical site[s] in which struggles over the organization and concentration of emotional and political investment and moral affiliation are taking place. These battles over identity involve the powerful manipulation of group symbols and strategies of articulation and rearticulation of public slogans and popular discourses. The signs and symbols are used to make identity and define social and political projects. (p. 333)

These 'group symbols' comprise a bond between individuals and the institution, and between individuals and a broader intragroup popular reverence for Dixie South whiteness—a bond that repositions the white subject as central authority of social privilege. Gottdiener (1994) explains that the empowering nature of the signifying systems are a result of strategically implemented "producer codes"—a concept which suggests the social construction of the sign, both by the intermediaries who control it and the consumers who reinvent and embody it. At Ole Miss, every element of the Colonel Reb brand is an interconnected sign, woven into the system of signification that connects the corporatized academy as a universal sign to the politics of Dixie South whiteness.

The University of Mississippi now finds itself immersed in the discursive universe of faux racism and the "compromised" logics of veneer reconciliation. The administration has in recent years moved toward disassociating the institution with symbolic racism, yet only superficially—in the form of a negotiation between the call for social justice and the preservation of the commodity brand. That an institution such as the University of Mississippi publicly attempted to come to terms with "its archaic investments in whiteness only in the context of an increasingly lucrative, racially marked system of collegiate athletic is telling"(King & Springwood, 2001). Despite repeated calls for the banishment of Colonel Reb on the Ole Miss campus, the university has allowed for his image to remain on licensed merchandise, public documents, and on campus and in the football stadium. The Chancellor recently, and defiantly, charged:

> To allay fears of those who believe we are abandoning our history and heritage, please know: 1) we are the Ole Miss Rebels and will continue to present ourselves under that name; 2) the song Dixie remains in our repertoire of school spirit songs and will be played at sporting events; 3) Colonel Rebel is an official trademark of the university and will continue to be included among our registered names, appear on merchandise and in public presentations. (Khayat, 2003, p. 1)

The continued life of the Ole Miss mascot thus bears "an indelible stain and frequently evoke[s] discomfort, if not disdain, precisely because [it] represents a problematic or vile formulation of whiteness, relying...upon symbols and sentiments of white supremacy that are no longer deemed acceptable or appropriate"(King & Springwood, 2001, p. 154)—marking the symbolic territories of the inside (whiteness) and the outside ("[re]visions"of an alternative symbolic politic).

And so at the impasse of the Colonel's symbolic purchase and what State Senator Michael Gunn, during ceremonies held on the Ole Miss campus to observe "Confederate Memorial Day," suggested is "a national conspiracy to exterminate the vestiges of our heritage" (quoted in King & Springwood,

2001, p. 140), the University of Mississippi must reconcile the identity politics of their neo-Confederate[d] mascot. For the white majority, the consciousness of the symbol follows the senator's declaration: "Make no mistake...we are the victims of a nationwide conspiracy perpetuated by the Left
to exterminate any vestiges of our precious Southern heritage. When Ole
Miss uses my tax money to pay hate-mongers like Johnnie Cochran to speak
on campus and call my Southern heritage racist, I'm offended"(quoted in
King & Springwood, 2001, p. 140). Many white Southerners such as Gunn
frequently have attempted to locate the debate of Southern symbols around
notions of "Southern pride" and traditional Southern values, and the victimization trope of a "happy and guilt-free revisionism" (Gallagher, 2003, p.
154), disregarding that the logics of racism and white centrality are inseparable from these imaginary spaces (Vanderford, 1996).

However, if there has been an assault on the signified heritage culture
from which these symbols stand, it has not come from the left or its progressive politics, but rather from the Ku Klux Klan, the Nationalists, and
other resilient advocates for white supremacy in Mississippi. Any defense
of the markers of Southern culture should start by confronting the meaning
makers who have in recent years mobilized these symbols for racial terrorism, not progressive Southern polity. A popular detritus among many white
members of the Ole Miss imagined community is the rejection of the notion of "reparations," whereby these individuals feel a sense of oppression
brought about by Affirmative Action and 'reverse racism.' By locating the
Colonel Reb issue as "an attack on culture," the intermediaries have aggress-
ively navigated a collective sense of disenfranchisement among the white
majority. Perhaps this retaliatory posture of the paranoid center following
'attacks' on Dixie South heritage culture signals the dualistic mechanism of
the signifiers of Southern history at play: "At best, they are instances of im-
perialist nostalgia and at worst, whether or not intentionally, they function
as forms of symbolic terror" (King & Springwood, 2001, p. 141).

Thus, the Colonel symbolizes a history of privilege and under privilege;
and what is at stake in these debates is the ability of those groups historically
empowered by their involvement with the university (and its symbols) to
protract structures of inequity whilst feigning, and framing, the order of
things under the guise of 'heritage.' In much the same way that the of
abundance of 'white victimization' public pedagogies in the early Obama
Era (think: Glenn Beck, Rush Limbaugh, Michael Savage) have sought to
frame the discussion to 'limits of [white] freedom' without reconciling how
one's freedoms are inextricably linked through history to another's socio-
political internment, defenders of the Colonel's place at Ole Miss often fail
to consider how symbolic and commercial import are created out of these
axes of history.

More importantly, the symbolic affectivity of the system of neo-Confederate signs active in the Ole Miss popular works because each reconstitutes
an ideological blanket that empowers members of the visible white center
(cf. Grossberg,1992). In other words, the import of Colonel Rebel is derived
from his ability to conjoin the collective conscious of Dixie South whiteness

to the gestures, practices, and distributional power of the lived experience. As a living symbol, the Colonel extracts the inequality of racial dominance, or as Stuart Hall (1981) suggested, they are representative of a "continuous and unequal struggle, by the dominant culture, constantly [trying] to disorganize and reorganize popular culture; to enclose and confine its definitions and forms within a more inclusive range of dominant forms"(p. 233). As such, the power-knowledge dynamic imbedded in these symbols was created by the dominant group, the hyper-white, hypermasculine center, to colonize the discursive landscape and the active bodies therein with a signifying system that memorializes the Old South and its hierarchical 'heritage.' The Colonel is the discursive canvas through which contemporary history is written and revised, and by which the specters of the Old South remain inescapable.

This reorientation of social operations in the 'tradition' of the Old South is rationalized as a product of dual erasure, whereby "the first is an erasure that has emptied these symbols of their past, but only because they had to be, to ensure their continued presence in a post-civil rights era"; and the second is "an erasure based on a denial of the contemporary manifestations of white supremacy and the existence of racial stratification and institutional racism"(King & Springwood, 2001, p. 142). In this process of scoring through, or filtering, the historicized meanings of the neo-Confederacy, the University of Mississippi and its power elite are actively refurbishing the symbols of the Old South to crystallize the symbolic gesticulations of a more "comfortable," less complicated [racially divided] Dixie heritage. As the chancellor recently expostulated: "We are deeply disappointed that some would inject race into the discussion"(Khayat, 2003, p. 1). Again evoking another tired trope invasive throughout discussions of race and racism in contemporary America (H. A. Giroux, 2005)—that of the 'race card'—the chancellor effectively eliminates the lived consequences of signified racism from the dialogue.

In other words, those populations that have been physically, financially, and psychologically tortured over the past 300 years are expected to arbitrarily divorce the signifier from the signified at the command of the non-reflexive center. According to the chancellor's logic, the signifier and the signified should be ordered around a preferred reading, one which is predicated on the notion that the 'real' cause of the Civil War was states' rights, that the institution of slavery has had no lasting impact on the region or the University, and that, despite repeated interjections to the contrary from Black students on campus, the Colonel is a symbol for all of the university's students. However, as one student detractor suggested:

> These traditionalists rely on a string of lies, half-truths and garbled inconsistencies. There is not a "liberal" conspiracy against these symbols, but a conspiracy of truth. The jingoistic cliché of "heritage, not hate" is often deployed in such a discussion. The South maintains a tainted history, however, one filled with racially-motivated violence and oppression, a heritage of hatred. (Niemeyer, 2005, p. 2)

What neo-Confederate defenders of the symbolic South such as Chancellor Khayat fail to realize is that: (a) many Black Mississippians see the "suffering of ancestors" in the cultural and symbolic flesh of Colonel Reb (R. E. Bonner, 2002, p. 178), and (b) by standing up in defense and cashing the checks generated by the flesh politics of the Colonel, these intermediaries are authorizing the plantation-era logics of white power through the Colonel's normative embodiment of hegemonic [white] identity politics.

The Spectacle of Dixie South Whiteness

Up to this point I have argued that a *visible center of Dixie South whiteness* established by the first wave of European settlers and plantation pioneers has been carried through the generations through *embodied imagery* (i.e. Archie and Eli Manning, Trent Lott, or John Vaught), *social praxis* (i.e. the waving of the Confederate or the singing of 'Dixie'), and the Old South geometrics of the Ole Miss campus (i.e. the Lyceum, the Grove, etc.). Importantly, this visibility—and the body pedagogics through which corporealities are made meaningful—carries not only the weight of a tumultuous regional history, but also ties the threads of race-, class-, and gender-based oppression and hierarchy from which that fractious social fabric has been woven onto the present. In this new 'economy of visibility' (McDonald, 2005, p. 248), such institutions of whiteness, spectacles of whiteness, and corporeal celebrations of the white symbolic territorialize and colonize subjected bodies in disciplined (physical and imagined) white spaces (Kintz, 2002). In the dialectic traditions of many of Twentieth Century Marxist thinkers we have been in dialogue with throughout this text, I have further argued that what makes Ole Miss relevant, and significant, are the ways in which history, pedagogy, ideology, and praxis interface to produce and remain productive of both spectacles of Dixie South whiteness—spectacles of embodiment, of space, of body knowledge, of neo-Confederate praxis, and so on—and broader 'recovery movement' (J. Kincheloe, 2008) spectacles of race, patriarchy, and capital.

In this chapter, I turn my focus away from the *representations of the body* and toward bodily practice as discursive formation and public pedagogy. In the surrealist spirit of the Situationist International (who acronymoniously referred to themselves as the 'SI'), in this chapter I offer a conjuncturally-sensitive, radically-contextual interpretation of *spectacular embodiments of Dixie South whiteness.* More than race protests and counter-protests, more than the spatial imaginaries of the Lyceum or the Circle, more than the celebration of 'campus cuties' or William Faulkner, today Ole Miss is best known in the national popular for the tailgating[1] spectacles which take place on the campus prior to, during, and following each Ole Miss home football event. In the central campus greenspace, the Grove, a colossal assemblage of [white-bodied] Ole Miss constituents produce one of the most unique college football experiences in the South and in the country. The *Sporting News* rated the spectacle among 'college football's greatest traditions' and described the Grove as "the Holy Grail of tailgating sites" (Stewart, 2003, p. 6). In listing America's 'top sports colleges,' *Sports Illustrated* named Ole Miss the nation's 'No. 1 tailgating school' ("Tailgating top 10," 2004, p. 1).

Tens of thousands of Rebel supporters converge upon the Grove each Saturday during football season to celebrate their university's football team (or perhaps, to celebrate themselves). A *Sports Illustrated* writer who attended the first home football game of the 2004 season celebrated the Grove in this way: "in Oxford lies, as promised, the most magical place on all of God's green, football-playing Earth: the Grove. A school of red and white and blue tents swimming in a shaded 10-acre forest of oak tress, floating in an ocean of good will and even better manners" (Duerson, 2004, p. 11). ESPN personality Mel Kiper, Jr. lauded the Grove: "We witnessed an amazing scene in the Grove just outside Vaught-Hemingway Stadium. An estimated 30,000 fans, and more tents than you could imagine, took the term 'tailgating' to a completely new level" (quoted in Stewart, 2003, p. 6).

A complex assemblage of symbols of the Confederacy, Old South gentility, and the splendors of hyper-white orthodoxy awaits the spectator of the 'Grove Society.' The term 'Grove Society' itself holds intricate and multifarious meanings: In the first instance, it refers to the human interactions within the Grove space during home football games which constitute the spectacle of the Grove. In the second, 'Grove Society' refers to the society of the conservative white South, the broader cultural and political body which has historically shaped social relations in Mississippi and beyond. Finally, the term is directly taken from season-ticket sales and promotional materials produced by the Athletic Department of the University of Mississippi; a creative branding strategy which in some ways forges a link between the first two descriptions. The alumni supporter group which financially supports Ole Miss Rebel athletics is referred to as the 'Grove Society,' a strategically organized foundation for the profit-making impetus of the institution. Members of the Grove Society are asked to financially 'give back' to the University, in order to ensure that "beauty, comfort, and solitude" re-

---

1. 'Tailgating' is the popular phenomenon in American football where sports fan congregate in the hours leading up to the event to 'cook-out,' drink alcoholic beverages, and engage in conversations pertaining to the upcoming event.

main a "unique part of [Ole Miss] heritage" ("The Grove Society," 2004, p. 2).

That 'comfort,' I suggest, is both a product and marker of the distinctive formation of an all-permeating whiteness. Surrounded by a spatial discourse marked as terrestrial, 'Southern,' and matriculating through time and practice in the realm of uncontested white reign, the Grove Society becomes more than a symbol of longevity, it becomes a formation of power through which the practices of Dixie South whiteness have evolved into an extension of the broader power regimes of the region. In sum, my use of the term 'Grove Society' in this chapter parallels Guy Debord's notion of a 'society of the spectacle,' an expansive socio-cultural configuration constituted through the assemblage of a vast array of spectacles (in this instance, local spectacles), each of which links the individual to the broader networks of spectacular society.

The Grove Society

Echoing the self-described qualities of Ole Miss's 'Grove Society,' my initial inclination in describing the spectacle of the Grove was also that of 'Southern comfort.' Both in the ingestion of pre-game mixtures of whiskey and the racial and habitus homogeneity, the Grove is more than ambiguous social space. It indeed is a "cathedral of pleasure" (Foucault, 1984a, p. 251); a cathartic realm in which its constituents can imbibe all the fruits of a collectively imagined self-hood. The Grove as spectacular space is constructed through placation; offering an intoxication of the comfortable; a flanerie[2] of the highest order—the familiar and the superlative. As the touring journalist from *SI* deduced, "There are rules here in the Grove. And ways of communicating that I couldn't comprehend" (Duerson, 2004, p. 10). The code of a unifying (divisive) Southern ethic is both encoded and decoded in a language unique to the Grove. Those unique ways of communicating are 'measured' by visibly performativity, in dress, gait, posture, activity, and conformity. One such 'rule' is the conduct and decoration of the bodily canvas: "I didn't know the rules at the Grove, rules like . . . Dress as if you're attending a baptism" (Duerson, 2004, p. 11). And the spectators of the Ole Miss sporting spectacle imbibe, gulping their collective whiteness as:

> . . . they drink bourbon and eat boiled peanuts and finger sandwiches from sterling-silver platters and serving dishes arranged by caterers and frantic moms on elaborate tabletops. They partake in front of flat-screen TVs with DirecTV, underneath chandeliers and amongst intricate candelabras and or-

---

2. The 'flaneur' is different from a Situationist participant of derive, in that "the flaneur symbolizes the privilege or freedom to move about the public arenas of the city observing . . . [and] consuming the sights through a controlling but rarely acknowledged gaze" (Pollock, 1988, p. 67), while participant of derive seeks to disrupt the class-, race-, and gender- based indifferences through refusal of forms of surveillance of that nature.

THE SPECTACLE OF DIXIE SOUTH WHITENESS

nate flower arrangements. And when football calls, they pay people like Andre, at the Rebel Rousers tent, to stand guard. (Duerson, 2004, p. 11)

The distinctive cultural practices within the Grove space are more than a metaphor of the centrality of whiteness in the spectrum of representative power at Ole Miss. The Grove spectacle permeates the consciousness of the Ole Miss collective, in the first instance bringing to the life the embodiment of an imagined and physically identifiable center.

The practices of 'being white' within the Grove spectacle have created a new culture industry based around the fetishization of spectacular whiteness. Through the modalities of adornment and deportment, the reification of the body politic is dispersed through, and onto, the politicized and spectacularized body. Symbolic garments, branded tailgating tents, themed provisions, and a variety of Confederate signifiers litter the green space in the center of campus on football Saturdays. On such days of *carnivale*, the organic space in the center of campus is transferred into a spectacle of Dixie South whiteness, upon which layers of a conservative 'ideological blanket' and commodity whiteness are interwoven within into spectacular space. My notes from a pep-rally held on the Ole Miss campus prior to the first spring practice/scrimmage of 2005[3] are suggestive of the spectacular nature of the Grove communal:

> Amidst the pom-poms and giant 'M' signs, fashioned after the stars and bars of the Confederacy, the team walked through the Grove to the stirs of Dixie and the chants of 'Hotty Toddy.' The sprit of Dixie takes on a material from in the Grove, as witnessed by the proliferation of Confederate flags, the images of an Old South mascot, and a culture industry fueled by the themed commercialization of every aspect of the Grove space, all the way down to the 'Hotty Toddy Potty' (the portable restroom situated on both the north and south sides of the Grove) (Fieldnotes)

The solidarity of spectacular commodity whiteness is constructed through the ocular preponderance of white-skinned agents operating in the Grove space. From my observations during the final home football game of the 2004 season, I offer the following crudely objectified, if not objectionable remarks:

> Throughout my observations at the football events over the past few seasons, the most striking illustration of spectacular homogeneity is the racial solidarity of the Grove spectators. Almost every fan/spectator in the Grove is white, and the few individuals of color who are present are typically bound to roles such as food servant, traffic officer, student-athlete, and hospitality shuttle driver. (Fieldnotes)

These observations echo those made by a writer for the *Chronicle of Higher Education*, who wrote: "just as at the game, blacks are virtually invisible in the Grove—except when the football squad . . . parades through the crowd en route to the stadium" (Lederman, 1993, p. A52). For the spectator of the Grove society, this symbolic unification of the racialized body creates

---

3. This was the first practice for the football team under the direction of its new head coach, Ed Orgeron.

THE CLASS OF 1865

a panoptic spectacular space, whereby commodity fetishization is material-ized through the possibilities of an atomized corporeal collective. In other words, the reign of an uncontested white space (the Grove) creates a codi-fied solidarity, as the embodied signification of Dixie South whiteness per-meates throughout, encapsulating young and old, masculine and feminine, black and white (Frederick, 1999).

To further illustrate the relations of spectacle and subjectivity active within the Grove Society, and following Richard Giulianotti (2002), I (somewhat arbitrarily) concluded that there are (at least) four predominate striations, or permutations, from which the politics of Dixie South white-ness are performed within the Grove: the preferred whiteness acted out by an older, upper-class constituency; the infantilized expressions of Dixie South whiteness embodied in the white-bodied youths of the Grove society; the aristocratic court of princes and princesses of Ole Miss—fraternity and sorority members; and the black-bodied, disciplined, marginalized, and ob-jectified 'Other.' I will now, in turn, offer a series of brief vignettes that might better illustrate the *place* of each group within such a taxonomy of spectatorship comprising the *spectacle of Dixie South whiteness.*

The Class of 1865

The first group, largely constituted by affluent alumni of the university and the region's white bourgeoisie, represents the old guard Ole Miss subjectiv-ity. From fieldnotes taken during the first home game, I offer the following description of what I came to refer to as 'the Class of 1865'[4]:

> The most prevalent group is comprised of the older fans and alumni who gathered quite early in the day (and all of the Groves habitants had set—or had someone set—their tents up the night before to stake their claim on the pro-visional space). Many of the men spend their time watching college football games, as a solid majority from this group has televisions (often flat screen) with satellite dishes. Meanwhile, the women from the group are busy con-structing and tending to large profusions of foodstuffs, often arranged in a buffet-style set-up. Some of these sub-congregational women are assisted in their endeavors by hired servants, most of whom are black men. The net-work of pods which organize the Grove tailgaters is littered with Confederate, school, state, and local flags hanging from the sea of Ole Miss logoed tents. Further, there are a number of banners which signify where the tailgaters reside (i.e. "Rebel Fans from Senatobia"). These individuals are often dressed in casual, yet up-scale clothing. (Fieldnotes)

For this first 'group' of tailgating spectators, the spectacle of Dixie South whiteness is expressed through the symbolic gesticulations of race, gender,

---

4.The colloquial use of the term 'Class of 1865' refers to the year the Civil War ended, and classes at the University of Mississippi resumed. There was no graduating class that year, since none of the students of the University returned following the war. So my use of the term is suggestive of the missing class of the 'Lost Cause,' and how the rites of graduation are often synonymous with the passage of the fallen fathers of the imagined Confederacy.

and social class and the commodification of representational wares. This faction is defined by whiskey-swilling charter members of the 'Good Ole Boy' network at Ole Miss who playfully consume the labors and fares of the matrons of spectacle and the black-bodied servants such as 'Andre at the Rebel Rousers tent' (Duerson, 2004). There is solidarity in the experiential discourse of the Grove spectacle, a distinctive 'rhythm of time and space' (Lefebvre, 2004), class and race—as twill and plaid trousers, penny loafers, red 'Ole Miss'-themed polo shirts dominate a cacophonous hyper-branded geometric topography. Such spectacular imagery is both product and producer of spectacular governance, which according to Debord (1990):

> ... now possesses all the means necessary to falsify the whole of production ad perception, [it] is the absolute master of memories just as it is the unfettered master of plans which shape the most distant future. It reigns unchecked; *it executes its summary judgments*. (thesis 4)

Written into the text of this spurious tentscape, the politics of race are performances of memorialized politics (and the politics of memory) of Dixie South whiteness through the symbolic (an onslaught of Colonel Rebs and Confederate flags), the conversant (the soft murmur of the white masculine communal), and the embodied (the phenotypical phalanstery). The Rebel-sporting flaneur, or masculine connoisseur of the Grove space, is drowned in the libations of hyper-normativity of which he is an active agent in reproducing.

The relationship between the masculine flaneur of Dixie South whiteness and the social order in which he perpetuates can be defined by the Marxist notion of *zoon politikon*. For Marx (1977), "Man (sic) is in the most literal sense of the word a *zoon politikon*, not only a social animal, but an animal which can develop into an individual only in society" (1977, p. 346). This notion resonates in Debord's (1967/1994) theory as well, as particularly in his synthesis of Hegelian and Marxist positions on historical materialism:

> It is because human beings have thus been thrust into history, and into participation in the labor and the struggles which constitute history, that they find themselves obliged to view their relationships in a clear-eyed manner. . . . As for the subject of history, it can only be the self production of the living: the living becoming master and possessor of its world—that is, of history—and coming to exist as consciousness of its own activity. (thesis 74)

While the collective conscious of humans (and the identification of the agent to that collectivity) is a product of imagined historical activity, the cultural praxis within the spectacle is the coming together of the spectator with the power-knowledge thrust of the spectacle. At Ole Miss, the racialized power-knowledge conundrum exists, and is preponderated through the active subjectification of humans in the language of history, hierarchy, and privilege. In Debord's (1981b) words, such a cultural formation is "the reflection and prefiguration of the possibilities of organization of everyday life in a given historical moment; a complex of aesthetics, feelings and mores through which a collectivity reacts on the life that is objectively determined by its economy" (p. 45).

The symbolic economy of representation in the Grove, and particularly that of its most powerful group, leads to a clandestine practice of conjectural racism. The symbolic, 'solid South' is in the first instance recognizable by the constellation, mobile-like ornamentation of the Grove landscape. From my fieldnotes taken on October 30, 2004[5]:

> ... on the eastern edge of the Grove there were a number of tailgaters flying various symbols and flags. The most popular of which were flags with the image of Colonel Reb, the university's sporting mascot. There were also a number of confederate flags hanging from the sea of tents in and around the Grove area. Some of the flags featured the transfusion of a Confederate backdrop with the image of Colonel Reb centered in the middle of the 'Southern Cross.' Of particular interest was an inflated figure of a football player hanging from a pole of a nearby tent. The figure was suspended from the pole by some strings, which almost made it look like an Auburn (the opponent on this day) clad voodoo doll hanging from a noose. If I were the only person who observed this, I might not have thought much about it. However, a number of individuals at the tent nearby also commented on the suspended figure, and I overheard tailgating neighbors to the north mention its close resemblance of a 'black man hanging from a tree.'

Such are the axiom and praxis of an uncontested whiteness transmitted trough the sanitized ether of similarity and difference, whereby the profusion of white bodies gives way to the diffusion of a practiced racial discourse.

In the midst of the tentscape of Dixie South whiteness, as the combative black bodies ready themselves for sporting malice, the whispers from a hyper-racist contemporaneous orthodoxy rattle throughout cover of magnolias in the Grove. For example, within my first few minutes on site in the early morning hours prior to the University of Memphis/Ole Miss game,[6] one such verbal interaction with a member of the controlling class came to fruition:

> The tailgating party to the immediate south of where we were located had begun to fraternize with my group, telling stories and offering predictions on the upcoming game. On his way back from the "pisser," on of the neighboring tailgaters, a middle-aged white man, stopped by our area to speak with us. He said, in a soft, almost timid voice: "Any of ya'll mind if I tell ya'll a nigger joke?" While I wanted to answer in negative, I held my tongue and my company all agreed that they did want to hear the joke. So the elderly man proceeded: "There was this nigger who had bought himself a hang glider. He had ordered it customized from the manufacturer in the color black, and so he had to wait a few days for it to get to him. He kept waiting . . .waiting . . . finally, on the day it arrived he was so excited to use it that he took it straight out of the box and climbed up a nearby hill. In the valley there was a man and his son

---

5. Some of my fieldnotes are written in the present tense, while others are presented in the past tense. Those written in the present were taken on site in real time, while those in past tense were recorded in intervals on site (within the immersive experiences of Ole Miss) as breaks from observation allowed.

6. For each Ole Miss home game, I adorned neutral, yet color-coordinated attire. For example, in dressing up for the Memphis game, I wore khaki shorts and a blue shirt, as blue is the official color of both Ole Miss and the University of Memphis.

hunting for deer. The nigger took off and he was flying high in the sky, when the son said 'daddy, what's that?' The father said, 'I don't know son, it looks like a giant bat. Shoot it!' So the son took out his rifle and fired a shot. The son asked, 'did I get him daddy?' The daddy said 'Well, I'm not sure if you got the bat, but you made it let loose of that nigger it was carrying." And so my day began. (Fieldnotes)

This is but one example of a number of overt racist offerings I noted during my time at the Grove. More disturbing than the content of the bigoted yarn is the hegemonic normalization of spoken racism inscribed in the geometric and anthropological space, one which is allowed to permeate all vectors within the Grove. In the first instance, the Grove society is an incarnation of the pervasive race-based 'spectacularization' (Belanger, 2000) of hegemonic Dixie South whiteness.

Children of the Grove

Unlike the elder statesmen and 'Ole Misses' of the 'Grove Society,' the younger generation of Ole Miss supporter-subjects traipsing through the wooded area on football Saturdays act within the frames of the prevailing order of Dixie South whiteness in a very different way. These children of the Grove are often outfitted in sport themed apparel (depending on gender) and more adolescent versions of bourgeoisie Ole Miss garb. These adolescents are typically at play in the Grove, frolicking about the wooded football wonderland while their parents are found socializing, drinking beer, and eating foodstuffs. In this instance, the important power relationship is perhaps not parental governance over the youthful subject, but the discursive regimes of surveillance which act upon the children of the Grove through the unified and the symbolic. My fieldnotes from a game between Ole Miss and Arkansas State University begin to tell the story of symbolic space in relationship to juvenile spatial practice:

> One of the first things I took notice of, which I had not recorded from previous games, was the degree to which young children are integrated into the logics of gender defined roles within the spectacle. A majority of the young boys I observed were dressed in some sort of football uniform, with the uniform of choice being an Eli Manning Ole Miss jersey. Some of them were even clad in full regalia, including football pants, pads, and helmets. These boys were engaged in various football activities, with many of them simulating a rendition of the sport form which was about to take place inside Vaught-Hemmingway Stadium. The young girls were often dressed in Ole Miss cheerleader outfits or spring dresses, and spent their time with such activities as choreographing various dance-like maneuvers and cheers and helping the mothers with the preparation of their masterpiece foodworks. (Fieldnotes)

In the first instance, much like any other form of sporting spectacle, these children learn their gender roles within sport (and society) through the practices of a gendered sporting polarity: hegemonic masculinity of the sporting combative versus preferred femininity of the submissive ornamental. Secondly, and perhaps more unique to the Grove Society, these young individuals are subjected to the creation of an idealized habitus, or a preferred 'class consciousness' of the Dixie South gentility. In this way, the emulating body becomes a site for pedagogical interplay: whereby "The body is not an object to be studied in relation to culture, but is to be considered as the subject of culture, or in other words as the existential ground of culture" (Csordas, 1990, p. 5)

The notion of such a class consciousness is best articulated in the Situationist papers fashioned during Debord's brief, fruitful, and somewhat tumultuous relationship with Henri Lefebvre. Their dialogue on mental and physical spaces of subordination to the spectacle harvested interesting trajectories for both Debord's theory of the spectacle and Lefebvre's later conceptualizations on everyday life (Ross, 1997). In reading the *Society of the Spectacle*, it becomes evident that Debord's theory and practice were greatly influenced by his predecessor's critique of everyday life. As Jappe (1999) noted regarding the history of the Situationist International, "a main preoccupation of the Situationists during the first years of the SI was the realm of *everyday life*, its critique and its revolutionary transformation" (p. 72). Debord (2002) describes the affects of ideology on everyday life in this way:

> The repression of practice and the antidialectical false consciousness that results from that repression are imposed at every moment of everyday life subjected to the spectacle—a subjection that systematically destroys the "faculty of encounter" and replaces it with a *social hallucination*: a false consciousness of encounter, an "illusion of encounter." In a society where no one can any longer be *recognized* by others, each individual becomes incapable of recognizing his own reality. Ideology is at home; separation has built its own world. (thesis 217)[7]

This notion of an 'illusion of encounter' is the centrifugal force which shapes relationships within the spectacle, and is consecrated upon the small bodies of the children operating within the Ole Miss Grove spectacle. For Debord (1967/1994), social progress is belied by the affectivity of "rebellious tendencies among the young" to permeate the existing hegemonic regimes and "generate a protest that . . . clearly embodies a rejection of the specialized sphere of the old politics, as well as of art and *everyday life*" (p. 86, italics added). The early installations of the indoctrination project of Dixie South whiteness, and particularly the semiotic and lived traditions of local gentility, are inscribed into (learned by) the youthful bodies of the Grove Society through cultural practices such as those found in the Grove. Immersed in a society of Dixie South privilege, many of these young people are subjected to the cultural politics of an upper-class, white, conservative habitus. From the tailgating extravaganza which precluded a home football game versus Vanderbilt University, I recorded the following notes:

> There is something interesting at work here in the Grove. The children's playground filled with flying footballs and miniature dance routines has an adult feel to it. The dress (often resembling the attire of their parents), mannerisms,

---

7. The notion of 'encounter' is derived from Joseph Gabel's *False consciousness: An essay on reification* (1975).

and interactions of the youths very closely resembles the actions of their elders. (Fieldnotes)

The Grove spectacle becomes both a cathedral of whiteness and disciplinary social space for the inscription of spatial and ideological markers of traditionalism, racial orthodoxy, and hyper-religiosity. For Debord (1990), spectacles such as the one found in the Grove indoctrinate modern society's youth in such a way:

> The erasure of the personality is the fatal accompaniment to an existence which is concretely submissive to the spectacle's rules, ever more removed from the possibility of authentic experience and thus from the discovery of individual preferences. (thesis 12)

Debord theorizes that to subvert the prevailing 'false consciousness' of 'the everyday' implicated the routinization of functions within everyday life, which create a disconnect between social awareness and social production, spectators must cease contribute to the postulations of the spectacle by producing the wants for spectacular society through subconscious fetishisms. The complacency and implicitness of the young in producing both the Grove spectacle and the Society of Dixie South Spectacle signal the reign of hegemonic Dixie South whiteness rather than a contested and contestable space of the politics of representation.

Landed Gentry of the Neo-Confederacy

A third subject position acting in the celebration of Ole Miss whiteness and its sporting politics has developed out of the spectacular bodily praxis of younger generations and the historical/cultural politics of the institution. This group, which consists of the post-pubescent student population, and particularly the white members of the campus Greek system, often define the popular imaginary of politicized identity politics of the campus. Ole Miss is known throughout the state and region as a producer of state and Federal politicians, high-ranking lawyers and judges, and powerful businessmen. As I have suggested earlier, at Ole Miss, affiliation leads to access of the "Good Ole Boy" network (Weeks, 1999, p. C1). The discursive terrain constructed by the uninterrupted fluidity with which these bodies float through the Grove space reiterates the territoriality of white hegemons within the context. From my fieldnotes, I offer the following initial description of this spectator group:

> The group made most evident by their style of dress was comprised of members of the student body. The male members of the student body were most often clad in khakis, button-up shirts, and ties, while the ladies were often dressed in summer dresses and high-healed shoes. Despite the fact that it was raining, the walkways throughout the Grove were highly congested, perhaps a product of the overwhelming number of people in the Grove and the limited walk space allowed by the overflow of Ole Miss tents. Most of the students were in tents which identified them as either in a fraternity of sorority, by way of their banners. The interactions between students was similar to that of their older counterparts, with the men lounging, consuming foods and bever-

ages while women, most of whom belonged to sororities (identifiable by their donning of various symbols), were socialized and wondering about the Grove. (Fieldnotes)

Again, for this group, the burden of whiteness becomes a form of governance, as the prescriptions of expressive whiteness and the embodied deportment of the politics of representation shape social action.

These spectators of the Grove spectacle are defined out of the discourse of sameness, and of the lack corporeal possibilities presented to them. Surrounded by a phantasmagoria of Confederate whiteness, "social life is so colonized by the . . . administrative techniques, so saturated in an accumulation of spectacles, that people are more like spectators than active agents, occupying roles assigned to them in a state of passive contemplation" (Pinder, 2000, pp. 361-362). From my observations prior to the Ole Miss versus University Tennessee home football game, I noted the following interpretations:

> There is no doubt that while the older alumni and boosters control the activities of the Grove (by way of their role as provider), the students, and particularly those in Greek organization, are the lifeblood of the tailgating festivities. They are the first to arrive, and often the last to leave the event, and for them, more than any other group, the Grove is a stage, a theater for expressing their beauty, their power, their wealth, and their solidarity. Interlopers, such as those wearing orange on this day, are met as such, outsiders to the clan-like cohesion of this imagined community. While the students are producers of social relationships, they seem to fail to connect how their unity in dress, deportment, gait, and behavior reproduce the social hierarchies of their predecessors. (Fieldnotes)

This unknowing [re]productivity, in which the visible center is expressed through the traditions of deport and dress,[8] becomes the organizing principle by which the spectacle of Dixie South whiteness is reproduced. As Homi Bhabba (1994) has argued, ambivalence is at the epicenter of such a colonial power structure. Through the uncritical reification of a nostalgic and uniformed acculturation of preferred Euro-American deportment, and the accessorized discomfort for the black 'exotic,' whiteness has remained at the core of identity politics within the spectacle.

I also noted that during the Ole Miss home games, students express the codified language of whiteness through a number of performative 'traditions':

> I entered the stadium approximately one hour prior to kick-off, and immediately went straight to my seat in the Ole Miss season ticket holder section (the section adjacent to the student section). All of the events (both on and off the field) leading up to kickoff were similar to other college football games, with the exception of two. . . . Prior to the singing of the national anthem, and pri-

---

8. Ole Miss students pride themselves on being the 'best dressed' student fans in all of college sport, a tradition which was enacted to pay tribute to the University Greys, who upon traveling to Jackson for meetings with the Confederate Council, were lauded for their handsome attire. By wearing their 'Sunday best,' these students are seen as paying homage to their Confederate forefathers, as well as distinguishing themselves by way of sophisticated attire.

or to the playing of the school's alma mater, the Ole Miss band played 'Dixie,' 'From Dixie with Love,' and 'Dixie Fanfare.' 'Dixie was played again in the
second half of the game. Secondly, the students, in a spectacle of unanimity,
chanted the school's fight song, 'Hotty Toddy,' following every positive event
produced by their team on the field. (Fieldnotes)

Engagement with these spectacular practices links the individual to the
spectacle (both the local and broader spectacle), and embellishment of the
body through the feminine faunal and the decorative Confederate creates
that space of alienation, whereby the spectator is disengaged from the popular, from the spectacle (Debord, 1990).

The admonishment of the alien, both by the empowered subject in rejecting the non-comfortable embodied and practiced space, and the marginalizing of subjectivities operating outside the Grove-encrusted norm,
creates a spatiality dominated by racial reclusion and symbolic reification.
In *The Society of the Spectacle*, Debord offers numerous inferred references
to *The History of Class Consciousness*, particularly extracting two ideas from
Lukács' (1971) essential text. First, it is quite evident that Lukács' *History
and Class Consciousness* (Lukács, 1971) greatly influenced *The Society of the Spectacle* (1967/1994) through the episteme that capitalist development produces
elements that both "deflect and encourage the proletariat's recognition of
its position" (Plant, 1992, p. 16). This state of unconsciousness, created by
the forces of alienation and the mind-numbing reign of the spectacle, reproduces the social inequities imbedded in the spectacle (where the powerful retain power, all in the service of the spectacle). In Lukács' (1971) terms,
the materialization of a divide between the material and ideological lies
"in the realization that the real motor forces of history are independent
of man's (psychological) consciousness of them" (p. 47). Therefore, an individual functions unconsciously within a society bound by dominant economic, cultural, and social structures.

This notion of the unwritten language of control is extrapolated and expounded upon throughout *The Society of the Spectacle* as the means by which
the spectacle reproduces itself (Debord, 1967/1994). The class-, gender-, and
race-conditioned unconsciousness, much like Bourdieu's notion of habitus, is reflective of the genealogical forces of whiteness which have persisted
throughout the longevity of Ole Miss, and which are transmitted by way
of social practice within the spaces of privilege at the university. In many
ways, the conduct of the practitioners of campus privilege (those wealthy
members of the sorority and fraternity class) is similar to that of business
class elites—there is a certain mystique about their gait, posture, and dress.
Everything is slowed down, never a hurried moment, never a thought of
disruption or confrontation. Fraternity men dressed in khaki pants and
collared shirts motion to one another in subtle, convivial mannerisms.

This seemingly telepathic connection is demonstrative of a realized affective bond to the inculcations of the visible center and the internalized
habitus-responses to the bodily discourses of the visible center. Sorority women, in an almost ritualistic fashion, parade across the Grove space, fratern-
izing with old and young, seeing the festival and perhaps more importantly,

being seen. This pageant of masculine bourgeois whiteness is captured in the following observation:

> The Grove is like a Confederate Ball,[9] as the men and women of campus dressed in their best attire promenade in a spectacle of conspicuous gentility. During my last trip (of the day) through the Grove, I encountered the following: First, while walking across the path which crosscuts the center of the Grove, I passed some Ole Miss fraternity men (as marked by their pins below the collar of their shirts) who were heckling passersby wearing the opposition's (The University of Memphis) colors. The men chanted "at least we don't tailgate in a parking lot" and "you'll work for us someday." These were but a few excerpts from the choral of class demarcation I have seen up to this point. Second, I noticed considerable consumption of 'toddies' (alcohol) by members of the fraternity groups in the Grove. (Fieldnotes)[10]

Following Debord, the human agent at Ole Miss reproduces and engages the spectacle often without knowledge of this relationship. Debord refers to this all-encapsulating reticence as "new obscurantism," or "the general resignation of the populace, the complete loss of logic, [and] the universal progress of venality and cowardice"(Debord, 1990, thesis 24). The power-knowledge dynamic written into the performances of Dixie South whiteness by Ole Miss coeds "implies a class-conditioned *unconsciousness* of one's own socio-historical and economic conditions, this condition [of the spectacle] is given as a definite structural relation, a definite formal nexus which appears to govern the whole of life" (Debord, 1981f, p. 52). The student subject as spectator is thus transformed into both a conduit of embodied politics of the hierarchical body politic, and the imagined representational space of corporeality which reaffirms the impulses of such a hierarchy.

Warriors and Servants

The fourth and final group of individuals in the Grove spectacle nomenclature is comprised of individuals who define themselves through, and are defined by, their black-bodied 'Otherness.' Within the physical and imagined boundaries of the Grove Society, spectacular practice becomes its

---

9. Which is an actual event on the Ole Miss campus, hosted bi-annually by Kappa Alpha fraternity.

10. Conversely, the women of the Grove, and particularly sorority women, have a distinctive way of expressing a seemingly natural class-based deportment. They spend hours preparing themselves for the Grove, hustle back-and-forth from the carnival to their sorority houses to ensure maximal beauty, and then gallivant across the Grove (unlike their masculine counterparts, who tend to remain less mobile) as if they had conducted themselves in this way since childhood (Fieldnotes). The imaged layering of Ole Miss women and the Grove have simultaneously defined both the emphasized femininity of the Grove Society and the gendered politics at Ole Miss for a broader mass constituency. In a *Sports Illustrated On Campus* article (2003a) entitled: "The 100 Things You Gotta Do Before You Graduate (Whatever the Cost)," number three on the list was "Tailgate in the Grove at Ole Miss, the 10-acre, debutante-stacked meadow on campus" (p. 4).

own discursive formation which emits an ether of solidarity for white bodies within that space, while black-bodied 'trespassers' are relegated to the physical and subjective margins. At Ole Miss sporting events, White bodies occupy spaces of privilege. Perhaps the best example of this is the Walk of Champions: a ceremonial pregame parade where predominantly Black-bodied gladiators (the Ole Miss football team) march through the center of the campus amidst a throng of Confederate flag–emblazoned, exclusively White spectators and supporters. During this spectacle within the spectacle, White, soft-bodied fanatics clad in khaki pants, collared shirts, and ties croon in admiration as a subjugated corps of predominantly black hard-bodied combatants—each dressed in a seemingly awkward juxtaposition of Dixie South fashion (attire very similar to the style garnered by the older, exclusively White onlookers: shirt, tie, khaki pants)—intersect the otherwise exclusively White space. As the visiting journalist from *Sports Illustrated* proclaimed, the players "walk like 'champions.' Read: in their best shirts and ties. Like adults" (Duerson, 2004, p. 11).

That is, they dress up in a way that will be deemed satisfactory by the disciplinary gaze of an Old South White patriarchy. Before the Arkansas State University versus Ole Miss fixture, I described the Walk of Champions in my notes in this way:

> In the midst of a congregated throng at the northwestern edge of the Grove, in front of the Student Union, I witnessed one of the signature moments of the Grove experience: the "Walk of Champions." The "Walk of Champions" is a ritual on the Ole Miss campus where student athletes, most of whom are black, walk to the stadium across the Grove a few hours prior to the kickoff. As the athletes walk in a single-file fashion through the Confederate flag-waving, red, blue, and white clad spectator group, they are greeted with the strains of "Dixie" (the entire band is present and blaring), sung by the white-bodied harmonious (in the sense of corporeal homogeneity, not singular verbosity) chorus. The Colonel (Colonel Rebel) lords over the procession, approvingly applauding his sporting minions while waving the flag of *his* ancestors. Cheerleaders lead the fans in a variety of chants, such as "Go, Ole Miss," with crescendo being the spirited rendition of "Hotty Toddy" (the same song the all-White student population barked in protest as James Meredith attempted to integrate the University during the Civil Rights Era). (Fieldnotes)

In the first instance, this gestalt of sporting Ole Miss transposes the logics and conventions of Dixie South Whiteness onto instrumental athletic deportment, as disciplined Black bodies march to the fashions, rhythms, and surveillance of the purveying gaze of Dixie South Whiteness. As King and Springwood (2001) argue, under such regimes, "the black athlete has been constructed as a *site* of pleasure, dominance, fantasy, and surveillance . . . in a post-civil rights America, African Americans have been essentially invented, policed, and literally (re)colonized through Euro-American idioms such a discipline, deviance, and desire" (p. 101).

In the second instance, the interplay of racially encoded and decoded bodies, a bevy of Ole South signifiers, and the material realities of a still-iniquitous power structure at the institution and throughout the region re-inscribe the territorialized boundaries of race and place. Through the flag's unwavering presence at these Ole Miss sporting spectacles, the political, material, and social power structure of the past converges onto both dominant and alternative subjectivities of performative South Whiteness. Being "White" in these neo-Confederated sporting spaces implies a membership in the history represented by its most relevant symbol—a history of domination. By way of refraction, being "black" or embodying the "other" is a meaningful expression of subjectivity—subjectification to subordinated politics of race at the institution, in the region, and in American social life more generally.

The solidarity of spectacularized Dixie South Whiteness is constructed through the visible preponderance of fair-skinned agents operating in the Grove space. I had the following observations during the final home football game of the 2004 season:

> Throughout my observations at the football events of the season, the most striking illustration of spatial/racial homogeneity lies in the racial solidarity of the Grove spectators. Of those who occupy space in the Grove prior to and after Ole Miss home football games, white bodies dominate the spaces of privilege therein. I have yet to see a group of African-American "tailgaters" in the Grove. (Fieldnotes)

These observations echo those made by a writer for the *Chronicle of Higher Education*: "Just as at the game, blacks are virtually invisible in the Grove—except when the football squad . . . parades through the crowd en route to the stadium" (Lederman, 1993, p. A52). For the spectator of the Grove spectacular, this symbolic unification of the racialized 'body/subject' creates a theater of spectacular power, whereby Confederate fetishization is resurrected, brought to life through the possibilities of an atomized corporeal collective. The markers of the confederacy outline its spectacular machinations, whereby the collective assembly of white bodies conscribes what Pierre Bourdieu (1990) refers to as a 'hidden pedagogy.' Bourdieu suggests that bodily practices such as those of the Grove do not:

> . . . become habitual simply as a result of explicit rules—rather dispositions can be collectively orchestrated—a group's structuring principles are made body by the hidden persuasion of a hidden pedagogy which can instill a whole cosmology. (p. 69)

In the Ole Miss context, the reign of an uncontested White space as delineated by the territorial flags of the Confederacy creates a deportmental solidarity, interlocking embodied signification of Dixie South Whiteness (which permeates throughout, encapsulating young and old, masculine and feminine, black and White) with the Old South order of things that has historically oppressed those operating on the margins (Frederick, 1999).

Debord, following David Riesman, refers to the notion of a 'lonely crowd,' in which the system—for both Riesman and Debord, capitalism's systematic grasp over the individual—creates division in order to create unity amongst individuals. For Riesman and his co-authors, individuals in the 'lonely crowd' can be classified into three types, two of which serve our purposes here (Riesman, Glazer, & Denney, 2001). 'Tradition-directed people' are those individuals who rigorously obey ancient rules, and seldom thrive in modern, rapidly changing societies. These individuals are both part of the 'lonely crowd,' and displaced from its inertia by their inability to create agency (Fulford, 2001). A second type of individual within Riesman's lonely crowd is typed as the 'inner-directed' person. This social agent acts out life in the manner she or he was trained in infancy—tending to be confident and perhaps also rigid in their demeanor (Riesman et al., 2001).

While delving too far into the typological fulcrum of *The Lonely Crowd* might prove problematic (as a number of detractors have pointed to the manuscript's overt positivism as a shortcoming of Riesman's signature text), it is interesting that these two figurations of individuals within the society of the spectacle accurately describe many of those individuals who embody, and perform, the strident whiteness of the Dixie South. These actors, or spectators within the lonely crowd, reproduce a society which brings people together only to spread them apart, as the spectacle "eliminates geographical distance only to reap distance internally in the form of spectacular separation" (Debord, 1967/1994, thesis 167). Consequently, two forms of isolationism emerge in the Grove Society: one as a result of a segregated cartography of the spectacle through the proximal logics of white supremacy (the collective space of 'tradition-directed people'); the other is an anthropological map in which symbols of difference, and the distance to embodied normativity, act upon the demarcated outsider. As such, there is but a liminal borderland within which expressions of blackness within the boundary logics of Dixie South whiteness—those operating outside both Riesman's typology and Oxford's hyper-normativity—can construct, and be constructed into, a space of empowerment. Here I want to outline the ways in which fear of alienation from spectacle whiteness leads to a unified white orthodoxy in the Grove. This form of white alienation in turn creates more oppressive forms of alienation for the black-bodied outlier—and eventually superficial empowerment through the dual processes of sterilization and false authorization.

In the first instance, the fetishization of Dixie South whiteness within the Grove Society has created a distinguishable isolationism, as expressions of collectivity are embodied, signified, and identified through a cohesive, recognizable, phenotypical whiteness. The ritualistic engagement with the Grove spectacle brings individuals closer together, only to spread them apart again by way of 'images of need' and narratives of want. As such, the social interactions of the Grove Society constitute a more tangible procession of the "clowns of the spectacle" (Debord, 1990, thesis 28) bound to the spectacular logics of the society from which they were borne, rather than the collection of autonomous agents creating new 'situations' of their disposition.

According to Debord (1967/1994), "separation is the alpha and the omega of the spectacle" (thesis 25). 'Separation,' in this regard, refers to the forces of alienation which shape the individual experience, always there, never attainable:

The more [the spectator] contemplates, the less he (sic) lives; the more he identifies with the dominant images of need, the less he understands his own life and his own desires. The spectacle's estrangement from the acting subject is expressed by the fact that the individual's gestures are no longer his own; they are the gestures of someone else who represents them to him. The spectator feels at home nowhere, because the spectacle is everywhere. (thesis 30)

The relationship between human action and the spectacle is an important one in conceptualizing human agency and the construction of the spectacle. French social theorist Roland Barthes (1957/1972) uses the terms *spectacle* and *gesture* interchangeably, each referring to the interplay of action, representation, and alienation between man and society. The *gestures* of a spectacular society become immersed in the logics of the spectacle, obsequiously binding the subject into the laws and power dynamics of the prevailing social order. The relationship between individuals of the spectacle is such that "individuals are linked to the spectacle in a one-way relationship while maintaining their isolation" (Ritzer, 2001, p. 185). In the spectacle of Dixie South whiteness found in the Grove, the white-bodied "front-row spectators" (Debord, 1990, thesis 21)[11] made flesh in the developed forms of each group defined above (the elder statesmen of Dixie South whiteness, the children of the Grove, and the princes and princesses of Oxford) serve the spectacle by way of their alienation, and further alienate those resigned to the spaces of idiosyncrasy.

This form of alienation, which produces the binaries of docile, eager whiteness and reticent blackness within the 'Grove Society' is reproduced through two primary apparatuses: (1) the segregation of spaces of whiteness and blackness;[12] and (2) the sterilization of black-bodied infiltrators of white spaces. The spectacle recreates itself through the conditions of its own existence—by creating "pseudo-needs" (Debord, 1967/1994, thesis 51) from which the spectators are linked to the spectacle, and to one another, through the gestures and interactions within spectacular society. For the white-bodied 'front row spectator' of the Grove spectacle, there is unity in practices of consuming spectacle, engaging both the commodity whiteness (symbolic, reified) and the experiential discourses of the Grove spectacular.

Conversely, black-bodied campus subjects are often relegated to the margins, both in their spatial displacement outside the Grove and their imagined disengagement from the ideological corpus of representational politics and the politics of identity within the Ole Miss space. Black individuals in the racialized spectacle are subjected to:

---

11. For Debord, these types of spectators "are stupid enough to believe they can understand something, not by making use of what is hidden in front of them, but by believing what is revealed" (Debord, 1990, thesis 21).

12. I use the term 'blackness' here, as opposed to the objectified 'black body' trope, to suggest that whereas black bodies in this space are often disempowered or objectified, blackness is a discursive formation which presents the possibility of an alternative (to whiteness) modality of power/knowledge. Objectified black bodies at Ole Miss offer little space for contesting white dominance, whereas blackness, even in a liminal manifestation, offers the possibility of carving out a space of empowerment.

> ... a logic of dehumanization, in which African peoples [are] defined as having bodies but not minds: in this way the superexploitation of the black body as a muscle-machine [can] be justified. (Mercer, 1994, p. 138)

Throughout my observations, I took notice that black students very rarely participated in the Grove spectacle, instead opting to create their own tailgating festivals outside the Grove space:

> After I toured the Grove for an hour or so, I headed up to Fraternity Row to see if any of the campus men were tailgating on the ground of their fraternity houses. To my surprise (perhaps due to the am hour), most of the fraternities had no organized parties, sans one chapter. The men Phi Beta Sigma had a full-blown front yard festival going on. This was my first encounter with any collective assemblage of black-bodies throughout the campus. . . . Upon reflection of my observations today, I can only recall seeing black students engaging the celebration of Ole Miss on one occasion, at the Phi Beta Sigma house early in the day. (Fieldnotes)

Interestingly, Phi Beta Sigma is the only black fraternity with a house on Fraternity Row.[13] More interestingly, the concentrated gathering of black coeds outside the Phi Beta Sigma house, coupled with the lack of black bodies in the Grove during that same time, is suggestive of the physical and symbolic resistance to a hyper-territorial, visible center occupied by campus whites.

If Fraternity Row lies on the x-axis (along with the Grove and Lyceum) of power at Ole Miss, then my trip up the y-axis in the hours prior to the next home game further reinforced such an interpretation:

> There is a flurry of white-bodied sorority women bouncing back-and-forth between Sorority Row and the Grove, clad in heeled shoes and flowered dresses (imagine the Kentucky Derby without the decorative headwear). Beyond the more pronounced, grandiose houses which are occupied by white sorority members are two women's Pan-Hellenic houses, those of Alpha Kappa Alpha and Delta Sigma Theta. Both houses have ten to twenty students gathered outside. At the Alpha Kappa Alpha house, the students are grilling, listening to forms of music I did not find in the Grove (and which I was unable to identify the artists), tossing a football (note: two of the men at the party), dancing (only sporadically) and conversing. At the neighboring Delta Sigma Theta house, the mood is a little less festive, as the women which occupy the front yard space in front of the house are arranged in an almost semi-circular formation, situated on lawn chairs and engaged in discussion. (Fieldnotes)

In this instance, the geometric spatial separation created by the ideological and symbolic fences which partition the Grove and its spectators from 'the outside'—holding in Dixie South whiteness while keeping out representations of alternative identity politics—reinforces the 'comfortableness' of whiteness in the Grove, and the alienation of its outliers.

Secondly, the reassuring possibilities of uncontested, oligarchic whiteness and the near-subservience of ancillary blackness in the Grove spectacle

---

13. Obviously the black fraternity system offers an even more interesting social space for interrogating the intersections of gender, race, and social class at Ole Miss than I develop here, and would certainly be an interesting course of study and one which would help round out this thread of research.

are reproduced through clearly defined, antebellum-esque roles of super-or-dination/subordination. While there are few black-bodies operating within the imagined Grove space (the cognitive spaces of active agents able to seize the privileges of hierarchical identity politics) the geometric Grove is not without a multitude of black individuals operating in that space. However, black individuals of the Grove spectacle more often occupy roles of facilita-tion, such as traffic officer, security guard, or food servant:

> One of the first things that caught my attention was the fact that most of the traffic officers ushering the automobiles around the university's campus were black. Furthermore, the workers who were shuttling people around the cam-pus via golf carts were also largely black. However, when I entered the Grove, the color and social activities changed dramatically. For example, I only saw seven black individuals inside the boundaries of the Grove. Five of whom were working a servers in some of the extravagant tailgating set-ups, while the other two were walking through the area outfitted in University of Memphis jerseys. (Fieldnotes)

The momentary corporeal facade of phenotypical variance is soon displaced by the stark realization that black bodies of the Grove space represent a re-configuration of the Old South social hierarchical logics—whereby the in-strumental black body serves as immobilized producer of spectacle white-ness and re-enforcer of race-based hierarchies.

The historically defined roles of black individuals in Dixie South spaces are rearticulated through the politics of being in the spectacle, whereby the seemingly empowered (traffic officers, etc) become minions of the spec-tacle. By empowering the campus black bodies, yet sterilizing blackness as an accommodatingly oppositional discursive formation, Dixie South white-ness holds sway over the center as well as its margins. As such, under the auspices of the spectacle, the logics of preferred deportment, performativ-ity, and ideology penetrate all aspects of racialized representation, identi-fication, and signification within the discursive lexicon of Grove spectator-ship.

Following Debord (1967/1994), such social and cultural traditions cannot be altered from within (by the practices of actors within the spectacle) as long as the spectators within the Grove Society embrace, and its foot soldiers surrender to, the dominant conditions of Dixie South hegemonic whiteness. In the local sense, the black bodied athlete at Ole Miss thus becomes subjected to "a spectacle of surveillance that is actively engaged in representing authority, visualizing deviance, and publicizing common sense" (Reeves & Campbell, 1994, p. 49). The alternating juxtaposition of black body as "savage, bestial, and uncivilized" is thus governed by a central ether and disciplinary gaze of the "restrained, cerebral, and civilized white European" spectator (D. L. Andrews, 1996b, p. 127).

Within such regimes of normative power of the spectacle, grated from Antonio Gramsci's notion of 'hegemony,' whiteness becomes the organiz-ing logic of the both spectacle and spectator[ship]. For Gramsci (1999), *he-gemony* is essential the sway under which a society's "dominant group" is able to celebrate and legitimate one way of doing things to the discredit of alternative ways (p. 12). In other words, hegemony is the dominance of one group over other groups, with or without the threat of force. As such, the dominant party can dictate the terms of social and cultural exchange to its advantage (Gramsci, 1999). With regard to Ole Miss, such hegemonic formations create a standard whereby cultural perspectives become skewed to favor the dominant group—the arbiters of Dixie South whiteness. By moving into, onto, and over the historical and cultural terrains of nonwhite subjects, Dixie South hegemons secure "a partial recovery of their erased selves, from imaginary expressions of libido, bellicosity, aggression, expressive spontaneity, and deviance" (King & Springwood, 2001, p. 161).

Theorizing Spectacular Whiteness

To make sense of how these bodies of the spectacle, through their public arrangement and performances, create power, I return to the work of Guy Debord. While Foucault has led us through the ways in which [the] formation[s] of discourse organize human activity, and the politics of identity at Ole Miss, and Lefebvre has guided the conceptualization of various forms of space in framing the ideological and material manifestations of a Dixie South cultural economy, Debord's theory can help us better understand how practices of the body, in the spatial panopticon that is Ole Miss, not only discipline the active body, but also fuse the practices of the spectacular event with the impetuses of the body politics and the politics of enfleshment within the Dixie South. Debord's seminal work, *The Society of the Spectacle* (1967/1994), weaves a complicated, yet concise synthesis of the classic social theory of Karl Marx, Georg Lukács' (1971) neo-Marxian reading of Marx's notions of reification and class consciousness, Gramsci's (1999) interrogations of hegemonic power, and Henri Lefebvre's (1991) theoretical interpretations of the sociology of everyday life, to formulate a multifarious account of the contemporary social and economic condition. In its most concretized form, the localized spectacle refers to "particular events or spaces. In this manner it has been prominent in attempts by geographers and other critics to address the emphasis on visual components and strategies within late modern culture" (Pinder, 2000, p. 357). While Debord tends to over-determine the economic relations of the spectacle (commodity fetishism, alienation, class consciousness, and consumer culture), he crafts a useful epistemological and theoretical framework from which we can understand the cultural politics of the spectacle.

The tendency of contemporary social critics has been to dismiss Debord's project as a conjectural intellectual theory, or to misappropriate Debordian theory by concentrating on one core aspect of *The Society of the Spectacle*—the singular spectacular event (Tomlinson, 2002). As Tomlinson (2002) suggests, social critics have for too long "taken [spectacular events] for granted by labeling them as spectacles, without any full developed sense of the conceptualization of the spectacular" (p. 45). This caricaturization of Debordian theory both complicates our understanding of his conceptualization of the spectacle and overlooks the nuances of a complex set of theses devoted to social critique. Jappe (1999) posits "there must be very few present-day authors whose ideas have been so widely applied in distorted form" (p. 1). The most problematic application of Debordian theory amongst scholars of physical culture is the [mis]appropriation of the notion of the 'spectacle' to describe singular exhibitions of the spectacular—such as 'prolympic' sporting events, television and mass produced mediations of the popular, and filmic reinventions of past, present, and future—without forging articulations of the spectacle to the structural formations from which, and to which, those spectacles are bound.

Loosely defined as anything from the mass mediation of sport (Gruneau, 1989), to the US sporting mega-event (Real, 1975), to the generic 'symbolic and ceremonial dimensions' (Tomlinson, 1996) of bodily movement, these configurations have oftentimes failed to delve into the complex ways in which cultural phenomena function dialectically with and within what Debord (1967/1994) refers to as the broader *society of the spectacle*. Those who simply evoke the Debordian spectacle to describe the sporting mega-event and its ancillary elements ignore the central thesis of Debord's (1967/1994) position, where he explains, "The spectacle appears at once as society itself, as a part of society and as a means of unification" (p. 12). That unity of discourse (the cohesiveness of the visible center), the imperceptibility of spectacular practice from the formations of the broader spectacle, is at the center of the forthcoming analysis on what could be considered the *new theater of operations in Southern culture* (Debord & Wolman, 1981).[14]

Debord's theory of late modern society illuminates the ways in which 'spectacles,' in their individualized form, creates a spatial (ideological, symbolic, and embodied) collectivity amongst spectators through their engagement with, and fetishization of, commodified and commercialized cultural forms. To be a *part of the spectacle* means to become *part of the society of the spectacle*, the formation of new technologies of the self create new identities, and the creation of new possibilities to delight oneself through the spectacle (Best & Kellner, 1999). However, equally as significant, to reproduce the power imbedded in the spectacle, Debord asserts that the spectacular society must reinvent itself, always marking and remaking itself as something new, something yet to be attained. The two-part outcome of the spectacle is thus alienation and class consciousness (Debord, 1997), as the individual in spectacular society is reinvented through engagement with the commodity and its signifiers. For the spectator, the distance between what one has and what one wants, who one is and who one wants to be, and so on, is always siphoned through the spectacle; forever interpellating, always impossible (Debord, 1967/1994). This paradox, in turn, creates an emotional distance from the spectacle, a return to the Marxian notion of alienation, but through consumption rather than production (Debord, 1991). The spectat-

---

14. The Situationist International refer to aerial photography, and particularly the variety which depict the activity within the cityscape, as the 'new theater of operations in culture'.

or systematically becomes part of the spectacle, incessantly consuming and engaging the modalities of the spectacle to locate herself or himself within the popular discourses of networks of representation and signification (Debord, 1981a, 1981c). The spectating body thus becomes an extension of the spectacle; colonized by the prevailing logics of power and representation.

In this way, individual bodies of the Grove Society becomes both products and producers of the discursive formation which stitches embodied whiteness, hierarchical ideology, and representational space and spaces of representation together in a cohesive articulation of *spectacular Dixie South whiteness*. In other words, the spectacular bodily practices within the Ole Miss empirical both unite, and separate, the practices of representation (and representational practices) within society of the Dixie South spectacle. Through cultural spectacles, dominant regimes of power are able to instill, propagate, and reproduce the iniquitous social relationships organized therein (Grossberg, 1985). As such, the society of the spectacle, the manifold, multi-layered articulations of power in contemporary society, is more than the singular event, more than the formation of dominant media forms. Debord's spectacle is described by Stephen Best and Douglas Kellner (1999) in this way:

> In one sense, it refers to a media and consumer society, organized around the consumption of images, commodities, and staged events. But the concept also refers to the vast institutional and technical apparatus of contemporary capitalism, to all the methods power employs, outside of direct force, to relegate subjects to passivity and to obscure the nature and effects of capitalism's power and deprivations. Under this broader definition, the educational system and the institutions of representative democracy, as well as the endless inventions of consumer gadgets, sports, media culture, and urban and suburban architecture and design, are all integral components of the spectacular society. Schooling, for example, deploys sports, fraternity and sorority rituals, bands and parades, and various public assemblies that indoctrinate individuals into dominant ideologies and submissive behavior. (p. 132)

Understood in these terms, we can situate Ole Miss at the center of the *society of the Dixie South spectacle*. A spectacle of [Dixie South] whiteness that is both embodied in the practices and principles the institution, and transmitted and diffused through those formations. Rephrasing Debord (1990), the practices and politics of the visible center have 'spread to the furthest limits on all sides, while increasing the density of the centre' (thesis 2).

Not only in furthering our understanding of the spectacle in its particular form, but in understanding the contemporary context where these social practices occur, Debord's commentary on the postmodern implications of practiced consumerism adds heuristic benefits to the study of contemporary frames of the politics of representation (Bracken, 1997).[15] At Ole Miss, this platitude of spectacularized whiteness is a significant problematic which complicates social relations in contemporary spaces of representation—the integrated spectacle as manifest through the individual. As Debord (1967/1994) posits, "spectacular consumption preserves the old culture in congealed form, going so far as to recuperate and rediffuse even its negative manifestations; in this way, the spectacle's cultural sector gives overt expression to what the spectacle is implicitly in its totality—*the communication of the incommunicable*" (thesis 192, author's italics).

The spectator in this society of Dixie South whiteness is both bound to and immersed in the spatial and imaged discourse—an individual "who is utterly undiscoverable" (Benjamin, 1973, p. 420), as well as affixed to the local by way of intolerance for the unknown 'out there' and the possibilities of similar intolerance within the outside world. Lefebvre, borrowing from the Situationists, refers to the notion of 'interior colonization,' which is the "new concentration of capital, personnel, and administrative techniques on realms such as consumption, leisure, and urban space" (Pinder, 2000, p. 366). The interior colonization of the Ole Miss spectator makes the individual both anonymous and seemingly autonomous, able to shift between and within the formations of prevailing power relations.

Not all spectators of the Dixie South spectacle encounter the 'Grove Society' in the same way. However, the pervasive presence of these bodily practices, and the ideologies for which they stand, constitute and reconstitute the reified relationship between individuals 'that assume, in their eyes, the fantastic form of a relation between things' (Marx, 1976). In other words, reified Dixie in the fanatical practices of neo-Confederates of the Grove not only locate whiteness at the center of Southern social relations, but accumulate a spectacular *cache* which unto itself becomes the unifying principle upon which the integrated spectacle is organized. Through the reified imaginary of Dixie South whiteness, the integrated spectacle of Dixie South whiteness thus maintains its dominance over all sways of social and cultural life therein. In sum, articulations between the concrete and the abstract, the local and the [global] popular, the spectacle and spectacular society, are illustrative of the power dynamics at work in any given social formation. In other words, the affectivity of the local spectacle is an important expression of the degree to which, if not medium for, spectacular power is exercised on the everyday experience of individuals.

---

15. In the age of hyper-consumption, Debord suggests, "In form as in content the spectacle serves as the total justification for the conditions and aims of the existing system" (1994, p. 13). In other words, the dialectic of the semiotics assigned to commercial goods and social experiences by cultural intermediaries, and the broader social forces that inform the consumer sensibilities toward consumption, are the core interrelationship within Debord's society of the spectacle (Best & Kellner, 1999). Consumers, or more accurately, spectators, are located in the discursive landscape of the spectacular—carving their identity out of the commodified pluralities of representation (Debord, 1990).

Coda

A Return to the Visible Center

Throughout this book I have tried to formulate an account of the inter-locking dynamics of race, physical culture, and power-knowledge at Ole Miss. I have, in the words of Lawrence Grossberg (1992), attempted to construct an analysis that "describes how practices, effects, and vectors are woven together, where the boundaries are located and where the fault lines lie" (p. 64). To return to the thesis I set out at the beginning, then, I have endeavored to map the social technologies which operate on the Ole Miss student subject; and how those technologies (and techniques) have constituted, and perpetually reconstitute, a preferred identity politics emanating from, and gravitating toward, the dominion of the [neo-]Con-federate whiteness. And while those politics were never static nor natur-al—having adapted and changed across various historical contexts—I came to realize that the dominant representations and praxes of Dixie South whiteness today look all too similar to those of plantation days of the Old South. Through *codes of the familiar*, the disciplinary gaze of the center of so-cial power still operates on "Othered', as well as white, bodies throughout the campus; whereby the complexities of pluralistic Southern blacknesses become colonized, if not generalized, under the hegemonic structures of knowledge and power (always reinventing the homogenous alternative) and whiteness in post-Civil Rights America becomes reorganized through the spectacular performances of enfleshment.

In spite of the reality that Southern society is more complex than these simplified, dichotomous discursive formations tend to allow, the arbitration of knowledge and power thereof has persistently returned to a centralized hierarchical binary structure—a social regime whereby whiteness (as well as class and patriarchy) defines the dominant formations of everyday life. In 'deconstructing Dixie,' I have sought to problematize the ways in which the politicized body acts within, and serves to reinforce, the prevailing logics of the racially-motivated body pedagogic. Thus my central focus has been how the 'political anatomy' (i.e. the political and politicized body) of the Dixie South is organized around a *visible center* of strident whiteness: the discursive, subjective, politicized centrifuge of power relations in the region. That center, through the dynamic [re]constitution of identity and the overt gesticulations of privilege, is made legitimate not in the society halls of the Ku Klux Klan or the Nationalists, or in the legislative halls in Jackson, but rather in the performative corporealities of a preferred whiteness which, through various interactions with the symbolic (Confederate flags and 'Dixie'), the spatial (the plantation aesthetic of the built environment and Confederate Memorials), and the spectacular (the integrated spectacle of the Grove Society), reinforce (or make necessary) the non-necessary correspondence between the ideologies of white supremacy and the practices of representation. The subjected body thus emerges as a product of various disciplinary constraints introduced within the paramount institutions of the neo-Confederacy, as well as a disciplined space from which the dominant order of cultural politics in the Dixie South can be created and reproduced.

Along the way, I learned that the formulation of hegemonic whiteness and the discursive formations of the visible center rely on a complex network of apparatuses and institutions to promote the new old pedagogies and new technologies of superlative Southern whiteness. As I attempted to illustrate here, the University of Mississippi still stands as one such 'crucible' of popularized, homogenous, Southern white governmentality and the central apparatus for subjectifying the student body. Thus whiteness at Ole Miss is both interpellative—as "the institution's image attracts students who yearn as much for its conservative, traditional nature as for the beauty of its campus and the quality of its education" (Lederman, 1993, p. A51)—and organizes the pedagogical terrain therein; whereby generational conglomerations of *bodies of privilege* and *bodies of difference* wrestle with the historical conjunctures of bodily subjectification and ideological indoctrination.

To close this analysis, I want to end with a brief discussion on the political and socio-cultural implications of how, increasingly—in the realms of body culture, sport, public pedagogy, and the national popular—*Ole Miss* 'matters.' Far beyond an isolated institution of higher learning situated in north Mississippi, Ole Miss matters as a politically-influential, popular-pedagogical, and economically-dialectic locus of the contemporary Dixie South. The institutionalized white subject position(s) hailed by, and organized through, the normalizing performative politics at Ole Miss surfaces out of, and contributes to, the constantly shifting US political asthenosphere. As such, the dominant subjectivities, performativities, and body pedagogics at

Ole Miss comprise an important cultural *assemblage* for not only understanding the identity politics of the Dixie South and the governance of corporeality, but also the attenuation, or consolidation, of the dominant and alternative technologies of the racialized-, gendered-, and classed-self in re-centering the hegemonic order of social relations in post-Civil Rights USA.

Therefore, my use of the term 'return' in the chapter title is sardonically veiled in the assumption that there was some sort of newly surfacing power for the white, masculine, wealthy visible center—which, of course, fails to acknowledge the structural realities of a diachronically-burdened historical materialism. As such, it is with caution that I refer to the 'return' of the visible center, and perhaps would be more appropriately served by framing the forthcoming argument in the notion of *the [r]elucidation of the risen center*. In other words, and in an effort to avoid allying the principle thesis of this coda with those social critics who in recent years have announced the 'death of the subject' (see Heartfield, 2002)—and thereby dismissed the active subjectifying processes at work in the social realm—I will instead position my contemplations of a 'return' of the visible center in the public sphere as a contextually-specific *sine qua non* of hegemonic power and the articulations of identity, power, and discourse. In this way, we might surmise that the inner-workings of Ole Miss sit within what has been referred to as a broader 'recovery movement.' This movement, as Joe Kincheloe (2008) has argued, is in general terms comprised of new and reinvigorated systems, practices, and matrices of social, political, and economic power. As Kincheloe (2008) suggested, in an increasingly interconnected 'global society'—subjected to the laws of the 'global marketplace' (and the coalescence of sociocultural and economic dimensions therein)—this procession of hierarchical litigious, commercial, social, religious, and political praxis now works to protect and strengthen 'traditional,' iniquitous forms of social, political, and economic power.

Following Ernesto Laclau (1996b), I therefore argue that there was never a 'death' of the *visible center* as either subject, subject position, of subjective formation, but rather through the ages Dixie South whitenesses—and the pedagogical systems that brought it to life on the Ole Miss campus as elsewhere—were constantly *adapting while staying the same*. In this way, whiteness bares inflections of the Old South while shifting-shape to meet the conjunctures of power and knowledge *in situ* (that is, in context). Amidst the transformations in identity and cultural politics brought forth by the Emancipation Proclamation, *Brown versus Board of Education*, and post-Civil Rights era politics of the state and the self, Ole Miss stands out from its peers as an institution that remained anchored to dominant axioms of Old South whiteness (Drake & Holsworth, 1996). In turn, as political and market interventions periodically disrupt 'normal' social life in the region, the politics of separatism and hierarchy intervene; refocusing 'normalcy' around the institution's white body pedagogics (and more overt white supremacist and patriarchal stylings such as those on offer in the public sphere by Glenn

Beck, Rush Limbaugh, etc. and in secret practice [e.g. the upsurge in white supremacist group membership]).

Following Laclau (1996b), I see these politics of dominant subject position[ality] not as a reprise from disenchantment, but an intensified subjectivity in the context of a post-national, postmodern 'proliferation of particularistic political identities'; and as a contextually-fleeting, non-absolute shift back to whiteness as local (and transnational) discourse of entitlement. For Laclau (1996b), the 'epistemological obstacle' of the individual subject in contemporary Western society emanates from the colonizing imperatives of subjectivity, whereby the 'death of the death of the subject' (a counter-narrative to the intellectual sacking of the subject) is suggestive of the arrival of new technologies of the self:

> The re-emergence of the subject as a result of its own death; the proliferation
> of concrete finitudes whose limitations are the source of their strength; the
> realization that there can be 'subjects because the gap the 'the Subject' was
> supposed to bridge is actually unbridgeable. (p. 21)

The rise, or 'return,' of the visible center has at once become increasingly transparent in the public, spectacular discourses of identity and representation in contemporary US society and all-the-more problematic; a product of the structurally articulated promise of complete agency (anti-dialectic individuality) and the impossibility of escape from those structures from which that agency is meant to be separated.

As conservative, 'traditional' cultural and political economies increasingly organize the distribution of technologies of the self and the performative pedagogies of individualism through the collective narratives of whiteness, the amalgamated logics of the body politic of the Right and the politics of the body unite under the formations of localized discourse, racial representation, and lived experience. The anti-pluralistic affectivity of the institution suggests that while not all subjects of the Dixie South share a common culture, the preferred vision of whiteness in the context of post-plantation, post-Civil Rights Ole Miss is deeply rooted in the triumvirate affectivity of: an antiquated gendered subjective/objective experience as demonstrated in the docility of 'campus cuties' and the patriarchal order of campus leadership; a class-based aristocracy where privilege and wealth are cemented in the confines and conduct of University Greeks; and most obviously, and subversive, and simultaneously *perceptible*, spectacle of white supremacy. And as those institutionalized bodies are projected onto the popular sphere, they authorize (whether due to the subject's intention of not) both the politics of representation and the pedagogical formations by which those politics are made powerful. "We do not simply exist as bodies, be we also *have* bodies. We have bodies not just because we are born *into* bodies but because we *learn* our bodies, that is, we are taught how to think about our bodies and how to experience our bodies" writes Peter McLaren (1988), "And in a similar fashion our bodies invent us through the discourses they embody" (p. 62). For whiteness at Ole Miss, much like in other prominent social institutions of the contemporary US South, is not discreet enterprise.

The 'Southernization' of America?

Despite marked ideological shifts within the racial politics of the US South over the past few decades, an historically-bound regime of racial hierarchy still prevails. That regime—moored in, and bound to, the logics of modernity and modernist conceptions of identity—has been constructed out of hierarchized binarisms in order to perpetuate the discursive and lived formations of social power. To some degree, this stems from collective idioms of entitlement; from historically-grounded social hierarchies built on years of slavery and land ownership (Hale, 1999). The 'new identities' of the South can be genealogically traced back to the *investments of whiteness* garnered by the first wave of European immigrants into the Dixie South, particularly the early 1800s. In a series of decisive moments since, Ole Miss has functioned as a central site for smoothing over the schisms of difference and equality; often institutionalizing the systems of subjectivity within a broader hegemonic order of white power. Within local and popular discursive formations, notions of 'race' are closely linked to ideas about 'ownership' and 'citizenship'—the former expressed in the ownership of wealth, the ownership of identity (and thus whiteness), the ownership of 'Ole Miss,' the ownership of nostalgia, and of autonomous delineations of 'Southernness' and an ethnicized 'Southern ethic,' and the latter in the declarations of *communitas* and configurations of the subjected collective. In the articulated interplay of universalism and particularism, many institutional technologies of the South have been used to stimulate and reinvent the antediluvian politics of difference in the *lingua franca* of the present, in the dialectic of 'Otherness' borne of 'the positive and the negative' (Laclau, 1996a). The discursively-constituted politics of difference, along with the positive undercurrent afforded whiteness and the contradictions of alternative politics, guarantees "continuity of difference by [always marking off] the other . . . by the constant renegotiation of the forms of its presence" (Laclau, 1996a, p. 53).

Ole Miss, however, is not the singular source for [re]producing the hegemonic acumen of monolithic whiteness in the Dixie South, but rather a 'nodal point' (Laclau & Mouffe, 1985) along an evolving network of racialized, gendered, and classed pedagogies, ideologies, and corporealities. These racialized body pedagogics, in competing and multifarious complexities, are created and mobilized in the subjectifying processes of a broader complex of normativity (Hall, 1992b). Through the interrelations of consumer capitalism, networks of social capital, and political institutions, the collective conscious is reinscribed through the "multifarious forms of undomesticated subjectivities in an objective totality" (Laclau, 1996a, p. 20). Thus, Dixie South whiteness emerges not as a formation exclusive to Ole Miss, rather Ole Miss is but one disciplinary space where the social formation of racialized power and the preferred meaning of whiteness are normalized, operationalized, and diffused.[1]

In the South, the longitudinal project of colonizing alternative discourses of subjectivity and uniting the visible center has been further promulgated through the efforts of several integral social institutions. In the academy, Ole Miss and similar educational organizations promote the extension of an antiquated, idealized 'Southern cerebralism.' The vestiges of Dixiecrat polity still shape the legislative bodies of many Southern states, as political leaders (such as Zell Miller, George W. Bush, and Ron Paul) secure 'moderate' Democrat and 'conservative' Republican seats while legislating a resolutely 'traditionalist' US polity.[2] Amidst the enclave of Confederate flags and religio-nationalistic propaganda, the correctional/judicial structures of the South still litigate and police under the guise of façadist social justice, as black men of the South are nearly five times more likely to face incarceration than their white counterparts (*State rates of incarceration by race*, 2004) and an Anglo-centric vision of Jesus 'guides' the morality of the secular South. The all-white congregations of many Southern churches gaze at pulpits and the religious leaders upon them who proffer 'a return to Christian values,' and thus, veiled in the language of new South asceticism, call for the 'elimination' of racialized social deviance (from the visible center) and promotions of scriptural domesticity. Health care systems of the South neglect poor black individuals, and indict 'community failings' and the 'poor individual choices' of the black working classes, rather than acknowledge the failings of the many city, state, and federal public works. In large part due to George W. Bush's 'No Child Left Behind' Act, military recruiters now concentrate their most intense recruitment efforts for black (and increasingly first generation immigrants from Latin America) students in working class neighborhoods of the South, and school leaders must accommodatingly identify those students who would make the best candidates for military service.[3]

These institutions organize the cultural exchanges of the racialized body, the evermore Confederatized American symbolic, and an ideology of white prerogative; all of which become conjoined and congealed through the op-

---

1. Ole Miss is the archetypal 'new Old South' (Rubin, 2002) institution, but more importantly is also an active apparatus in the broader reconstruction of a socially paleo-conservative, fiscally neoliberal US (ideological and physical) empire (Hardt & Negri, 2000). Distinctively Southern, yet decidedly familiar, Ole Miss functions to indoctrinate, and concurrently symbolize, the centrality of local embodiments of power and exclusivity, and is an important social space because it offers that connection between the individual and the collective through the corporeal and the symbolic.

2. While Miller and Bush are more commonly referred to as social conservatives, and champions [neo-]liberal economic policy, Edwards' conservativism lies in his appeal to the 'traditional' values of the South: anti-abortion, pro-politico-religiosity, and emblematic of an idealized Southern work ethic.

3. If these school officials fail to comply with the military take-over of student livelihood, they stand to lose substantial government funding and significant teaching jobs.

erationalized synthesis of the symbolic and the material. Within the 'racial imagery of white people', the universalism of whiteness becomes visible, and is made powerful, through the distribution of corporeal signifiers and ideological locations of seemingly 'non-located and disembodied positions of knowledge' (Dyer, 1997). In other words, by making central aspects of power visible, whiteness can act in a panoptic way; with numerous social outposts ordering social power, capital, and the politics of race and representation in systematic regime of oppression and normalization. But one has to step back here, for this is paradoxically a disembodied *embodiment*.[4]

More to the point, I would argue that in contemporary American life, the *body pedagogics of Ole Miss are everywhere*. Looking out over the vast panoply of media politics, consumer cultures, and postmodern performativities, we can see that Ole Miss is but a signpost on the super-expressway of mass-mediated spectacles, celebrities, and symbols *en route* to monolithic whiteness.[5] Within the contemporary US mass/popular discourse, the normative narrative of distinctive Southern cultures has helped forge that

---

4. The claim to embodiment, too, serves as a marker of whiteness and its privileges, the legacy of the Christian story of a God who became man, and revalorized, while transcending, the human body and saving it from mortality. For example, in the fall of 2005, numerous Christian-based, hyper-white conservative coalitions boycotted toy brand 'American Girl,' citing the parent company's support of one of the nation's oldest girl's advocacy groups, Girls, Inc. American Girl, whose often patriotic products have long had a loyal following among conservatives, was boycotted by the Mississippi-based American Family Association, whose members were urged to demand that American Girl halt support for Girls Inc., which it called 'a pro-abortion, pro-lesbian advocacy group' (Crary, 2005). This conservative group, as well as numerous other religious-Right organizations, cited Girls, Inc.'s efforts to support a girl's right to have access to contraception and support for girls dealing with issues of sexual orientation as reasons for the boycott. Perhaps, as is the case in many Southern cities these organizations prefer the interventions of groups like 'Love in Action International,' a Delta South-based ministry that provides prevention and treatment for behaviors like homosexuality and drug addiction. Just as these and other social institutions are fashioned to delineate racial difference, locate the marginalized and authorize normativity, and oppress or colonize the 'Other' and reaffirm the centrifugal forces of the orthodox center in many communities of the South, these institutions of access, power, and universalism are most certainly at work in other regions of the nation and globe.

5. The operational focus of the visible center is fixed on the homogenization of the cultural possibilities of the subject, eliminate pluralism or assimilate particularism under the sway of normative regimes of capital accumulation (and alienation through labor and consumption), cultural universalization, and objective marginalization:

> Difference and particularisms are the necessary starting point, but out of it, it is possible to open the way to a relative universalization of values which can be the basis for popular hegemony. The universal and its open character certainly condemns all identity to an unavoidable hybridization. (Laclau, 1996b, p. 65)

link between the consumable politics of the [conservative, white] South and the consumer poetics of the self. The popularized vision of the monolithic South has littered the filmic mainstream in Hollywood iterations such as *Days of Thunder, The Dukes of Hazzard, Mississippi Burning, Heart of Dixie, O' Brother Where Art Thou?, Deliverance,* and *Slingblade*. The popular sphere is further saturated with the country western musical exploits of Toby Keith, Alan Jackson, Gretchen Wilson, Dolly Parton, and Faith Hill and the hybrid rock/country offerings of Kid Rock, Lynard Skynard, and Credence Clearwater Revival. Southern sporting men such as Peyton Manning, Eli Manning, and Lance Armstrong now occupy a permanent space on the ESPN rotation of programs. During his protracted tenure, President George W. Bush was quick to identify himself as a 'man of the South.'[6] Bush's predecessor, Bill Clinton, was similarly lauded for his ability to translate his distinctive 'Southernness' into votes from the Northern and Southern moderate faction. In sum, increasingly, when it comes to mainstream American culture, *the South matters*. And the current US President Barack Obama, in what many commentators suggests was an effort to 'Southernize' his black vernacular, adopted and refined performances of bodily and linguistic 'Southernness' in his successful 2008 Presidential campaign.

The mainstreaming of the Dixie South belies the trend that, in recent years, the American popular (political, religious, cultural, and economic) has taken a southerly turn. This shift is considered by many scholar/commentators to be suggestive of 'the spread of Dixie' to the cultural economy of America: what some refer to as a broader process of the 'Southernization of America' (Cowden, 2001; Egerton, 1974; Phillips, 2006). Whether referred to as the 'Southernization of the nation' (Cowden, 2001), the 'Americanization of Dixie,' or 'the Southernization of America' (Egerton, 1974; Phillips, 2006), idiosyncratically 'Southern' personalities, ideologies, and institutions have increasingly come to permeate US mass culture. To this end, the dialectical homogenizing forces of American social technologies are now symbiotically bound to the collective configurations of the South. Proponents of this notion of a 'Southernization of America' point to examples such as the influx of country western radio stations, the popularity of Southerly programming, and the import of the World Wrestling Entertainment (WWE) and NASCAR (Newman, 2007).

These forms of 'helluvafella' mass culture present 'mainstream America' with a universally-accepted populist refuge—a non-threatening, exclusive, almost 'comforting' alternative to the usual manifestations of commercialized cosmopolitanism and narrativized multiculturalism. In these unsettled economic times, where the failings of capital have stimulated new public debates around *entitlement* (of belonging, of health care, of the right to exist with the domestic space) and citizenship (what it means to be an American), the mass culture industries have retreated to tired dichotomous racialized

---

6. And many have argued that his opponent in the 2000 election, Al Gore, lost the election because he failed to reassure his home state of Tennessee that he had not lost his 'Southernness.'

logics and obsequious pedagogical embodiments. In this new binary, popular figures such as Jeremiah Wright, Terrell Owens, Kanye West, Jesse
Jackson, or Al Sharpton and organizations such as Acorn or the NAACP
are strategically positioned in the popular realm as antithetical to 'mainstream American' values; a dominant discursive formation that increasingly
celebrates white [Southern] equivalent celebrities such as NASCAR drivers
Clint Boyer or Dale Earnhardt, Jr.—a couple of 'good ole' boys' out there
just having some reckless fun; Tim McGraw or Toby Keith, a pair of pure-
bred songsmiths; or new-wave Bible-reading, cowboy-hat-wearing 'sons of
the South.' In this way, sport, country music, and a number of other mass
culture institutions thus constitute not only a locus of conservatism (of
the ideologies and traditions of chivalry, hypermasculinity, and 'traditional'
conceptions of race and ethnicity), but also of the 'normal' and 'natural'
socio-political trajectories of the nation. This expansion of Southern tribal-
ism(s) indicates an 'authorization' of the South, the normalization of Southern polity, and the universalization of Southern traditions and Southern
hierarchies.

There is, of course, a counter argument to theories of Southernization,
one which suggests that Southern culture is being co-opted by the forces
of commercial capitalism rather than obtaining any sort of mainstream recognition of culturally distinct nuances. In this thesis, 'the South' is becoming more 'Americanized'; bringing it further under the sway of late capitalism. From this perspective, it might be argued that the overrepresentation
of Southern cultural forms in the main—particularly the import of Southern religion, music, sport, and politics—is defined by the homogenizing processes and normative technologies of the mass culture industries. The relevance of George Wallace in the last century, for example, or the Southern favor of Nixon's republicanism, is suggestive of the incorporation of a
Southern political economy into an incessantly vigilant national conservative monoculturalist project. Under such a conceptual frame, *Southernized
Americana* is thus articulated as the amalgamated currency of populist culture; a co-optation of regional nuance for the purposes of capital or political accumulation. This line of thought perhaps falls in line with other debates regarding the negation(s) of the global and the local, and of the heterogeneous and the homogenizing forces of global capital. Problematically, this
frame of analysis tends to privilege the local, sympathizing with the seemingly inimitable rather than critically deconstructing the political power invested and operating in and between the local (as *distinctively Southern*) and
the global.

Perhaps there is a third hypothesis from which we can conceptualize the
increased relevance of the imaginary South—and the formative role that
contemporary institutions such as Ole Miss, and figures such as Trent Lott
or Eli Manning—plays in both cultural diffusion and cultural territorialization. Just as these symbolic figurations have come to embody the visible
center's normative vision for contemporary 'America,' and simultaneously
establish the common ground of a populist dream for monolithic whiteness,
the geographic boundaries and imaginary spaces of the center are galvanized

in the assimilative moorings of the 'recovery movement.' Perhaps we are not in the midst of a Southernization of America, nor an Americanization of the South, but rather we are engulfed by new governmentalities of the old visible center (which are so succinctly, and efficiently identified and identifiable with Dixie South imagery, values, and ideologies)—and a return to Southern inflections of socio-political power brought forth by the South's increased relevance.

The affectivity of this imaginary South is predicated not only on such regimes of internalized governance and conformity, but the prevailing cultural economy's own self-expansion through the *laissez-faire* inventories of popular conscious, collective memory, and mobilized ideology (Barthes, 1972; Hutton & Giddens, 2000; Rosenstein, 2001; Tindall, 1989; Young, 1990). This dialectic of history (as framed by discourses of an idealized South) and paleo-conservative ideology has been crassly articulated by popular Mississippi politico Richard Barrett (2005) in this way:

> . . . plantation life was idyllic, compared to social-chaos of modern day, regarded by many as a model for 'race relations,' to hold a burgeoning Negro birthrate and primitive mentality in tow. There were no gang-bangs, car-jackings, or 'wilding.' There, certainly, were no voting districts drawn to install Negroes in office, no 'quotas' to place Negroes in schools and no 'affirmative action' to elevate Negroes in the workplace. Negroes stayed 'in their place' and government, property, constitutional-rights, family and society, itself, were all safe and secure. In short, America was neither African nor Mexican nor alien, in any way. America was American. (p. 1)

Rather than conceptualizing the Southerly shift of mainstream US cultural economy as mass diffusion or intrusion, we might best be served by considering how the South's increased weight in the popular sphere signals the episodic [eternal] return of hegemonic centrality to hetero-normative, white, masculine, Christian conservativism. In the context of a highly contested state of warfare, a divided public conscious of issues of abortion and social welfare, and a fracturing body politic in the expanded global economy, the identity of the social agents, rationalistically conceived under the 'interests' of the dominant faction, and the transparency of the means of representation in relation to what is represented, are "the two conditions which permit the exteriority of the hegemonic link to be established" (Laclau & Mouffe, 1985, p. 55). The conflation of individual interests and the assimilative politics of the center and 'the lack'[7] thus give way to the rise of new hegemonic machinations and, in the case of the contemporary US, the return to the traditional politics envisaged and embodied in the Old South. Paraphrasing Stuart Hall (1984), the widening racial divide and the rise of the visible center is attributable to the three-part reunion and re-emergence of: neo-liberal economic privilege, New American solipsism, the recalcitrance of a disempowered white center, and the rise of a new cultural economy of racism.

---

7. The constant subjectification of the individual to the alienating forces of contemporary social configurations.

Society of the Spectacular South

It has been argued that over the past twenty years, neoliberal economics and paleo-conservative individualism have achieved imminent domain over an eminently national and vastly global frontier by symbolically reconciling two historical strains that are, in reality, marked by correspondent contradictions: "the social gospel of traditional values and the economic gospel of the free market" (Kintz, 2002, p. 735). In the US Presidential election of 2004, the deciding factor for many 'swing voters' was the Right's ability to locate and articulate a populist platform built on the 'traditional America values' embodied by George W. Bush: familial patriarchy (and anti-women's rights); the end of 'reverse discrimination' (and the return to anti-affirmative action white reign); inherited egalitarianism (and the anti-socialist welfare for the disadvantaged); heteronormative closed-door sexuality (and focused attacks on American lesbian and gay communities); overpopulation regulation (and anti-immigration, anti-Latina/o laws); pro-'family'; pro-Judeo-Christian; and pro-police (pro-gun) statism—all of which were mobilized to interpellate the political sensibilities of the visible center and its expanded peripheries (J. R. Brown, 1998; Crosby, 1997; Hochschild, 1998; J. L. Kincheloe, et al., 1998; McGowan, 1998). The 'populist unity' (Hall, 1984) of the visible center became narrativized in the vernacular of a paranoid Christian Right (where prayer in schools became more important than the quality of education in those schools), the bio-power of anti-abortionists usurped the humanitarianism of social welfare for the dying poor, and social security became less a matter of ensuring livelihood for the elderly, and more about securing the economic welfare of the wealthy and the corporate than providing health care to impoverished children. Consequently, progressiveness, feminism, and blackness were framed as counternarratives to the discursive machinations of the visible center; antithetical to 'traditional' conceptions of family, labor, asceticism, and faux meritocracy (Ware & Back, 2001). In securing the vote of the self-identified white middle-class, the Republican Party was able to secure majority power in the Senate and the House, connecting the technologies of the Right to the politics of the self for the dominant faction of voting Americans.

That paranoia of fleeting dominance is evidenced by the notion that white residents of the United States believe that 'whites' are a minority in the United States. In a 1996 poll, white respondents estimated that the white population of the Unites States was approximately 49.9 percent—while the accurate figure was 74 percent (D. R. Roediger, 2002, p. 10). This panic from the center has transcended the imperfect science of 'race,' as "white men (the future minority) are [now seen as] the new persecuted majority . . . women and people of color are perceived as *the* restraints on white men's realization of the American way of life" (Cole & Andrews, 2001, p. 111). And so in the face of a perceived transitory white male hegemony, the many civic and political institutions within the US and the West (and beyond) have come to *authorize* relevance, and relativize *citizenship*, around the normative center of conservative ideologies and performative whiteness. This notion of citizenship suggests that tension exists between the contradictory forces of representational ownership (entitlement of the subject and the subject position) and the contested boundaries of belonging, and according to Chantal Mouffe (1992), for the white majority 'there is no hope of a final reconciliation.' And thus the fragile nature of whiteness, and the political paranoias of the dominant faction, make institutions such as Ole Miss all the more imperative for advancing the Right-ward shift of the new American cultural and political economies.

At the impasse of a North/South, black/white, Left/Right political and cultural divide, and as the dominance of white masculinity in the political, corporate, cultural, and religious spheres has recently been narrativized as 'dissipating,' the Right's call to arms in the defense of 'core American principles' and a corrosive cultural economy meant defending the moral majority from the threats of 'bleeding heart' liberalism and 'reverse racism' (Thandeka, 2002):

> today, white people—above all, white men—have been put on the defensive. What they have taken for granted as the fruits of hard work and virtue is now decried by others as the undeserved advantages of privilege born of racism and the correlative evils of sexism and class domination. Seeing their economic and political dominance challenged by forces over which they have no control—loss of jobs to foreign competition, depreciation of marketable skills and qualifications, and decline in wages, salaries, and benefits due to downsizing, the opening up of competitive labor markets, and so on—they feel more insecure than ever about their place in the world. . . . A less overtly racist (and sometimes nonracist) reaction is principled opposition to policies, such as immigration and affirmative action, that supposedly violate the rights of American workers in general and, more specifically, the rights of white men. (Ingram, 2005, pp. 248-249)

Popular discourses of individual wealth and intrinsic equality have thus been articulated out of the fashionable 'dual unity' of neoliberal capitalism and social conservativism. The 'legitimacy' of the Right is further concretized by the ideological sway and representative regimes of subjective/subjectivized political alienation. In other words, the politics of the subject, and the subjective politics of the 'recovery movement,' became conjoined in the collapsing power dictums of legitimated self-interest (of the white majority) during the 'troubled times' of multi-cultural America (Laclau & Zac, 1994). As Ruth Frankenberg (1997) suggests, "white people's conscious racialization of others does not necessarily lead to a conscious racialization of the white self" (p. 5). Importantly, such non-reflexive sensibilities of entitlement, coupled with what comedian Jon Stewart refers to as the 'white Christian persecution complex,' inform not only the public discourse, the national discourses of race, class, gender, and generationality.

Federal interventions which impeded the pursuit of individual wealth, and particularly those which structurally reconciled the iniquitous history of a political economy of racism such as equal opportunity and affirmative action measures,[8] have been met with fanatical resistance from the white Right, and in the post-Reagan insurgence of neoliberal self-actualization, tormented the Left in the public discourse and the popular electorate (Thandeka, 2002). To protect white power and white wealth, the Right successfully interpellated the refractory sensibilities of the moral majority and spread the new technologies of paleo-conservativism:

> Many white middle-class Americans consider affirmative action as a policy to be unfair because it is alleged to rely on racially based preferences. Yet studies demonstrate that this same group of Americans chooses to live in predominantly white neighborhoods, work in racially segregated occupations, and, if given the opportunity, hire white employees rather than African Americans. (Pierce, 2003, p. 54)[9]

The new disciplinarity of idealized individual freedoms and the discourses of 'liberal individualism' (Pierce, 2003) thus promise the demise of social welfarism and the elimination of 'big government spending' on social programs for the poor and the underserved, while simultaneously expanding the wealth of the white Right through expansive military programs, a top-heavy 'trickle-down' economy, and diversion of public subsidies to the private sector. The purging of economic constraints have translated into the limitless, unchallenged expansion of economic and political exigencies of the visible center and the rise of a new politics of individualism and conservative pluralism. Ironically, the idiosyncratic nature of the most recent iterations of the 'great moving Right show' features the inculcation of the (alienated) subject by way of promising collectivity through atomism. In other words, the politics of the Right and the subjectifying processes of the body politic intersect at the interpellative discourses of the center: a spontaneous storyline which conjures up the presuppositions of whiteness and centralized power through the veneer diffusion of individual freedom (Laclau & Zac, 1994).

The autonomous ideologies and centralized governance of the Right has increasingly equated to the homogeneity of the cultural politics of red-state

---

8. In an editorial offered up by the *Daily Mississippian* Editorial Board in 2005, the student-authors condemned the scholarship opportunities reserved specifically for black students entering the UM law school, citing that such measures "should be cast aside [as they] cannot help in our progress toward a truly color-blind society" (Carrington, Shovel, & Salu, 2005, p. 2). They continued, "the money that funds these scholarships adds up pretty quickly, and could certainly be put to better use . . . Perhaps, though, one of the most negative impacts that these scholarships may have is that of diffusing incentive among black students who are aspiring to law school" (Carrington et al., 2005, p. 2). This ultra-conservative logic of the white center continues: "If you tell any group that they don't need to do anything in order to qualify for substantial scholarships, it will certainly decrease their incentive to perform to the full extent of their abilities in the undergraduate programs" (Carrington et al., 2005, p. 2)

9. The body of research that Jennifer Pierce (2003) refers to includes work by Dovidio, Mann, and Gaertner (1989); Drake and Holsworth (1996); Massey and Denton (1993); Tomascovic-Devey (1993); and Wilson (1997).

America. In the collapsing condition of the post-nation, 'ethnonational-ist' or transnational imagined community of ethnic commonality (Tambi-ah, 1996) has come to usurp the pluralistic ethnic nationalism(s) of the loc-al. First, the striking correlations between contemporary 'Red State' polit-ical identities and the politics of antediluvian slave statists problematically overlaps with the segregationist Old South; to the mainstream popular con-servative agenda under the racially divisive tenets of power, exclusion, and superiority. In other words, while very few conservative white voters in red state America would support the re-institutionalization of slavery, the hier-archical system of oppression which has long operated in these regions (as well as most of their 'blue-state' counterparts) is no longer articulated in res-istance to Federalism or discourses of white supremacy, but rather through the steadfast 'traditions' of a value-system which privileges the white, mas-culine, 'American' center. The appeal of George Bush, and the victories of both the 2000 and 2004 elections (or those victories of Reagan or the elder Bush), are thus not only indicative of the Rightward shift of American polit-ics, but of the reign of an inward-looking self-interest polity of the visible center.

In the summer of 2005, Democratic National Committee Chairperson Howard Dean criticized the disenfranchising politics of the conservative American bloc, telling a forum of journalists and minority leaders that the Republican Party is "not very friendly to different kinds of people, they are a pretty monolithic party . . . it's pretty much a white, Christian party" (quoted in Marrinucci, 2005, p. 1). While Dean received a substantial amount of public criticism for his comments, he rightly identified the at-tractive nature of the 'W' brand and its luminaries to white red-state Amer-ica, as well as the unalterable core of whiteness and the tantamount cor-relation between racialized polity and the 'values' of the Right (Thandeka, 2002). In recent years, the 'great moving Right show' has successfully cap-tured the attention (and votes) of an expanded audience by 'operationaliz-ing' the subjective liberties of *laissez faire* neoliberalism and the interpos-itions of multicultural social interdependencies (Rains, 1998). Second, the fall of centralized governmental regimes in Eastern Europe and Asia and the cultural and military colonization of an 'axis' of opposition has further given licensure to an omnipresent, or integrated, spectacle of collective American exceptionalism and [re]centralized social power in the form of individual-ized conservative politics. In other words, economic, political, and cultural power is now organized around a collective configuration of conservative, 'traditional' white masculinity, and the central nodes or knowledges acting to reproduce 'ethnocentric monoculturalism' (Sue, 2004) are found in new technologies of media, military, and medicine.

When the Levee Breaks

I hate the way they portray us in the media. You see a black family, it says, 'They're looting.' You see a white family, it says, 'They're looking for food.' And, you know, it's been five days [waiting for federal help] because most of the people are black. . . . We already realize a lot of people that could help are at war right now, fighting another war—and they've given them permission to go down and shoot us! . . . George Bush doesn't care about black people! – Kanye West (quoted in Moraes, 2005, p. C01)

By way of a conclusion I want to briefly return to Ole Miss—back to the Mississippi Delta and the cultural politics that define social relations therein. To understand the political weight of institutions of whiteness such as Ole Miss, and the complex social interplay between the visible center of whiteness and its marginalized ancillaries, perhaps we need look no further than the pages of local and national print news-media. A review of popular media representations of Dixieland bodies of Hurricane Katrina in late 2005—the greatest natural disaster ever endured by US citizens—brings into sharp relief the popular body pedagogics of the contemporary US South. Inundated with images of elderly women wading through a swamp of human feces, mothers and fathers breaking down the doors to corporate foodstuff big boxes so that they might feed their starving children, and waterworn, bloated corpses floating down Canal Street, American spectators were reminded of the under-told story of a racially-determined crisis of underprivilege in the South.

Those images were soon replaced in the popular discourse with the recurring narrative of the 'greedy,' 'uncivilized,' 'deplorable' black looter. As these (mostly) poor (almost exclusively) black families desperately waded through rising waters and then government red tape to escape the drowning city (relocating in Texas, northern Mississippi, and Tennessee), Barbara Bush, matriarch of the most powerful family in US politics at the time, lauded her son's Federal interventions, citing: "What I'm hearing, which is sort of scary, is they all want to stay in Texas." She continued by suggesting that since "most were underprivileged anyway," an arrangement where these folks were herded into giant sporting venues throughout the South was "working very well for them" (quoted in "Barbara Bush calls evacuees better off," 2005). In the chaotic aftermath of the hurricane, and as Kanye West made clear during a televised hurricane relief program (see epigraph), the social and economic disparities of black and white America could not be made more clear than by the contextual intersection brought to life by such a disaster.

The political institutions which had already buried many of these people in a under-water social catchment before the levees broke had already organized social life and spatial organization in the region under a unilateral order of class and racial difference—both for the purpose of a more perfect union and for the creation of a more delineated binary (control crime, foster development, attract capital)—as the moral highlanders and their economies of privilege translated their race and class citizenship into an escape from the flood, the riots, and the problems of the black underclass. Black bodies, on the other hand, were left behind, left to wade through feces and frothy, disease-ridden sludge, while the city's wealthy white party took holiday and sipped frothy lattes and watched the demise of their neighbors. And thus, public debates coalesced around the hyper-centralized logics of 'responsibility,' rather than the growing disparities of opportunities in New Orleans, south Mississippi, and beyond. In other words, in the post-9/11 moment, one where bumper stickers and lapel pins reminded Americans of the sufferings of white America at the hands of the dark-bodied terrorist cell, equally grave tragedies suffered by those outside the center, and directly resultant from antihumane politics of a domestic, corrosive body politic, are quickly forgotten and the project of reclaiming white dominance becomes refocused through Bush-like talking heads who point to the 'struggles ahead' in conquering 'those who oppose the American way of life.'

The intrusive fusion of conservative politics and 'traditional' conceptions of race were further publicized in a study reported by a number of television and print media platforms two weeks after Katrina. The study's findings promised, in the unsettling times of disaster, Americans' "longstanding assumptions on race, safety, and spending had shifted":

> After a crisis with indisputable elements of race and class—searing images of mostly poor, mostly black New Orleans residents huddled on rooftops or waiting in lines for buses—some Americans worry about strains in the nation's social fabric. ("AP poll: Katrina changed Americans' thinking," 2005, p. 1)

Unfortunately, these 'new' attitudes about race, social class, and impoverishment were nothing more than a return to the politics of white privilege and self-focus, as 55%of respondents said evacuees from Katrina have turned up in their cities or communities, thus "raising concerns about living conditions for the refugees, vanishing jobs for locals and—among one in four respondents—increased crime . . . and gang violence" ("AP poll: Katrina changed Americans' thinking," p. 1). These 'new' attitudes Americans have toward race, one which means that the threat of 'gang violence and crime' flowing out of New Orleans and into the suburbs of white America, threatens to disrupt the way of life for many within the visible center. Norman Denzin (1991) refers to the populist view of divided America as a form of "new cultural racism" (p. 7), as "symbolic articulations of the color white, Christian iconography, and the alleged benevolent superiority of white bodies are ubiquitous in North American popular culture" (McDonald, 2005, p. 246), and thus black identities, and the cultural realities of poor black Americans, are pushed to the periphery.

In a survey reported in the pages of *USA Today* on September 12, 2005, when asked 'do you have a favorable or unfavorable opinion of the Republican Party?', 74% of black respondents chose 'unfavorable.' When asked if 'George W. Bush does-or does not- care about black people' (obviously in reference to the West indictment), 72% of black respondents answered 'no, he does not,' while only 26% of white respondents thought that the President 'does not care' about black Americans. Perhaps most tellingly, the convictions of many white Americans were unwavering in their support of Bush and his administration, as nearly 50% of white respondents thought the President did a 'good' or 'very good' job in immediately responding to the natural disaster, while only 15% of black respondents shared that sentiment. After a crisis with indisputable elements of race and class—searing images of mostly poor, mostly black New Orleans residents huddled on rooftops or waiting in lines for buses—some Americans worry about strains in the nation's social fabric.

As Benjamin Barber (1996) points out, "just beyond the horizon of current events lie two possible political futures—both bleak, neither democratic" (p. 7). He describes the two principal political forces of our post-modern society—tribalism and globalism—as opposite and antithetical in every way but one: they may both be threatening to democracy. With regard to the former, Barber characterizes the forces of 'retribalization'—the condition in national states in which "culture is pitted against culture, people against people, [and] tribe against tribe," or what he refers to as the *Jihad* principle. Counteractively, the pressures of cultural homogenization, or what he calls the *McWorld* principle, are forged out of the conjunctural logics of post-industrial consumerism, monocultural identity politics, and discontented alienation of the disenchanted spectator. While *McWorld* promises prosperity, unity, and stability, but at the cost of independence, community and identity, *Jihad*, distributes a vibrant local identity and a sense of community, but guarantees a parochialism predicated on difference. The notion of Jihad, and Barber's own theorizing on contemporary society, is often used to refer to the 'insurgent,' vigilante-types of the Middle East. In the rise of the visible center, the parochialism of the South is woven into the discursive fabric of the nation and national identity politics. The Jihadism of the US conservative Right is symmetrically perfected through the homogenizing forces of unidirectional polity (the politics of hegemonic white individualism), through mass culture with a distinctively Southern feel, and through institutions which serve to normalize dominant formations of representation, and of the hypermasculine, hyper-white technologies of the self.

Just north of New Orleans in Oxford, Mississippi, arbiters of this new cultural racism pedagogically parade an idealized white past and a reified bifurcated present, the re-tribalization of the Old South through the new technologies of the imagined collective will act to further delineate the anti-progressive politics of 'the double.' In other words, through the institutionally-divisive practices of surveillance and hyper-disciplinarity, the fetishization of a revisionist iconography, the respatialization of physical and ideological power, and the spectacular embodiments of the neo-Confederacy, whiteness and the cultural politics which give whiteness power are not only extracted, but *acted out* and reinvented within contemporary Ole Miss. As that regime of normativity which actively locates the privileges of citizenship, and marks off whiteness as a culturally empowered discursive space, different forms of subjectivity become centralized or marginalized and the [post-]Civil War battle lines are reinserted into the conjoining symbolic discourses of 'American' culture, economic hierarchy, political power, and representational divisiveness. Thus, the center becomes the cultural locale by which hyper-masculine white supremacy is channeled and articulated, whereby Ku Klux Klan marches at Ole Miss no longer evoke the same affective response from the student subjects of Oxford, in part because the ideologies they promote are already deeply affirmed by more popularized discursive embodiments of Dixie South whiteness.

What then, is to be done about Ole Miss? As I have tried to reinforce throughout this book, it is important here to remember that the vast majority of Ole Miss students, academic and technical staff members, alumni, and other constituents are well-intentioned supporters of cultural plurality. And yet, as I have tried to make clear, the body pedagogics that inform race relations at Ole Miss have been slow in changing over the years. Looking back in order to look forward, I am reminded of the words offered by Martin Luther King, Jr. upon hearing of the dreadful murders of Civil Rights workers James Chaney, Michael Schwerner, and Andrew Goodman in 1964. When asked by reporters who he thought was responsible for the murders, King declared that *the who* was far less important than *the what*. *The what* that still afflicts the everyday lives of people of color in the Dixie South is the reign of white supremacy, and some people's investments in a contextually-specific, intangible, and grossly-malleable Dixie South whiteness.

And yet, if *the what* that plagues the Deep South's emancipatory potential is this possessive investment in whiteness and the protraction of race-based body pedagogies through the ages, then I might suggest that Ole Miss's institutional[ized] place with Dixieland might present a unique platform through which we might envisage, enact, and perform new pedagogies; pedagogies that embrace cultural difference and celebrate local plurality. In this way, while it has long been an important site for re[producing] *the what* that carried forward inequity through the generations, Ole Miss holds the potential to become that space where the pedagogical work of *the who* **replace** the structural legacies to which they are bound; where Ole Miss teachers, students, athletes, and stakeholders capture an emancipatory agency in a place where race, gender, and class have for too long categorized, colonized, and put in place those bodies of the institution.

What I am proposing here is a radical pedagogy that exposes, pries loose, and sweeps away Dixie South whiteness (and its racist lineage). As pedagogues and influential figures in ushering in the next generation of Mississippi's leaders, teachers must recognize that the knowing body is incontrovertibly linked to the broader social, political, and economic formations of which it is a part. And those "educators and cultural workers who are compliant and collaborative with such dehumanization must hold themselves responsible for the 'stripping away' of those possible futures arching towards hope" (McLaren, 1999, p. xi). In turn, teachers must create what Freire (1970/2006) refers to as 'cultural circles' around the human body—dialogic pedagogical contexts that bring together diverse bodies and cultural experiences, and nurture the emancipatory, integrative, and constructivist potentialities that are made possible by the coalition. For in their hands and minds, these young people of the South hold a wealth of catalytic possibilities. In the classrooms and lectures auditoria, share the histories of the oppressed (rather than valorize the histories of the oppressor). Come together in ways where body knowledges empower rather than disempower; where the body is not a commodity in the chains of the education-industrial-complex but a conduit to the circle of humanity.

This is a call for a bodily pluralism that by way of its very existence dismantles the homogenizing processes and recovery movements that I detailed here. The individuals acting within the Ole Miss campus space are indeed subjects of history and socio-political formations, but are always capable of 'radical resignification'; capable of remaking the subject from within. Cast(e) the next Eli Manning (or Michael Spurlock) not in the mould of his segregation fathers or that of his Confederate grandfathers, but of an icon of enfleshed humanitarianism. Make use of your embodiment as student-athlete to contest the system of exploitation that brought you to Ole Miss, and continue to hinder your academic success once there. We can learn a lot from such an athletic body through "a discourse that can be used to interrogate schools as ideological and material embodiments of a complex web of relations of culture and power, on the one hand, and as socially constructed sites of contestation actively involved in the production of lived experiences on the other" (H. Giroux, 1985, p. 23).

This is a call for new spectacular body pedagogic on the Ole Miss campus—like that on offer November 21, 2009. After new Ole Miss Chancellor Dan Jones announced that the University would be seeking alternatives to the band's ritual of Playing "From Dixie with Love' during Ole Miss sporting events (the song that ends with the crowd chanting: "The South will Rise Again!"), the Ku Klux Klan of Mississippi announced that they would hold a protest prior to the Ole Miss versus Louisiana State University football context that Saturday. I leave the description of what followed to the words of Kevin Cozart, a senior at the University and the coordinator for operations at Ole Miss's Sarah Isom Center for Women and Gender studies:

> Under an overcast sky and greeted with a wall of boos and calls to leave, a few members of the Mississippi Chapter of the Ku Klux Klan rallied on the campus of the University of Mississippi this morning . . . for less than ten minutes. Little could be heard of any message they attempted to convey. Dressed in the highly recognizable robes, the ten Klansmen that showed up simply stood and waved their banners of hate and ignorance from the portico of Fulton Chapel, a fitting place since it is the home of the Theatre Department's productions. The sizable crowd that had gathered to see them was extremely hostile regardless of color, race, creed or university affiliation. After all of the fanfare, bravado and planning (including the use of bomb sniffing dog around the area), the brief appearance by the Klansmen [was] the very definition of anti-climactic.
>
> The real story of the day was the students, faculty, staff and alumni who gathered peacefully and read the University's creed in unison repeatedly a few hundred feet from where the Klan had gathered. Organized by One Mississippi, a student group working towards greater social integration at Ole Miss, protesters wore shirts that said "TURN YOUR BACK ON HATE… (I live by the UM Creed)" and stickers with one simple word: "Unity." Before and after the rally, they talked to fans in town for the game about their message and plan to make their way through the 10-acre, park-like Grove, passing out copies of the UM creed to fans.
>
> Today, the members of the real Ole Miss family were not afraid to show their faces. They were not afraid of the Klansmen. They stood with their

backs to them. They stood together to say with one voice that Ole Miss "believe(s) in respect for the dignity of each person." They stood as the leaders of a new Mississippi, a Mississippi that her citizens and a nation can be proud of. ("Klan outnumbered by protestors," 2009)

Indeed, this spectacular practice of bodily resistance became the stuff of progressive blog fete and YouTube legend. This is not a singular event in the University's recent history of resistance to racism and racist praxis. However, the degree to which students, fans, boosters, alumni, and faculty came together to *make pathetic* those bodily practices once-normalized within that campus space offers perhaps the most significant (to date) spectacle of resistance upon which a new, more equitable body pedagogic and body politic can be forged.

This is also a call to dare to imagine a different Ole Miss; to deviate from the now-normal, seemingly natural qualities of a spatial fabric that for too long have re-inscribed race onto its spaces; a call to paint the Union walls with the rainbow colors of the LBGT Movement; to wash the Grove in the colors of Africa. The prospect of such acts of spatio-ideological 'dissent' will no doubt trouble many who inhabit the campus space, which perhaps is the point. While some see beauty and solitude in the campus's neo-plantation aesthetic, others rightfully writhe about the phantasms of the Old South brought back to life in the etchings, stonework, brick coloring, and geographic layout of the Ole Miss campus. Lastly, writing as a biological descendant of the Confederacy, I can predict with some certainty that Ole Miss will be a much better place the day it parts ways with Colonel Reb, his Dixie Confederate stylings, and the flag that bears his imprint. While these symbolic arrangements have certainly been good for business in tough economic times (and certainly for United States' public universities), they suffocate any progress the University might make in the coming years with regard to racial equality (symbolic or otherwise).

In the dialectic spaces between the classroom, disciplinary, iconographic, spatial, symbolic, and spectacular bodily pedagogies of Ole Miss and the broader 'recovery movement' is where power has been wielded and accumulated over the years; but it is also in those spaces—in the contested and contestable spaces of the mind, of history, of the body, and of knowledge—where a new, better South may arise.

Epilogue

Notes on a Homecoming

I was born and raised in the South. I grew up deep inside the foothills of the Appalachian Mountains in the small town of Cosby, Tennessee. Cosby is situated between Asheville, North Carolina, and Knoxville, Tennessee—abutting the northeastern border of the Great Smoky Mountains National Park. For most East Tennesseans, Cosby is best known as the town that served as a major artery for moonshine bootleggers traversing the winding back roads through to North Carolina during the prohibition era. The remoteness of the town, and the topographic bottleneck created by Mount Camerer and English Mountain, made Cosby the ideal place for inconspicuous passage to the west (and back) for North Carolinian moonshiners (Higgs, Manning, & Miller, 1995; Salstrom, 1996).[1]

Today, Cosby is situated in one of the poorest counties in one of the poorest states in the American South. Cosby's commercial modalities have historically revolved around a modest agricultural economy and augmented by an unstable manufacturing sector (Whisnant, 1995). During the Industrial Revolution (and post-industrialization thereafter), the geographic remoteness of Cosby and surrounding townships isolated the region from the modernizing American industrial economy (Salstrom, 1996). And a result, today a vast majority of townspeople draw their employ in a panoply of part-

---

1. Handling shipments of moonshine is often called "whiskey-running" or simply "running" it. During Prohibition cars were "souped up" to create a more maneuverable and faster car to better traverse the mountainous terrain between East Tennessee and West North Carolina.

time, low-wage, unskilled, no-benefit 'McJobs' on offer in neighboring Sevier County (Ritzer, 1998a, 2004); home of the oft-visited mega-touristscapes known as Gatlinburg, Pigeon Forge, and Sevierville.

Like my peers—and as a child who grew up on the downside of Ronald Reagan's trickle-down economics—I came to understand my own subsistence existence within Cosby's post-industrial 'hillbilly' class as a extension of the *natural* 'order of things.' The story I learned *to tell myself about myself* went something like this: as a daughter of an 'egalitarian America,' my mother made a series of poor choices in her late adolescent years, and I was born to bear the burden of her 'misguided' agency. In spite of the fact that my mother worked two jobs—and eventually married my dad who contributed through the part-time, low-wage construction work he could sporadically secure—my brother and I were made to believe we were the proverbial 'drain on the system'; children of parents who sometimes relied on welfare, food stamps, and government aid to subsidize an annual household earnings regime that never eclipsed the $20,000 threshold.

Framed by the discursive throws of the Reagan-Bush I [neo-]conservative meritocracy, my family had become a countercurrent to a resurgent free-market American ethos. We were, as the 'skin of my yellow country teeth' constantly reminds me, the embodiments of contemporaneous Appalachian poverty. Throughout my youth, I spent many a winter's nights endeavoring to bathe myself by siphoning hot water from our kitchen sink and into an animal-feeding trough located in the front yard of our mountainside homestead. As a single-car family, my dad, brother, and I made nightly 20-mile midnight pilgrimages to pick-up mom from her job as a waitress in Gatlinburg. Thinking back, I am reminded of how my adolescent social life was stifled by the absence of telephone service in our home; a condition that was further complicated by an intermittent awareness of the American popular due to long periods where our household was without television. While other kids were mesmerized by the consumer cultures of Air Jordan, I was as a 12-year old preoccupied with fitting into the hand-me-down basketball shoes my friends had used the season prior. In short, it can be said that in the 1980s and early 1990s America, our upbringing wreaked of Appalachian poverty.

Over time, my peers and extended family alike taught me to loath my parents for failing to acculturate into the region's systems of scarce capital. Furthermore, I learned to frame those failings in the *epistemes* and rhetoric of a pastoral evangelical ascetic: generations before us had realized their place within the South's iniquitous cultural economy by subjecting their bodies to systems of accumulation, subjecting their everyday experience to the hierarchical thrust of a nation's manifest destiny, and subjecting their faith to an unwavering faith in God's plan for true believers. We were, after all, Americans.

More importantly, we were young white men of the South. With Reagan's early brand of neoliberalism as ideological backdrop, our failing post-industrial identities became contested and negotiated around the subjectification of power and suffering. Like folks in many Southern towns, those of us who grew up in Cosby learned to mobilize a vicious *mélange* of racism, patriarchy, and fundamentalism in rescuing our collective sense of 'Self' in an otherwise subordinated everyday experience. From the outset, we were students to a compulsory, compensatory pedagogy of exclusivity. For Cosby was—and not by accident—a town comprised of exclusively white inhabitants. Local lynch-mob vigilantes and Jim Crow separatists had nurtured, and continue to produce, a culture of white terrorism meant to ensure that my hometown remains, as it is commonly referred to, 'pure' or 'nigger-free.'

Further, as anyone who has spent an evening at the Three-Way Inn (the town's only bar in an otherwise 'dry county') or the neighboring Newport Speedway racetrack can attest, Cosby is a place where 'men can be men.' Paradoxically, it was my experience growing up that those Appalachian patriarchs who spent Saturday night at the Three Way Inn were the first to perfunctorily fill the pews of the area's multitude of Evangelical churches the following Sunday morning. It was also my experience that the church, perhaps more than any social institution, actively nurtured pedagogies of race-, sexuality-, and gender-based oppression within the community. As a child, it was not uncommon for me to find myself sitting pulpit-side to a Sunday morning sermon, listening to [white, masculine] pastors evoke a common 'end-times' pedagogy for the purposes of proselytizing indoctrination; or to lambaste what they frequently referred to as 'the disease of miscegenation'; or to draw out a protracted campaign against 'the threat of homosexuality.' Looking back, I can see now how incessant promotion of these cultures of intolerance (and 'tolerance') made for good spiritual and cultural enterprise—casting dispersions upon the 'Other' and congealing solidarity for the visible center, and thus extracting social power over the [mythologized] 'Other' in an otherwise disenfranchising late capitalist condition.[2]

Moreover, and despite my parents' best efforts, my adolescent tongue reflected this vile ethnocentric *communitas*. It was my experience growing up that slurs such as "nigger," "bitch," "faggot," and so on were commonly deployed in communal exercises of linguistic and symbolic violence over the imaginary 'Other.' Such vernacularism was not simply a slippage back to 'Old South' parlance, but rather a contrived mobilization of a narrative borne of, and reinforcing, dominant notions of *difference* and a sense of superiority amongst local hetero-masculine whites. Through this bucolic, heteronormative racism, my milieu and I were able to locate our sense of 'Self' in relation to the demonized and mythologized 'Other.' Building upon the Sartrean (1992) term 'project' (*projet*) and the Heideggerian (1962) notion of 'throwness,' I draw upon the work of French feminist philosopher Simone de Beauvoir to explain how the 'self' and the 'other' are produced in such powerfully diametric ways:

---

2. In much the same way as Americans today vilify the abstracted Muslim 'Other,' a mythological enemy through which discursive structures of power can be cast upon, and thus made real.

It's not *for* the other that each transcends oneself; one writes books . . . invents machines . . . craved nowhere; nor is it for the self (*pour soi*) because the "self" (*soi*) exists only through the same project which throws one into the world . . . we need the other so that our existence becomes established and necessary. . . . My acts, my works, my life: it's only by these objects that I . . . can communicate with (and through) the other. (quoted in Fullbrook & Fullbrook, 1994, pp. 96-97)

It is important to note the ways in which de Beauvoir articulates Sartre's (1992) double notion of the self: both as an 'objective' and objected being (*soi*) 'thrown into the world' and as a being that is aware of itself (*pour soi*). Thus, my own 'Self'-location—limited by the economic and cultural *frames* into which I was 'thrown'—constricted the pluralistic potentiality of my *pour soi*; and equally so of the imaginary 'Other' against which my sense of self was *framed*.

And yet as I matured, and availed myself to new and diverse structures of language, ideology, and identity, the more I came to realize how my 'objective' and objected being was produced by parochial structures of racism, misogyny, and homophobia. I came to realize, having yet to formulate a deeply Marxist sensibility, that while I had been free to make my own history, I had not done so under conditions of my own choosing. During my teenage years—as I matriculated through the East Tennessee educational system—I became increasingly aware of the structural forces acting upon my changing sense of 'self.' And as such, my discontent with the race-, class-, and gender-based politics of the local festered. As an example of my uneasiness with the ethnocentrism of my home place, and, yet my inability to acknowledge how those same forces shaped by own worldview, I offer the following poem which was written half a lifetime ago:

The ~~Rune~~ Ruin of Two Lives

Black man . . .
struggled through life, trying to survive
no chance to be normal, have a house, a wife
painful to live, it was all that he could do
destruction and bloodshed were all that he knew

White man . . .
family name, labeled the best
admired and loved, some said he was blessed
gracing his peers with all of his knowledge
valedictorian—high school and college

Black man . . .
nothing to live for, world of hell
deaths of friends and stories to tell
alcohol and drugs, world of illusions
no meaning to life, just basic confusion

White man . . .
expectations of greatness, family pride
the world his oyster, feelings aside
he knew his worth, as did others
qualities to uphold, Oh! . . .how they smother

a bullet shot here, a bullet shot there
two lives taken in the midnight air
expectations fulfilled, expectations ceased
both men free at last . . . to rest in peace

I offer this poem not as an example of any sort of enlightenment toward 'diversity' that I might have experienced during my formative years, but rather as an insight to my heightened (albeit ill-refined) structuralist proclivities at the time (as constrained by my impressions of 'different' ethnic experiences). Up to that point, I had never attended school with anyone from a 'racial category' outside my own. While I was aware of the problematic treatment of the racialized 'Other' through local racist discourse, my portrait of the "black man" in this poem is nothing more than an erudite simulacrum founded on interpretations of popular mediated representations of African-Americans.

Upon reflection, I suppose that if the author is written into those verses, then my own sense of self was somewhere between the two men, wrestling with the [neo]conservative priorities of a parochially-imagined meritocratic whiteness and the struggles to maintain livelihood in the economic determinism of a post-Reagan neoliberal condition. Despite an ill-informed sense of history, I went on to employ various forms of *poesis* in re-imagining the Jewish experience in Nazi Germany and the religious persecution of peoples of the Middle East and Eastern Europe. Nonetheless, there was still a discernable prejudicial bent to my interpretive voice; one I have been struggling to eliminate ever since.

In the words of fellow Southerner Richard Wright (1945/1998), 'this was the culture from which I sprang.' Under these socio-economic conditions, I fell into a habitus of contingencies (Bourdieu, 1998a): working class in the context of neoliberalism, Southern whiteness in tenuous times of multiculturalism (and its myriad distortions), and heteronormative masculinity at the anti-gay, anti-choice Biblical crossroads. Having spent most of my life oscillating between the boundaries of oppression, however, both structuralists and individualists alike might have predicted my turn toward a life of a cultural and economic polemicist. Perhaps an exorcism of that habitus, or more likely an exercise in scholarly *re-imagineering of my own South*, such an existence bore an ongoing intellectual project comprised in one part value-laden sociology of Southern body cultures and one part political economy of late capitalist forms of embodiment; a project reflective of an eradication of the 'self' in search of a more humane pedagogical modality.

Re-Placing My [New] Self

In the years since, in and through my own research, I have tried to craft a politically-committed, contextually-radical critique of contemporary physical cultures of the US South—and particularly those cultures of exploitation, inequality, and oppression that haunt the South in which my old self was formulated—while articulating the practices of the local to the broader formations of oppression acting upon the everyday experience. I have sought to make use of my white, Southern, hetero-masculine body to illuminate and thus complicate the oppressive structures and iniquitous cultural physicalities of what I have to referred to as the 'New Sporting South.' At once an exercise in mimesis and a resurrection of my former self, my various research encounters over the past few years have in some ways constituted a rediscovery of my own whiteness, my own Southern-ness, and my own masculinity; for, as Peter McLaren (1999) eloquently puts it, "we all have unfinished business with the history of our body" (p. ix). Through ethnographic engagement with the Southern sporting fields in Mississippi and in other areas throughout the South (see Newman, 2007; Newman & Giardina, 2008, 2009), I have both employed, and been made aware of, a habitus-based contextually-important, historically-constituted performative politics.

As such, this type of engaged qualitative research has revealed an [auto]ethnographic dialectic; whereby a politically-driven intellectual project—bent on contextualizing, and thus problematizing, the seemingly banal nature of Southern sporting fixtures such as college football and stock car racing—both constitutes, and is constitutive of, my 'ethnographic self' (Coffey, 1999). In other words, as I further immersed my 'Self' in the sport and body cultures of the US South, and Ole Miss in particular, the more I came to realize how 1) the 'auto' in any auto-ethnographic rendering of the qualitative world illuminates and is illuminated by the empirical encounter; 2) the empirical encounter is itself produced by, and its actors are subjected to, individual and collective structural and discursive histories; and 3) the qualitative boundaries of 'the field' are set and reset based on those histories. In short, and following Spry (2001), performing my 'ethnographic self' has meant producing meaning in and through my own body, whereby the body "is like a cultural billboard for people to read and interpret in the context of their own experience" (p. 719); further, it meant blurring, or perhaps imploding, the traditional anthropological binaries of 'insider' and 'outsider,' as well as what it means to 'go native.'

While the selected episodes described in this book reveal but part of what has become my near decade-long fixation with the sporting and body cultures of the US South, each nonetheless speaks to issues of representation, access, and [self-]identification that have arisen in my attempts to, borrowing a crude anthropological idiom, 'go native' again. I returned to the South in hopes of finding something different from that which formed my own experiences as a youth, but expected to be confronted by the structures and practices of oppression, racism, and sexism that I had, if only in my mind, left behind. In either case, I did so for political reasons: to write about and celebrate a more humane sporting South, or to excavate the most derisive and antihumane cultural politics that still *make* the sporting local. In short, I did so in hopes of crafting what Laurel Richardson (2000) refers to as 'evocative representations' of a *better South* (see Ellis, 1997). For mine was a transgressive endeavor with transformative aspirations, and through these "narrative performances," following Linda Park-

Fuller (2000), I sought to reveal "what has been kept hidden, a speaking of what has been silenced—an act of reverse discourse that struggles with the preconceptions borne in the air of dominant politics" (p. 26).

However, the more time I spent at Ole Miss—relocated in the sport cultures of my youth (with a genteel twist)—the better I was able to trace a series of ostensibly inescapable patterns of oppression: 1) the cultures of racism, sexism, patriarchy, and ableism are still highly active within these local pedagogies and spectacles; 2) my white skin, Southern drawl, 'hillbilly' vernacular, and masculine deportment allowed access to the most exclusive/ divisive of these social spaces (whereas others might have been denied); 3) to prolong engagement with various groups, 'I' often 'performed' my 'old' Southern self (laughing at racist jokes, admiring Confederate flag-emblazoned garb, etc.) (see Buber, 1937/2000 for a better explanation of 'I-thou'); and 4) in an effort to create change (through critical interrogation of the sporting empirical), I was most often 'read' as a [re]productive agent of these residual, regressive cultural politics (see R. Williams, 1977).

Reflecting on the Problem of 'Hillbilly' Double Consciousness

Borrowing from W. E. B. Du Bois (1903/1996), it might be argued that I have since been wrestling with my own strange *hillbilly double consciousness*. In other words, as I have reflected upon my new [intellectual, Left, progressive, pedagogical, transgressive] 'self' as well as an sharpened my awareness of how others perceive an alternative [Southern, white, masculine, hillbilly, sport-loving] 'self' within empirical space, I have synthesized identity and performativity into both a perceivable cultural politic and a seemingly perceptive, if not introspective, performative intellectualism. Indeed, following Hargreaves and Vertinsky (2007), such dimensions of embodiment are never neutral (p. 10)—not only those forms of embodiment we within the fields of qualitative inquiry and cultural studies labor to problematize, but also our own bodies as social organisms. Both within the fields of cultural inquiry and within the amalgamated performances of the everyday—as pedagogues, mentors, field workers, advocates, activists, and 'researchers'—engaged [auto]ethnographers situate their embodied 'selves' into those realms which has heretofore been described as the amorphous 'field' (Madison, 1999; Selzer & Crowley, 1999). As Ronai (1992) suggests, ours are bodies amongst bodies, of embodiment, and within the discourses, rhetoric, and praxis of cultural physicality. And as Paula Saukko (2005) makes clear, such a research dynamic negotiates "the dialogic space between the Self of the researcher and the Other world of the person being researched" (p. 348).

As for me, that type of engaged, empirical, qualitatively-dialogic research was not always an encounter of the Self and the Other, but often the strange reunion of my new 'performative' (Judith Butler, 1997) researcher self with my old Southern self. Tami Spry (2001) distinguishes these two researcher 'selves' through her textual binary of 'being here' and 'being there,' and in so doing agues that we must "reflect critically upon their own life experien-

ce, their constructions of self, and their interactions with others within so-
ciohistorical contexts" (p. 711). In the fields of the socio-cultural everyday,
however, I was constantly reminded of the 'dialectics of everyday' (Neuman, 1996), whereby the routines of my new Self were continually made
subjective (in both forms of the word): at once 1) an empowering act (or
so it would seem) where I went back to my proverbial 'roots' to develop
strategies for a re-politicized Southern kinesis and 2) having failed to escape
the specters of neoliberalism and now existing in the realm of the corporatized university, these encounters proved to be productive in enhancing my
knowledge-based market value. Regarding the latter, I was able to publish
various research articles and in doing so grow the brand equity of the institutions from which I draw employ. Furthermore, as John Beverley (2005)
points out, the transition from storyteller *in situ* to author allowed for a "parallel transition from *gemeinschaft* to *gesellschaft*, from a culture of primary and
secondary orality to writing, from a traditional group identity to the privatized, modern identity that forms the subject of liberal political and economic theory" (p. 548).

But here is where things get complicated. While in the 'field,' I was most
often 'read' as 'one of the crowd' or a member of the imagined communities in which I was engaging. Not accidentally, I labored—if by slipping into
habitus—to "render my account credible" through, as Clifford Geertz (1988)
argues, "rendering [my] person so." In other words, I was what Geertz refers
to as an 'I-witness' (pp. 78-79); a researcher-observer for whom the 'I' was
perceived to be in place. And while in most cases that would only mean that
I found myself interacting with Ole Miss students engaged in the banal-
ity of their existence within those spaces (drinking a beer, talking sports or
politics, playing cards, eating a bratwurst, etc.), there were more than a few
times I found myself in situations such as those described earlier; where individuals and groups mobilized bodily practice or spoken language as a form
of what Pierre Bourdieu (1993, 1998a) calls 'symbolic violence' against a demonized or marginalized 'Other.' In these circles, much like the cultural
circles of my youth, spoken and unspoken [patriarchal and racist] 'bioso-
cial' (Rabinow, 1992) praxis undergirded a more sinister, divisive, and violent
territorialism. Unlike traditional forms of race-, class-, and gender-based violence (e.g., lynching, 'bum bashing,' or sexual abuse), the shared physical,
phenotypcial, and cultural characteristics of the Southern *biosociality* operating within these sporting spaces projected oppressive forms of inclusivity
and thus exclusivity. To borrow from the later phenomenological parlance
of Edmund Husserl (1970), I was re-inhabiting an intersubjectivity (*Inter-
subjektivität*) of corporeal sameness and ideological difference; thus further
splitting the dichotomies of I-thou, us-them, and insider-outsider into, and
between, discursive, material, practiced, and ideological realms.

As my work at Ole Miss progressed, I became increasingly concerned
about how my own Southern, white body—against my best intentions—was
becoming a site of identity-based power within these spaces. In the first
instance, that power was productive in the sense that I was able to use it

through research outcomes to create new pedagogies of sporting whiteness. But to do this, I had to make myself *visibly invisible*—using my body to gain access to research sites and moments but not forcing my new 'self' onto the lived experiences I encountered. I came to deduce that there was a 'visible center' of identity politics at work within these empirical spaces, one that celebrated hetero-patriarchal Southern whiteness as the dominant cultural corporeality. And despite diachronically-disposed ideological and physical disjunctures, I was becoming part of that visible center. In short, I was *blending my white, Southern, masculine self in with the crowd.*

In large part due to my choice of research sites—those sporting and social spheres most deeply-saturated by neo-Confederate forms of unchallenged whiteness, and dialoging with the 'white reign' that exists within those spaces (J. L. Kincheloe & McLaren, 1998; J. L. Kincheloe & Steinberg, 2006; J. L. Kincheloe, et al., 1998)—my body became a symbol of conformity amongst thousands of other similarly white bodies. Like most spectators at these events, I did not wear a Confederate flag t-shirt or less subtle race-based signifiers, and yet my white skin was cloaked by the 'ideological blanket' (J. Baudrillard, 1983b) that covers these Southern [sporting] spaces. As Michael Giardina and I have argued elsewhere (Newman & Giardina, 2008), because the discursive practices of a racist few still hold sway over these spectacles, the racially-exclusive symbolic both colonizes those bodies operating within these spaces and territorializes these social formations as exclusively white domains.[3] And like the conscientious majority, mine became one such colonized body.

Thus in the second instance, by standing idle or only offering a begrudging smirk while various forms of symbolic violence were being enacted—indeed by becoming part of 'us' instead of part of 'they'—I was reproducing local power iniquities along the lines of class, gender, sexuality, and race. Mine was read as a body acting *of*, and *in*, solidarity—and thus complicity; a body that in turn collaborated in the production of violence and oppression over the race-, gender-, or class-based 'they.' Indeed, I was simultaneously *'homeless'* in the South and *at home*; forced to reconcile what Edward Said (1996) refers to as the 'dream-nightmare' of the discursive, imaginary, and real cultural fabrics of my own Southern identity, Southern dialect, and perceivably (and perceived) Southern body.

---

3. Further, my masculinity was often co-opted by the visible center; where it was assumed by those I met that as a man operating in these spaces, women were to subordinate themselves to me. And my Southern drawl instantly located me into two distinctly parochial habituses (working class in NASCAR spaces, capitalist class at Ole Miss)—each bound to the Old South schisms of a plantation cultural and political economy (see Bourdieu, 1998).

On the Messy Business of Articulating Reflexivity

As numerous scholar-researchers have suggested, the rigorous, qualitative investigation of the body is at once a political project "dedicated to the contextually based understanding of the corporeal practices, discourses, and subjectivities through which active bodies become organized, represented, and experienced in relation to the operations of social power" (D. L. Andrews, 2008, p. 54) and an embodied enterprise. Regarding the former, Robert Sparkes (1995) reminds us that we are *interpreting*, and thus recreating through text, representations of the human condition:

> No textual staging can ever be innocent. Whose voices are included in the text, and how they are given weight and interpreted, along with questions of priority and juxtaposition, are not just textual strategies but are political concerns that have moral consequences. How we as researchers choose to write about others has profound implications, not just for how readable the text is but also for how the people the text portrays are 'read' and understood (p. 159).

In short, the researcher is using the body to at once create representation (of the self and the other), regulation (of the researcher body in moving about space), and resistance (to the structures of oppression operating within those spaces).

Perhaps equally imperative, with regard to the latter, researchers of the body are creating conditions of interpretation whereby the corporeal inflections of the 'present author' are staged, performed, and 'read' *in situ* within various psychogeographic and corporeal-cultural boundaries. For these are not *author-evacuated texts*, as Clifford Geertz (1988) would argue; and ours is not a positivistic science of *convenient absence*. Rather, in seeking to contextualize, and thus problematize, the power relations of the body through various ethnographic encounters, researchers are placing their own body and identity politics within the realms of the empirical. By making use of the human body to better understand power relations layered onto, evoked by, and exchanged within bodies, the researcher in some ways projects her or his own bodily knowledges and dispositions onto the corporeal cartographies of everyday life (for an insightful overview, see J. Richardson & Shaw, 1998). As such—and at the collisions of histories, multiple subjectivities, structure and agency, researched and researcher, and body with body—those of us 'doing' qualitative research on the body must 1) acknowledge the [inter]subjective nature of bodily encounter; 2) maintain, to borrow from Maurice Merleau-Ponty (1973), a constant sense of 'corporeal reflexivity'; and 3) limit the symbolic violence created in research contexts where bodily encounters produce power, inequality, exploitation, or oppression.

Drawing on my own research, it was my experience in various ethnographic detours through the 'new New South' that the bodies of both researched and researcher were indeed sites of social power; and that self-presentation and the performances of selfhood and identity were in the first instance physical in nature. The body was, a Derrida (1974) reminds us, that most transcendental of signifiers. Moreover, the closer in contact bodies came within one another, the more powerful each became. Let me explain: problematizing how "the active body is culturally regulated, practiced, and materialized. As are power and power relations, so is the active body, and its related experiences, meanings, and subjectivities, dialectically linked to social and historical contingencies" (D. L. Andrews, 2008, p. 53) became an active pursuit of placing my own body in the spaces where bodily practice, social power, and sporting identity intersected. For my ends, the more concentrated exclusively white, patriarchal, and parochial the corporeal praxis, the greater depth of observation and interaction I was able to produce toward the political ends of my research projects. Conversely, as my white masculine body and Southern dialect joined these spectacular amalgams of physicality, it added to the increased cultural dominion of the visible center over these socially-exclusive spaces.

Thus, it can be argued that, following the Hegelian-Frankfurt School theoretical synthesis offered by Phil Carspecken (1999), as empirical subjectivities and contingencies (such as those I discussed earlier) collide, they do so at and around the human body in the form of meaningful and important *intersubjectivities*. In other words, the subjective (in a Freireian sense of subjection to power) and objective (that of the physical corpus) intersect at various discursive formations and practices of embodiment (J. Butler, 1993). As such, the interpretive and project of post-positivistic (Lincoln & Denzin, 2000), qualitatively-grounded politico-cultural kinesis is produced through dialogic encounters between bodies; whereby the intersubjective research act is an exchange of bodily interpretations (between the researcher and the researched) and embodied performances (again between the researcher and the researched).

In turn, and in looking back on my research encounters, I have found that the complexities of reflexivity toward, and about, the research act extend beyond the dialectics of language, representations, and reciprocity. They extend beyond Bourdieu's (1992) critique of Weber's 'value-free' sociological imperative and Foucault's (1994b) re-conceptualizations of *a priori* assumptions regarding Western structures and organization of knowledge in *The Order of Things*. Perhaps what I am arguing for here is a heightened, re-engaged sense of what Merleau Ponty's refers to as 'corporeal reflexivity.' A self-awareness of the researcher as 'embodied subject' (see Vasterling, 2003), both a discursive property in the physical world and an agent subjected to the existential structures acting upon those discourses.

In 'reading for the best' of the phenomenologist's work,[4] as Stuart Hall (1986a) would put it, we can surmise that Merleau-Ponty's model of *intercorporeality* illuminates the meaning-making processes active within and

---

4. For a more detailed reconciliation of Sartre's idea of being-for-itself and Merleau-Ponty's phenomenological conceptions of self-discovery of fundamental meaning see Kujundzic and Buschert's (1994) article titled "Instruments of the Body." For our purposes here, let it be suffice to over-simplify the role of the body in each theorist's work is complex, but that each acknowledge various relational interdependencies between the body, conceptions of the body, and the physical and ideological worlds.

between bodies and the power-knowledge relations produced within the bodily encounters we seek to better understand (Kelly, 2002). Rosalyn Diprose's (2002) synthetic interpretations of Merleau-Ponty's imperative for 'corporeal reflexivity' are worth quoting here at length:

> ... and while it may seem as if my corporeal reflexivity is already in place before the world or the other, which would allow the imaginary in my body to dominate, it is also the case that it is the other's body entering my field that 'multiplies it from within,' and it is through this multiplication, this decentering, that 'as a body, I am exposed to the world' (Merleau-Ponty, 1973, p. 138). This exposure to the world through the disturbance of the other's body 'is not an accident intruding from outside upon a pure cognitive subject ... or a content of experience among many others but our first insertion into the world and into truth' (ibid., p. 139) (pp. 183-184).

Much like Deleuze's (1988) notion of "the double," discourses of the body produce embodiments; meaningful texts projected out of similarity and difference. I am thus reminded that of Deleuze's famous dictum that identification is the "interiorization of the outside" (Deleuze, 1988, p. 98), the connection between the external discourses of identity and the internal definitions of the self. And by thrusting our researcher-bodies into cultural fields of bodily texts (through adornment, gesticulation, physicality, musculature, deportment, etc.), we must not only remain aware of how our bodies are intruding upon the bodies of others, but also of how we are engaging and producing various 'differential processes.'

This, of course, leads to my third and final point. Up to now I have argued that the best qualitative inquiries of the body—those which intercede on the anti-humane structures, practices, and symbolic acts within cultures of the active body—make use of both physical and ideological praxis to, as Laclau and Mouffe (1985) posited, *articulate* the human experience with broader contextual forces. These connections are meant to highlight "any practice establishing a relation among elements such that their identity is modified as a result of the articulatory practice" (Laclau & Mouffe, 1985, p. 105).[5] As Jennifer Daryl Slack (1996) quite carefully postulates, articulation is both that connection between broader contextual formations and the em-

---

5.These days, articulation's theoretical legacy is most often situated within Stuart Hall's work with the New Left and the Center for Contemporary Cultural Studies (CCCS) and his (1976) metaphoric lorry in conceptualizing the dialectic theory and method of articulation:

> 'articulate' means to utter, to speak forth, to be articulate. It carries that sense of language-ing, of expressing, etc. But we also speak of an 'articulated' lorry (truck): a lorry where the front (cab) and back (trailer) can, but need not necessarily, be connected to one another. The two parts are connected to each other, but through a specific linkage, than can be broken. An articulation is thus the form of the connections that can make a unity of two different elements, under certain conditions (p. 141).

pirical moment which we seek to establish, and at the same time the meth-odological *episteme* under which we operate. On the articulation of context and practice, and with particular regard to the ways in which practice pro-duces context, she writes: "The context is not something *out there, within which practices occur or which influence the development of practices.* Rather, *iden-tities, practices, and effect generally, constitute the very context in which they are practices, identities, or effects*" (p. 125, emphasis in original). As such, ours is not simply an exercise in context-mapping or abstracted corporeal cartography, but of using the political and politicized body to engage and interact with human action—articulatory praxis which produces, and is produced by, so-cial, political, and economic context.

I have further argued heretofore that the best of cultural analyses of the body are those which operate *from the ground up*; by developing carefully-crafted critical representations and performance texts of empirical embod-iment and praxis; those 'thick' (Geertz, 1973), rich representations of prac-tice that come through human interaction—through sharing knowledge and experience with other human beings. Those critical analyses are typic-ally generated by way of a conscientious, often stifling, self-awareness of the researcher and the research act (see Langellier, 1999). In critical studying the cultures of the body, we seek to better understand context through bod-ily practice, and the oppressive and liberatory potential of the human body as constrained by contextual forces.[6]

But if I have made anything clear here, I hope it is that such an engaged, interventionist, reflexive, reciprocal, and practiced method can sometimes get messy. Engaged studies of the body, following Rossman and Rallis (2003), are thus complicated projects of the "recursive, iterative, messy, te-dious, challenging, full of ambiguity, and exciting" (p. 4). In reflecting upon my own research, and my own body as a site of power within Southern social spaces, I have become increasingly frustrated at how, as an embodied sub-ject—and in spite of my best efforts to raise consciousness and thus bring

---

6. As Norman Denzin (2002) suggests, such radically-contextual, articulatory methods are those which:

1. Unsettle, criticize and challenge taken for granted, repressed meanings;
2. Invite moral and ethical dialogue, while reflexively clarifying their own moral position;
3. Engender resistance, and offer utopian thoughts about how things can be made different;
4. Demonstrate that they care, that they are kind;
5. Show, instead of tell, while using the rule that less is more;
6. Exhibit interpretive sufficiency, representational adequacy, and authentic adequacy;
7. Foster political, functional, collective and commitment.

about change to the iniquitous order of things in the South in which was raised—those corporeal power-knowledge structures that I my-self was trying to situate in context *were ultimately articulating me*. By projecting bodily performance of complicity in the 'new New South', I had failed to reject, or my embodied self had been overdetermined by, the dominant politics of white hetero-masculine privilege at work within these empirical spaces. Following Paula Saukko (2005), I tried to "forge the micro and the macro in a way that [did] not reduce the local experiences to props of social theories" (Saukko, 2005, p. 345), but that engagement brought be in close reflection with my former self.

And thus I have become all the more aware of the duality of subjectivity; at once a subject with some agency in shaping various experience (such as those in the research field), and yet subjected to the power imbedded in my own body, and our own performances (or past and present), and of my own Southern self. So I do not offer any answers on this front, but only use these reflections on the 'Self,' the body,' and the politics of reflexivity and articulation to call for a messier, bottom-up qualitative engagement with the body; a contemplative method of articulation(s) that situates the *body amongst bodies* and framed through both the *soi* and the *pour soi*. Instead, I defer to the late Alan Ingham (1997), who, in laying the groundwork for the academic discipline which has come to be known as 'physical cultural studies' and attending to its embodied-ethnographic imperative, sharply postulated:

> In 'physical culture,' all of us share genetically endowed bodies, but to talk about physical culture requires that we try to understand how the genetically endowed is socially constituted or socially constructed, as well as socially constituting and constructing. In this regard, we need to know how social structures and cultures impact our social presentation of our 'em-bodied' selves and how our embodied selves reproduce and transform structures and cultures; how our attitudes towards our bodies relate to our self- and social identities (p. 176).

Hence, in studying the complex relations of the body, the self, and pedagogy—and representing the 'self' and the 'Other' in just and reflexive ways—we must be aware of, and limit the violence created by, our 'em-bodied selves' along the way. For research is a journey—a complicated, self-inhabiting one—but to forgo the journey, to disengage and let those iniquitous bodies culture and the power relations of embodiment stand uninterrupted holds far more dire consequence.

References

A new dean at Ole Miss (1969, July 18). *Time, 94, 53, 55.*

Aanerud, R. (1997). Fictions of whiteness: Speaking the names of whiteness in U.S. literature. In R. Frankenberg (Ed.), *Displacing whiteness: Essays in social and cultural criticism* (pp. 35-59). Durham: Duke University Press.

Adorno, T., & Horkheimer, M. (1979). The culture industry: Enlightenment as mass deception (abridged). In J. Curran, M. Gurevitch & J. Woollacott (Eds.), *Mass communication and society* (pp. 349-383). Beverly Hills: Sage.

Aiken, C. S. (1998). *The cotton-plantation South since the Civil War.* Baltimore, MD: Johns Hopkins University Press.

Ainley, P. (2004). The new 'market state' and education. *Journal of Education Policy, 19*(4), 497-514.

Alderman, D. H. (2000). A street fit for a king: Naming places and commemoration in the American South. *The Professional Geographer*(52), 673-684.

Alexander, B. K. (2004). Black skin/white masks: The performative sustainability of whiteness (with apologies to Frantz Fanon) *Qualitative Inquiry, 10*(5), 647-672.

Alford, P. (2005, January 26). Who's that in the seats? It's Colonel Too, that's who. *Northeast Mississippi Daily Journal,* p. A1.

Allen, J. (2002). Symbolic economies: The 'culturalization' of economic knowledge. In P. d. Gay & M. Pryke (Eds.), *Cultural economy* (pp. 39-58). London: Sage.

Allen, T. (1994). *The invention of the white race*. London: Verso.

Allison, C. B. (1998). Okie narratives: Agency and whiteness. In J. L. Kincheloe, S. R. Steinberg, N. M. Rodriguez & R. E. Chennault (Eds.), *White reign: Deploying whiteness in America* (pp. 229-243). New York: St. Martin's Press.

Alred, J. (1983, September 7). Letter to the Editor. *The Daily Mississippian*, p. 2.

Altavilla, J. (2004, May 9). Easy Eli: Manning begins to reveal himself. *Houston Chronicle*, p. 1.

Althusser, L. (1971). *Lenin and philosophy and other essays*. London: New Left Books.

Andrews, D. L. (1996a). Deconstructing Michael Jordan: Reconstructing postindustrial America. *Sociology of Sport Journal, 13*(4), 315-318.

Andrews, D. L. (1996b). The fact(s) of Michael Jordan's blackness: Excavating a floating racial signifier. *Sociology of Sport Journal, 13*(2), 125-158.

Andrews, D. L. (2006, November 4). *Toward a physical cultural studies*. Paper presented at the Annual conference for the North American Society for the Sociology of Sport Vancouver, BC.

Andrews, D. L. (2008). Kinesiology's *Inconvenient Truth*: The physical cultural studies imperative. *Quest, 60*(1), 46-63.

Andrews, D. L. (2008). Kinesiology's inconvenient truth and the physical cultural studies imperative. *Quest, 60*(1), 45-60.

Andrews, D. L., & Giardina, M. D. (2008). Sport Without Guarantees: Toward a Cultural Studies That Matters. *Cultural Studies <=> Critical Methodologies, 8*(4), 395-422.

Andrews, D. L., & Jackson, S. J. (2001a). Introduction: Sport celebrities, public culture, and private experience. In D. L. Andrews & S. J. Jackson (Eds.), *Sport stars: The cultural politics of sport celebrity* (pp. 1-19). London: Routledge.

Andrews, D. L., & Jackson, S. J. (Eds.). (2001b). *Sport Stars: The cultural politics of sporting celebrity*. London: Routledge.

Andrews, K. T. (2004). *Freedom Is a constant struggle: The Mississippi Civil Rights Movement and its legacy*. Chicago: University of Chicago Press.

Ang, I. (1989). *Watching Dallas: Soap opera and the melodramatic imagination*. London: Routledge.

Angry reaction (1993, March 3). *The Daily Mississippian*, p. 3.

AP poll: Katrina changed Americans' thinking (2005, September 23). Retrieved October 1, 2005

Apple, M. W. (1995). Cultural capital and official knowledge. In M. Berube & C. Nelson (Eds.), *Higher education under fire: Politics, economics, and the crisis of the humanities* (pp. 91-107). New York: Routledge.

Apple, M. W. (1997). Consuming the other: Whiteness, education, and cheap french fries. In M. Fine, L. Weis, L. C. Powell & L. M. Wong (Eds.), *Off white: Readings on society, race, and culture* (pp. 121-128). New York: Routledge.

Apple, M. W. (2001). *Educating the 'Right' way: Markets, standards, God, and inequality.* New York: Routledge-Falmer.

Applebome, P. (1997). *Dixie Rising: How the South is shaping American values, politics, and culture.* San Diego: Harcourt Brace.

'Archie Who' could be state's top seller (1969, December 8). *The Daily Mississippian,* p. 7.

Athletic heads go to meet; Ole Miss to play La Crosse (1925, December 4). *The Mississippi,* p. 1.

Atkinson, T. (2005). Introduction. In T. Atkinson (Ed.), *The Body* (pp. 1-11). New York: Palgrave Macmillan.

Augé, M. (1995). *Non places: Introduction to an anthropology of supermodernity.* London: Verso.

Ayers, E. L. (1993). *The promise of the New South: Life after Reconstruction.* Oxford, UK: Oxford University Press.

Ayers, E. L. (2007). *The promise of the New South: Life after Reconstruction.* New York: Oxford University Press.

Ayers, W. C. (1997). Racing in America. In M. Fine, L. Weis, L. C. Powell & L. M. Wong (Eds.), *Off white: Readings on society, race, and culture* (pp. 129-136). New York: Routledge.

Baca, L. R. (2004). Native images in schools and the racially hostile environment. *Journal of Sport and Social Issues, 28*(1), 71-78.

Bailey, T. P. (1969). *Race orthodoxy in the South--and other aspects of the negro question.* New York: Negro Universities Press.

Baker, R. S. (1964). *Following the color line: American Negro citizenship in the Progressive Era.* New York: Harper & Row.

Baker, R. W. (1989). *Ole Miss football: The John Vaught Era, 1947-1970.* Unpublished M. A. Thesis, University of Mississippi, Oxford, MS.

Baldwin, R. (1993, April 16). 'Dixie' symbol of 'abominable ideology'. *The Daily Mississippian,* p. 2.

Bale, J. (1994). *Landscapes of modern sport.* Leicester: Leicester University Press.

Ballard, M. B. (2004). *Vicksburg: The campaign that opened the Mississippi.* Chapel Hill, NC: University of North Carolina Press.

Barbara Bush calls evacuees better off (2005, September 7). *New York Times,* p. online.

Barber, B. R. (1996). *Jihad vs. McWorld: How globalization and tribalism are reshaping the world.* New York: Ballantine Books.

Barkun, M. (1994). *Religion and the racist right: The origins of the Christian identity movement.* Chapel Hill, NC: University of North Carolina Press.

Barnett, C. (1999). Culture, government and spatiality: Reassessing the 'Foucault effect' in cultural-policy studies. *International Journal of Cultural Studies, 2*(3), 369-397.

Barnett urges stand (1965, May 13). *The Mississippian*, p. 1.

Barnhart, T. (2003, November 23). LSU 17, Ole Miss 14: Tigers take control in West. *Atlanta Journal-Constitution*, p. 1E.

Barrett, R. (2005). The myth of Southern isolation Retrieved March 20, 2005, from http://www.nationalist.org/docs/instruct/civics.html

Barrett, R. H. (1965). *Integration at Ole Miss*. Chicago: Quadrangle Books.

Barthes, R. (1957/1972). *Mythologies*. New York: Hill & Wang.

Barthes, R. (1972). *Mythologies*. New York: Hill & Wang.

Bartlett, M. (2003, September 10). Students vote for Col. Reb. *The Daily Mississippian*, p. 1.

Baudrillard, J. (1981). *For a critique of the political economy of the sign* (C. Levin, Trans.). St. louis, MO: Telos Press.

Baudrillard, J. (1983a). *Simulation and simulacra*. Anne Arbor, MI: University of Michigan Press.

Baudrillard, J. (1983b). *Simulations*. New York: Semiotext[e].

Baudrillard, J. (1988). *Jean Baudrillard: Selected writings*. London: Polity.

Baudrillard, J. (1989). *America* (C. Turner, Trans.). London: Verso.

Bauman, Z. (2002). *Society under siege*. Malden, MA: Blackwell.

Beatriz, M., & Patterson, D. (1998). America's racial unconscious: The invisibility of whiteness. In J. L. Kincheloe, S. R. Steinberg, N. M. Rodriguez & R. E. Chennault (Eds.), *White reign: Deploying whiteness in America* (pp. 103-121). New York: St. Martin's Press.

Becker, E. (1983, April 13). Rebel flag not just a symbol. *The Daily Mississippian*, p. 2.

Belanger, A. (2000). Sport venues and the spectacularization of urban spaces in North America. *International Review for the Sociology of Sport, 35*(3), 378-397.

Benjamin, W. (1969). *Illuminations*. New York: Schocken Books.

Benjamin, W. (1973). *Illuminations*. London: Fontana.

Benjamin, W. (1999). *The arcades project* (H. Eiland & K. McLaughlin, Trans.). Cambridge, MA: The Belknap Press of Harvard University Press.

Bentham, J. (1995). Panopticon. In M. Bozovic (Ed.), *The panopticon writings* (pp. 29-95). London: Verso.

Benz, R. (1983, April 15). BSU reaction questioned. *The Daily Mississippian*, p. 2.

Berry, C. C. (1987). *A history of higher education for women in Mississippi*. Unpublished Master's thesis, University of Mississippi, Oxford, MS.

Best, S., & Kellner, D. (1999). Debord, cybersituations, and the interactive spectacle. *Substance*(90), 129-154.

Beverley, J. (2005). *Testimonio*, subalternity, and narrative authority. In N. K. Denzin & Y. S. Lincoln (Eds.), *The sage handbook of qualitative research* (3rd ed., pp. 547-558303-558342). Thousand Oaks, CA: Sage.

Bhabba, H. (1994). *The location of culture*. New York: Routledge.

Bibbs, C. (1983a, October 25). Six biracial task forces set. *The Daily Mississippian*, p. 1.

Bibbs, C. (1983b, November 2). Klan frat party garb upsets Black group. *The Daily Mississippian*, p. 1.

Bilbo endorses removal of Ole Miss to capital (1928, January 20). *The Mississippian*, pp. 1, 8.

Billington, R. A., & Ridge, M. (2001). *Westward expansion: A history of the American frontier*. Albuquerque, NM: University of New Mexico Press.

Bishop, R. (2009). It hurts the team even more : Differences in coverage by sports journalists of White and African-American athletes who engage in contract holdouts. *Journal of Sports Media, 4*(1), 55-84.

Black, D. P. (1997). *Dismantling black manhood: An historical and literary analysis of the legacy of slavery*. New York: Garland Publishing.

Blaudschun, M. (2004, April 17). Manning looks like a throwback. *Boston Globe*, p. E3.

Blight, D. W., & Simpson, B. D. (Eds.). (1997). *Union and emancipation: Essays on politics and race in the Civil War era*. Kent, OH: Kent State University Press.

Bok, D. (2004). *Universities in the marketplace: The commercialization of higher education*. Princeton, NJ: Princeton University Press.

Bonner, F. (2003). *Ordinary television: Analyzing popular TV*. London: Sage.

Bonner, R. E. (2002). *Colors and blood: Flag passions of the Confederate South*. Princeton, NJ: Princeton University Press.

Bonnett, A. (1996). "White studies": The problems and projects of a new research agenda. *Theory, Culture & Society, 13*(2), 145-155.

Bonnett, A. (2000). *White identities: Historical and international perspectives*. London: Prentice Hall.

Bontemps, A. (2001). *The punished self: Surviving slavery in the Colonial South*. Ithaca, NY: Cornell University Press.

Boorstin, D. (1971). *The image: A guide to pseudo-events in America*. New York: Atheneum.

Borucki, W. (2003). "You're Dixie's football pride": American college football and the resurgence of southern identity. *Identities: Global Studies in Culture and Power, 10*(3), 477-494.

Bourdieu, P. (1977). *Outline of a theory of practice*. Cambridge, UK: Cambridge University Press.

Bourdieu, P. (1984). *Distinction: A social critique of the judgement of taste*. Cambridge: Harvard University Press.

Bourdieu, P. (1985). The social space and genesis of groups. *Social Science Information, 24*(2), 195-220.

Bourdieu, P. (1986a). The forms of capital. In J. G. Richardson (Ed.), *Handbook of theory and research for the sociology of education* (pp. 241-258). Westport: Greenwood Press.

Bourdieu, P. (1986b). The forms of capital. In J. G. Richardson (Ed.), *Handbook of theory and research for the sociology of education* (pp. 241-260). New York: Greenwood Press.

Bourdieu, P. (1990). *The logic of practice* (R. Nice, Trans.). Stanford, CA: Stanford University Press.

Bourdieu, P. (1993). *The field of cultural production*. New York: Columbia University Press.

Bourdieu, P. (1996). The work of time. In A. E. Komter (Ed.), *The gift: An interdisciplinary perspective* (pp. 135-147). Amsterdam: Amsterdam University Press.

Bourdieu, P. (1998a). *Distinction: A social critique of the judgment of taste* (R. Nice, Trans.). Cambridge, MA: Harvard University Press.

Bourdieu, P. (1998b). The state, economics and sport. *Culture, Sport, Society, 1*(2), 15-21.

Bourdieu, P., & Wacquant, L. J. D. (1992). *An invitation to reflexive sociology*. London: The University of Chicago Press.

Bracken, L. (1997). *Guy Debord: Revolutionary*. Feral House: Venice, CA.

Bratich, J. Z. (2003). Making politics reasonable: Conspiracism, subjectification, and governing through styles of thought. In J. Z. Bratich, J. Packer & C. McCarthy (Eds.), *Foucault, cultural studies, and governmentality* (pp. 67-100). Albany, NY: State University of New York Press.

Bratich, J. Z., Packer, J., & McCarthy, C. (2003). Governing the present. In J. Z. Bratich, J. Packer & C. McCarthy (Eds.), *Foucault, cultural studies, and governmentality* (pp. 3-22). Albany, NY: State University of New York Press.

Brattain, M. (2001). *The politics of whiteness: Race, workers, and culture in the modern South*. Princeton, NJ: Princeton University Press.

Breed, A. G. (2003, July 1). Dixie fading at Ole Miss. *Washington Times*, p. LN.

Brigance, G. (1951, November 16). Rebel yells again ring amid Dixie Week Parade, pep rally, and Herman Dance. *The Mississippian*, p. 7.

Brower, S. (1962a, September 20). Editorial. *The Mississippian*, p. 2.

Brower, S. (1962b, September 27). Meredith rejected again. *The Mississippian*, p. 1.

Brower, S. (1962c, September 28). Crowd cheers Barnett. *The Mississippian*, p. 1.

Brower, S. (1962d, October 1). Editorial. *The Mississippian*, p. 2.

Brower, S. (1962e, October 31). UM 'get tough policy' appears lost in crowd. *The Mississippian*, p. 2.

Brown, E. B. (2000). Negotiating and transforming the public sphere: African American political life in the transition from slavery to freedom. In J. Dailey, G. E. Gilmore & B. Simon (Eds.), *Jumpin'*

Jim Crow: Southern politics from Civil War to civil rights (pp. 28-66). Princeton, NJ: Princeton University Press.

Brown, J. R. (1998). Affirmative action and epistemology. In R. Post & M. Rogin (Eds.), *Race and representation: Affirmative action* (pp. 333-338). New York: Zone Books.

Brown, M. M. (1940). *The University Greys: Company A . Eleventh Mississippi Regiment, Army of Northern Virginia*. Richmond, VA: Garrett and Massie.

Brownstein, H. (1940, September 20). George will top bruiser is Rebs have good year. *The Mississippian*, p. 9.

Brumfield, P. (1970, February 27). Charges dropped. *The Daily Mississippian*, p. 1.

Buber, M. (1937/2000). *I and thou* (R. G. Smith, Trans. 1st Scribner Classics ed.). New York: Scribner.

Buck-Morss, S. (1991). *The dialectics of seeing: Walter Benjamin and the arcades project*. Cambridge: MIT Press.

Buck-Morss, S. (2000). *Dreamworld and catastrophe: The passing of mass utopia in East and West*. Cambridge, MA: MIT Press.

Burgin, R. (1954, November 26). Unreconstructed Rebels have made it the best Dixie Week ever held on campus. *The Mississippian*, pp. 1, 4.

Burnham, B. (2003, September 26). Between the goalposts. *The Clarksdale Press Register*, p. 12.

Butler, J. (1990). *Gender trouble: Feminism and the subversion of identity*. London: Routledge.

Butler, J. (1993). *Bodies that matter: On the discursive limits of "sex"*. New York: Routledge.

Butler, J. (1997). *Excitable speech: A politics of the performative*. London: Routledge.

Butler, J. (2000). Critically queer. In P. d. Gay, J. Evans & P. Redman (Eds.), *Identity: A reader* (pp. 108-118). London: Sage.

Cabaniss, A. (1971). *The University of Mississippi: Its first hundred years* (2nd ed.). Hattiesburg, MS: University & College Press of Mississippi.

Cagin, S., & Dray, P. (1988). *We are not afraid: The story of Goodman, Schwerner, and Chaney and the Civil Rights Campaign for Mississippi*. New York: Scribner.

Calkins, G. (2003, November 22). Manning returned for a year like this. *Commercial Appeal*, p. D1.

Campus States' Righters elect Bowen as leader (1948, July 29). *The Mississippian*, pp. 1, 4.

Canaan, J. E., & Shumar, W. (2008). Higher education in the era of globalization and neoliberalism. In J. E. Canaan & W. Shumar (Eds.), *Structure and agency in the neoliberal university* (pp. 1-32). New York: Routledge.

Carrington, B. (2001). Postmodern blackness and the celebrity sports star: Ian Wright, "race" and English identity. In D. L. Andrews & S. J.

Jackson (Eds.), *Sport Stars: The cultural politics of sporting celebrity* (pp. 102-123). London: Routledge.

Carrington, E., Scovel, A., & Salu, J. (2005, January 27). Buying diversity *The Daily Mississippian*, p. 2.

Carspecken, P. (1999). *Four scenes for posing the question of meaning and other essays in critical philosophy and critical methodology*. New York: Peter Lang.

Casey, E. S. (1997). *The fate of place: A philosophical history*. Berkeley, CA: University of California Press.

Cash, W. J. (1941/1991). *The mind of the South*. New York: Vintage.

Cassreino, T. R. (1983, October 21). Rebel flag: Group calls for support of Confederate symbols. *The Daily Mississippian*, p. 1.

Castells, M. (1985). High technology, economic restructuring, and the urban-regional process in the United States. *Urban Affairs Annual Reviews, 28*, 11-40.

Catalogue of the officers and students of the University of Mississippi (1866). (University Catalogue). Jackson, MS: University of Mississippi.

Catalogue of the officers and students of the University of Mississippi (1884). (University Catalogue). Jackson, MS: University of Mississippi.

Catalogue of the officers and students of the University of Mississippi (1887). (University Catalogue). Jackson, MS: University of Mississippi.

Catsam, D. (2003). Hiring a black head coach in 2003 is news? Yeah, unfortunately. *History News Network,* (1847), 1-2

Certeau, M. d. (1984). *The practice of everyday life*. Berkeley: University of California Press.

Chalmers, D. M. (1981). *Hooded Americanism: The history of the Ku Klux Klan* (3rd ed.). Durham, NC: Duke University Press.

Chancellor blames disturbances on news conference (1963, January 11). *Jackson Daily News*, pp. 1, 16.

Charm school opens today (1964, March 17). *The Mississippian*, p. 6.

Cheerer reform, race bill passed (1970, March 4). *The Daily Mississippian*, p. 1.

Chitham, R. (2004). *The classical orders of architecture*. Burlington, MA: Architectural Press.

Chomsky, N. (2002, September 29). Assaulting solidarity - privatizing education Retrieved June 1, 2005, from http://www.uct.ac.za/org/aa/chomsk.htm

Cleveland, R. (2000). *Vaught: The man and his legacy*. Birmingham, AL: Epic Sports.

Cleveland, R. (2003, June 19). Colonel not exactly a longtime tradition. *Clarion-Ledger*, p. 19.

Cobb, J. C. (1992). *The most southern place on earth: The Mississippi Delta and the roots of regional identity*. New York: Oxford University Press.

Cobb, J. C. (1999). *Redefining Southern culture: Mind and identity in the modern South*. Athens, GA: University of Georgia Press.

Coffey, A. J. (1999). *The ethnographic self: Fieldwork and the representation of identity*. Thousand Oaks, CA: Sage.

Cohodas, N. (1997). *The band played Dixie: Race and the liberal conscience at Ole Miss*. New York: The Free Press.

Collins, D. (Ed.). (1970). *Ole Miss*. Oxford, MS: University of Mississippi.

Confederate heroes (1899, unknown). *The University Record*, p. 1.

Connell, R. (1983). *Which way is up?* Sydney: George Allen and Unwin.

Connell, R. W. (1990). An Iron Man: The body and some contradictions of hegemonic masculinity. In M. A. Messner & D. F. Sabo (Eds.), *Sport, men, and the gender order: Critical feminist perspectives* (pp. 83-95). Champaign: Human Kinetics.

Cook, A. (1988, July 21). Black frat one step closer to move. *The Daily Mississippian*, p. 1.

Coombe, R. J. (1998). *The cultural life of intellectual properties: Authorship, appropriation, and the law*. Durham, NC: Duke University Press.

Corlew, J. (1963, September 24). Gun exposed: UM segegrated once again. *The Mississippian*, pp. 1, 4.

Coski, J. M. (2005). *The Confederate battle flag: America's most embattled symbol*. Cambridge, MA: The Belknap Press (Harvard University).

Cowden, J. A. (2001). Southernization of the nation and nationalization of the South: Racial conservatism, social welfare and white partisans in the United States, 1956-92. *British Journal of Political Science*, *31*(2), 277-301.

Cox, K. L. (2003). *Dixie's daughters: The United Daughters of the Confederacy and the preservation of Confederate culture*. Gainesville, FL: University Press of Florida.

Crang, M. (2000). Relics, places and unwritten geographies in the work of Michel de Certeau. In M. Crang & N. Thrift (Eds.), *Thinking space* (pp. 136-153). London: Routledge.

Crary, D. (2005, October 14). Groups threaten to boycott American Girl. *Associated Press*, pp. 1-2. from http://cnn.netscape.cnn.com/news/story.jsp?idq=/ff/story/0001/20051014/1834877091.htm&sc=1110&photoid=20031108NY121.

Crosby, F. J. (1997). Confessions of an affirmative action mama. In M. Fine, L. Weis, L. C. Powell & L. M. Wong (Eds.), *Off white: Readings on society, race, and culture* (pp. 179-186). New York: Routledge.

Crossley, N. (2007). Researching embodiment by way of 'body techniques'. In C. Shilling (Ed.), *Embodying sociology: Retrospective, progress and prospects* (pp. 80-94). Malden, Ma: Blackwell.

Csordas, T. J. (1990). Embodiment as paradigm for anthropology. *Ethos*, *18*(1), 5-47.

D'Souza, D. (1995). *The end of racism: Principles for a multiracial society*. New York: The Free Press.

Dabney, B. (1988, August 26). Black fraternity progressing after blaze dampens move. *The Daily Mississippian*, pp. 1, 8.

Dailey, J., Gilmore, G. E., & Simon, B. (2000). Introduction. In J. Dailey, G. E. Gilmore & B. Simon (Eds.), *Jumpin' Jim Crow: Southern politics from Civil War to civil rights* (pp. 3-6). Princeton, NJ: Princeton University Press.

Davis, K. (2007). Reclaiming women's bdies: Colonialist trope or critical epistemology? In C. Shilling (Ed.), *Embodying sociology: Retrospective, progress and prospects* (pp. 50-64). Malden, Ma: Blackwell.

Davis, L. E. (2005, March 1). Preserving 'Ole Miss' through traditions. *The Daily Mississippian*, p. 2.

De Cordova, R. (1990). *Picture personalities: The emergence of the star system in America*. Urbana/Chicago: University of Illinois Press.

Debord, G. (1967/1994). *The society of the spectacle* (D. Nicholson-Smith, Trans.). New York: Zone.

Debord, G. (Writer) (1981a). Critique of seperation, *Situationist international anthology*. Berkeley, CA: Bureau of Public Secrets.

Debord, G. (1981b). Definitions (K. Knabb, Trans.). In K. Knabb (Ed.), *Situationist international anthology* (pp. 45). Berkeley, CA: Bureau of Public Secrets.

Debord, G. (1981c). How not to understand Situationist books. In K. Knabb (Ed.), *Situationist International anthology* (pp. 265-266). Berkeley, CA: Bureau of Public Secrets.

Debord, G. (1981d). Introduction to a critique of urban geography (K. Knabb, Trans.). In K. Knabb (Ed.), *Situationist international anthology* (pp. 5-7). Berkeley, CA: Bureau of Public Secrets.

Debord, G. (1981e). Perspectives for conscious alterations in everyday life (K. Knabb, Trans.). In K. Knabb (Ed.), *Situationist international anthology* (pp. 68-75). Berkeley, CA: Bureau of Public Secrets.

Debord, G. (1981f). Theory of derive (K. Knabb, Trans.). In K. Knabb (Ed.), *Situationist international anthology* (pp. 50-54). Berkeley, CA: Bureau of Public Secrets.

Debord, G. (1990). *Comments on the society of the spectacle* (M. Imrie, Trans.). London: Verso.

Debord, G. (1991). *Panegyric* (J. Brook, Trans.). London: Verso.

Debord, G. (1997, Winter). Theses on cultural revolution. *October*, 90-92.

Debord, G. (2002). The society of the spectacle Retrieved February 16, 2002, from http://www.bopsecrets.org/SI/debord/index.htm

Debord, G., & Wolman, G. J. (1981). Methods of détournement (K. Knabb, Trans.). In K. Knabb (Ed.), *Situationist international anthology* (pp. 8-13). Berkeley, CA: Bureau of Public Secrets.

Defiant Barnett hailed at game (1962, September 30). *Commerical Appeal*, p. 1.

Deleuze, G. (1988). *Foucault*. Minneapolis, MN: University of Minnesota Press.

Deleuze, G. (1994). *Difference and repetition* (P. Patton, Trans.). New York: Columbia University Press.

Deleuze, G., & Guattari, F. (1983a). *Anti-Oedipus*. Minneapolis, MN: University of Minnesota Press.

Deleuze, G., & Guattari, F. (1983b). *On the line*. New York: Semiotext(e).

Delgado, R., & Stefancic, J. (1997). *Critical white studies: Looking behind the mirror*. Philadelphia, PA: Temple University Press.

Denzin, N. K. (1991). *Images of postmodern society: Social theory and contemporary cinema*. London: Sage.

Denzin, N. K. (2002). Confronting ethnography's crisis of representation. *Journal of Contemporary Ethnography, 31*(4), 482-490.

Denzin, N. K., & Lincoln, Y. S. (2000). Introduction: The discipline and practice of qualitative research. In N. K. Denzin & Y. S. Lincoln (Eds.), *Handbook of Qualitative Research* (2nd ed., pp. 1-29). Thousand Oaks, CA: Sage.

Derrida, J. (1974). *Of grammatology*. Baltimore: The Johns Hopkins University Press.

Derrida, J. (1976). *Of grammatology* (G. C. Spivak, Trans.). Baltimore, MD: The Johns Hopkins University Press.

Derrida, J. (1977). *Writing and difference*. London: Routledge & Kegan Paul.

Derrida, J. (1982). Differance *Margins of philosophy* (pp. 1-27). Chicago: University of Chicago Press.

Diprose, R. (2002). *Corporeal generosity: On giving with Nietzsche, Merleau-Ponty, and Levinas*. New York: State University of New York Press.

Dittmer, J. (1995). *Local people: The struggle for Civil Rights in Mississippi*. Champaign, IL: University of Illinois Press.

Dixie Week events may be reported by *Chicago Tribune* (1954, November 5). *Mississippian*, p. 1.

Dixon, F. (1913, February 8). Progess of the 19th Century lay in the rise of the individual. *The Mississippian*, p. 1.

Dodson, J. (1997, March 21). Ole Miss continues struggle with history. *The Daily Mississippian*, pp. 1, 8.

Dovidio, J. F., Mann, J., & Gaertner, S. L. (1989). Resistance to affirmative action: The implications of aversive racism. In F. Blanchard & F. Crosby (Eds.), *Affirmative action in perspective* (pp. 83-97). New York: Springer-Verlag.

Doyle, A. (1996). Bear Bryant: Symbol for the embattled South. *Colby Quarterly, 2*(1), 72-86.

Doyle, A. (2002a). An atheist in Alabama is someone who doesn't believe in Bear Bryant: A symbol for an embattled south. In P. B. Miller (Ed.), *The sporting world of the modern south* (pp. 247-275). Urbana, Ill: University of Illinois Press.

Doyle, A. (2002b). Turning the tide: College football and southern progressivism. In P. B. Miller (Ed.), *The sporting world of the modern south* (pp. 101-125). Urbana, Ill: University of Illinois Press.

Doyle, W. (2001). *An American insurrection: The battle of Oxford, Mississippi, 1962*. New York: Doubleday.

Dr. Hendleston talks on college spirit (1915, April 14). *The Mississippian*, p. 1.

Dr. J. P. Smith makes address (1912, March 30). *The Mississippian*, p. 1.

Drake, W. A., & Holsworth, R. D. (1996). *Affirmative action and the stalled quest for black progress*. Urbana, IL: University of Illinois Press.

Drape, J. (2003, November 22). Manning rewrites the family legacy. *New York Times*, p. D1.

Dreyfus, H., & Rabinow, P. (1983). *Michel Foucault: Beyond structuralism and hermeneutics*. Chicago, IL: The University of Chicago Press.

Du Bois, W. E. B. (1903/1996). *The souls of black folk*. New York: Penguin.

Dubois, D. (1948, July 22). Fifty-five Ole Miss students attend States' Rights meeting. *The Mississippian*, pp. 1, 3.

Duerson, A. (2004, September 23). Roadtrip: University of Mississippi. *Sports Illustrated On Campus*, 10-11.

Dumas, K. (1982, September 2). Hawkins responds to press. *The Daily Mississippi*, p. 1.

Duncan, M. C. (1993). Representation and the gun that points backwards. *Journal of Sport and Social Issues, 17*(1), 42-46.

"Dutch" Stengel coaching baseball (1914, February 18). *The Mississippian*, p. 1.

Dyer, R. (1979). *Stars*. London: BFI.

Dyer, R. (1986). *Heavenly bodies: Film stars and society*. London: BFI Macmillan.

Dyer, R. (1997). *White*. New York: Routledge.

Eakin, W. A. (1856, November 11). *Record book of the faculty minutes from the University of Mississippi (9th Session)*, Oxford, MS.

Eco, U. (1986). Function and sign: Semiotics of architecture. In M. Gottdiener & A. Lagopoulos (Eds.), *The city and the sign* (pp. 55-86). New York: Columbia University Press.

Egerton, J. (1974). *The Americanization of Dixie: The Southernization of America*. New York: Harper's Magazine Press.

Elias, N. (1982). *Power and Civility: The civilizing process* (E. Jephcott, Trans. Vol. 2). New York: Pantheon.

Ellis, C. (1997). Evocative autoethnography: Writing emotionally about our lives. In W. G. Tierney & Y. S. Lincoln (Eds.), *Representation and the text* (pp. 115-139). New York: State University of New York Press.

Ellison, R. (1952). *Invisible man*. New York: Random House.

Emmerich, W. (2005). Effort to change mascot is misguided Retrieved January 11, 2005, from http://www.saveolemiss.com/

Eskew, G. T. (1997). *But for Birmingham: The local and national movements in the civil rights struggle*. Chapel Hill, NC: University of North Carolina Press.

Evans, S. M. (1989). Myth against history: The case of Southern womanhood. In P. Gerster & N. Cords (Eds.), *Myth and Southern history: The New South* (pp. 141-155). Champaign-Urbana, IL: University of Illinois Press.

Fabijancic, T. (2001). The prison in the Arcade: A carceral diagram of consumer space. *Mosaic, 34*(3), 141-157.

Fair, G. (1970a, February 13). Dent, Nichols speak for campus blacks. *The Daily Mississippian,* pp. 4-5.

Fair, G. (1970b, February 26). . . . Finally gone too far. *The Daily Mississippian,* p. 1.

Fanon, F. (1986). *Black skin, white masks.* London: Pluto Press.

Farnell, B. (2004). Zero-sum game: An update on the Native American mascot controversy at the University of Illinois. *Journal of Sport and Social Issues, 28*(2), 212-215.

Faust, D. G. (1988). *The creation of Confederate nationalism: Ideology and identity in the Civil War South.* Baton Rouge, LA: Louisiana State University Press.

Fay, B. (1987). *Critical social science.* Ithaca, NY: Cornell University Press.

Feagin, J. R., & Vera, H. (1995). *White racism: The basics.* New York: Rooutledge.

Featherstone, M. (1982). The body in consumer culture. *Theory, Culture & Society, 1*(2), 18-33.

Ferber, A. L. (1998a). Constructing whiteness: The intersections of race and gender in US white supremacist discourse. *Ethnic and Racial Studies, 21*(1), 48-63.

Ferber, A. L. (1998b). *White man falling: Race, gender, and white supremacy.* Lanham, MD: Roman & Littlefield.

Ferguson, R. (1990). Introduction: Invisible center. In R. Ferguson (Ed.), *Out there: Marginalization and contemporary cultures* (pp. 9-14). New York: New Museum of Contemporary Art and MIT Press.

Fernandez-Balboa, J. M., & Muros, B. (2006). The hegemonic triumverate--ideologies, discourses, and habitus in sport and physical education: Implications and suggestions. *Quest, 58*(2), 197-221.

Fielding, H. (1999). Depth of embodiment: Spatial and temporal bodies in Foucault and Merleau-Ponty. *Philosophy Today, 43*(1), 73-85.

Fight erupts between Negro and classmate (1964, September 23). *The Mississippian,* p. 1.

Finley, J., & Yoste, E. (2001, November 8). Fraternity party under investigation *The Daily Mississippian,* p. Online.

First Dixie Week celebration gets into full swing (1950, December 1). *The Mississippian,* pp. 1, 8.

Fisher Fishkin, S. (1995). Interrogating "Whiteness", complicating "Blackness": Remapping American Culture. *American Quaterly, 47*(3), 428-466.

Flaherty, M. G. (2002). The crisis in representation: A brief history and some questions. *Journal of Contemporary Ethnography, 31*(4), 479-482.

Flautt, A. (1954a, November 5). Secession from Union, slave auction, Ku Klux Klan to highlight Dixie Week. *The Mississippian,* pp. 1, 8.

Flautt, A. (1954b, November 19). Star and bars are going up again; open season on Yankees starts Monday. *The Mississippian*, p. 1.

Foster, G. M. (1987). *Ghosts of the Confederacy: Defeat, the Lost Cause and the emergence of the New South, 1865-1913*. New York: Oxford University Press.

Foucault, M. (1975). *The birth of the clinic: An archaeology of medical perception*. New York: Vintage Books.

Foucault, M. (1976). *The archeology of knowledge and the discourse of language*. New York: Harper Colophon.

Foucault, M. (1977a). *Discipline and punish: The birth of the prison* (A. Sheridan, Trans.). New York: Vintage Books.

Foucault, M. (1977b). Nietzsche, genealogy, history. In D. F. Bouchard (Ed.), *Language, counter-memory, practice: Selected essays and interviews* (pp. 139-164). Ithaca, NY: Cornell University Press.

Foucault, M. (1978). *The history of sexuality* (Vol. 1). New York: Pantheon.

Foucault, M. (1980). Questions on geography. In C. Gordon (Ed.), *Power/knowledge: Selected interviews and other writings, 1972-1977* (pp. 63-77). New York: Pantheon.

Foucault, M. (1982a). Technologies of the Self. In H. G. a. P. H. H. L.H. Martin (Ed.), *Technologies of the Self* (pp. 16-49). Amherst, MA: University of Massachusetts Press.

Foucault, M. (1982b). The subject and power. In H. Dreyfus & P. Rabinow (Eds.), *Michel Foucault: Beyond structuralism and hermeneutics* (pp. 208-226). Chicago: University of Chicago Press.

Foucault, M. (1984a). Space, knowledge, and power. In P. Rabinow (Ed.), *The Foucault Reader* (pp. 239-256). New York: Pantheon.

Foucault, M. (1984b). Truth and power. In P. Rabinow (Ed.), *The Foucault Reader* (pp. 51-75). New York: Pantheon Books.

Foucault, M. (1988a). Technologies of the self. In L. H. Martin, H. Gutman & P. H. Hutton (Eds.), *Technologies of the self: A seminar with Michel Foucault* (pp. 16-49). Amherst, MA: University of Massachusetts Press.

Foucault, M. (1988b). *The history of sexuality, volume 1: An introduction*. New York: Vintage Books.

Foucault, M. (1994a). Maurice Florence (C. Porter, Trans.). In G. Gutting (Ed.), *The Cambridge companion to Foucault* (pp. 321-352). Cambridge, England: Cambridge University Press.

Foucault, M. (1994b). *The order of things: An archaeology of the human sciences*. New York: Vintage.

Foucault, M. (2001). Power/knowledge. In S. Seidman & J. C. Alexander (Eds.), *The new social theory reader: Contemporary debates* (pp. 69-75). London: Routledge.

Frankenberg, R. (1993). *The social construction of whiteness: White women, race matters*. Minneapolis: University of Minnesota Press.

Frankenberg, R. (1994). Whiteness and Americanness: Examining constructions of race, culture, and nation in white women's life narratives. In S. Gregory & R. Sanjek (Eds.), *Race* (pp. 62-77). New Brunswick: Rutgers University Press.

Frankenberg, R. (1994). Whiteness and Americanness: Explaining constructions of race, culture, and nation in White women's life narratives. In S. Gregory & R. Stanjek (Eds.), *Race* (pp. 62-77). New Brunswick, N.J.: Rutgers University Press.

Frankenberg, R. (1997). Introduction: Local whitenesses, localizing whiteness. In R. Frankenberg (Ed.), *Displacing Whiteness: Essays in social and cultural criticism* (pp. 1-34). Durham, NC: Duke University Press.

Frankenberg, R. (2001). The mirage of an unmarked whiteness. In B. B. Rasmussen, E. Klinenberg, I. J. Nexica & M. Wray (Eds.), *The making and unmaking of whiteness* (pp. 72-96). Durham, NC: Duke University Press.

Franklin, J. H., & Moss, A. A. (2000). *From slavery to freedom: A history of African Americans.* New York: McGraw-Hill/Knopf.

Frederick, C. R. (1999). *A good day to be here: Tailgating at the Grove at Ole Miss.* Unpublished Doctoral Dissertation, Indiana University, Bloomington, IN.

Frederickson, K. (2000). "As a man, I am interested in States' Rights": Gender, race, and the family in the Dixiecrat Party, 1948-1950. In J. Dailey, G. E. Gilmore & B. Simon (Eds.), *Jumpin' Jim Crow: Southern politics from Civil War to Civil Rights* (pp. 260-274). Princeton, NJ: Princeton University Press.

Frederickson, K. (2001). *The Dixiecrat revolt and the end of the solid South, 1932-1968.* Chapel Hill, NC: University of North Carolina Press.

Freeland, L. (1983a, April 13). BSU protests annual pictures. *The Daily Mississippian,* p. 1.

Freeland, L. (1983b, April 18). Officials hear black demands. *The Daily Mississippian,* p. 1.

Freire, P. (1970/2006). *Pedagogy of the oppressed.* New York: Continuum.

Friend, C. T., & Glover, L. (Eds.). (2004). *Southern manhood: Perspectives on masculinity in the Old South.* Athens, GA: University of Georgia Press.

Frow, J., & Morris, M. (2000). Cultural studies. In N. K. Denzin & Y. S. Lincoln (Eds.), *Handbook of Qualitative Research* (2nd ed., pp. 315-346). Thousand Oaks, CA: Sage.

Fulford, R. (2001, July 3). David Riesman's *The Lonely Crowd. The National Post,* p. LN.

Fullbrook, K., & Fullbrook, E. (1994). *Simone de Beauvoir and Jean-Paul Sartre: The remaking of a Twentieth-Century legend.* New York: BasicBooks.

Furr, F. (1942, October 30). University Greys approved as new campus organization. *The Mississippian,* pp. 1, 8.

Fusco, C. (2005). Cultural landscapes of purification: Sports spaces and discourses of whiteness. *Sociology of Sport Journal, 22*(3), 283-310.

Fusco, C. (2006). Spatializing the (Im)Proper Subject: The Geographies of Abjection in Sport and Physical Activity Space. *Journal of Sport & Social Issues, 30*(1), 5-28.

Gabriel, J. (1998). *Whitewash: Racialized politics in the media.* London: Routledge.

Gallagher, C. A. (2003). Playing the white ethnic card: Using ethnic identity to deny contemporary racism. In A. W. Doane & E. Bonilla-Silva (Eds.), *White out: The continuing significance of racism* (pp. 145-158). New York: Routledge.

Gamson, J. (1994). *Claims to fame: Celebrity in comtemporary America.* Berkeley: University of California Press.

Gamson, J. (2001). The assembly line of greatness: Celebrity in twentieth-century America. In C. L. Harrington & D. D. Bielby (Eds.), *Popular culture: Production and consumption* (pp. 259-282). Malden, Mass.: Blackwell.

Garland, L. C. (1870, October 5). *Record book of the faculty minutes from the University of Mississippi (20th Session)*, Oxford, MS.

Garland, L. C. (1872a, January 16). *Record book of the faculty minutes from the University of Mississippi (21st Session)*, Oxford, MS.

Garland, L. C. (1872b, January 23). *Record book of the faculty minutes from the University of Mississippi (21st Session)*, Oxford, MS.

Garland, L. C. (1874, March 24). *Record book of the faculty minutes from the University of Mississippi (23rd Session)*, Oxford, MS.

Garrett, H. E. (1964). Racial differences: There are such things. *Western Destiny*, 10-11.

Garrett, H. E. (1973, Fall). Intelligence linked to genetics. *Instauration, 5*.

Gaston, P. M. (1989). The New South creed: A study in Southern myth-making. In P. Gerster & N. Cords (Eds.), *Myth and Southern history: The New South* (pp. 17-32). Champaign-Urbana, IL: University of Illinois Press.

Geertz, C. (1973). *The interpretation of cultures: Selected essays.* New York: Basic Books.

Geertz, C. (1988). *Works and lives: The anthropologist as author.* Palo Alto, CA: Stanford University Press.

Genovese, E. D. (2003). *The political economy of slavery: Studies in the economy and society of the Slave South.* Middletown, CT: Wesleyan University Press.

Giddens, A. (1984). *The constitution of society.* Cambridge: Polity Press.

Giddens, A. (1990). *The consequences of modernity.* Cambridge: Polity Press.

Giddens, A. (1991). *Modernity and self-identity: Self and society in the late modern age.* Cambridge: Polity Press.

Gildea, W. (2002, August 4). At Ole Miss, passing the torch. *Washington Post*, p. D01.

Gilroy, P. (2004). Melancholia and multiculture. Retrieved March 22, 2004, from openDemocracy, Ltd.: http://www.opendemocracy.net/con-

tent/articles/PDF/2035.pdf?redirect2=/debates/article-1-111-
2035.jsp

Gilroy, P. (2005). *Postcolonial melancholia*. New York: Columbia University
Press.

Ginn, M. (Writer) (2003). The University Greys: From students to soldiers
[Documentary]. In M. Ginn, J. Schefflel & S. Miller (Producer).
Oxford, MS: Grandaddy's Farm Productions.

Giroux, H. (1985). Critical pedagogy, cultural politics and the discourse of
experience. *Journal of Education, 167*(2), 22-41.

Giroux, H. (2007). Cultural studies as a performative practice. In N. Denzin & M. Giardina (Eds.), *Contesting Empire, Globalizing Dissent:
Cultural Studies After 9/11* (pp. 213-230). Boulder: Paradigm.

Giroux, H. A. (1994). Living dangerously: Identity politics and the new cultural racism. In H. Giroux & P. McLaren (Eds.), *Between borders:
Pedagogy and the politics of cultural studies*. New York: Routledge.

Giroux, H. A. (1997a). Racial politics and the pedagogy of whiteness. In M.
Hill (Ed.), *Whiteness: A critical reader* (pp. 294-315). New York:
New York University Press.

Giroux, H. A. (1997b). Rewriting the discourse of racial identity: Towards a
pedagogy and politics of whiteness. *Harvard Educational Review,
67*(2), 285-320.

Giroux, H. A. (1997c). White squall: Resistance and the pedagogy of whiteness. *Cultural Studies, 11*(3), 376-389.

Giroux, H. A. (1998). Youth, memory work, and the racial politics of whiteness. In J. L. Kincheloe, S. R. Steinberg, N. M. Rodriguez & R. E.
Chennault (Eds.), *White reign: Deploying whiteness in America* (pp.
123-135). New York: St. Martin's Press.

Giroux, H. A. (2000). Public pedagogy as cultural politics: Stuart Hall and
the 'crisis' of culture. In P. Gilroy, L. Grossberg & A. McRobbie
(Eds.), *Without guarantees: In honour of Stuart Hall* (pp. 134-147).
London: Verso.

Giroux, H. A. (2001). Cultural studies as performative politics. *Cultural
Studies - Critical Methodologies, 1*(1), 5-23.

Giroux, H. A. (2001). Introduction: Critical education or training: Beyond
the commodification of higher education. In H. A. Giroux & K.
Myrsiades (Eds.), *Beyond the corporate university: Culture and pedagogy in the new millennium* (pp. 1-13). Lanham, MD: Rowman &
Littlefield.

Giroux, H. A. (2004). *The terror of neoliberalism: Authoritarianism and the ec-
lipse of democracy*. Boulder, CO: Paradigm.

Giroux, H. A. (2004). War talk, the death of the social, and disappearing
children: Remembering the other war. *Cultural Studies-Critical
Methodologies, 4*(2), 206-211.

Giroux, H. A. (2005). The conservative assault on America: Cultural politics, education and the new authoritarianism. *Cultural Politics, 1*(2),
139-164.

Giroux, H. A. (2006). *Stormy weather: Katrian and the politics of disposibility*. Boulder, CO: Paradigm.

Giroux, H. A. (2007). *The university in chains: Confronting the military-industrial-academic complex*. Boulder, CO: Paradigm.

Gitlin, T. (2001). *Media unlimited: How the torrent of images and sounds overwhelms our lives*. New York: Metropolitan Books.

Giulianotti, R. (2002). Supporters, followers, fans, and flaneurs: A taxonomy of spectator identities in football. *Journal of Sport & Social Issues, 26*(1), 25-46.

Gledhill, C. (Ed.). (1991). *Stardom: Industry of desire*. London: Routledge.

Goldfield, D. (2002). *Still fighting the Civil War: The American South and Southern history*. Baton Rouge, LA: Louisiana State University Press.

Goldfield, D. R. (2003). *Southern histories: Public, personal, and sacred*. Athens, GA: University of Georgia Press.

Gooden, R. (1985, July 11). Black enrollment declines; improved image necessary. *The Daily Mississippian*, p. 5.

Gore, J. M. (2001). Disciplining bodies: On continuity of power relations in pedagogy. In C. Paechter, R. Edwards, R. Harrison & P. Twining (Eds.), *Learning, space and identity* (pp. 167-181). Thousand Oaks, CA: Sage.

Gottdiener, M. (1994). Semiotics and postmodernism. In D. R. Dickens & A. Fontana (Eds.), *Postmodernism and social inquiry* (pp. 155-181). New York: The Guilford Press.

Gramsci, A. (1999). *Selections from the prison notebooks*. New York: International.

Greenwood, D. J., & Levin, M. (2000). Reconstituting the relationships between universities and society through action research. In N. K. Denzin & Y. S. Lincoln (Eds.), *Handbook of Qualitative Research* (2nd ed., pp. 85-106). Thousand Oaks, CA: Sage.

Gregor, A. J. (1961). On the nature of prejudice. *Eugenics Review, 52*(2), 217-224.

Grizzard, L. (1989, October 23). Ole Miss has it figured out. *The Daily Mississippian*, p. 2.

Grob, G. N. (2002). *The deadly truth: A history of disease in America*. Cambridge, MA: Harvard University Press.

Grossberg, L. (1985, December 11). The spectacle is the message. *In These Times*, 21.

Grossberg, L. (1992). *We gotta get out of this place: Popular conservatism and postmodern culture*. London: Routledge.

Grossberg, L. (1996). Identity and cultural studies: Is that all there is? In S. Hall & P. d. Gay (Eds.), *Questions of cultural identity* (pp. 87-107). London: Sage.

Grossberg, L. (1997). Bringing it all back home: Pedagogy and cultural studies *Bringing it all back home: Essays on cultural studies* (pp. 374-390). Durham: Duke University Press.

Grosz, E. (1994). *Volatile bodies: Toward a corproreal feminism*. Bloomington, IN: Indiana University Press.

Gruneau, R. (1989). Making spectacle: A case study in television sports production. In L. A. Wenner (Ed.), *Media, sports, & society* (pp. 134-156). Newbury Park, CA: Sage.

Guelzo, A. C. (2004). *Lincoln's Emancipation Proclamation: The end of slavery in America*. New York: Simon & Schuster.

Gurner, J. (1988, July 22). College Board approves lease to black group. *The Daily Mississippian*, p. 1.

Gutman, B. (1975). *Football superstars of the '70s*. New York: Julian Messner.

Gutman, H. S. (1977). *The black family in slavery and freedom, 1750-1925*. New York: Vintage.

Hale, G. E. (1998). *Making whiteness: The culture of segregation in the South, 1890-1940*. New York: Vintage Books.

Hale, G. E. (1999). We've got to get out of this place. *Southern Cultures, 5*(1), 54-66.

Hale, G. E. (2000). "For colored" and "for white": Segregating consumption in the South. In J. Dailey, G. E. Gilmore & B. Simon (Eds.), *Jumpin' Jim Crow: Southern politics from Civil War to civil rights* (pp. 162-182). Princeton, NJ: Princeton University Press.

Hall, S. (1980). Encoding/decoding. In S. Hall, D. Hobson, A. Lowe & P. Willis (Eds.), *Culture, media, language: Working papers in cultural studies, 1972-1979* (pp. 128-138). London: Hutchison.

Hall, S. (1981). Notes on deconstructing "the popular". In R. Samuel (Ed.), *People's history and socialist theory* (pp. 227-240). London: Routledge & Kegan Paul.

Hall, S. (1984). The rise of the new Right: The great moving Right show. *New Internationalist,* (133). Retrieved from http://www.newint.org/issue133/show.htm

Hall, S. (1985). Signification, representation, ideology: Althusser and the post-structuralist debates. *Critical Studies in Mass Communication*(2), 91-114.

Hall, S. (1986a). Gramsci's relevance for the study of race and ethnicity. *Journal of Communication Inquiry, 10*(2), 5-27.

Hall, S. (1986b). The problem of ideology: Marxism without guarantees. *Journal of Communication Inquiry, 10*(2), 28-44.

Hall, S. (1992a). Old and new identities, old and new ethnicities. In A. D. Smith (Ed.), *Culture, globalization and the world-system* (pp. 41-68). Minneapolis: University of Minnesota Press.

Hall, S. (1992b). The question of cultural identity. In S. Hall, D. Held & A. McGrew (Eds.), *Modernity and its futures* (pp. 273-325). Cambridge: Polity Press.

Hall, S. (1992c). The west and the rest: Discourse and power. In S. Hall & B. Gieben (Eds.), *Formations of modernity* (pp. 275-320). Cambridge: Polity Press.

Hall, S. (1995). The whites of their eyes: Racist ideologies and the media. In G. Dines & J. M. Humez (Eds.), *Gender, race, and class in media: A text-reader* (pp. 18-22). Thousand Oaks, CA: Sage.

Hall, S. (1996). Introduction: Who needs 'identity'? In S. Hall & P. d. Gay (Eds.), *Questions of cultural identity* (pp. 1-17). London: Sage.

Hall, S., & Gay, P. d. (Eds.). (1996). *Questions of cultural identity*. London: Sage.

Hall, S., & Jameson, F. (1990, September). Clinging to the wreckage: A conversation. *Marxism Today, 28-31.*

Hardt, M., & Negri, A. (2000). *Empire*. Cambridge, MA: Harvard University Press.

Hargreaves, J., & Vertinsky, P. (Eds.). (2007). *Physical culture, power, and the body*. London: Routledge.

Harrison, B. N. (1858, December 13). *Record book of the faculty minutes from the University of Mississippi (11th Session)*, Oxford, MS.

Harrison, B. N. (1859a, May 23). *Record book of the faculty minutes from the University of Mississippi (11th Session)*, Oxford, MS.

Harrison, B. N. (1859b, October 10). *Record book of the faculty minutes from the University of Mississippi (12th Session)*, Oxford, MS.

Harrison, B. N. (1859c, October 24). *Record book of the faculty minutes from the University of Mississippi (12th Session)*, Oxford, MS.

Harrison, B. N. (1859d, December 4). *Record book of the faculty minutes from the University of Mississippi (12th Session)*, Oxford, MS.

Harrison, B. N. (1860a, May 7). *Record book of the faculty minutes from the University of Mississippi (12th Session)*, Oxford, MS.

Harrison, B. N. (1860b, February 13). *Record book of the faculty minutes from the University of Mississippi (12th Session)*, Oxford, MS.

Harrison, B. N. (1860c, June 23). *Record book of the faculty minutes from the University of Mississippi (12th Session)*, Oxford, MS.

Harrison, B. N. (1860d, November 5). *Record book of the faculty minutes from the University of Mississippi (13th Session)*, Oxford, MS.

Harrison, B. N. (1861a, January 14). *Record book of the faculty minutes from the University of Mississippi (13th Session)*, Oxford, MS.

Harrison, B. N. (1861b, March 11). *Record book of the faculty minutes from the University of Mississippi (13th Session)*, Oxford, MS.

Harrison, B. N. (1861c, April 7). *Record book of the faculty minutes from the University of Mississippi (13th Session)*, Oxford, MS.

Harrison, B. N. (1861d, May 2). *Record book of the faculty minutes from the University of Mississippi (13th Session)*, Oxford, MS.

Hartigan, J. (1997a). Establishing the fact of whiteness. *American Anthropologist, 99*(3), 495-505.

Hartigan, J. (1997b). Unpopular culture: The case of 'white trash'. *Cultural Studies, 11*(2), 316-343.

Hartley, J. (1999). *Uses of television*. London: Routledge.

Hartman, A. (2004). The rise and fall of whiteness studies. *Race & Class, 46*(2), 22-38.

Harvey, D. (1989a). *The condition of postmodernity: An enquiry into the origins of cultural change.* Oxford: Blackwell.

Harvey, D. (1989b). *The condition of postmodernity: An inquiry into the origins of cultural change.* Oxford, UK: Blackwell.

Harvey, D. (1998). University, Inc. *The Atlantic Monthly, 282*(4), 112-116.

Harvey, D. (2001). *Spaces of capital: Towards a critical geography.* New York: Routledge.

Hawk, E. Q. (1943). *Economic history of the South.* Westport, CT: Greenwood Press.

Heartfield, J. (2002). *The 'death of the subject' explained.* London: Perpetuity Press

Heidegger, M. (1962). *Being and time.* New York: Harper & Row.

Hendrickson, P. (2003). *Sons of Mississippi.* New York: Alfred A. Knopf.

Henley, J. (1983, April 19). Letters from the students. *The Daily Mississippian* p. 2.

Hermaean Society has long and proud history on university campus (1934, February 24). *The Mississippian,* p. 1.

Herrnstein, R. J., & Murray, C. (1994). *The bell curve: Intellegence and class structure in American life.* New York: The Free Press.

Higgins, R. (2003, August 24). 'Easy' decision - with NFL on hold, Eli plans to savor last season in Oxford. *Commercial Appeal,* p. M3.

Higgs, R. J., Manning, A. N., & Miller, J. W. (Eds.). (1995). *Appalachia inside out: Culture and custom.* Knoxville, TN: University of Tennessee Press.

Hill, M. (1997). *Whiteness: A critical reader.* New York: New York University Press.

Hill, R. A. (1983, April 20). Letters from students. *The Daily Mississippian,* p. 2.

History of the Lyceum Building (1952). (Internal Document). Oxford, MS: University of Mississippi.

Hobsbawm, E., & Ranger, T. (Eds.). (1983). *The invention of tradition.* Cambridge: Cambridge University Press.

Hochschild, J. (1998). Affirmative action as culture war. In R. Post & M. Rogin (Eds.), *Race and representation: Affirmative action* (pp. 347-352). New York: Zone Books.

Hoelscher, S. (2003). Making place, making race: Performances of whiteness in the Jim Crow South. *Annals of the Association of American Geographers, 93*(3), 657-686.

hooks, b. (1992). *Black looks: Race and representation.* Boston: South End Press.

hooks, b. (1997). Representing whiteness in the black imagination. In R. Frankenberg (Ed.), *Displacing whiteness: Essays in social and cultural criticism* (pp. 165-179). Durham: Duke University Press.

hooks, b. (2000a). Eating the other: Desire and resistance. In J. B. Schor & D. B. Holt (Eds.), *The consumer society reader* (pp. 343-359). New York: The New Press.

hooks, b. (2000b). *Where we stand: Class matters.* New York: Routledge.

hooks, b. (2003). *Teaching community: A pedagogy of hope.* New York: Routledge.

Horwitz, T. (1999). *Confederates in the attic: Dispatches from the unfinished Civil War.* New York: Vintage.

Houston, K. (2004, October 15). Ventress grafitti holds decades of memories *The Daily Mississippian,* p. 1.

Howard, R. C. (1917, November 7). Patriotism key note of program. *The Mississippian,* p. 1.

Howell, J. W., Andrews, D. L., & Jackson, S. J. (2002). Cultural and sport studies: An interventionist practice. In J. Maguire & K. Young (Eds.), *Perspectives on the sociology of sport* (pp. 151-177). Greenwich, CT: JAI Press.

Humber, J. (1962, October 1). Death, injuries from campus rioting. *The Mississippian,* pp. 1, 4.

Hume, A. (1928). Appeal to Board of Trustees. Oxford, MS: University of Mississippi.

Hummer, S. (2003, November 9). Manning's arm, Auburn's hands hoist Rebels. *Atlanta Journal-Constitution,* p. 3F.

Hunt, J. (2002). *The last battle of the Civil War: Palmetto Ranch.* Austin, TX: University of Texas Press.

Hurdle, F. (1987, October 23). Wave a flag, drink a pint and yell a cheer. *The Daily Mississippian,* p. 2.

Husserl, E. (1970). *The crisis of European sciences and transcendental phenomenology.* Evanston: Northwestern University Press.

Husserl, E. (1973). *Experience and judgment.* Evanston: Northwestern University Press.

Hutton, W., & Giddens, A. (Eds.). (2000). *On the Edge: Living with global capitalism.* London: Jonathan Cape.

Ignatiev, N. (2003). Whiteness and class struggle. *Historical Materialism, 11*(4), 227-235.

Ingham, A. G. (1997). Toward a department of physical cultural studies and an end to tribal warfare. In J. Fernandez-Balboa (Ed.), *Critical postmoderism in human movement, physical education, and sport* (pp. 157-182). Albany: State University of New York Press.

Ingham, A. G. a. F. (1997). Toward a department of physical cultural studies and the end to tribal warfare. In J.-M. Fernandez-Balboa (Ed.), *Critical postmodernism in human movement, physical education, and sport: Rethinking the profession* (pp. 157-182). New York: State University of New York Press.

Ingram, D. (2005). Toward a cleaner white(ness): New racial identities. *The Philisophical Forum, 36*(3), 243-277.

Intruders in the dust (1966, September 23). *Time, 88,* 26.

Irons, P. (2004). *Jim Crow's children: The broken promise of the Brown decision.* New York: Penguin.

Jameson, F. (1984). Postmodernism, or the cultural logics of late capitalism. *New Left Review*(146), 53-92.

Jameson, F. (2001). *Postmodernism, or, the cultural logic of late capitalism.* Durham, NC: Duke University Press.

Jappe, A. (1999). *Guy Debord* (D. Nicholson-Smith, Trans.). Berkeley, CA: University of California Press.

Johnson, A. S. (1951). *The Confederate cause: Yesterday and today.* Paper presented at the Sons of Confederate Veterans Meeting.

Johnson, D. (1983). *Body.* Boston: Beacon Press.

Johnson, W. (1999). *Soul by soul: Life inside the antebellum slave market.* Cambridge: Harvard University Press.

Judge Kimbrough speaks on athletics (1918, March 27). *The Mississippian,* p. 1.

Kanengiser, A. (2002, December 12). Black students allegedly behind racist graffiti. *The Mississippi Clarion-Ledger,* p. Online.

Kanengiser, A. (2003a, November 15). Saving the Colonel. *Clarion-Ledger,* p. 2F.

Kanengiser, A. (2003b, Augustg 30). UM group hoping to save 'Colonel'. *The Clarion-Ledger,* p. 5.

Kelly, S. D. (2002). Merleau-Ponty on the body. *Ratio, 15*(4), 376-391.

Kennedy, S. (1959/1992). *Jim Crow Guide: The way it was.* Boca Raton, Fl: Florida Atlantic University Press.

Khayat, R. (1996, April 2). Khayat promises changes at Ole Miss. *The Daily Mississippian,* pp. 1, 4.

Khayat, R. C. (2003, July 13). Ole Miss has Rebels, 'Dixie,' mascot - and a future. *Clarion-Ledger,* p. 1.

Kilpatrick, J. J. (1962). *Southern case for school segregation.* New York: Crowell-Collier.

Kincheloe, J. (Producer). (2008, January 8, 2009) Interview with Joe Kincheloe for the 150th Anniversary of the Faculty of Education at McGill University. Podcast retrieved from http://freire.mcgill.ca/content/joe-kincheloe-interviewed.

Kincheloe, J. L., & McLaren, P. L. (1998). Rethinking critical theory and qualitative research. In N. K. Denzin & Y. S. Lincoln (Eds.), *The landscape of qualitative research: Theories and issues* (pp. 260-299). Thousand Oaks, CA: Sage.

Kincheloe, J. L., & Steinberg, S. R. (1998). Addressing the crisis of whiteness: Reconfiguring white identity in a pedagogy of whiteness. In J. L. Kincheloe, S. R. Steinberg, N. M. Rodriguez & R. E. Chennault (Eds.), *White reign: Deploying whiteness in America* (pp. 3-29). New York: St. Martin's Press.

Kincheloe, J. L., & Steinberg, S. R. (2006). An ideology of miseducation: Countering the pedagogy of empire. *Cultural Studies <=> Critical Methodologies, 6*(1), 33-51.

Kincheloe, J. L., Steinberg, S. R., Rodriguez, N. M., & Chennault, R. E. (Eds.). (1998). *White reign: Deploying whiteness in America.* New York: St. Martin's Griffin.

King, C. R. (2002). Defensive dialogues: Native American mascots, anti-Indianism, and educational institutions. *Simile, 2*(1).

King, C. R., Davis-Delano, L., Staurowsky, E., & Baca, L. (2006). Sports mascots and the media. In A. A. Raney & J. Bryant (Eds.), *Handbook of sports and media* (pp. 599-575). London: Lawrence Erlbaum Associates.

King, C. R., Leonard, D. J., & Kusz, K. W. (2007). White power and sport: An introduction. *Journal of Sport & Social Issues, 30*(1), 3-10.

King, C. R., & Springwood, C. F. (2000). Fighting spirits: The racial politics of sports mascots. *Journal of Sport and Social Issues, 24*(3), 282-304.

King, C. R., & Springwood, C. F. (2001). *Beyond the cheers: Race as spectacle in college sport.* Albany, NY: State University of New York Press.

King, C. R., Staurowsky, E. J., Baca, L., Davis, L. R., & Pewewardy, C. (2002). Of polls and race prejudice: Sports Illustrated's errant "Indian Wars". *Journal of Sport & Social Issues, 26*(4), 381-402.

Kintz, L. (2002). Performing virtual whiteness: George Gilder's techno-theocracy. *Cultural Studies, 16*(5), 735-773.

Kirby, V. C. (1989). Corporeographies. *Inscriptions: Journal for the Critique of Colonial Discourse, 5*(2), 103-119.

Klarman, M. J. (2004). *From Jim Crow to civil rights: The Supreme Court and the struggle for racial equality.* London: Oxford University Press.

Klein, N. (1999). *No Logo: Taking aim at brand bullies.* New York: Picador.

Knottnerus, J. D., Monk, D. L., & Jones, E. (1999). The slave plantation system from a total insitution perspective. In T. J. Durant & J. D. Knottnerus (Eds.), *Plantation society and race relations: The origins of inequity* (pp. 17-28). Praeger: Westport, CT.

Kriehn, T. (1970a, February 25). Tensions flair, blacks protest. *The Daily Mississippian,* p. 1.

Kriehn, T. (1970b, February 26). Eighty-nine blacks arrested. *The Daily Mississippian,* pp. 1, 8.

Kriehn, T. (1970c, October 12). Rebels win fourth straight. *The Daily Mississippian,* p. 8.

Kristeva, J. (1980). The bounded text. In L. S. Roudiez (Ed.), *Desire in language: A semiotic approach to literature and art* (pp. 36-63). New York: Columbia University Press.

Ku Klux Klan reorganized (1921, February 16). *The Mississippian,* p. 1.

Kujundzic, N., & Buschert, W. (1994). Instruments and the body: Sartre and Merleau-Ponty. *Research in Phenomenology, 24*(2), 206-215.

Kusz, K. (2007). *Revolt of the white athlete: White masculinities, sport, and contemporary American culture.* New York: Peter Lang.

Kusz, K. W. (2001). "I want to be the minority": The politics of youthful white masculinities in sport and popular culture in 1990s America. *Journal of Sport & Social Issues, 25*(4), 390-416.

Laclau, E. (1996a). *Emancipation(s)*. London: Verso.

Laclau, E. (1996b). Universalism, particularism, and the question of identity. In E. N. Wilmsen & P. McAllister (Eds.), *The politics of difference: Ethnic premises in a world of power* (pp. 45-58). Chicago: The University of Chicago Press.

Laclau, E., & Mouffe, C. (1985). *Hegemony and socialist strategy: Towards a radical democratic politics.* London: Verso.

Laclau, E., & Zac, L. (1994). Minding the gap: The subject of politics. In E. Laclau (Ed.), *The making of political identities* (pp. 11-39). London: Verso.

Ladd, T., & Mathisen, J. A. (1999). *Muscular Christianity: Evangelical Protestants and the development of American sport.* Grand Rapids, MI: Baker Books.

Lamb, B., & Sperber, M. (2000). Interview: *Beer and Circus* Retrieved April 23, 2005, from http://www.booknotes.org/Transcript/?ProgramID=1590

Lane, M. (1993). *Architecture of the Old South.* New York: Beehive Press.

Langellier, K. (1999). Personal narrative, performance, performativity: Two or three things I know for sure. *Text and Performance Quarterly, 19*(1), 125-144.

Latham, M. (1962, October 11). Magazine looks for talent. *The Mississippian,* p. 3.

Latimer, J. (2009). Introduction: Body, knowledge, worlds. In J. E. Latimer & M. W. J. Schillmeier (Eds.), *Un/knowing bodies* (pp. 1-22). Malden, MA: Blackwell.

Lattimer, J. (2009). Introduction: Body, knowledge, words. In J. Lattimer & M. Schillmeier (Eds.), *Un/knowing bodies* (pp. 1-22). Malden, MA: Blackwell.

Lawrence, B. (1962, April 4). Brad 'speaks for you'. *The Mississippian,* p. 4.

Lederman, D. (1993, October 20). Old times not forgotten. *The Chronicle of Higher Education, 15,* A51-A52.

Lee, S. P., & Passell, P. (1979). *A new economic view of American history.* New York: W. W. Norton & Co.

Lefebvre, H. (1991). *The production of space* (D. Nicholson-Smith, Trans.). Malden, MA: Blackwell.

Lefebvre, H. (2004). *Rythmanalysis: Space, time and everyday life.* London: Continuum.

Let's keep the Colonel at Ole Miss (2004). Retrieved December 16, 2004

Levin, D. M. (1987). Clinical stories: A modern self in the fury of being. In D. M. Levin (Ed.), *Pathologies of the modern self* (pp. 479-537). New York: New York University Press.

Lewis, J. (1975). *Max Weber and value-free sociology.* London: Lawrence and Wishart.

Liberty bulletin (1962). (1 ed., pp. 1-3). Oxford, MS.

Lincoln, Y. S., & Denzin, N. K. (2000). The seventh moment: Out of the past. In N. K. Denzin & Y. S. Lincoln (Eds.), *Handbook of Qualitative Research* (2nd ed., pp. 1047-1065). Thousand Oaks, CA: Sage.

Lincoln, Y. S., & Guba, E. G. (2000). Paradigmatic controversies, contradictions, and emerging confluences. In N. K. Denzin & Y. S. Lincoln (Eds.), *Handbook of Qualitative Research* (2nd ed., pp. 163-188). Thousand Oaks, CA: Sage.

Lipovetsky, G. (1994). *The empire of fashion: Dressing modern democracy* (C. Porter, Trans.). Princeton, NJ: Princeton University Press.

Lipsitz, G. (1998). *The possessive investment in whiteness: How white people profit from identity politics*. Philadelphia: Temple University Press.

Litwack, L. F. (1998). *Trouble in mind: Black Southerners in the age of Jim Crow*. New York: Vintage/Knopf.

Lomax, W. A. (1927, October 21). Where are we headed? *The Mississippian*, p. 4.

Lomax, W. A. (1928, April 6). On the University Library. *The Mississippian*, p. 4.

Long live the Colonel (1953, October 15). *Oxford Eagle*, p. 1.

Lopez, I. F. H. (1998). *White by law: The legal construction of race*. New York: New York University Press.

Lord, W. (1965). *The past that would not die*. New York: Harper & Row.

Lott, E. (2001). The mirage of an unmarked whiteness. In B. B. Rasmussen, E. Klinenberg, I. J. Nexica & M. Wray (Eds.), *The making and unmaking of whiteness* (pp. 214-233). Durham, NC: Duke University Press.

Lowe, D. M. (1995). *The body in late-capitalist USA*. London: Duke University Press.

Lukács, G. (1971). *History and class consciousness: Studies in Marxist dialectics* (R. Livingstone, Trans.). Cambridge, MA: The MIT Press.

Lury, C. (1996). *Comsumer culture*. Piscataway, NJ: Rutgers University Press.

Lyon, E. W. (1923, March 30). Ole Miss - Its religious character. *The Mississippian*, p. 2.

Madison, D. S. (1999). Performing theory/embodied writing. *Text and Performance Quarterly, 19*(1), 107-124.

Mahar, C. (1990). Pierre Bourdieu: The intellectual project. In R. Harker, C. Mahar & C. Wilkes (Eds.), *An introduction to the work of Pierre Bourdieu: The practice of theory* (pp. 26-57). London: Macmillan.

Mahoney, M. (1997). The social construction of whiteness. In R. Delgado & J. Stefancic (Eds.), *Critical white studies: Looking behind the mirror*. Philadelphia: Temple University Press.

Malin, B. (2003). Memorializing white masculinity: The late 1990s "crisis of masculinity" and the "subversive performance" of Man on the Moon. *Journal of Communication Inquiry, 27*(3), 239-255.

Malone, R. (1997, October 29). Illegal inserts found in Friday's DM. *The Daily Mississippian*, p. 1.

Mandel, E. (1975). *Late capitalism*. London: NLB.

Mandelbaum, M. (2001). A note on history as narrative. In G. Roberts (Ed.), *The history and narrative reader* (pp. 52-58). London: Routledge.

Manning, A., Manning, P., & Underwood, J. (2000). *Manning: A father, his sons, and a football legacy*. New York: HarperEntertainment.

Marcoulatos, I. (2001). Merleau-Ponty and Bourdieu on *embodied significance. Journal for the Theory of Social Behaviour, 31*(1), 1-27.

Marcus, G. E., & Fischer, M. M. J. (1986). *Anthropology as cultural critique: An experimental moment in the human sciences*. Chicago: University of Chicago Press.

Marcuse, H. (1964). *One dimensional man: Studies in the ideology of advanced industrial society*. Boston: Beacon Press.

Marrinucci, C. (2005, June 7). In S.F., Dean calls GOP 'a white Christian party'. *San Francisco Chronicle*, p. 1A.

Marshall, P. D. (1997). *Celebrity and power: Fame in contemporary culture*. Minneapolis: University of Minnesota Press.

Martin, C. H. (2002). Integrating new year's day: The racial politics of college bowl games in the American south. In P. B. Miller (Ed.), *The sporting world of the modern south* (pp. 175-199). Urbana, Ill: University of Illinois Press.

Marx, K. (1976). *Capital, Vol. 1* (B. Fowkes, Trans.). Middlesex: Penguin Books.

Marx, K. (1977). Grundrisse. In D. McLellan (Ed.), *Karl Marx: Selected writings* (pp. 345-387). Oxford: Oxford Unviersity Press.

Mason, N. (1964, October 14). Beatniks are a lost cause. *The Mississippian*, p. 5.

Mason, S., & Yarbrough, B. (1989, September 21). UM to hear case; frat apologizes. *The Daily Mississippian*, pp. 1, 8.

Massey, D., & Denton, J. (1993). *American apartheid: Segregation and the making of the underclass*. Cambridge: Harvard University Press.

Mauss, M. (1934/1973). Techniques of the body. *Economy and Society, 4*(1), 70-88.

McCarthy, C. (1998). Living with anxiety: Race and the renarration of public life. In J. L. Kincheloe, N. Steinberg, N. Rodriguez & R. Chennault (Eds.), *White reign: Deploying whiteness in America* (pp. 329-341). New York: St. Martin's Press.

McDonald, M. G. (2005). Mapping whiteness and sport: An introduction. *Sociology of Sport Journal, 22*(3), 245-255.

McDonald, M. G., & Andrews, D. L. (2001). Michael Jordan: Corporate sport and postmodern celebrityhood. In D. L. Andrews & S. J. Jackson (Eds.), *Sport Stars: The cultural politics of sporting celebrity* (pp. 20-35). London: Routledge.

McDonough, T. (2002). Situationist space. In T. MacDonough (Ed.), *Guy Debord and the Situationist International: Documents and texts* (pp. 241-165). Cambridge, MA: The MIT Press.

McGowan, M. O. (1998). Diversity of what? In R. Post & M. Rogin (Eds.), *Race and representation: Affirmative action* (pp. 237-250). New York: Zone Books.

McIntosh, P. (1990). White privilege: Unpacking the invisible knapsack. *Independent School, 49*(2), 31-36.

McIntyre, A. (1997). *Making meaning of whiteness: Exploring the racial identity of white teachers.* Albany, NY: State University of New York Press.

McLaren, P. (1988). Schooling the postmodern body: Critical pedagogy and the politics of enfleshment. *Journal of Education, 170*(3), 53-83.

McLaren, P. (1999). Foreword. In S. B. Shapiro (Ed.), *Pedagogy and the politics of the body: A critical praxis* (pp. ix-xxiii). New York: Garland Publishing.

McLeod, R. (1985, July 26). White males deserve fair shake. *The Daily Mississippian,* p. 2.

McMillen, N. R. (1971). *The Citizen's Council: Organized resistance to the Second Reconstruction, 1954-64.* Urbana, IL: University of Illinois Press.

McPherson, T. (2003). *Reconstructing Dixie: Race, gender, and nostalgia in the imagined South.* Durham, NC: Duke University Press.

McWhite, S. L. (2002). *Echoes of the Lost Cause: Civil War reverberations in Mississippi from 1865 to 2001.* Unpublished PhD Dissertation, University of Mississippi, Oxford, MS.

Mercer, K. (1994). *Welcome to the jungle: New positions in black cultural studies.* New York: Routledge.

Meredith, J. (1966). *Three years in Mississippi.* Bloomington, IN: Indiana University Press.

Meredith, J. (1982, October 1). Highlights of Meredith speech. *The Daily Mississippian,* p. 1.

Meredith, J., Marshall, B., & Doar, J. (2002, September 30). *James Meredith and the integration of Ole Miss,* John F. Kennedy Library and Foundation.

Merleau-Ponty, M. (1945/2002). *Phenomenology of perception* (C. Smith ed.). London: Routledge.

Merleau-Ponty, M. (1968). *The visible and the invisible* (A. Lingis, Trans.). Evanston: Northwestern University Press.

Merleau-Ponty, M. (1973). *Consciousness and the acquisition of language* (H. J. Silverman, Trans.). Evanston: Northwestern University Press.

Merleau-Ponty, M. (1993). *The Merleau-Ponty aesthetics reader: Philosophy and painting* (M. Smith, Trans.). Evanston: Northwestern University Press.

Merrifield, A. (2000). Henri Lefebvre: A socialist in space. In M. Crang & N. Thrift (Eds.), *Thinking space* (pp. 167-182). London: Routledge.

Mesny, A. (2002). A view on Bourdieu's legacy: Sens pratique v. hysteresis. *Canadian Journal of Sociology, 27*(1), 59-67.

Meyer Jr., W. E. H. (1995). Culture-wars/gender-scars: Faulkner's South vs. America. *Journal of American Culture, 18*(4), 33-42.

Meyer, K. E. (1962, October 5). Dixie's last stand. *New Stateman, LXIV*, 441.

Miller, P. B. (2002). The manly, the moral, and the proficient: College sport in the new south. In P. B. Miller (Ed.), *The sporting world of the modern south* (pp. 17-51). Urbana, Ill: University of Illinois Press.

Miller, P. B. (Ed.). (2002). *The sporting world of the modern south*. Urbana, Ill: University of Illinois Press.

Miller, T. (2001). *Sportsex*. Philadelphia: Temple University Press.

Miller, T., Govil, N., McMurria, J., & Maxwell, R. (2001). *Global Hollywood*. London: BFI.

Moore, B. (1985, July 11). UM gets $100,000 to help minorities. *The Daily Mississippian*, pp. 1,4.

Moraes, L. d. (2005, September 3). Kanye West's torrent of criticism. *Washington Post*, p. C01.

Morris, W. (1983). Issues *Ole Miss* (pp. 63). Oxford/University, MS: University of Mississippi.

Morrison, T. (1987). *Beloved*. New York: Knopf.

Morrison, T. (1992). *Playing in the dark: Whiteness and the literary imagination*. New York: Vintage.

Mostly politics: Old Ku Klux Klan an absolute necessity (1921, October 11). *The Mississippian*, pp. 1-2.

Mouffe, C. (Ed.). (1992). *Dimensions of radical democracy*. New York: Verso.

Mukerji, C., & Schudson, M. (1991). Introduction: Rethinking popular culture. In C. Mukerji & M. Schudson (Eds.), *Rethinking popular culture: Contemporary perspectives in cultural studies* (pp. 1-62). Berkeley, CA: University of California Press.

Munro, R. (1996). A consumption view of self: Extension, exchange and identity. In S.Edgell, K. Hetherington & A. Warde (Eds.), *Consumption matters: The production and experience of consumption* (pp. 248-273). Oxford: Blackwell.

Myers, G. (2004, September 3). Archie not one to start trouble. *Daily News (New York)*, p. 116.

Naipaul, V. S. (1989). *A turn to the South*. New York: Vintage.

Nayar, P. (2009). *Seeing stars: Spectacle, society, and celebrity culture*. Thousand Oaks, CA: Sage.

NCAA might expand Confederate flag ban: South Carolina baseball, football may not be able to host postseason games (2006, August 2). Retrieved August 2, 2006, from http://www.msnbc.msn.com/id/14138981/

Nettleton, M. (1983, April 22). Flag verdict rejected. *The Daily Mississippian*, p. 1.

Neuman, M. (1996). Collecting ourselves at the end of the century. In C. Ellis & A. Bochner (Eds.), *Composing ethnography: Alternative forms of qualitative writing* (pp. 172-200). London: Alta Mira Press.

New misery at Ole Miss (1968, August 30). *Time, 92*, 37.

Newitz, A., & Wray, M. (1997). What is "white trash"? Stereotypes and economic conditions of poor whites in the United States. In M. Hill (Ed.), *Whiteness: A critical reader* (pp. 168-184). New York: New York University Press.

Newman, J. I. (2007). A detour through 'NASCAR Nation': Ethnographic articulations of a neoliberal sporting spectacle. *International Review for the Sociology of Sport, 42*(3), 289-308.

Newman, J. I., & Beissel, A. S. (2009). The limits to 'NASCAR Nation': Sport and the 'recovery movement' in disjunctural times. *Sociology of Sport Journal,* 26(4), 517-539.

Newman, J. I., & Giardina, M. D. (2008). NASCAR and the 'Southernization' of America: Spectatorship, subjectivity, and the confederation of identity. *Cultural Studies <=> Critical Methodologies, Forthcoming.*

Newman, J. I., & Giardina, M. D. (2009). Onward Christian drivers: Theocratic nationalism and the cultural politics of 'NASCAR Nation'. In S. R. Steinberg & J. L. Kincheloe (Eds.), *Christotainment: Selling Jesus through popular culture* (pp. 51-82). Boulder, CO: Westview Press.

Niemeyer, B. (2004, September 29). Athletics over academics. *The Daily Mississippian,* p. 2.

Niemeyer, B. (2005, March 2). Traditions of a racist past. *The Daily Mississippian,* p. 2.

Nora, P. (1989). Between memory and history: Les lieux de Memoire. *representations*(26), 7-.

North, D. C. (1966). *The economic growth of the United States, 1790-1860.* New York: W. W. Norton & Co.

Nossiter, A. (1997, May 4). Ground zero. *The New York Times* Retrieved March 7, 2005, from http://www.nytimes.com/books/97/05/04/reviews/970504.04nossitt.html

O'Rourke, D. K. (2004). *How America's first settlers invented chattel slavery: Dehumanizing Native Americans and Africans with language, laws, guns, and religion.* New York: Peter Lang Publishing Group.

O'Shea, G. (1964, October 27). A girl's guide to football. *The Mississippian,* p. 3.

O'Shea, M. (1925). *Public education in Mississippi: Report of a study of the public education system.* Jackson, MS: State of Mississippi.

Oberholtzer, E. P. (1917). *A history of the United States since the Civil War.* New York: Macmillan Company.

Oglesby, J. (1989, April 22). Problem is system-wide. *The Daily Mississippian,* p. 2.

Ole Miss (1962, October 21). *New York Times,* p. 20.

Ole Miss leads the South with interest in mid-winter sports (1924, March 7). *The Mississippian,* pp. 1-2.

Ole Miss men prepare for country's call (1917, April 12). *The Mississippian,* p. 1.

Ole Miss students favor segregation (1956, January 27). *The Mississippian*, p. 1.

Omi, M., & Winant, H. (1993). On the theoretical concept of race. In C. McCarthy & W. Critchlow (Eds.), *Race, identity, and representation in education* (pp. 3-10). New York: Routledge.

Osborne, H. (1970). *Aesthetics and art theory: An historical introduction.* New York: Dutton.

Osborne, R. T. (1960). Racial differences in mental growth and school achievement: A longitudinal study. *Psychological Reports, 2*, 233-239.

Park-Fuller, L. (2000). Performing absence: The staged personal narrative as testimony. *Text and Performance Quarterly, 20*(1), 20-42.

Peck, J. (2000). Keep your room clean: How to uncover corporate and military influence on your campus. In G. D. White & F. C. Hauck (Eds.), *Campus, Inc.: Corporate power in the ivory tower* (pp. 405-417). Amherst, NY: Prometheus Books.

Peirce, R. (1983, April 20). Letters from the students. *The Daily Mississippian*, p. 2.

Perkins, J. (1963, May 10). 'We don't comprehend': Iowan says of Ole Miss. *The Mississippian*, p. 3.

Personnel of annual style show is released by 1934 'Ole Miss' (1933, November 11). *The Mississippian*, p. 1.

Pewewardy, C. D. (2001). Educators and mascots: Challenging contradictions. In C. R. King & C. F. Springwood (Eds.), *Team spirits: The Native American mascots controversy* (pp. 257-280). Lincoln, NE: University of Nebraska Press.

Pewewardy, C. D. (2004). Playing Indian at halftime The controversy over American Indian mascots, logos, and nicknames in school-related events. *Clearing House, 77*(5), 180-185.

Phillips, K. (2006). *American theocracy: The peril and politics of radical religion, oil, and borrowed money in the 21st Century.* London: Viking Penguin.

Philo, C. (2000). Foucault's geography. In M. Crang & N. Thrift (Eds.), *Thinking space* (pp. 205-238). London: Routledge.

Physical Ed classes plan demonstration (1927, April 8). *The Mississippian*, pp. 1, 4.

Pierce, J. L. (2003). 'Racing for innocence': Whiteness, corporate culture, and the backlash against affirmative action. *Qualitative Sociology, 26*(1), 53-70.

Pike's, E's: Abusive? (1983, September 26). *The Daily Missisisppian*, pp. 1, 7.

Pinder, D. (2000). 'Old Paris is no more': Geographies of spectacle and anti-spectacle. *Antipode, 32*(4), 357-386.

Plant, S. (1992). *The most radical gesture: The Situationist International in a posmodern age.* London: Routledge.

Points of interest at the University of Mississippi (1984). Oxford, MS: University of Mississippi.

Profs sign statement on recent happenings (1962, October 9). *The Mississippian,* p. 1.

Program for Religious Emphasis Week (1938). Oxford, MS: University of Mississippi.

Pulitzer, I. (1950, December 8). Dixie Week is all over - but the shouting; save Confederate Jack for next year. *The Mississippian,* p. 2.

Rabinow, P. (1984). Introduction. In P. Rabinow (Ed.), *The Foucault Reader* (pp. 3-29). New York: Pantheon Books.

Rabinow, P. (1992). Artificiality and Enlightenment: From sociobiology to biosociality. In J. Crary & S. Kwinter (Eds.), *Incorporations* (pp. 190-201). New York: Zone Press.

Racial study completed (1962, October 10). *The Gulf Coast Gazette,* p. 1.

Raines, S., Freeland, L., Cassreino, T. R., Haeavey, L., Pitcock, F., & Miskelly, R. (1983, April 19). Rumors stir protest. *The Daily Mississippian,* p. 1.

Rains, F. V. (1998). Is the benign really harmless?: Deconstructing some 'benign' manifestations of operationalized white privilige. In J. L. Kincheloe, S. R. Steinberg, N. M. Rodriguez & R. E. Chennault (Eds.), *White reign: Deploying whiteness in America* (pp. 77-102). New York: St. Martin's Griffin.

Rands, R. (1963, May 3). Anthropologist looks at 'Race and Reason'. *The Mississippian,* pp. 3-6.

Rawls, W. (1982, September 4). Black cheerleader balks at waving the 'Rebel' flag. *New York Times,* p. 6.

Read, S., & Freeland, L. (1983, April 12). The needed symbol? *The Daily Mississippian,* p. 2.

Readings, B. (1996). *The university in ruins.* Cambridge, MA: Harvard University Press.

Real, M. R. (1975). Super Bowl: Mythic spectacle. *Journal of Communication,* 25(1), 31-43.

Rebel underground (1962). University of Mississippi.

Redmond, S., & Holmes, S. (2007). Introduction: What's in a reader? In S. Redmond & S. Holmes (Eds.), *Stardom and celebrity: A reader* (pp. 1-12). Los Angeles: Sage.

Reed, B. E. (1983, April 21). Demands provoke negation of progess and traditon. *The Daily Mississippian,* p. 2.

Reed, J. S. (1986). *The enduring South: Subcultural persistence in mass society.* Chapel Hill, NC: University of North Carolina Press.

Reeves, J. L., & Campbell, R. (1994). *Cracked coverage: Television news, the anti-cocaine crusade, and the Reagan legacy.* Durham: Duke University Press.

Richardson, J., & Shaw, A. (Eds.). (1998). *The body in qualitative research.* London: Ashgate.

Richardson, L. (2000). Writing: A method of inquiry. In N. K. Denzin & Y. S. Lincoln (Eds.), *Handbook of Qualitative Research* (2nd ed., pp. 923-948). Thousand Oaks, CA: Sage.

Richardson, W. G. (1856, September 16). *Record book of the faculty minutes from the University of Mississippi*, Oxford, MS.

Ricoeur, P. (2004). *Memory, history, forgetting*. Chicago: The University of Chicago Press.

Riesman, D., & Denney, R. (1970). Football in America: A study in cultural diffusion. In J. W. Loy & G. S. Kenyon (Eds.), *Sport, culture, and society* (pp. 306-319). London: Macmillan.

Riesman, D., Glazer, N., & Denney, R. (2001). *The lonely crowd: A study of the changing American character*. New Haven, CT: Yale Note Bene.

Ritzer, G. (1993). *The McDonaldization of society: An investigation into the changing character of contemporary social life*. Thousand Oaks: Pine Forge Press.

Ritzer, G. (1998a). McJobs: McDonaldization and its relationship to the labor process. In G. Ritzer (Ed.), *The McDonaldization thesis: Explorations and extensions* (pp. 59-70). London: Sage Publications.

Ritzer, G. (1998b). *The McDonaldization thesis: Explorations and extensions*. London: Sage.

Ritzer, G. (2001). *Explorations in social theory: From metatheorizing to rationalization*. London: Sage.

Ritzer, G. (2004). *The McDonaldization of society* (Revised New Century Edition ed.). London: Sage.

Robbins, C. G. (2004). Racism and the authority of neoliberalism: A review of three new books on the persistence of racial inequality in a color-blind era. *Journal for Critical Education Policy Studies, 2*(2), 1-16.

Robinson, D. (1979, October 29). Naming the UM horse. *The Daily Mississippian*, p. 2.

Rodriguez, N. M. (1998). Emtying the content of whiteness: Toward an understanding of the relation between whiteness and pedagogy. In J. L. Kincheloe, S. R. Steinberg, N. M. Rodriguez & R. E. Chennault (Eds.), *White reign: Deploying whiteness in America* (pp. 31-61). New York: St. Martin's Press.

Roediger, D. R. (1997). White looks: Hairy apes, true stories, and Limbaugh's laughs. In M. Hill (Ed.), *Whiteness: A critical reader* (pp. 35-46). New York: New York University Press.

Roediger, D. R. (2002). *Colored white: Transcending the racial past*. University of California Press: Berkeley, CA.

Rojek, C. (2001). *Celebrity*. London: Reaktion Books.

Ronai, C. R. (1992). The reflexive self through narrative: A night in the life of an erotic dancer/researcher. In C. Ellis & M. G. Flaherty (Eds.), *Investigating subjectivity: Research on lived experience* (pp. 102-124). Thousand Oaks, CA: Sage.

Rosenstein, J. (2001). In whose honor?, mascots, and the media. In C. R. King & C. F. Springwood (Eds.), *Team spirits: The Native American mascots controversy* (pp. 241-256). Lincoln, NE: University of Nebraska Press.

Ross, A. (1988). *Universal abandon?: The politics of postmodernism*. Minneapolis: University of Minnesota Press.

Ross, K. (1988). *The emergence of social space: Rinbaud and the Paris commune*. Minneapolis, MN: University of Minnesota Press.

Ross, K. (1997). Lefebvre on the Situationists: An interview. *October, 79*, 69-83.

Rossman, G. B., & Rallis, S. F. (2003). *Learning in the field: An introduction to qualitative research* (2nd ed.). Thousand Oaks, CA: Sage.

ROTC celebrates the Old South (1948, December 1). *The Mississippian*, p. 1.

Rowe, D. (1995). *Popular cultures: Rock music, sport and the politics of pleasure*. London: Sage.

Rubin, R. (2002). *Confederacy of silence: A true tale of the new Old South*. New York: Atria Books.

Russell, D. M. (1935, November 30). Hail politics! *The Mississippian*, pp. 1, 4.

Rutherford, J. (2005). Cultural Studies in the corporate university. *Cultural Studies, 19*(3), 297-317.

Rybczynski, W. (2000). *A clearing in the distance: Frederick Law Olmsted and America in the 19th Century*. New York: Scribner.

Sage, G. H. (1990). *Power and ideology in American sport: A critical perspective*. Champaign: Human Kinetics.

Said, E. (1996). *Representations of the intellectual: The 1993 Reith Lectures*. New York: Vintage.

Salstrom, P. (1996). Appalachia's informal economy and the transition to capitalism. *Journal of Appalachian Studies, 2*(2), 213-233.

Sandoval, C. (1997). Theorizing white consciousness for a post-empire world: Barthes, Fanon, and the rhetoric of love. In R. Frankenberg (Ed.), *Displacing whiteness: Essays in social and cultural criticism* (pp. 86-106). Durham, NC: Duke University Press.

Sansing, D. (1982, September 10). Professor comments on the flag. *The Daily Mississippian*, pp. 1,8.

Sansing, D. G. (1990). *Making haste slowly: The troubled history of higher education in Mississippi*. Jackson, MS: University of Mississippi Press.

Sansing, D. G. (1999). *The University of Mississippi: A Sesquicentennial history*. Jackson, MS: University of Mississippi Press.

Sartre, J.-P. (1992). *Being and nothingness*. New York: Washington Square Press.

Saukko, P. (2005). Methodologies for cultural studies: An integrative approach. In N. K. Denzin & Y. S. Lincoln (Eds.), *The sage handbook of qualitative research* (3rd ed., pp. 343-356). Thousand Oaks, CA: Sage.

Schickel, R. (1985). *Intimate strangers: The culture of celebrity in America*. Chicago: Ivan R. Dee.

Schlesinger, A. M. (1997). *The vital center: The politics of freedom*. New York: Transaction.

Scott, A. F. (1989). After suffrage: Southern women in the Twenties. In P. Gerster & N. Cords (Eds.), *Myth and Southern history: The New*

South (pp. 81-100). Champaign-Urbana, IL: University of Illinois Press.

Seidman, S. (1998). *Contested knowledge: Social theory in the postmodern era* (2nd ed.). Malden, Mass.: Blackwell.

Selzer, J., & Crowley, S. (1999). Rhetorical bodies. In B. Dickson (Ed.), *Reading maternity materially* (pp. 297-313). Madison, WI: University of Wisconsin Press.

Semali, L. (1998). Perspectives of the curriculum of whiteness. In J. L. Kincheloe, S. R. Steinberg, N. M. Rodriguez & R. E. Chennault (Eds.), *White reign: Deploying whiteness in America* (pp. 177-190). New York: St. Martin's Press.

Sessions, C. (1963, June 13). NAACP leader slain. *The Mississippian*, p. 1.

Shapiro, S. B. (1999). *Pedagogy and the politics of the body*. New York: Grland Publishing.

Shearer, L. (1963, November 1). Why do women go to college? *The Mississippian*, p. 5.

Sheriff Ford remains calm and restrained (1963). *The Mississippian*, p. 3.

Shilling, C. (2003). *The body and social theory* (2nd ed.). London: Sage.

Shilling, C. (2007). Introduction: Sociology and the body. In C. Schilling (Ed.), *Embodying sociology* (pp. 2-18). Oxford: Blackwell.

Shoup, F. A. (1867a, March 9). *Record book of the faculty minutes from the University of Mississippi (16th Session)*, Oxford, MS.

Shoup, F. A. (1867b, May 23). *Record book of the faculty minutes from the University of Mississippi (16th Session)*, Oxford, MS.

Shoup, F. A. (1867c, June 19). *Record book of the faculty minutes from the University of Mississippi (16th Session)*, Oxford, MS.

Shuey, A. M. (1958). *The Testing of Negro Intelligence*. Lynchburg, VA: J.P. Bell Company.

Sigelman, L. (1998). Hail to the Redskins? Public reactions to a racially insensitive team name. *Sociology of Sport Journal, 15*(4), 317-325.

Silver, J. W. (1966). *Mississippi: The closed society*. New York: Harcourt, Brace & World.

Silver, J. W. (1984). *Running scared: Silver in Mississippi*. Jackson, MS: University Press of Mississippi.

Silverman, K. (1988). *The acoustic mirror: The female voice in psychoanalysis and cinema*. Bloomington: Indiana University Press.

Simmel, G. (1918/1971). *Georg Simmel on individuality and social forms*. Chicago: University of Chicago Press.

Simmons, B. (1963, November 1). Local coeds air views. *The Mississippian*, p. 5.

Sims, P. (1996). *The Klan* (2nd ed.). Lexington, KY: University Press of Kentucky.

Sindelar, M. (2003, October 10). Officials terminate search for mascot: Lack of support cited for end *The Daily Mississippian*, p. Online.

Sixteenth annual catalogue of the officers and students of the Industrial Institute and College of Mississippi, 1900-1901 (1901). Columbus, MS: Industrial Institute and College of Mississippi.

Skerrett, J. T. (2002). *Literature, race, and ethnicity: Contesting American identities.* New York: Longman.

Slack, J. D. (1996). The theory and method of articulation in cultural studies. In D. Morley & K. H. Chen (Eds.), *Stuart Hall: Critical dialogues in cultural studies* (pp. 112-127). London: Routledge.

Slaughter, S. (2006). Academic freedom and the neoliberal state. Unpublished Unpublished Research Paper. University of Georgia.

Slaughter, S., & Leslie, L. (2000). Professors going pro: The commercialization of teaching, research, and service. In G. D. White & F. C. Hauck (Eds.), *Campus, Inc.: Corporate power in the ivory tower* (pp. 140-156). Amherst, NY: Prometheus Books.

Slaughter, S., & Rhoades, G. (2004). *Academic capitalism and the new economy: Markets, state, and higher education.* Baltimore, MD: The Johns Hopkins University Press.

Sleeter, C. E. (1993). How white teachers construct race. In C. McCarthy & W. Critchlow (Eds.), *Race, identity, and representation in education* (pp. 157-171). New York: Routledge.

Sleeter, C. E. (1996). White silence, white solidarity. In N. Ignatiev & J. Garvey (Eds.), *Race traitor* (pp. 257-265). New York: Routledge.

Smart, B. (1983). *Foucault, Marxism and critique.* London: Routledge.

Smith, J. (1963a, December 13). Dr. Silver charges with further charges. *The Mississippian,* pp. 4-5.

Smith, J. (1963b, October 2). Shifts popular on campus. *The Mississippian,* p. 7.

Smith, M. M. (1998). *Debating slavery : Economy and society in the antebellum American South.* Cambridge, UK: Cambridge University Press.

Smith, N., & Katz, C. (1993). Grounding a metaphor: Towards a spatialized politics. In M. Keith & S. Pile (Eds.), *Place and the politics of identity* (pp. 67-83). New York: Routledge.

Soja, E. (1989). *Postmodern geographies.* London: Verso.

Soja, E., & Hooper, B. (1993). The spaces that difference makes: Some notes on the geographical margins of the new cultural politics. In M. Keith & S. Pile (Eds.), *Place and the politics of identity* (pp. 183-205). London: Routledge.

Soja, E. W. (1996). *Thirdspace: Journeys to Los Angeles and other real-and-imagined places.* Oxford: Blackwell Publishers.

Solterdijk, P. (1987). *Critique of cynical reason.* Minneapolis: University of MInnesota Press.

Somerson, W. (2004). White men on the edge: Rewriting the borderlands in *Lone Star. Men and Masculinities, 6*(3), 215-239.

Sorrels, W. W., & Cavagnaro, C. (1976). *Ole Miss Rebels: Mississippi football.* Huntsville, AL: Strode.

Sparkes, R. (1995). Writing people: Reflections on the dual crises of representation and legitimation in qualitative inquiry. *Quest, 47*(1), 158-195.

Sperber, M. (2000). *Beer and circus: How big-time college sports is crippling undergraduate education.* New York: Henry Holt.

Springwood, C. F. (2004). "I'm Indian too": Claiming Native American identity, crafing authority in mascot debates. *Journal of Sport & Social Issues, 28*(1), 56-70.

Spry, T. (2001). Performing autoethnography: An embodied methodological praxis. *Qualitative Inquiry, 7*(6).

Spurrier: Flag should come down from S.C. Statehouse (2007). Retrieved April 16, 2007, from http://sports.espn.go.com/ncf/news/story?id=2837735

Stampp, K. M. (1989). *Peculiar institution: Slavery in the ante-bellum South.* New York: Vintage.

Stanton, F. L. (2005). *Songs from Dixie Land.* Whitefish, MT: Kessinger.

Starobin, R. S. (1970). *Industrial slavery of the Old South.* London: Oxford University Press.

State of Mississippi; House and Senate Concurrent Resolution, No. 125(1956).

State rates of incarceration by race (2004). Washington, DC: The Sentencing Project.

Staurowsky, E. J. (1998). In whose honor? American Indian mascots in sport. *International Review for the Sociology of Sport, 33*(4), 411-413.

Staurowsky, E. J. (2001). Sockalexis and the making of the myth at the core of Cleveland's "Indian" image. In C. R. King & C. F. Springwood (Eds.), *Team spirits: The Native American mascots controversy* (pp. 82-108). Lincoln, NE: University of Nebraska Press.

Staurowsky, E. J. (2004). On the legal and social fictions that sustain American Indian sport imagery. *Journal of Sport & Social Issues, 28*(1), 11-29.

Staurowsky, E. J. (2004). Privilige at play: On the legal and social fictions that sustain American Indian sport imagery. *Journal of Sport and Social Issues, 28*(1), 11-29.

Staurowsky, E. J. (2007). "You know, we are all indian": Exploring white power and privilege in reactions to the NCAA Native American policy. *Journal of Sport & Social Issues, 30*(1), 61-76.

Stead, A. (1982, October 25). Klan stages peaceful march over weekend. *The Oxford Eagle,* p. 1.

Stewart, S. (2003, October 31). Grove tailgating setup becomes big business. *The Oxford Eagle,* p. 6.

Stowe, D. W. (1996). Uncolored people: The rise of whiteness studies. *Lingua Franca, 6*(6), 68-77.

Strong, P. T. (2004). The mascot slot: Cultural citizenship, political correctness, and psuedo-Indian sports symbols. *Journal of Sport & Social Issues, 28*(1), 79-87.

353

Students protest 'Dixie' at Ole Miss (1993, March 4). *Clario-Ledger*, p. B1.

Stunt Night '64 (1964, March 17). *The Mississippian*, pp. 4-5.

Sue, D. W. (2004). Whiteness and ethnocentric monoculturalism: Making the 'invisible' visible. *American Psychologist, 59*(8), 761-769.

Sweat, N. S. (1948, August 5). States' Rights group lists its principles, eight resolutions. *The Mississippian*, p. 2.

Tailgating top 10 (2004, August 20). *Associated Press*, p. 1.

Tambiah, S. J. (1996). The nation-state in crisis and the rise of ethnonationalism. In E. N. Wilmsen & P. McAllister (Eds.), *The politics of difference: Ethnic premises in a world of power* (pp. 124-143). Chicago: The University of Chicago Press.

Thandeka (2002). *Learning to be white: Money, race, and God in America*. New York: Continuum.

The Grove Society (2004). (pp. 1-6). Oxford, MS: University of Mississippi Athletic Department.

The Ku Klux ably defended (1922, October 6). *The Mississippian*, p. 1.

'The Mississippi Flood' picked as name for athletes (1929, November 23). *The Mississippian*, p. 1.

The University of Mississippi (1912). Unpublished Pamphlet. The University of Mississippi.

The Y.M.C.A stands for clean muscular Christian manhood (1912, February 17). *The Mississippian*, p. 4.

Thomas, K. (2000, February 15). GHM slurs not an anomaly; racism hides in everyone. *The Daily Mississipian*, p. Online.

Though the heavens fall (1962, October 12). *Time, 80,* 19-22.

Tierney, W. G., & Rhoads, R. A. (1995). The culture of assessment. In J. Smyth (Ed.), *Academic work* (pp. 99-111). Buckingham, UK: Open University PRess.

Tindall, G. B. (1989). Mythology: A new frontier. In P. Gerster & N. Cords (Eds.), *Myth and Southern history: The New South* (pp. 1-16). Champaign-Urbana, IL: University of Illinois Press.

Todd, H. P. (1951, February 5). *Industrialization in the South and its relation to agriculture*. Paper presented at the Joint Crops and Soils Section, Memphis, TN.

Tomascovic-Devey, D. (1993). *Race and gender at work*. Ithaca, NY: IRL University Press.

Tomlinson, A. (1996). Olympic spectacle: Opening ceremonies and some paradoxes of globalization. *Media, Culture & Society, 18*(4), 583-602.

Tomlinson, A. (2002). Theorising spectacle: Beyond Debord. In J. Sugden & A. Tomlinson (Eds.), *Power games: A critical sociology of sport* (pp. 44-60). London: Routledge.

Tuan, Y. F. (1974). *Topophilia*. Englewood Cliffs, NJ: Prentice-Hall.

Tuana, N., Cowling, W., Hamington, M., Johnson, G., & MacMullan, T. (Eds.). (2002). *Revealing male bodies*. Bloomington, IN: Indiana University Press.

Tulloch, H. (1999). *The debate on the American Civil War era*. Manchester University Press: Manchester, UK.

Tullos, L. (1983, September 2). Reb flags wave a pep rally. *The Daily Mississippian*, p. 1.

Tumulty, K. (2002, December 12). Trent Lott's segregationist college days. *Time, 160*, 16.

Turnage, H. (1948, August 12). States' Right Movement favored in student poll. *The Mississippian*, p. 4.

Turner, B. S. (1992). *Regulating bodies: Essays in medical sociology*. London: Routledge.

Turner, D. (1983, April 21). Rebel flag: Half mast. *The Daily Mississippian*, p. 1.

Turner, D., & Nettleton, M. (1983, April 14). Blacks may 'protest' Klan pics. *The Daily Mississippian*, p. 1.

Turner, G. (2004). *Understanding celebrity*. London: Sage.

Turner, G., Bonner, F., & Marshall, P. D. (2000). *Fame games: The production of celebrity in Australia*. Melbourne: Cambridge University Press.

Tzonis, A., & Lefaivre, L. (1986). *Classical architecture: The poetics of order*. Boston, MA: The MIT Press.

UM should honor Black History Month with diverse monuments (2000, February 17). *The Daily Mississippian*, p. 2.

University adopts new nickname - Rebels (1936, May 5). *The Mississippian*, p. 1.

van Ingen, C. (2003). Geographies of gender, sexuality and race: Reframing the focus on space in sport sociology. *International Review for the Sociology of Sport, 38*(2), 201-216.

van Ingen, C. (2004). Therapeutic landscapes and the regulated body in the Toronto Front Runners. *Sociology of Sport Journal, 21*(3), 253-269.

Vanderford, H. (1996). What's in a name? Heritage or hatred: The school mascot controversy. *Journal of Law and Education, 25*(4), 381-388.

Vasterling, V. (2003). Body and language: Butler, Merleau-Ponty and Lyotard on the speaking embodied subject. *International Journal of Philosophical Studies, 11*(2), 205-223.

Vaught, J. (1971). *Rebel Coach*. Memphis, TN: Memphis State University Press.

Vertinsky, P., & Hargreaves, J. (2007). *Physical culture, power and the body*. London: Routledge.

Waddell, J. (1891). *Memorials of academic life*. Richmond, VA: Presbyterian Committee of Publications.

Waddell, J. N. (1848, November 6). *Record book of the faculty minutes from the University of Mississippi (1st Session)*, Oxford, MS.

Waddell, J. N. (1851, April 1). *Record book of the faculty minutes from the University of Mississippi (3rd Session)*, Oxford, MS.

Waddell, J. N. (1852, September 27). *Record book of the faculty minutes from the University of Mississippi (5th Session)*, Oxford, MS.

Waddell, J. N. (1853a, February 1). *Record book of the faculty minutes from the University of Mississippi (5th Session)*, Oxford, MS.

Waddell, J. N. (1853b, June 23). *Record book of the faculty minutes from the University of Mississippi (5th Session)*, Oxford, MS.

Waddell, J. N. (1853c, September 26). *Record book of the faculty minutes from the University of Mississippi (6th Session)*, Oxford, MS.

Waddell, J. N. (1853d, December 5). *Record book of the faculty minutes from the University of Mississippi (6th Session)*, Oxford, MS.

Waddell, J. N. (1854a, March 7). *Record book of the faculty minutes from the University of Mississippi (6th Session)*, Oxford, MS.

Waddell, J. N. (1854b, May 16). *Record book of the faculty minutes from the University of Mississippi (6th Session)*, Oxford, MS.

Wade, W. C. (1998). *The fiery cross: The Ku Klux Klan in America* (2nd ed.). Oxford, UK: Oxford University Press.

Walton, G. W. (1995). *The Lyceum*. Paper presented at the Dedication of the Renovated Lyceum, Oxford, MS.

Ware, V., & Back, L. (2001). *Out of whiteness: Color, politics, and culture*. Chicago: University of Chicago Press.

Watterson, J. S. (2000). *College football: History, spectacle, controversy*. Baltimore: Johns Hopkins University Press.

We will not surrender (1962, September 14). *Clarion-Ledger*, p. 1.

Weber, M. (1958/2002). *The Protestant ethic and the spirit of capitalism* (S. Kalberg, Trans.). Los Angeles: Roxbury Publishing Company.

Weeden, T. L. (1993, March 2). Play 'Dixie' damnit. *The Daily Mississippian*, p. 2.

Weeks, L. (1999, January 7). Two from Ole Miss, hitting it big. *Washington Post*, p. C1.

Weiss, G. (1999). *Body images: Embodiment as intercorporeality*. New York Routledge.

Weissberg, L. (1999). Introduction. In D. Ben-Amos & L. Weissberg (Eds.), *Cultural memory and the construction of identity*. Detroit: Wayne State University Press.

Wellman, D. (1997). Minstrel shows, affirmative action talk, and angry white men: Marking racial otherness in the 1990s. In R. Frankenberg (Ed.), *Displacing whiteness: Essays in social and cultural criticism* (pp. 311-332). Durham, NC: Duke University Press.

Wells, L. (1980). *Ole Miss football*. Oxford, MS: Sports Yearbook Company.

Whannel, G. (2002). *Media sports stars: Masculinities and moralities*. London: Routledge.

Whisnant, D. (1995). Cultural values and regional development. In R. J. Higgs, A. N. Manning & J. W. Miller (Eds.), *Appalachia inside out* (pp. 192-193). Knoxville, TN: University of Tennessee Press.

White, G. D., & Hauck, F. C. (Eds.). (2000). *Campus, Inc.: Corporate power in the ivory tower* Amherst, NY: Prometheus Books.

Whiteside, K. (2003, November 7). QB Manning has Mississippi close to end of 40-year wait. *USA Today*, p. 6C.

Why did Mississippi vote on state flag lose? (2001, April 27). *Socialist Worker*, p. 2.

Wiegman, R. (1995). *American anatomies: Theorizing race and gender*. Durham, NC: Duke University Press.

Williams, E. (1962, October 31). Mob demonstrates at Meredith's dorm. *The Mississippian*, p. 1.

Williams, E. (1963, April 12). Should Communists speak here? *The Mississippian*, p. 3.

Williams, J. J. (2001). Franchising the university. In H. A. Giroux & K. Myrsiades (Eds.), *Beyond the corporate university: Culture and pedagogy in the new millennium* (pp. 15-28). Lanham, MD: Rowman & Littlefield.

Williams, R. (1977). *Marxism and literature*. Oxford: Oxford University Press.

Williams, R. (1981). *The sociology of culture*. New York: Schoken Books.

Williamson, J. (1984). *The crucible of race: Black/white relations in the American South since emancipation*. New York: Oxford University Press.

Wilson, J. Z. (2002). Invisible racism: The language and ontology of 'white trash'. *Critique of Anthropology, 22*(4), 387-401.

Wilson, W. J. (1997). *When work disappears: The world of the new urban poor*. New York: Vintage Books.

Winant, H. (1992). Amazing grace. *Socialist Review, 75*(19), 162-183.

Winders, J. (2003). White in all the wrong places: White rural poverty in the postbellum US South. *Cultural Geographies, 10*(1), 45-63.

Woodward, C. V. (1971). *Origins of the New South, 1877-1913*. Baton Rouge, LA: Louisiana State University Press.

Woodward, C. V. (1989). The search for Southern identity. In P. Gerster & N. Cords (Eds.), *Myth and Southern history: The New South* (pp. 119-132). Champaign-Urbana, IL: University of Illinois Press.

Works both ways: Freedom discussed (1962, October 18). *The Mississippian*, p. 1.

Wray, M., & Newitz, A. (1997). *White trash: Race and class in America*. New York London: Routledge.

Wright, G. (1978). *The political economy of the Cotton South: Households, markets, and wealth in the Nineteenth Century* New York: W. W. Norton & Company.

Wright, H. K., & Grossberg, L. (2001). 'What's going on?' Larry Grossberg on the status quo of cultural studies: An interview. *Cultural Values, 5*(2), 133-162.

Wright, R. (1945/1998). *Black boy: A record of childhood and youth*. New York: Harper.

Yafa, S. (2005). *Cotton: A revolutionary fiber*. London: Penguin.

Yates, D. L. (1999). Plantation-style social control: Oppressive social structures in the slave plantation system. In T. J. Durant & J. D. Knottnerus (Eds.), *Plantation society and race relations: The origins of inequity* (pp. 29-40). Praeger: Westport, CT.

Young, R. C. (1990). *White mythologies: Writing history and the West.* London: Routledge.

Zizek, S. (1989). *The sublime object of ideology.* London: Verso.

Breinigsville, PA USA
10 August 2010
243397BV00002B/3/P